TAKING SIDES

Clashing Views in

Human Resource Management

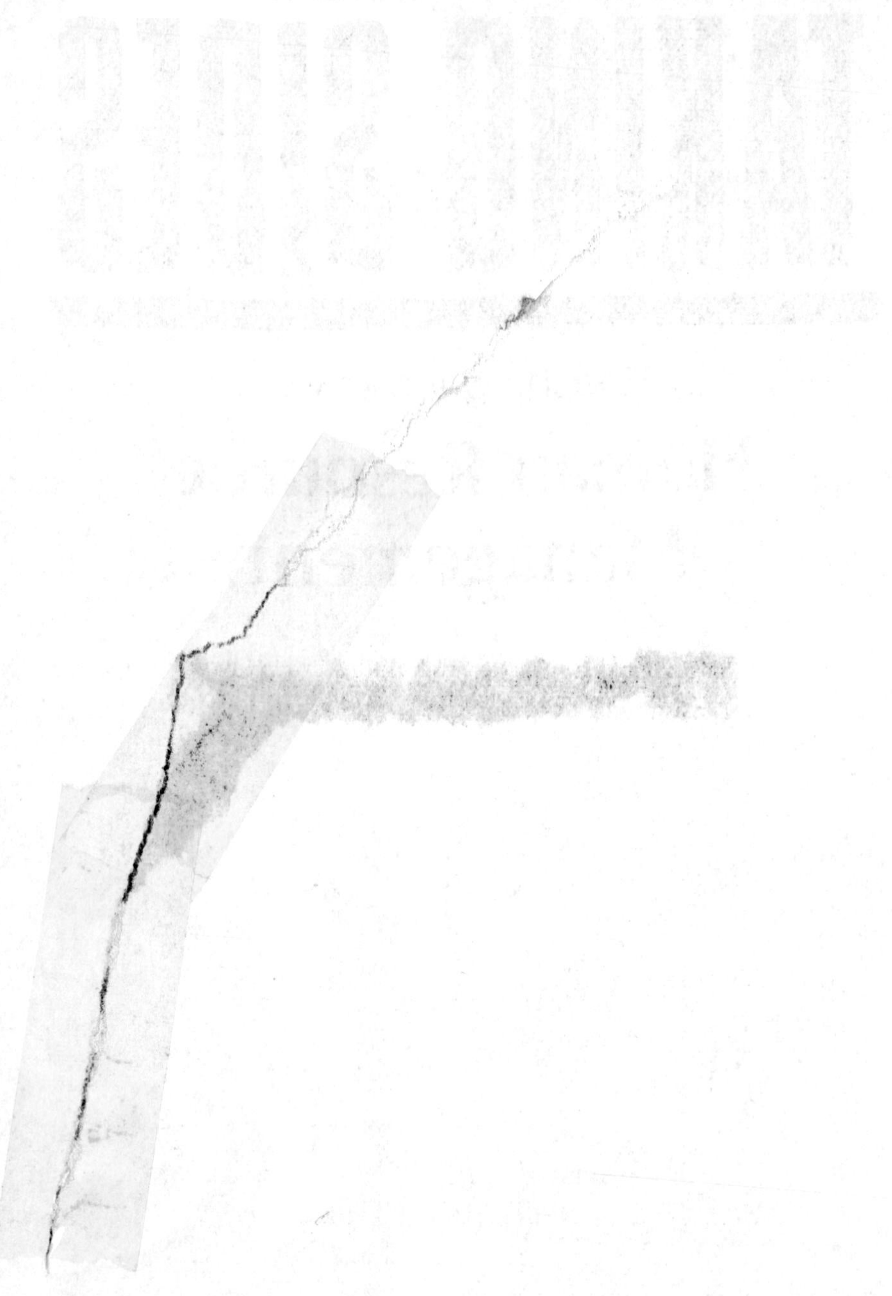

TAKING SIDES

Clashing Views in

Human Resource Management

SECOND EDITION

Selected, Edited, and with Introductions by

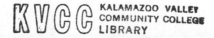

Pramila Rao
Marymount University

The McGraw-Hill Companies

TAKING SIDES: CLASHING VIEWS IN HUMAN RESOURCE MANAGEMENT, SECOND EDITION

Published by McGraw-Hill, a business unit of The McGraw-Hill Companies, Inc., 1221 Avenue of the Americas, New York, NY 10020.

This book is printed on acid-free paper.

Taking Sides is published by the **Contemporary Learning Series** group within the McGraw-Hill Higher Education division.

1 2 3 4 5 6 7 8 9 0 DOC/DOC 1 0 9 8 7 6 5 4 3 2

MHID: 0-07-352736-X
ISBN: 978-0-07-352736-9
ISSN: 2152-9795 (print)
ISSN: 2152-9809 (online)

Managing Editor: *Larry Loeppke*
Developmental Editor: *Dave Welsh*
Permissions Coordinator: *DeAnna Dausener*
Senior Marketing Communications Specialist: *Mary Klein*
Lead Project Manager: *Jane Mohr*
Design Coordinator: *Brenda A. Rolwes*
Cover Graphics: *Rick D. Noel*
Buyer: *Nicole Baumgartner*
Media Project Manager: *Sridevi Palani*

Compositor: MPS Limited
Cover Image: © Radius Images/Getty Images RF

www.mhhe.com

Editors/Academic Advisory Board

Members of the Academic Advisory Board are instrumental in the final selection of articles for each edition of TAKING SIDES. Their review of articles for content, level, and appropriateness provides critical direction to the editors and staff. We think that you will find their careful consideration well reflected in this volume.

TAKING SIDES: Clashing Views in HUMAN RESOURCE MANAGEMENT

Second Edition

EDITOR

Pramila Rao
Marymount University

ACADEMIC ADVISORY BOARD MEMBERS

Editors/Academic Advisory Board continued

Editors/Academic Advisory Board continued

Preface

I have never in my life learned anything from any man who agreed with me.

—Dudley Field Malone

The well-bred contradict other people; the wise contradict themselves.

—Oscar Wilde

This volume contains 40 selections, presented in a pro and con format, which provide the readers with 20 interesting debate topics in human resource management (HRM). We encourage professors to consider each of the HRM selections throughout the semester to involve and engage their students in lively classroom discussions.

The Greeks identified debates as one of the best methods to develop rhetoric and holistic skills. The Greek philosopher Protagoras, considered the "father of debates," used to conduct debates on several issues to get participants get a profound understanding on the subject. He believed that studying rhetoric will develop people to be better prepared in their professional and personal lives as it teaches them how to be both persuasive and convincing. The Greeks placed a tremendous importance on the power of speaking and regarded it as an important educational activity. Aristotle regarded rhetoric to involve the three concepts of *logos, ethos,* and *pathos* (logic, character, and emotion). His philosophy suggested that speakers use reason, personality, and emotion for any public forums.

In the United States, debates had their origins in the well-known presidential debates. While such political discussions began in the nineteenth century during the Lincoln era, it was the first televised debates between former President John Kennedy and Richard Nixon that set the stage for the widely publicized televised presidential debates that absorb the media and audience today. In the eighteenth century, Ivy League schools began to include the works of great debaters so that students may learn how to understand any topic from both the pro and con standpoints. The first academic debate competition in the United States was held in 1881. After this, several colleges began to introduce debates in their educational curriculum as it was considered important. In the late nineteenth century, academic debate prompts were often chosen from the book series, *The American Debater,* which had insightful debate questions on diverse subject topics. The book also provided valuable suggestions to debaters as to how to prepare cogently for their debates.

In the academic world, debates are considered a very engaging teaching method as it requires students to be active participants of the learning process. Students have to identify learning resources, develop their own understanding on the learning material, create a position on the topic, and discuss their subject knowledge with their peers. A debate-style learning format allows students to engage in critical thinking, become active learners, build their own knowledge, participate collaboratively, think quickly (for rebuttals), develop public speaking skills, and develop listening skills. While this method might seem to place the burden of learning squarely on students, the outcome of such independent learning is enormous. Debates also provide students an opportunity to take a public stand and support their viewpoints—an important competency in the business environment. Generally, business leaders make their decisions after understanding both sides to an issue as it allows for better judgments.

Each selection issue has an *Issue Summary* or brief synopsis of the YES and NO readings that helps to set the stage for the debates. This is followed by an introduction that usually involves a historical introduction, definition of important terms, relevant statistics, high-profile court cases (wherever relevant), rhetorical questions, and a summary of both the YES and NO readings. This edition also provides an international perspective to each selection as students are encouraged to acquire a global view on management perspectives. This is followed by a common ground perspective that provides a middle standpoint on the issue. This section introduces readers to alternate viewpoints and additional questions on the topic. Each section also has discussion questions related to the learning goals of the debate prompt. Each section also has a list of suggested readings that will help readers glean a better understanding of the debate topic. There is also a section providing the biography of all the contributors of the issue articles at the end of the book. This section provides their professional and academic background for readers to understand their credibility on the subject matter.

It is very important that students do not limit their scholarly readings mainly to the YES and NO articles and suggested readings sections. Students should conduct their own research and identify new articles related to the topic to develop new and additional perspectives. Such an increased understanding on the topic will provide participants enhanced subject knowledge and also make debates more lively and engaging.

This is the second edition of Taking Sides in human resource management (HRM). It includes 20 topics, which were carefully selected after conducting a market research survey on the importance of these topics to human resource management. Scholars from various universities identified these topics as relevant topics in HRM. This book also provides an instructor's resource guide with test questions (multiple-choice and essay).

I would like to acknowledge the support and inspiration of my family that made this writing project possible again. My immense thanks goes to Marymount University and both my Dean (James Ryerson) and Chair (Dr. Virginia Bianco-Mathis) who have always been very supportive of my professional development. And finally, my students convinced me that they really enjoy the learning process in debates; they tell me "I cannot wait for our next class debate!"

Pramila Rao
Marymount University

Contents In Brief

UNIT 1 Legal Environment 1

Issue 1. Is Affirmative Action Still Necessary? 2

Issue 2. Will the Americans with Disabilities Act Amendments Act (ADAAA) Be Abused in the U.S. Workplace? 16

Issue 3. Has the Sarbanes–Oxley Act Helped U.S. Corporations? 28

Issue 4. Should Employees Be Allowed to Wear Symbols of Faith in the Workplace? 44

UNIT 2 Talent Acquisition 63

Issue 5. Are Social Networking Sites Good Recruitment Sources? 64

Issue 6. Are Personality Tests Good Predictors of Employee Performance? 81

Issue 7. Is Cognitive Ability Testing a Good Predictor of Work Performance? 98

Issue 8. Would Mandatory Background Checks for All Employees Reduce Negligent Hiring Lawsuits? 113

UNIT 3 Women in Corporate Levels 129

Issue 9. Do Women Make Better Business Leaders? 130

Issue 10. Does the Glass Ceiling Still Exist in U.S. Organizations? 153

UNIT 4 Employee Performance and Organizational Productivity 167

Issue 11. Does Increased Dependence on Laptops, Cell Phones, and PDAs Hurt Employee Productivity? 168

Issue 12. Do Unions Help Organizational Productivity? 188

UNIT 5 Compensation and Performance Appraisal 201

Issue 13. Has Merit Pay Lost Its Meaning in the Workplace? 202

Issue 14. Is Forced Ranking an Effective Performance Management Approach? 217

Issue 15. Is the U.S. Executive Pay Model Flawed? 233

UNIT 6 The Effect of HRM Practices 255

Issue 16. Does Attracting, Developing, and Retaining the Millennial Generation Require Significant Changes to Current HRM Practices? 256

Issue 17. Do Human Resource Management (HRM) Practices (Such as Selection, Training, Performance Management, and Compensation) Contribute to Increased Firm Performance? 272

UNIT 7 Global HRM 291

Issue 18. Is Overseas Outsourcing a Good U.S. Business Strategy? 292

Issue 19. Is the Sweatshop Concept Adopted by the U.S. Manufacturers Overseas Ethical? 312

Issue 20. Are U.S. Companies Adaptive to Local Practices Overseas? 327

Contents

Preface viii

Correlation Guide xx

Topic Guide xxiii

Introduction xxv

UNIT 1 LEGAL ENVIRONMENT 1

Issue 1. Is Affirmative Action Still Necessary? 2

YES: David L. Chappell, from "If Affirmative Action Fails . . . What Then?" *New York Times* (May 8, 2004) *6*

NO: Jonathan Kaufman, from "Fair Enough? Barack Obama's Rise Has Americans Debating Whether Affirmative Action Has Run Its Course," *Wall Street Journal* (June 14, 2008) *9*

David L. Chappell, a columnist and public speaker, believes that affirmative action programs are still required as our society continues to live in racial segregation in tacit and non-tacit ways. He feels that affirmative action programs will benefit individuals who are truly in need of better opportunities in academe or the corporate world. Jonathan Kauffman, education editor at Bloomberg, believes that affirmative action programs should refocus their overarching goals so that the truly disadvantaged get opportunities to advance. He emphasizes how President Obama, an African American, is the highest political leader today, making policymakers question that affirmative action programs need to be readdressed.

Issue 2. Will the Americans with Disabilities Act Amendments Act (ADAAA) Be Abused in the U.S. Workplace? 16

YES: Dina Berta, from "Labor Lawyers: Changes to Americans with Disabilities Act May Lead to More Workplace Discrimination Suits," *Nation's Restaurant News* (October 2008) *20*

NO: Victoria Zellers, from "Make a Resolution: ADA Training," *HR Magazine* (January 2009) *22*

Award-winning writer Dina Berta suggests that the ADA (Americans with Disabilities Act) has always been controversial because it was difficult to define and understand. Now that the act has been redefined to ADAAA (Americans with Disabilities Act Amendments Act), it will allow more employees to fall under the disability category, which could increase the number of lawsuits. Legal attorney Victoria Zellers argues that sufficient training of HR professionals could substantially reduce litigation expenses for organizations. The HR department should be proactive to understand and provide for the special needs of their employees.

Issue 3. Has the Sarbanes–Oxley Act Helped U.S. Corporations? 28

YES: Edward Cone, from "Learning to Live with SOX," *CIO Insight, 1*(69), (2006) *31*

NO: C.J. Prince, from "Unintended Consequences," *Chief Executive*, vol. 205, (2005) *37*

The article offers interesting insights as to why the act is useful in the American corporate world. The article provides several examples to substantiate its points. C.J. Prince, a writer with 15 years experience, suggests that the Sarbanes–Oxley Act has placed a lot of burden on organizations. Today organizations are more concerned about their ethical rather than their strategic agenda.

Issue 4. Should Employees Be Allowed to Wear Symbols of Faith in the Workplace? 44

YES: Robert J. Grossman, from "Religion at Work," *HR Magazine* (December 2008) *48*

NO: Robert D. Ramsey, from "When Religion and Work Clash," *Supervision* (September 2007) *56*

Robert J. Grossman, professor of management, suggests that organizations should adopt a faith-friendly approach and allow employees to wear their symbols of faith. He provides examples of leading companies such as Coca-Cola and Ford Motors that have taken progressive steps regarding wearing symbols of faith and have observed positive HRM outcomes. Robert D. Ramsey, author and freelance writer, argues that accommodating religious requests might become a never-ending laundry list of requests that could hamper business goals and profits. Organizations should always keep their business interests and objectives as their top priority.

UNIT 2 TALENT ACQUISITION 63

Issue 5. Are Social Networking Sites Good Recruitment Sources? 64

YES: Jamie Vicknair, Dalia Elkersh, Katie Yancey, and Michael C. Budden, from "The Use of Social Networking Websites as a Recruiting Tool for Employers," *American Journal of Business Education*, vol. 3, no. 11, 7–12 (2010) *67*

NO: Daniel J. Solove, from "The End of Privacy?" *Scientific American*, vol. 299, no. 3 (September, 2008) *73*

Jamie Vicknair and colleagues suggest most employers use SNS as a preliminary screening tool. They state that though Gen Y applicants are aware of this trend, yet they post a lot of personal information online. This could have powerful consequences on their employment profile. Daniel J. Solove, a law professor at George Washington University, and also the author on several books on topics related to privacy, asserts that online information is not an accurate and honest source for recruiters. Gen Yers are more likely to post incorrect information when personal and business relationships become unpleasant.

Issue 6. Are Personality Tests Good Predictors of Employee Performance? 81

YES: Ira Blank, from "Selecting Employees Based on Emotional Intelligence Competencies: Reap the Rewards and Minimize the Risk," *Employee Relations Law Journal* (December 2008) *84*

NO: Erin White, from "Theory and Practice: Personality Tests Aim to Stop 'Fakers'; Some Say Tool's Accuracy Could Be Improved to Make Misrepresentations Harder," *Wall Street Journal* (Eastern Edition) (November 6, 2006) *93*

Ira Blank, litigation attorney, suggests that personality tests are excellent predictors of job performance because they identify several critical work-related skills needed in today's team and multicultural environment. Erin White, reporter for the *Wall Street Journal,* cites the studies of Dr. Griffith, which state that students always fake their personality when they realize the outcomes are different. Questions on these tests are so transparent that it is easy to manipulate the answers.

Issue 7. Is Cognitive Ability Testing a Good Predictor of Work Performance? 98

YES: Martha J. Frase, from "Smart Selections," *HR Magazine* (December 2007) *101*

NO: Rangarajan (Raj) Parthasarathy, from "Emotional Intelligence and the Quality Manager: Beauty and the Beast?" *The Journal for Quality and Participation* (January 2009) *106*

Martha Frase, freelance writer, suggests that cognitive ability tests are excellent predictors of work performance because they are objective, valid, and reliable. Further, these tests can be administered to a variety of job categories from entry to executive levels. Raj Parthasarathy, process improvement manager, states that emotional intelligence is the best predictor of job performance because it involves critical components of self and relationship management. Researchers are paying increasing attention to emotional intelligence (EI) as its components have positive consequences on job performance.

Issue 8. Would Mandatory Background Checks for All Employees Reduce Negligent Hiring Lawsuits? 113

YES: Lessing E. Gold, from "Security and the Law: Get a Background Check," *SDM Magazine* (October 2007) *117*

NO: Chad Terhune, from "The Trouble with Background Checks: Employee Screening Has Become a Big Business, but Not Always an Accurate One," *BusinessWeek* (June 2008) *119*

Lessing Gold, attorney and writer, contends that organizations have a liability in checking the background references of both their permanent or temporary applicants. He indicates how applicants with criminal records emerge back into the work environment with false records, potentially putting customers and coworkers in jeopardy. Chad Terhune, writer for *SmartMoney,* asserts that information from background checking companies is so inaccurate that it is very unfair to several whose employment records have become blemished. He feels that the unregulated nature of this industry could be one of the main reasons for such employment errors.

UNIT 3 WOMEN IN CORPORATE LEVELS 129

Issue 9. Do Women Make Better Business Leaders? 130

YES: Ann Pomeroy, from "Cultivating Female Leaders," *HR Magazine* (February 2007) *133*

NO: Herminia Ibarra and Otilia Obodaru, from "Women and the Vision Thing," *Harvard Business Review* (January 2009) *140*

Ann Pomeroy, who recently served as a senior writer for *HR Magazine,* illustrates with the example of Safeway how organizations have identified that women are better business leaders. She suggests that women have some innate characteristics that serve them well as leaders. INSEAD Professor Herminia Ibarra and her doctoral student, from their research study, suggest that women demonstrate low visionary skills. These business skills are very important for understanding the dynamic business environment and hence women may not be effective leaders.

Issue 10. Does the Glass Ceiling Still Exist in U.S. Organizations? 153

YES: Jessica Marquez, from "Gender Bias Found to Start Early in Career," *Workforce Management* (June 2009) *156*

NO: Anonymous, from "Women in the Economy (A Special Report)—Tales from the Front Lines: On How They Did What They Did," *Wall Street Journal* (p. R.6, 2011) *158*

Jessica Marquez, journalist at *Workforce Management,* suggests that women face a glass ceiling possibly because their careers begin much later and they have more career interruptions due to family commitments. The article provides examples of leading women in the corporate world. These professional women share their work stories and corporate recipes with the readers.

UNIT 4 EMPLOYEE PERFORMANCE AND ORGANIZATIONAL PRODUCTIVITY 167

Issue 11. Does Increased Dependence on Laptops, Cell Phones, and PDAs Hurt Employee Productivity? 168

YES: Paul Hemp, from "Death by Information Overload," *Harvard Business Review* (September 2009) *171*

NO: Michelle LaBrosse, from "Working Successfully in a Virtual World," *Employment Relations Today* (2007) *181*

Paul Hemp, a Harvard Law School graduate and editor of the *Harvard Business Review,* argues that our current society is facing loss of productivity due to excessive dependence on technology (such as BlackBerrys, cell phones, etc.), blurring boundaries between home and work. Michelle LaBrosse, one of the 25 Most Influential Women in Project Management, contends that modern technological devices allow employees to be connected to form virtual teams.

Issue 12. Do Unions Help Organizational Productivity? 188

YES: **AFL-CIO**, from "Unions Are Good for Business, Productivity, and the Economy," http://www.aflcio.org/joinaunion/why/uniondifference/uniondiff8.cfm (2009) *192*

NO: **Dennis K. Berman**, from "The Game—Dr. Z's Chrysler Predicament: Selling Unions on Sacrifice," *Wall Street Journal* (Eastern Edition) (April 24, 2007) *195*

The American Federation of Labor and Congress of Industrial Organizations (AFL-CIO) Web site identifies the work of Professor Harley Shaiken, from the University of California–Berkeley, who states the positive impact of unions on HRM outcomes. Dennis Berman, *Wall Street Journal* journalist and 2003 Pulitzer Prize winner, argues that the current state of the auto industry is mainly due to excessive demands of the unions. The high cost of maintaining labor is passed on to the consumers and reduces organizational profit margins.

UNIT 5 COMPENSATION AND PERFORMANCE APPRAISAL 201

Issue 13. Has Merit Pay Lost Its Meaning in the Workplace? 202

YES: **Fay Hansen**, from "Merit-Pay Payoff?" *Workforce Management* (November 2008) *205*

NO: **Susan J. Wells**, from "No Results, No Raise." *HR Magazine* (vol. 50, no. 5, pp. 76–80, 2005) *210*

Fay Hansen, contributing editor for *Workforce Management,* provides studies of leading professors from Stanford and MIT which suggest that merit pay has lost its meaning because employees are not being actually rewarded for performance. They assert that this compensation system is not distinguishing between success and failure and hence has lost its meaning in the workplace. S. J. Wells, a writer for *HR Magazine,* contends that organizations should become rigorous in establishing a pay-for-performance culture. She provides examples of organizations that have established such practices successfully.

Issue 14. Is Forced Ranking an Effective Performance Management Approach? 217

YES: **Alex Blyth**, from "Cull or Cure?" *Personnel Today* (May 2007) *220*

NO: **Gail Johnson**, from "Forced Ranking: The Good, the Bad, and the Alternative," *Training* (May 2004) *223*

Alex Blyth reiterates the thoughts of Microsoft leaders on forced ranking. This performance approach is very good at identifying the underperformers and rewarding the stars. Gail Johnson, former editor of *Training* magazine, suggests this method is flawed because it encourages a very competitive and dysfunctional work environment.

Issue 15. Is the U.S. Executive Pay Model Flawed? 233

YES: Sarah Anderson, John Cavanagh, Chuck Collins, Mike Lapham, Sam Pizzigati, from "Executive Excess 2007," at the Institute for Policy Studies, http://www.ips-dc.org/reports/#84 (2007) *237*

NO: Robert B. Reich, from "The Economic Argument for CEO Pay," *Wall Street Journal* (Eastern Edition) (September 14, 2007) *248*

Compensation expert and IPS Fellow Sarah Anderson and her colleagues argue that U.S. CEOs are substantially overpaid in a 2008 study conducted for the Institute for Policy Studies. Professor Reich from Berkeley states that the capitalistic system promotes a principle of supply and demand. There are very few qualified executives, so they are in high demand. Executives have distinguished educational and work records that result in their elaborate pay levels.

UNIT 6 THE EFFECT OF HRM PRACTICES 255

Issue 16. Does Attracting, Developing, and Retaining the Millennial Generation Require Significant Changes to Current HRM Practices? 256

YES: Charles Woodruffe, from "Generation Y," *Training Journal* (July 2009) *260*

NO: Dana Kyles, from "Managing Your Multigenerational Workforce," *Strategic Finance* (2005) *266*

Charles Woodruffe is an author and CEO of a company that focuses on managing winning talent. He states that Gen Yers might need a new set of management practices as the current practices might not be very congruent with their personality needs and characteristics. This generation has experienced accomplishments and rewards right through their lives and will have the same expectations at the workplace. Dana Kyles, freelance writer for *BusinessWeek* and *Strategic Finance* magazines, informs readers that it is possible for multiple generations to work harmoniously together. Several HRM practices appeal to all the generations unanimously and organizations should try and identify these common practices.

Issue 17. Do Human Resource Management (HRM) Practices (Such as Selection, Training, Performance Management, and Compensation) Contribute to Increased Firm Performance? 272

YES: Anonymous, from "Google's Lessons for Employers: Put Your Employees First," *HR Focus* (vol. 85, no. 9, pp. 8–9, September 2008) *276*

NO: Keith H. Hammonds, from "Why We Hate HR," *Fast Company* (vol. 97, pp. 40–47, 2005) *278*

This article interviews the senior HRM leader in Google Inc. to identify how HRM practices have contributed to their phenomenal success and growth of the organization. Lazlo Bock, HRM leader of Google, insists that it is his HRM practices and the Google employees that make his organization outstanding. Keith Hammonds, former executive editor of *Fast Company* magazine, suggests that HRM leaders are never in the forefront in most organizations. Hence, HRM departments do not provide any substantial profits or growth in organizations.

UNIT 7 GLOBAL HRM 291

Issue 18. Is Overseas Outsourcing a Good U.S. Business Strategy? 292

YES: **John E. Gnuschke, Jeff Wallace, Dennis R. Wilson, and Stephen C. Smith,** from "Outsourcing Production and Jobs: Costs and Benefits," *Business Perspectives* (Spring 2004) *296*

NO: **Murray Weidenbaum,** from "Outsourcing: Pros and Cons," *Executive Speeches* (August/September 2004) *303*

Professor John Gnuschke and colleagues from the University of Memphis insist that outsourcing is a good business strategy as it creates higher profits, delivers cheaper products, and reduces customer response time. Most multinationals are taking advantage of the outsourcing trends as the benefits surpass the costs. Professor Murray Weidenbaum from Washington University suggests that there are several barriers to a smooth outsourcing process such as language barriers, technology glitches, and intellectual rights. Outsourcing has become a national topic, making employees aware of this global labor trend.

Issue 19. Is the Sweatshop Concept Adopted by the U.S. Manufacturers Overseas Ethical? 312

YES: **Tara J. Radin and Martin Calkins,** from "The Struggle Against Sweatshops: Moving Toward Responsible Global Business," *Journal of Business Ethics* (vol. 66, nos. 2–3, pp. 261–272, 2006) *315*

NO: **Dennis G. Arnold and Laura P. Hartman,** from "Beyond Sweatshops: Positive Deviancy and Global Labor Practices," *Business Ethics: A European Review* (vol. 14, no. 3, pp. 206–210, July 2005) *321*

Professor Radin and Professor Calkins provide a very informative view as to why sweatshops still exist despite all their controversies. They also provide several alternatives for organizations while adopting sweatshop manufacturing facilities overseas. The Web sites showcase how women are generally exploited in sweatshops and how Walmart abused its employees in its overseas facilities.

Issue 20. Are U.S. Companies Adaptive to Local Practices Overseas? 327

YES: **Mike Hughlett,** from *Strong Amid Slowdown Worries Sitting Pretty: McDonald's Overseas Sales Are Surging as It Adapts Successful U.S. Operations to Local Tastes, Styles of Its International Restaurants* (McClatchy—Tribune Information Services, 2008) *331*

NO: **Jaya Halepete, K. V. Seshadri Iyer, and Soo Chul Park,** from "Wal-Mart in India: A Success or Failure?" *International Journal of Retail & Distribution Management* (vol. 36, no. 9, pp. 701–713, 2008) *334*

Hughlett, a food reporter, provides evidence of how McDonald's has innovatively created different menus to ensure their consumers are happy. Further, the company also has paid attention to local management practices to enhance its corporate success. Assistant Professor Halepete and her colleagues do an excellent case analysis of Walmart in Germany, Korea, and India, providing evidence of how important cultural values are in making or breaking a company.

Contributors 346

Correlation Guide

The *Taking Sides* series presents current issues in a debate-style format designed to stimulate student interest and develop critical thinking skills. Each issue is thoughtfully framed with an issue summary, an issue introduction, and a postscript. The pro and con essays—selected for their liveliness and substance—represent the arguments of leading scholars and commentators in their fields.

Taking Sides: Clashing Views in Human Resource Management, 2/e is an easy-to-use reader that presents issues on important topics such as *talent acquisition, women in corporate levels, employee performance and organizational productivity, and compensation and performance appraisal*. For more information on *Taking Sides* and other *McGraw-Hill Contemporary Learning Series* titles, visit http://www.mhhe.com/cls.

This convenient guide matches the issues in **Taking Sides: Human Resource Management, 2/e** with the corresponding chapters in four of our best-selling McGraw-Hill Human Resource textbooks by Noe et al., Cascio, Bernardin, and Ivancevich/Konopaske.

Taking Sides: Human Resource Management, 2/e	Human Resource Management, 8/e by Noe et al.	Managing Human Resources: Productivity, Quality of Work Life, Profits, 9/e by Cascio	Human Resource Management, 6/e by Bernardin	Human Resource Management, 12/e by Ivancevich/ Konopaske
Issue 1: Is Affirmative Action Still Necessary?	**Chapter 3:** The Legal Environment: Equal Employment Opportunity and Safety **Chapter 5:** Human Resource Planning and Recruitment	**Chapter 3:** The Legal Context of Employment Decisions	**Chapter 3:** The Legal Environment of HRM: Equal Employment Opportunity **Chapter 5:** Human Resource Planning and Recruitment	**Chapter 1:** Human Resource Management
Issue 2: Will the Americans with Disabilities Act Amendments Act (ADAAA) Be Abused in the U.S. Workplace?	**Chapter 3:** The Legal Environment: Equal Employment Opportunity and Safety **Chapter 6:** Selection and Placement **Chapter 13:** Employee Benefits	**Chapter 3:** The Legal Context of Employment Decisions **Chapter 5:** Planning for People **Chapter 7:** Staffing **Chapter 15:** Safety, Health, and Employee Assistance Programs	**Chapter 3:** The Legal Environment of HRM: Equal Employment Opportunity **Chapter 4:** Work Analysis and Design **Chapter 10:** Compensation: Base Pay and Fringe Benefits **Chapter 14:** Employee Health and Safety **Chapter 12:** Managing the Employment Relationship	**Chapter 7:** Recruitment **Chapter 17:** Promoting Safety and Health
Issue 3: Has the Sarbanes–Oxley Act Helped U.S. Corporations?		**Chapter 3:** The Legal Context of Employment Decisions	**Chapter 1:** Human Resource Management in a Changing Environment	
Issue 4: Should Employees be Allowed to Wear Symbols of Faith in the Workplace?	**Chapter 3:** The Legal Environment: Equal Employment Opportunity and Safety	**Chapter 16:** International Dimensions of Human Resource Management	**Chapter 3:** The Legal Environment of HRM: Equal Employment Opportunity	**Chapter 1:** Human Resource Management

Taking Sides: Human Resource Management, 2/e	Human Resource Management, 8/e by Noe et al.	Managing Human Resources: Productivity, Quality of Work Life, Profits, 9/e by Cascio	Human Resource Management, 6/e by Bernardin	Human Resource Management, 12/e by Ivancevich/ Konopaske
Issue 5: Are Social Networking Sites Good Recruitment Sources?	**Chapter 5:** Human Resource Planning and Recruitment	**Chapter 6:** Recruiting	**Chapter 5:** Human Resource Planning and Recruitment	**Chapter 7:** Recruitment **Chapter 8:** Selecting Effective Employees
Issue 6: Are Personality Tests Good Predictors of Employee Performance?	**Chapter 9:** Employee Development	**Chapter 7:** Staffing	**Chapter 6:** Personnel Selection	**Chapter 8:** Selecting Effective Employees
Issue 7: Is Cognitive Ability Testing a Good Predictor of Work Performance?	**Chapter 9:** Employee Development	**Chapter 7:** Staffing	**Chapter 6:** Personnel Selection	**Chapter 8:** Selecting Effective Employees
Issue 8: Would Mandatory Background Checks for all Employees Reduce Negligent Hiring Lawsuits?	**Chapter 6:** Selection and Placement	**Chapter 7:** Staffing	**Chapter 6:** Personnel Selection	**Chapter 8:** Selecting Effective Employees
Issue 9: Do Women Make Better Business Leaders?	**Chapter 5:** Human Resource Planning and Recruitment **Chapter 6:** Selection and Placement **Chapter 9:** Employee Development	**Chapter 1:** Human Resources in a Globally Competitive Business Environment **Chapter 4:** Diversity at Work **Chapter 5:** Planning for People **Chapter 10:** Managing Careers	**Chapter 3:** The Legal Environment of HRM: Equal Employment Opportunity	**Chapter 5:** Human Resource Planning
Issue 10: Does the Glass Ceiling Still Exist in U.S. Organizations?	**Chapter 1:** Human Resources in a Globally Competitive Business Environment **Chapter 9:** Employee Development	**Chapter 3:** The Legal Context of Employment Decisions	**Chapter 3:** The Legal Environment of HRM: Equal Employment Opportunity **Chapter 4:** Work Analysis and Design **Chapter 9:** Career Development	**Chapter 5:** Human Resource Planning **Chapter 14:** Career Planning and Development
Issue 11: Does Increased Dependence on Laptops, Cell Phones, and PDAs Hurt Employee Productivity?	**Chapter 1:** Human Resource Management: Gaining a Competitive Advantage	**Chapter 1:** Human Resources in a Globally Competitive Business Environment	**Chapter 12:** Managing the Employment Relationship	**Chapter 13:** Training and Development
Issue 12: Do Unions Help Organizational Productivity?	**Chapter 14:** Collective Bargaining and Labor Relations	**Chapter 11:** Pay and Incentive Systems **Chapter 13:** Union Representation and Collective Bargaining	**Chapter 13:** Labor Relations and Collective Bargaining	**Chapter 15:** Labor Relations and Collective Bargaining
Issue 13: Has Merit Pay Lost its Meaning in the Workplace?	**Chapter 12:** Recognizing Employee Contributions with Pay	**Chapter 11:** Pay and Incentive Systems	**Chapter 11:** Rewarding Performance	**Chapter 9:** Performance Evaluation and Management **Chapter 11:** Compensation: Methods and Policies
Issue 14: Is Forced Ranking an Effective Performance Management Approach?	**Chapter 8:** Performance Management	**Chapter 9:** Performance Management	**Chapter 7:** Performance Management and Appraisal **Chapter 11:** Rewarding Performance	**Chapter 9:** Performance Evaluation and Management

(Continued)

Taking Sides: Human Resource Management, 2/e	Human Resource Management, 8/e by Noe et al.	Managing Human Resources: Productivity, Quality of Work Life, Profits, 9/e by Cascio	Human Resource Management, 6/e by Bernardin	Human Resource Management, 12/e by Ivancevich/ Konopaske
Issue 15: Is the U.S. Executive Pay Model Flawed?	**Chapter 12:** Recognizing Employee Contributions with Pay	**Chapter 11:** Pay and Incentive Systems	**Chapter 10:** Compensation: Base Pay and Fringe Benefits	**Chapter 10:** Compensation: An Overview **Chapter 11:** Compensation: Methods and Policies
Issue 16: Does Attracting, Developing, and Retaining the Millennial Generation Require Significant Changes to Current HRM Practices?	**Chapter 1:** Human Resource Management: Gaining a Competitive Advantage **Chapter 2:** Strategic Human Resource Management **Chapter 8:** Performance Management	**Chapter 2:** The Financial Impact of Human Resource Management Activities **Chapter 4:** Diversity at Work **Chapter 5:** Planning for People	**Chapter 3:** The Legal Environment of HRM: Equal Employment Opportunity **Chapter 5:** Human Resource Planning and Recruitment **Chapter 6:** Personnel Selection	**Chapter 5:** Human Resource Planning **Chapter 7:** Recruitment **Chapter 8:** Selecting Effective Employees
Issue 17: Do Human Resource Management (HRM) Practices (Such as Selection, Training, Performance Management, and Compensation) Contribute to Increased Firm Performance?	**Chapter 1:** Human Resource Management: Gaining a Competitive Advantage **Chapter 2:** Strategic Human Resource Management **Chapter 8:** Performance Management	**Chapter 2:** The Financial Impact of Human Resource Management Activities **Chapter 9:** Performance Management	**Chapter 1:** Human Resource Management in a Changing Environment **Chapter 7:** Performance Management and Appraisal	**Chapter 2:** A Strategic Management Approach to Human Resource Management **Chapter 9:** Performance Evaluation and Management **Chapter 13:** Training and Development **Chapter 14:** Career Planning and Development
Issue 18: Is Overseas Outsourcing a Good U.S. Business Strategy?	**Chapter 1:** Human Resource Management: Gaining a Competitive Advantage **Chapter 15:** Managing Human Resources Globally	**Chapter 1:** Human Resources in a Globally Competitive Business Environment	**Chapter 2:** The Role of Globalization in HR Policy and Practice	**Chapter 4:** Global Human Resource Management
Issue 19: Is the Sweatshop Concept Adopted by the U.S. Manufacturers Overseas Ethical?	**Chapter 15:** Managing Human Resources Globally	**Chapter 1:** Human Resources in a Globally Competitive Business Environment **Chapter 16:** International Dimensions of Human Resource Management	**Chapter 2:** The Role of Globalization in HR Policy and Practice	**Chapter 4:** Global Human Resource Management
Issue 20: Are U.S. Companies Adaptive to Local Practices Overseas?	**Chapter 15:** Managing Human Resources Globally	**Chapter 1:** Human Resources in a Globally Competitive Business Environment **Chapter 16:** International Dimensions of Human Resource Management	**Chapter 2:** The Role of Globalization in HR Policy and Practice	**Chapter 4:** Global Human Resource Management

Topic Guide

This topic guide suggests how the selections in this book relate to the subjects covered in your course. You may want to use the topics listed on these pages to search the Web more easily. On the following pages, a number of Web sites have been gathered specifically for this book. They are arranged to reflect the issues of this Taking Sides reader. You can link to these sites by going to http://www.mhhe.com/cls.

All issues and their articles that relate to each topic are listed below the bold-faced term.

Affirmative Action

1. Is Affirmative Action Still Necessary?

Background Checks

8. Would Mandatory Background Checks for All Employees Reduce Negligent Hiring Lawsuits?

Compensation

13. Has Merit Pay Lost Its Meaning in the Workplace?
14. Is Forced Ranking an Effective Performance Management Approach?
15. Is the U.S. Executive Pay Model Flawed?

Disabilities

2. Will the Americans with Disabilities Act Amendments Act (ADAAA) Be Abused in the U.S. Workplace?

Employee Performance

11. Does Increased Dependence on Laptops, Cell Phones, and PDAs Hurt Employee Productivity?
12. Do Unions Help Organizational Productivity?
14. Is Forced Ranking an Effective Performance Management Approach?

Faith in the Workplace

4. Should Employees Be Allowed to Wear Symbols of Faith in the Workplace?

Global HRM

18. Is Overseas Outsourcing a Good U.S. Business Strategy?
19. Is the Sweatshop Concept Adopted by the U.S. Manufacturers Overseas Ethical?
20. Are U.S. Companies Adaptive to Local Practices Overseas?

HRM Practices

16. Does Attracting, Developing, and Retaining the Millennial Generation Require Significant Changes to Current HRM Practices?
17. Do Human Resource Management (HRM) Practices (Such as Selection, Training, Performance Management, and Compensation) Contribute to Increased Firm Performance?

Legal Environment

1. Is Affirmative Action Still Necessary?
2. Will the Americans with Disabilities Act Amendments Act (ADAAA) Be Abused in the U.S. Workplace?
3. Has the Sarbanes–Oxley Act Helped U.S. Corporations?
4. Should Employees Be Allowed to Wear Symbols of Faith in the Workplace?

Organizational Productivity

11. Does Increased Dependence on Laptops, Cell Phones, and PDAs Hurt Employee Productivity?
12. Do Unions Help Organizational Productivity?

(Continued)

Talent Acquisition

5. Are Social Networking Sites Good Recruitment Sources?
6. Are Personality Tests Good Predictors of Employee Performance?
7. Is Cognitive Ability Testing a Good Predictor of Work Performance?
8. Would Mandatory Background Checks for All Employees Reduce Negligent Hiring Lawsuits?

Technology

11. Does Increased Dependence on Laptops, Cell Phones, and PDAs Hurt Employee Productivity?

Testing

5. Are Personality Tests Good Predictors of Employee Performance?

Unions

12. Do Unions Help Organizational Productivity?

Women in Corporations

9. Do Women Make Better Business Leaders?
10. Does the Glass Ceiling Still Exist in U.S. Organizations?

Introduction

Today human resource management (HRM) leaders are playing the role of strategic partners in their organizations. Organizations today compete with one another to offer the best HRM practices, realizing that their employees are their most valuable assets. Human resource management includes recruitment, selection, training and development, performance appraisal, compensation, and labor management practices.

There are several examples of organizations in the American corporate that offer excellent work-related practices. Google Inc., the Internet leader, has 15 gourmet restaurants on their corporate campus and provides free breakfast, lunch, and dinner for their 20,000 employees every day. Container Store, the storage retailer, offers its employees 50–100 percent above the industry wages and flexible work schedules. SAS, the number one *Fortune* 500 firm in 2010, mandates a work week of only 35 hours.

How did the HRM journey begin? Research suggests that the employee–employer relationships workers began during the medieval times. It started with the various craft associations of carpenters, masons, among others creating an apprenticeship environment. Early apprentices were encouraged to live and learn from their masters about their trade and work. In the course of being apprenticed, the masters took care of their apprentices, providing them with shelter, food, and compensation. This dependent association set the stage for an employment relationship between a worker and his master or an employee and employer.

These paternalistic work relationships slowly faded with the advent of steam engines and the Industrial Revolution. The Industrial Revolution began in the mid-eighteenth century, introducing the concept of mass production and employment of thousand workers in the factories. Machines slowly began to replace time-consuming labor and employees were hired to mainly perform repetitive labor tasks. Henry Ford, the founder of the Ford Motor and father of mass production, is said to have commented that employees do not need brains but only brawn for their work.

The concept of division of labor also began as employees began to specialize in their jobs. This created a tremendous increase in production of goods, making organizations very profitable. However, slowly a rift between employers and employees began to emerge. Employees complained of poor motivation, low wages, and deplorable conditions. Employees began to realize that they do not have a voice to protect their interests and work-related needs. Therefore employees began to form labor groups so that they could have balance of power at the work place. However, there were no federal acts established at that time that supported employees or recognized them as a source of bargaining power.

In the late 1870s, Frederick Taylor pioneered the scientific management movement with revolutionary suggestions that management should be viewed as a science to enhance workplace productivity. Science is generally based on data and experiments—similarly he suggested that job performance should be based on hard core data. His scientific research, referred to as the time and motion studies, was conducted in steel factories to identify the underlying cause as to why employees were not functioning at their best performance levels. Therefore he recorded the time employees took to complete their assigned tasks. This study provided three important results; first, this study provided evidence that employees should be selected based on their knowledge, skills, and abilities (KSAs). For instance, he observed several steel workers struggle to move heavy tons of steel, indicating that these employees were physically not the most qualified for their jobs. Second, the study indicated that jobs should be defined well into tasks, duties, and responsibilities (TDRs) so that it will allow for better work outcomes. Finally, there should be work incentives or rewards for employees performing their jobs well. His management concept was embraced by manufacturing facilities throughout the country. Organizations that adopted his school of thought observed increased profits and employee satisfaction, suggesting that job performance can be regarded as a science. His research also introduced the piecework incentive scheme to motivate employees to increase their productivity. The scientific management was the dominant management approach until the early 1930s.

Around 1883, the Pendleton Act was introduced, establishing that applicants take competitive exams to be selected for federal positions. This step established the process of test-taking in hiring and also recognized that merit is an important selection criterion. Prior to the establishment of this act, selecting applicants for the federal services was largely based on nepotism, resulting in the staffing of unqualified applicants. The importance of different HRM practices was slowly beginning to take shape and form in the work environment.

Toward the end of the nineteenth century, the employment conditions in factories were becoming very miserable. The employees felt they were being largely exploited by their employers. Employees wanted to establish a formal communication system with their employers. Employees perceived a better communication with the management would help in an equitable workplace. The emergence of the welfare secretaries was an initiative to help the employers and the employees communicate cordially. The welfare secretaries were predominantly women who mainly looked after employees who needed special care. They slowly included work-related functions to their care-giving roles. The welfare secretaries began to act as liaisons between the management and the employees and also played neutral in their roles.

Around the early 1900s, industrial psychologists began to study the effect of applicants' mental characteristics on job performances. Hugo Munsterberg, chair of the psychology department at Harvard, pioneered this school of thought with the launching of his book *Psychology and Industrial Efficiency*. The book provided three main theses: (1) how to hire the most qualified, (2) how to get maximum productivity, and (3) how to improve work techniques. He developed and conducted simulation tests in several job professions to demonstrate that mental characteristics are important predictors of job performance. World War I provided a great opportunity to conduct these tests on thousands of applicants and identify the results of the test scores on job performance.

It was around the early 1900s that the term "personnel" first appeared in print. The civil service commissions primarily used this term in their annual reports to indicate specific labor needs. Organizations hired personnel specialists and began to identify these departments by several names, such as "Welfare," "Sociological," "Employment and Service," and "Personnel and Training." The primary purpose of these personnel departments was to provide for the well-being of employees in terms of safety, training, and benefits.

However, while the goal of these departments was to help employees, some companies' personnel departments were considered quite invasive. A case in point—from 1914 to 1917, the Sociological Department of Ford Motor Company had a policy that required their management employees to visit their employees' homes. This was mainly to ensure that their employees' lifestyles were not considered too deviant from the expected norms. Employees who did not meet the organization's standards of living styles were either dismissed or denied company profits. Subsequently, this practice was abolished due to the injustice and unfairness caused to several employees.

Around the 1920s, behavioral psychologists contributed another breakthrough research, the Hawthorne studies, in understanding human resource management better. This research investigation, conducted from 1924 to 1933 at the Western Electric company in Chicago, studied the effects of working conditions (such as lighting and temperature) on job performances and productivity. The study provided mixed results, with some experiments suggesting that working conditions did impact job performance while others indicated that they did not. As a result of such irrational results, the organization conducted a deeper research investigation with the help of researchers from the Harvard Business School. Researchers Elton Mayo, an industrial researcher, and his associate Fritz Roethlisberger identified that human factors contributed more than environmental factors in enhancing productivity. Their study, referred to as the Relay Assembly Test Room, identified six women working in the company to understand the effect of working conditions on productivity. However, after a year, the research concluded that these employees did not place much importance on their working conditions. However, they deeply valued the human factors involved at the workplace—how their supervisors treated them, how their co-workers interacted with them, and how they were recognized for their work. Organizations slowly began to realize the importance of having a nurturing work environment instead of a robotic atmosphere.

In 1935, the National Labor Relations Act (Wagner Act) was established, which was another major step for employees to champion for equality at the workplace. This act allowed employees to work together as an entity (a labor union) and collectively bargain for their interests. The mutual agreement between any management and their employees is referred to as the collective bargaining agreement. It is a comprehensive document that includes all work-related practices and interests of the concerned labor unions. Although employees could form labor unions even prior to the formation of this act, employers were generally against and very anti-union. Employees were fired for participating in any unionized activities and hence became very fearful and hesitant to join labor unions. However, this federal act mandated that employers cannot interfere in the formation of labor unions and also have to bargain in good faith with their labor unions. This also saw the formation of labor relations departments in organizations to manage the employment relationship between employees and employers.

In 1964, federal law of the Title VII or the Civil Rights Act brought increased attention to the importance of work-related practices. The act prohibits workplace discrimination based on race, sex, color, or national origins. The law recognized that employees should be treated fairly in their work environments. It introduced several other federal acts over the decades (Equal Pay Act of 1963, Age Discrimination in Employment Act of 1967, Rehabilitation Act of 1973, Americans with Disabilities Act of 1990, Civil Rights Act of 1991, Sarbanes–Oxley Act of 2002) to ensure impartiality at the workplace. Although the importance of HRM was strongly acknowledged, this department was still regarded as being administrative in function.

In the 1970s and 1980s, the business world witnessed several important trends such as increased globalization, intense domestic competition, changes in workforce demographics, and reduced firm productivity. These trends made HRM departments mindful of employees' job performances. Traditionally, strategic models dictated that organizations compete mainly on the basis of external market factors. However, the new model suggested that organizations consider their internal resources, such as their HRM practices and their employees, as their significant organizational assets.

Around the early 1980s, academic scholars also began to identify an interest in organization's internal resources. In 1984, Birger Wernerfelt introduced the term resource-based view to emphasize how effective HRM practices can contribute to any organization's strategic goals. However, it was in the 1990s that Jay Barney laid the foundation to this concept with his revolutionary resource-based view theory or RBV. This theory identified that HRM practices that are valuable and unique can contribute to increased firm performance. Therefore, an increased awareness that employees and their HRM practices can provide organizations with sustainable competitive advantages became entrenched.

The U.S. corporate world provides several examples of HRM practices that are exclusive and inimitable. The Internet leader Google Inc. allows their employees to decide their own work schedules with a 70-20-10 job policy (main project, personal development, and creativity). This practice allows employees to choose to work on any innovative ventures apart from their main responsibilities. The electronic retailer, Best Buy, has revolutionized the concept of the traditional work hours through their ROWE (results-only work environment) program. Employees need to demonstrate their work results on a weekly basis and are not required to be physically present at work every day. The ROWE program has demonstrated 35 percent increase in work productivity and 50 percent decrease in employee turnover.

In the hospitality industry, Ritz-Carlton's daily employee line ups, elaborate talent-hiring process, and $2,000 frontline empowerment culture are applauded in several industries. Booz Allen, a management consulting firm, recognized as a leader in training and development, offers its employees annually $5,000 in tuition reimbursement. The organization considers graduate education and professional development of its employees a very important strategic priority. W.L. Gore & Associates, a manufacturing and an award winning company, emphasizes a work environment that does not provide any professional designations (manager, director, vice-president, etc.) that are usually prevalent in any organization. The management of this company believes a lack of job titles helps build an efficient and productive team culture.

In 1997, Ulrich, a leading scholar, contributed to the strategic orientation of HRM by providing a four-role model of HRM. He suggested that HRM professionals have four specific organizational roles: administrative expert, change agent, employee advocate, and strategic partner. Each role allows HRM professionals to deliver effective organizational outcomes. As an administrative expert, the HR leader is the authority on identifying effective HRM practices to employees. As a change agent, the HR leader must be proactive to adapt HRM practices in step with the dynamic business environments. As an employee advocate, HRM leaders support employees' concerns and also champion their causes. Finally, as a strategic partner, HRM leaders contribute to the strategic orientation of their organizations.

In 2005, Ulrich and Brockbank also proposed the "HR value proposition," suggesting that HRM leaders can contribute to the performances of their organizations in the context of five important components. The external environment (legal, competition, etc.) offers important guiding principles for HRM managers in developing their practices. The HRM leaders must be mindful of creating and providing positive outcomes to all their stakeholders. The HRM managers should develop practices that make the firms clearly stand out in the marketplace. HRM professionals must take proactive roles in understanding the business orientations of their organizations. HRM leaders must learn to wear different caps as they play multiple roles in their organizations.

In the last decade, HRM is witnessing yet another transformation—the emergence of e-HRM (electronic human resource management). E-HRM is the process of using technology for any human resource management practices. E-HRM has provided HRM leaders with two important options for (1) self-service and (2) outsourcing. Organizations are predominantly using e-recruitment, e-learning, virtual teams, and online benefit—planning which allow employees to personally perform some HRM functions. Technology has also redefined the meaning of the workplace as employees work increasingly with their laptops, PDAs, and cell phones, converting their personal spaces into offices. In addition, organizations can outsource certain HRM functions to external vendors that they do not consider to be their core activities. Organizations also outsource HRM functions if it proves to be more cost-effective. Practitioners and scholars suggest that e-HRM could possibly enhance the strategic orientation of human resource professionals as they will devote more time on the long-term activities of the organizations.

Yet several studies suggest mixed results on the roles performed by HRM leaders in their organizations. A 2002 research by SHRM (Society of Human Resource Management) indicated that only 34 percent of the organizations' HRM leaders performed any strategic role. Even after such a long journey, HRM does not seem to be as prominent as finance, marketing, and sales. And the debate continues whether HRM leaders have a prominent place at the board level. What could be the reasons for this?

A 2002 study done by Accenture on HRM practices suggests that HRM leaders do not have strategic leadership because the effectiveness of the HRM practices on firm profits is still not on the agenda of many organizations' HRM departments. While it is very clear to identify the output of any sales or production departments, it is more difficult to get tangible results from HRM departments. HRM leaders are not able to clearly articulate how their staffing practices impact firm performance or how their training practices enhance bottom-line profits. A holistic approach to HRM such that the various practices are interrelated to provide a comprehensive people system will also be very valuable in its effectiveness.

On the other hand, a 2010 consulting study on 3,000 respondents suggested that HRM is an active contributor in the company's business orientation. The business world has become a global marketplace and HRM is stepping in to play a strong role in this globalization process. Organizations are actively seeking new markets and opportunities in emerging economies. The use of technology is also helping HRM become a very strong player in any business. For instance, the use of social media for recruiting and blogs for informal training has transformed how HRM functions are traditionally performed. Experts predict that 60–70 percent of the organizations will use LinkedIn or other social media to attract their applicants in the future.

Studies also suggest that HRM leaders can also contribute to augmenting the innovation of their firms. HRM practices of staffing, training, and performance appraisal and compensation should reward the same criterion (innovation) such that employees realize the value and importance of this competency to the organizational culture. For instance, identifying applicants during hiring who will demonstrate creativity and rewarding employees in the appraisal process who demonstrate such skills. Organizations that adopt a comprehensive HRM approach will ensure instilling a culture of high performing values.

What does the future hold for HRM professionals? As the business world is becoming globalized and information is getting more digitized, HRM departments have to proactively develop their agenda for enhancing the organization's value. Further, these leaders will be held more accountable for their tactical input as organizations are trying to outsource routine administrative work to allow HRM leaders to have quality time for business planning. Consequently, there is a very strong emphasis on adopting human resource management metrics to predict a strong relationship between HRM practices and organizational effectiveness. Human resource management practices have come a long way from the early days of informal apprenticeship to the current existence of electronic practices.

References

Bradley, R. (1995, October). Lessons in productivity and people. *Training & Development, 49*(10), 56.

Esdaille, M. & Alleyne, S. (2004). HR growth. *Black Enterprise, 34*(11), 85–92.

Friedman, B. (2007). Globalization implications for human resource management roles. *Employee Responsibilities and Rights Journal, 19*(3), 157.

Glaspie-Ellis, F. (2006). From paper-pusher to strategic partner: The changing role of the human resource professional. Minneapolis, Minnesota: Dissertation, Capella University.

Greenwood, R. (2004). Employee privacy issues of the early 20th century: 1900 through Hawthorne studies. *Journal of Applied Management and Entrepreneurship, 9*(1), 94–99.

Gubman, E. (2004). HR strategy and planning from birth to business results. *Human Resource Planning, 27*(1), 13–23.

Jamrog, J. & OverHolt, M. (2004). Building a strategic HR function: Continuing the evolution. *Human Resource Planning, 27*(1), 51–63.

Landy, F. (1997). Early influences on the development of industrial and organizational psychology. *Journal of Applied Psychology, 82*(4), 467–477.

Levering, R. & Moskowitz, M. (2007). In good company. *Fortune, 155*(1), 94–114.

Vosburgh, R. (2007). The evolution of HR as an internal consulting organization. *Human Resource Planning, 30*(3), 11–23.

Ulrich, D. & Brockbank, W. (2005). *HR value proposition*. Harvard Business School Press, Boston, MA.

Web Sites

http://www.chartcourse.com/article_SAS.html: SAS institute: Best Places to Work.

http://www.netmba.com/mgmt/scientific/: Frederick Taylor and Scientific Management.

http://www.ourdocuments.gov/doc.php?flash=old&doc=48: Pendleton Act (1883).

http://faculty.frostburg.edu/mbradley/psyography/hugomunsterberg.html: Internet Source for Biographies on Psychologists: Hugo Munsterberg.

http://www.cipd.co.uk/subjects/hrpract/hrtrends/pmhist.htm: Personnel Management: A Short History.

http://www.u-s-history.com/pages/h1612.html: National Labor Relations Act.

http://www.valuebasedmanagement.net/methods_barney_resource_based_view_firm.html: RBV Barney.

http://www.shrm.org/hrdisciplines/orgempdev/articles/Pages/2011ODPredictions.aspx: Study: HR Expected to Become "Power Hitter" in 2011.

http://www.shrm.org/Research/Articles/Articles/Pages/Human_20Resource_20Management_20and_20Innovation.aspx: Human Resource Management and Innovation.

http://www.workforce.com/article/20060309/NEWS02/303099992#: Small Groups, Big Ideas.

Internet References . . .

The History of Affirmative Action Policies

This Web site is maintained by NPC productions and frequently produces articles on various current issues. This site has also received several awards for its content and presentation.

http://www.inmotionmagazine.com/aahist.html

Affirmative Action History—A History and Timeline of Affirmative Action

This Web site provides information on several current domestic and international events. It started as an authoritative answer to all kinds of factual questions since 1938—first as a popular radio quiz show, then starting in 1947 as an annual almanac, and since 1998 on the Internet at http://www.infoplease.com.

http://www.infoplease.com/spot/affirmative1.html

Facts About the Americans with Disabilities Act

This Web site is maintained by the U.S. Equal Employment Opportunity Commission (EEOC), which is responsible for enforcing federal laws.

http://www.eeoc.gov/facts/fs-ada.html

Americans with Disabilities Act

This Web site, Answers.com, is the place where reference information and Q&A content come together to deliver the best answers on the Internet.

http://www.answers.com/topic/americans-with-disabilities-act

Sarbanes–Oxley Essential Information

This site provides details such as the definition, its intent, and consequence of noncompliance.

http://www.sox-online.com/basics.html

The History of Sarbanes–Oxley

This site provides information on the main components of the act.

http://ezinearticles.com/?The-History-of-Sarbanes-Oxley&id=143573

Findlaw

Findlaw is a legal resource for up-to-date online legal information on relevant employment topics.

http://employment.findlaw.com/employment/employment-employee-discrimination-harassment/employment-employee-religion-discrimination-top/employment-employee-religion-workplace.html

Religion and the Workplace

Entrepreneur is a Web site that provides answers for several work-related concerns or issues.

http://www.entrepreneur.com/management/legalcenter/legalissuescolumnistjeffreysteinberger/article184334.html

UNIT 1

Legal Environment

What rights should employees have? Should federal laws support employees? HRM practices in the U.S. corporate world enjoy a very strong federal support. This section addresses some laws that have been introduced to attain an equal opportunity work environment. Affirmative action was introduced in the 1960s to reduce racial discrimination while the Americans with Disabilities Act appeared in the early 1990s to mitigate disability discrimination. The Sarbanes–Oxley Act was introduced in the early 2000s as a result of the corporate scandals the U.S. corporate world witnessed. Should employees be allowed to express their religion at the workplace? What kind of federal interventions do we need to make the work environment fair and just?

- Is Affirmative Action Still Necessary?
- Is the Americans with Disabilities Act Being Abused in the U.S. Workplace?
- Has the Sarbanes–Oxley Act Helped the U.S. Corporations?
- Should Employees Be Allowed to Wear Symbols of Faith in the Workplace?

ISSUE 1

Is Affirmative Action Still Necessary?

YES: David L. Chappell, from "If Affirmative Action Fails . . . What Then?" *New York Times* (May 8, 2004)

NO: Jonathan Kaufman, from "Fair Enough? Barack Obama's Rise Has Americans Debating Whether Affirmative Action Has Run Its Course," *Wall Street Journal* (June 14, 2008)

Learning Outcomes

After reading this issue, you should be able to:

- Gain an understanding of the challenges of affirmative action programs.
- Describe the University of Michigan court case and its implications on affirmative action.
- Discuss the case of *Brown v. Board of Education* and its consequences on affirmative action.
- Identify how affirmative action programs are adopted in other countries.
- Define the terms preferential treatment and reverse discrimination.

ISSUE SUMMARY

YES: David L. Chappell, a columnist and public speaker, believes that affirmative action programs are still required as our society continues to live in racial segregation in tacit and non-tacit ways. He feels that affirmative action programs will benefit individuals who are truly in need of better opportunities in academe or the corporate world.

NO: Jonathan Kauffman, education editor at Bloomberg, believes that affirmative action programs should refocus their overarching goals so that the truly disadvantaged get opportunities to advance.

He emphasizes how President Obama, an African American, is the highest political leader today, making policymakers question that affirmative action programs need to be readdressed.

The term affirmative action was introduced by President Kennedy in 1961 to address the issue of racial discrimination that existed at that time. It was federally mandated in 1965 by the issuing of Executive Order 11246. The main goal was to remedy past acts of discrimination against protected groups (such as African Americans, women) who did not have similar labor opportunities in the workforce. Affirmative action is legally mandated for all federal contractors ($50,000 and 50 or more employees) and can also be a legal settlement in discrimination law suits.

Affirmative action is implemented through utilization analysis and affirmative action plans. The utilization analysis is a statistical method of comparing percentages of the organization's internal labor force with those of the external labor force. The affirmative action plans provide goals as to remedy any underrepresentation of protected groups.

The consequences of affirmative action being implemented in the 1970s and 1980s were that educational institutions saw a reduction of achievement gaps between white and minority students. Further in the 1990s, as the businesses became increasingly global, they benefited from a diverse qualified work force that was able to provide better work solutions.

However, preferential treatment and reverse discrimination have become contentious outbursts of affirmative action plans. Preferential treatment is the process of proactively hiring underutilized groups into the organization's workforce. Reverse discrimination is when dominant groups (such as white males) begin to feel discriminated against during the employment process as a result of preferential treatment. A high-profile reverse discrimination court case is that of Alan Bakke, a qualified white male student, who was refused medical school admission in 1978 due to a quota system (a predetermined number) adopted by school during the admission process. The quota system kept 16 seats out of 100 seats for minority applicants. The outcome of this case resulted in courts prohibiting the use of quota systems in any admission process.

The Supreme Court ruling in 2003 supported the view that affirmative action plans can be applied to students at the university level. The judges affirmed that a diverse university student population will help students understand the dynamics and nuances of today's global work force. Organizations are becoming increasingly global in their interactions today with almost 700 out of 1,000 large U.S. firms stating that their international operations exceed those of their domestic operations. Proactive affirmative efforts will also gradually mitigate the racial disparity experienced at high-profile U.S. universities. Affirmative action will attract protected individuals to careers and universities they might have not considered if there were no such programs. Do we not want see a diverse society?

Chappell states celebrating the 50th anniversary of *Brown v. Board of Education* is a well-deserved victory for affirmative action proponents. In *Brown v. Board of Education,* racial segregation in public schools was deemed unlawful as it went against the tenets of the Constitution. The case began when an African American Linda Brown was not allowed to attend a white elementary school near her house. She had had to walk quite a distance to get to her "black" elementary school. Her father, with other disgruntled parents, sued the board of education. The board of education argued that as separation between races was the norm at that time, it would only help both races to experience this concept in their schooling also. The board suggested that great American leaders attended "segregation schools"—hence such schools should not carry a negative connotation. The case was heard initially in the district court and subsequently in the Supreme Court. In 1954, the Supreme Court made the hallmark decision to ban segregation of races in public schools.

Chappell suggests while this law is clearly put into practice today, racial segregation continues to permeate at other levels. Ms. Cashin, a law professor from Georgetown, supports this viewpoint, contending that the first step in creating this segregation problem is real-estate properties. Housing properties are becoming very largely racially segregated as real-estate agents sell properties as "black or white" neighborhoods. They imply to customers that they will feel at home if they choose "racially appropriate" neighborhoods. Racial segregation is further strengthened by federal housing laws that make sure the properties are distinguished by economic classes creating racially based neighborhoods. This racial segregation of neighborhoods has unfortunately created public schools systems that are seemingly dominated by one race or the other. While we do not have obvious racial segregation in schools, neighborhoods have created their own closed societies and racial schools. This definitely dampens academic opportunities for certain races, making affirmative action still a necessity.

Chappell reiterates that affirmative action laws are still required as races live and experience predominantly in their own separate cliques. However, affirmative action programs need to refocus on groups who are truly disadvantaged today. These programs need to address the needs of racial groups who are economically disadvantaged and truly need the help of federal interventions. Such groups would benefit tremendously as they have been unfairly left behind and affirmative action programs would provide them meaningful education or appropriate work. Though the Michigan law school case supported affirmative action at university levels, the judge concluded hoping that affirmative action programs might not be needed 25 years hence. This was disturbing for many who feel that this program is still *sine quo non* (essential).

However, opponents of affirmative action plans feel that providing preferential treatment sets a stigma suggesting their performance (academic or job) requires federal intervention and support. Employees and students have expressed negative behavior because of preferential treatment. Further, it attributes any individual's hard work for academic or job admission to be a result of external factors. Further, opponents argue that if we continue with affirmative action mandated three decades ago, the U.S. society continues to live in shades of black and white. Do we still want to live in a color-biased society?

Critics are skeptical about affirmative action programs as they observe Senator Obama rise to be president of the United States. The nation witnessed an African American individual reaching the highest political position in the nation today. Further, we have several women and African American individuals holding high positions in political, academic, and corporate life. This program was enacted initially in 1960s to provide opportunities for special groups who were denied employment and academic opportunities. Today we see these "protected" people in the highest corporate boardrooms and educational institutions. Do we need affirmative action programs still?

Opponents of affirmative action are convinced that affirmative action results in reverse discrimination. Reverse discrimination suits continue to dominate legal courtrooms even today. Recently, white and Hispanic firefighters in New Haven, Connecticut, won a reverse discrimination suit as the city of Connecticut threw out the test scores of white and Hispanic employees on a promotional exam as African Americans firefighters did not receive high scores on the same tests. The city management threw the tests out as they feared lawsuits from African Americans about the promotional test being racially based. The firefighters won as they claimed their race and skin color was discriminated against for further employment opportunities.

A concluding twist to this debate is whether such programs are quintessentially American. Have other countries initiated federal programs for disadvantaged groups? In fact—yes they do. India provides affirmative programs to people from different castes (distinct labor groups) and Malaysia offers support to different ethnic groups (Muslims and Chinese). These groups are truly disadvantaged and the local governments have taken proactive action to help in their personal advancement.

YES  **David L. Chappell**

If Affirmative Action Fails . . . What Then?

The 50th anniversary of the *Brown v. Board of Education* decision this month is a well-deserved feel-good moment for civil rights strategists, but it is only a temporary distraction from the deep conflicts that remain.

Many people earnestly believe that aggressive remedies like affirmative action are still necessary to eliminate the inequality at which Brown made only a glancing blow. Even the most ardent supporters of affirmative action are frustrated, however, because of its persistent unpopularity and its very limited success in closing the academic and economic gaps between black and white Americans.

The Supreme Court's decision last year involving the University of Michigan Law School, though it defended a form of affirmative action, appears to put a 25-year limit on the court's tolerance of even the most scrupulously moderate considerations of race. In the companion decision on Michigan's undergraduate program, the court banned broader forms of affirmative action altogether.

So what now?

Of the shelfload of new books that try to answer that question, "The Pursuit of Fairness: A History of Affirmative Action" by Terry H. Anderson (Oxford University Press) is a good place to get your bearings. Following the political scientist John David Skrentny and the historian Hugh Davis Graham, Mr. Anderson emphasizes the "ironies of affirmative action," the policies' logical contradictions and perverse effects. Mr. Anderson, a history professor at Texas A&M, defends many of the policies from simplistic attack. But he makes clear that the best defense of affirmative action has always been that the alternatives to it are even worse.

Mr. Anderson will surprise many with his reminder that the federal government did not commit itself to affirmative action until the Republican administration of Richard M. Nixon. Racial hiring preferences had been declared illegal after President Lyndon B. Johnson's brief experiment with them. Nixon revived them, Mr. Anderson says, partly from political calculations. Democratic liberals would be forced to defend and expand Nixon's affirmative action policy. Black hiring preferences would supersede white workers' hard-won seniority rights, thus driving a wedge between union members and black voters. Nixon was able to capitalize on the division by the end of his first term, turning against his own initiatives and other strong remedies, like court-ordered busing. As Nixon hoped, white rank-and-filers abandoned the Democrats in droves.

Opposition to affirmative action persisted, partly because racists resented black success. But people who were not racists also found it hard to justify violating the 14th Amendment's equal-protection clause to serve its deeper purpose. And when affirmative action worked at all, it tended to aid those who least needed aid: black students who had already qualified for university admission or come very close. That increasingly meant affluent black students with college-trained parents. Affirmative action offered little to those who suffered most from racism, the poor.

Sheryll Cashin, a law professor at Georgetown, offers the most refreshing path away from the confusion: integration, a goal so long out of fashion that it is ripe for revival. In "The Failures of Integration: How Race and Class Are Undermining the American Dream" (PublicAffairs), she warns upwardly mobile black parents that their growing separatism is a swindle even as she sympathizes with their desire to forgo fighting for acceptance in their neighborhoods. Black enclaves in leafy suburbs are now available. But one of the selling points of these enclaves—the huge racial discounts on nice houses that white buyers won't consider because too many neighbors are black—make the benefits short-lived. Real estate agents steer black buyers into these areas, emphasizing that they will "fit in." They don't mention that economic development is moving away from these areas or that underfinanced schools and services often explain much of the racial discount. Black enclaves are often closest to declining areas of the city.

Ms. Cashin addresses the white middle class with equal seriousness, seeing among them too many flight risks. They, too, are getting cheated. As the rich hunker down in gated communities or otherwise remove themselves from the common tax base, they stick the rest of America with the bill for their extended sewer lines and commuting time (increased road maintenance, pollution, accidents).

Ms. Cashin presents historical evidence that America's unusual stratification does not result from individual choices or market forces. Laws have trapped a desperate underclass in ghettos and ferried a decadent overclass away. The Federal Housing Administration, created in 1937, underwrote one-third of all new housing construction in its first 35 years. Its manual required that all properties "continue to be occupied by the same social and racial classes." The Interstate Highway Act (1956), in addition to subsidizing oil barons in Texas and Saudi Arabia, directly displaced 330,000 poor families, mostly black. State laws made things worse. A combination of new town charters (which encourage creation of low-tax havens), zoning laws (which artificially concentrate both poverty and wealth) and local building codes (which make housing affordable to a select stratum) have sharply segregated, and to some extent created, social classes.

The recent vintage of these policies is important. The widespread barriers—which are arguably more harmful than legal segregation or the lingering effects of slavery—created the world we live in today.

In "Silent Convenants: Brown v. Board of Education and the Unfulfilled Hopes for Racial Reform" (Oxford University Press), Derrick Bell tacks in the opposite direction from Ms. Cashin, insisting that separatism is unavoidable and that benefits can be had within it. It is significant that Mr. Bell, who provocatively posits that black people might have been better off without the Brown decision, still strongly supports affirmative action. White opponents of affirmative action were deluded, he writes: affirmative action never deprived them of opportunities or benefits. This is hard to square with Mr. Bell's advocacy of slave reparations. His logic seems to be: white people resisted giving black people their due when it cost them nothing. Why don't we try making them pay a lot of money instead?

Mr. Bell's main theme is the "interest convergence" theory he advanced 24 years ago—that white leaders grant concessions to black people only to prevent upheaval or otherwise serve their own interests. The theory was novel not so much for its realism as for the outrage that Mr. Bell conveyed when explaining it. Though many call him a cynic, Mr. Bell, a visiting professor at New York University Law School, still appears deeply hurt that white people do not voluntarily give up their privileges.

Mr. Bell's most practical section covers alternatives to school desegregation. He will irritate liberals and union supporters by advocating experiments with vouchers, along with charter schools and single-sex education. Unfortunately, he leaves the proposals underdeveloped. Showing advanced symptoms of academic celebrity, he may be too busy to put in the long hours of contemplation or to do the digging necessary to come up with fresh, factually rich arguments to vie with Ms. Cashin's.

Charles Ogletree Jr., a professor at Harvard Law School, names Mr. Bell as a mentor and is clearly on the celebrity track with him. Like Mr. Bell, he is a brilliant lawyer, but he writes evenhandedly in "All Deliberate Speed: Reflections on the First Half-Century of Brown v. Board of Education" (W. W. Norton), more like a judge than Mr. Bell, who is content to advocate one side. Mr. Ogletree shares Ms. Cashin's concerns about black flight and, like her, takes economic divisions, including those within the black population, very seriously. The best part of his book is an invigorating memoir of his rise from poverty. He found opportunity and hope in desegregation, which balance his disappointment with Brown's unfinished business.

Mr. Ogletree gives critics of reparations a fair hearing, though he ultimately rejects their arguments. His proposal for reparations, one of many in this wide-ranging book, is his most fully developed idea—perhaps because he is preparing a related suit, on behalf of victims of the Tulsa race riot in 1921. Since the Tulsa victims are few, and since they sustained direct injuries, their case sidesteps some of the objections to reparations for slavery: slavery was perfectly legal until 1865; its victims and perpetrators are long dead; only racists think guilt is genetically transferable. (So far, the Tulsa suit does not answer the objection that, politically, reparations are a pipe dream.)

If the suit helps revive black commitment to the freedom struggle, or white support, it will revive the most elusive part of the struggle's half-century-old heyday. If not, the frustrations of the affirmative-action era may not go away so much as change form.

Jonathan Kaufman

Fair Enough? Barack Obama's Rise Has Americans Debating Whether Affirmative Action Has Run Its Course

Warren, Mich.—Stan Sheyn, a white student who attends community college in this working-class Detroit suburb, supports Barack Obama for president. But he has no time for what he calls "double standards and propagation of victim mentality."

"The fact that a black man can run for the position of the President of the United States of America only corroborates that there is enough opportunity and equality for great things like that to happen," he says. "And that there is no need to create special advantages for any demographic group."

Electra Fulbright, a black small-business consultant in prosperous Southfield, Mich., couldn't disagree more.

"Obama's privileges and his accomplishments are minute compared to the black population at large," says Ms. Fulbright, who plans to vote for Sen. Obama. "When we talk about Obama, we are not talking about the average black American. There is injustice in this country, and until we correct it, we need affirmative action."

Few issues have been as incendiary in the workplace and on college campuses as affirmative action—in large part because so many blacks and whites have been personally affected by affirmative action, in ways both good and bad.

Now, Sen. Obama's rise is prompting some whites to ask—and some blacks to fear—the question: Does America still need affirmative action, given that an African-American has made it to the top of American politics?

The question has been asked before, as other blacks have risen to high positions. But Sen. Obama's swift ascent to the verge of the presidency may have created a turning point in the debate.

The issue of affirmative action is likely to dog Sen. Obama on the campaign trail as he seeks to win over white blue-collar voters in battleground states like Michigan. For many of these voters, affirmative action has been divisive since the 1970s. Ward Connerly, a prominent affirmative-action opponent, is seeking to place anti-affirmative action referendums on the ballot in

Arizona, Nebraska and Colorado. Voters would be asked to ban "preferential treatment" of women and minorities in state university admissions, the filling of state-funded jobs and awarding of state contracts.

White anger over affirmative action has diminished as the Supreme Court has systematically narrowed the scope of programs in colleges and the workplace. Still, the gap between black and white opinion remains wide.

More than half of blacks—57%—say the country should make "every effort to improve the position of blacks and minorities, even if it means giving preferential treatment," according to a poll conducted last year by the Pew Research Center, a non-partisan Washington think tank that studies social attitudes. Just 27% of whites agree with that view. The same poll shows that nearly half of whites—48%—believe the U.S. has "gone too far in pushing equal rights in this country." Far fewer African Americans—27%—agree.

Opinions about affirmative action vary depending on how researchers word their questions; support tends to grow, for example, when the question describes the programs in more detail. But the Gallup polling firm says that regardless of the wording, all of its surveys on affirmative action show blacks overwhelmingly support it, while whites tend to be much more divided.

Sen. Obama's success has also stirred an uncomfortable debate within the black community over who has reaped the gains of affirmative action. Some argue the policies skew toward middle-class blacks instead of poor blacks, and have favored too many individuals like Sen. Obama—people with a biracial background or the children of African and Caribbean immigrants, as opposed to blacks born in the U.S.

In a 2000 interview with the *Journal of Blacks in Higher Education,* Sen. Obama, then an Illinois state senator, said: "I have no way of knowing if I was a beneficiary of affirmative action either in my admission to Harvard or my initial election to the [Harvard Law] Review. If I was, then I am certainly not ashamed of the fact, for I would argue that affirmative action is important precisely because those who benefit typically rise to the challenge when given an opportunity."

Sen. Obama's newfound prominence has also prompted some successful blacks to wonder whether his achievements, and theirs, mean affirmative action should be modified to help poor and working-class whites.

"You have this traditional assumption that whites have made it and have it all—that 'because I am black, I am disadvantaged,' and 'because I am white, I am advantaged,'" says Rev. Carlyle Stewart, who holds degrees from the University of Chicago and Northwestern and heads a large middle-class black church in Southfield, a short drive from Warren. "It may be time to broaden that discussion."

Sen. Obama "believes that no one can deny that our country has made tremendous progress in the past 50 years," said campaign spokesman Tommy Vietor in a statement. "But the suggestion that somehow Senator Obama's campaign represents an easy shortcut to racial reconciliation is just not realistic." He said Sen. Obama believes "affirmative action in universities today is appropriate only if race is one of many factors. The Supreme Court has made that clear."

Republican presidential nominee Sen. John McCain opposes "affirmative action plans and quotas that give weight to one group of Americans at the expense of another," says McCain spokesman Tucker Bounds. "Plans that result in quotas, where such plans have not been judicially created to remedy a specific, proven act of discrimination, only result in more discrimination and violate the concept of equality of opportunity."

Affirmative action began in 1961, when President Kennedy issued an executive order declaring that federal contractors should "take affirmative action" to integrate their work forces.

The initiative broadened to include policies that favored women and minorities in hiring and promotion at work and in college admissions, the goal being to overcome past discrimination.

Many whites charged that this amounted to "reverse discrimination." In the landmark Bakke case of 1978, the Supreme Court narrowed the definition of affirmative action, declaring unconstitutional the use of some rigid quota systems. But it upheld the principle of affirmative action.

In 2003, a more-conservative Supreme Court again upheld the principle of affirmative action, but narrowed the interpretation still further, adding in a majority opinion, "We expect that 25 years from now, the use of racial preferences will no longer be necessary." Opponents of affirmative action recently filed another suit challenging affirmative action in Texas.

Many economists and sociologists agree that affirmative-action programs have helped spur the growth of the black middle and upper classes, defined as households making more than $40,000 a year. Today, this group accounts for about 40% of black households, up from about 25% in 1970, according to U.S. Census figures. During that same period, the percentage of white households in the middle class and above has risen to about 60%, from just under 50%.

Affirmative action policies have helped blacks gain access to large corporations and top universities, studies have shown, and the presence of blacks in these places has encouraged others to follow. The number of African Americans at the country's top 50 colleges and universities has doubled in recent decades, according to Harry Holzer, a Georgetown University economist. Women have benefited, too, especially in the 1970s and 1980s, when they began breaking into traditionally male-dominated fields.

Michigan's Macomb County is home to many of the fabled "Reagan Democrats," the conservative working-class whites who left the Democratic Party largely over social issues including race in the 1980s. Here, life has been changed by affirmative action and the rise of the black middle class. In the past five years, the African-American population has doubled to about 6% from about 3%, in part as blacks have left Detroit for safer suburbs with better schools.

Such changes make some whites here wonder why affirmative action is needed at all. "If blacks are living in the same houses that I am living in, and they can afford the same things I can afford, why shouldn't I have the same breaks as they do?" says Tony Licata, a professional photographer in Macomb County who is white and says he is leaning toward voting for Sen. McCain.

"Race should not be the deciding point about who gets what," says Jessalin Horne, a white working-class college student who plans to vote for Sen. Obama in the fall.

In conversations, many white blue-collar and middle-class workers in Macomb County said they blame competition from China, India and elsewhere for their job losses, not competition from blacks. But the economic battering that many poor and working-class whites have taken as Michigan's auto industry has shrunk makes some whites feel that it's their turn for a leg up.

"I have been a supporter of affirmative action, but it needs to be refocused—other groups need to be included," says Marceia Lugo, a divorced white mother of three whose mother and ex-husband have left Michigan to look for work. Ms. Lugo says she backed Sen. Clinton but will now vote for Sen. Obama. "I am not black, so I don't know those issues. But I have been poor, and I have had to struggle, so I should get special treatment."

A half-hour drive from Warren lies Southfield, Mich., a leafy, integrated middle-class and upper-middle-class suburb that is a testament to the impact of affirmative action. Barbara Talley, now a retired financial analyst and a Southfield resident, became one of the first black owners of a KFC franchise in the 1980s, after Rev. Jesse Jackson lobbied the company to sell more franchises to African Americans. Wanda Cook-Robinson, Southfield's black school superintendent, has been the first black in several teaching and administrative positions at area schools. "That wouldn't have happened without affirmative action," says Ms. Cook-Robinson.

Many blacks here don't want to lose the boost that they say affirmative action gives them. Stephen Kemp, a successful black funeral director in Southfield, sends his son to a $24,000-a-year private high school. His son, a junior, has been receiving letters from elite colleges wooing him to apply. "When they look at his application they see he is an African-American male—he has so much opportunity," says Mr. Kemp, who himself attended the University of Michigan. "Brown called him yesterday."

Mr. Kemp thinks it is fine that his son gets special attention, because diversity on campus benefits whites as well as blacks. "If you are getting a true education, that has to reflect all kinds of people," he says.

The election, especially Sen. Obama's success in winning white voters, has Mary Donaldson thinking that affirmative action is likely to fade away in coming years as the country continues to change. "My son is 9 years old. Just because he is black, he can't think he's going to get special treatment," says Ms. Donaldson, who works at a pre-school in Southfield and supports Sen. Obama. "I don't want him to totally depend on something like that."

Twyla Griffin, who works for a health-care company and attends church in Southfield, says she thinks bias lives on. "It's fear—'this black boy is going to take my little white Johnny's job,'" says Ms. Griffin. Affirmative action, she says, simply levels a still-tilted playing field.

"It would be great if Obama made all the decisions for us, but there are a lot of people who still have decision-making power who are still a little prejudiced," says Marilyn Hobbs, an intellectual-property manager who supports Sen. Obama.

James Jackson, a black banker and another Obama supporter, nods in agreement. He says he doesn't put his photograph on his business card like many of his white colleagues, because he thinks it will discourage white customers. "Race is a real issue still, no matter what happens in November," he says.

EXPLORING THE ISSUE

Is Affirmative Action Still Necessary?

Critical Thinking and Reflection

1. What suggestions would you have to mitigate the effects of racially segregated neighborhoods and schools?
2. If you were making the decision on the test scores that the New Haven firefighters took, what would you have done? Why?
3. Should policymakers identify new groups that should be included as "protected groups" in affirmative action? Which groups would you suggest and why?
4. Why do we need affirmative programs when we have protected group members as our president and Supreme Court judge?
5. Explain how the affirmative action programs in India are different from those of the United States?

Is There Common Ground?

The most important guiding principle of affirmative action is to provide and enhance opportunities to individuals who are truly disadvantaged either at the workplace or education. The word disadvantaged has many times carried wrongful interpretations, which has led to ugly lawsuits. Policymakers even suggest that EEOC identifies new groups that can be included in affirmative action programs. The affirmative program was established initially to protect women and African Americans in the 1960s as they were largely discriminated at that time. Today, we have females as leaders of *Fortune* 500 companies and African Americans leading the nation. Should we reconsider the focus of the affirmative action programs? What about other groups that are truly disadvantaged? For instance, what about economically disadvantaged groups? And economically disadvantaged groups who are white? Their skin color does not allow them to currently qualify for affirmative action. Why should they not benefit from such programs? What other groups of people do you think can benefit from being included in affirmative action programs?

Additional Resources

Barnes, R. (2009). *Justices Rule in Favor of White Firefighters in Racial-Bias Case.* http://www.washingtonpost.com/wp-dyn/content/article/2009/06/29/AR2009062901608.html

Gray, M. (2007, February). Nationwide attack on affirmative action. *Black Enterprise, 37*(7), 29.

Kronholz, J., Tomsho, R., and Forelle, C. (2003). High Court's ruling on race could affect business hiring. *Wall Street Journal* (Eastern Edition), p. A.1.

Marshall, A. (2003). U.S. Supreme Court tackles affirmative action in university admissions: Will the outcome affect corporate diversity efforts? *Employee Relations Law Journal, 29*(1), 96. Retrieved October 21, 2009, from ABI/INFORM Global (Document ID: 348086671).

Zaleski, J. (2004). The unfinished agenda of *Brown v. Board of Education. Publishers Weekly, 251*(12), 77–77.

http://law.jrank.org/pages/3291/Bakke-V-University-California-Appeal-1978.html: Bakke V. University of California Appeal: 1978—Reverse Discrimination Claimed.

www.cnn.com/2009/POLITICS/06/29/supreme.court.discrimination/index.html: High Court Backs Firefighters in Reverse Discrimination Suit.

http://www.csmonitor.com/2009/0423/p02s01-usju.html%20: Reverse-Discrimination Case Splits Supreme Court.

www.timeshighereducation.co.uk/story.asp?storyCode=177865§ioncode=26: Michigan Ruling Reaffirms Drive for Student Diversity.

www.watson.org/~lisa/blackhistory/early-civilrights/brown.html: *Brown v. Board Education.*

http://www.jewishworldreview.com/cols/sowell060503.asp: International Affirmative Action.

http://search.proquest.com/docview/398244133?accountid=27: Supreme Court Eases Way for Schools in Busing Cases—Major Ruling Sets Standard for Courts on Ending Desegregation Orders.

ISSUE 2

Will the Americans with Disabilities Act Amendments Act (ADAAA) Be Abused in the U.S. Workplace?

YES: Dina Berta, from "Labor Lawyers: Changes to Americans with Disabilities Act May Lead to More Workplace Discrimination Suits," *Nation's Restaurant News* (October 2008)

NO: Victoria Zellers, from "Make a Resolution: ADA Training," *HR Magazine* (January 2009)

Learning Outcomes

After reading this issue, you should be able to:

- Gain an understanding of the American Disability Act.
- Define employment terminology specific to the ADA.
- Understand how ADA is different from ADAAA.
- Understand the court cases and how it will be interpreted by ADAAA.
- Gain an international perspective of this act.

ISSUE SUMMARY

YES: Award-winning writer Dina Berta suggests that the ADA (Americans with Disabilities Act) has always been controversial because it was difficult to define and understand. Now that the act has been redefined to ADAAA (Americans with Disabilities Act Amendments Act), it will allow more employees to fall under the disability category, which could increase the number of lawsuits.

NO: Legal attorney Victoria Zellers argues that sufficient training of HR professionals could substantially reduce litigation expenses for organizations. The HR department should be proactive to understand and provide for the special needs of their employees.

The Americans with Disabilities Act (ADA) was introduced in 1990 to reduce discrimination against disabled people. This act is applicable to any organizations with 15 or more employees. Traditionally, society has treated people who are disabled differently. This federal act was instituted to mitigate this negative inclination in the society. This act was introduced as a federal intervention would help disabled people integrate better into the society and also help them achieve their economic independence. Currently, approximately 43,000,000 Americans have one or more physical or mental disabilities. This rate is increasing constantly as advancements in science have made it possible to diagnose several disorders.

The ADA defined disabled individuals as those who have a physical or mental impairment that drastically impairs their major life activities. The definition of "major life activities" includes walking, speaking, sitting, and reading, among several other activities specified. Specifically, an individual must demonstrate that he/she (a) has a physical or mental impairment that substantially limits one or more of his or her major life activities; (b) has a record of such an impairment; or (c) is regarded as having an impairment. The disabled categories also include "controlled impairment"—individuals who have conditions that are controlled with medication (for example, epilepsy) and also individuals who are perceived as disabled (for example, morbidly obese).

The ADA introduced several important employment terms to the American corporate world. *Essential functions* are defined as the tasks and duties that employees must perform to be effective in their jobs. *Marginal functions* are considered peripheral duties that are not critical to the jobs. Employers usually make hiring decisions based on the ability of individuals to perform essential job functions. *Reasonable accommodations* are adjustments that employers may provide for disabled employees (such as wheel chair access; Braille access). *Undue hardship* occurs when organizations perceive they might incur a lot of costs or difficulties in providing any accommodations to the disabled.

The main controversy with the ADA is the very strict interpretation of the word "disabled." This difficulty in interpretation of the word has led to several lawsuits. The number of disability legal suits that the EEOC (Equal Employment Opportunity Commission) receives is ranked third after sexual harassment and racial suits. The other contributing factor for increased lawsuits under ADA was the inability of employers to provide reasonable accommodations. It has been observed that employees and customers frequently sue organizations and retail establishments that do not provide reasonable accommodations. Small and mid-size establishments find it very difficult to make reasonable accommodations due to their budgetary constraints.

Two important court cases illustrate how the interpretation of word disabled can be lead to legal disputes. In *Sutton v. United Airlines*, twin sisters sued the airline when they were not hired due to severe myopia as airline pilots. The sisters claimed they were not hired because they were perceived as disabled. However, the court concluded that severe myopic problems do not classify as a disability as they did not impede the sisters from getting other jobs; also they functioned perfectly well with corrective measures (eyeglasses).

In *Toyota Motor Manufacturing v. Williams* the courts upheld and reversed decisions to reach a correct definition of the word disabled. The plaintiff, Ella Williams, sued Toyota after she developed carpal tunnel syndrome and requested reasonable accommodation. However, when the organization terminated her subsequently she sued under ADA claiming that she was fired because of her disability. The Supreme Court did not consider her condition a disability as it did not impair her major life activities.

The ADA has been amended to ADAAA from January 2009 in view of broadening the definition of disability. The term "major life activities" was redefined with an exhaustive list of activities such as walking, standing, lifting, eating, standing, lifting, bending, reading, writing, and sleeping, among several others including critical activities. Further, employers have to disregard mitigating factors when determining if individuals have a disability. *Mitigating factors* are defined as external factors that help disabled individuals reduce the impact of any disability (such as hearing aids or medications). However, corrective measures such as eyeglasses and contacts were excluded in assessing any disability. In addition, chronic illnesses that could reoccur (such as cancer) qualify as disabilities as such illnesses in their active stage would substantially limit an individual's life activity. Given such a broad expansion to disability, many more individuals will qualify as being disabled. Employers are very apprehensive they may face increased law suits. Will individuals abuse such a broad definition of the term disabled?

On the other hand, HRM professionals are confident that sufficient training is the key to reduce costly law suits. While organizations invest sufficiently enough in sexual harassment and diversity training, organizations do not spend enough for disability training. Disability training can make employers feel well-prepared and identify any loopholes in managing the process. During any hiring process disabled individuals should not be asked specifically about their disabilities but only whether they can perform the essential job functions required for their jobs. Further, experts suggest that HRM managers adopt a very collaborative approach with line managers about employees in understanding the broadened definition of the term "disabled." HR managers should be informed of employees who may be having problems with major life activities so that they can be prepared when such employee-related problems arise. The main goal for HRM departments and line managers is to develop a well-coordinated approach before such employee concerns become litigation. HRM professionals and hiring managers should also be familiar with the amendments of the act with an emphasis on how disability can be accommodated.

The new expanded definition of the ADAAA has created both concerns and answers to disability activists. The current broad definition has an exhaustive list of activities not included in the earlier version of the act and has included additional disability clauses. Therefore, more individuals would currently qualify as being considered disabled. For instance, the current ADAAA requires disabilities to be considered without mitigating factors—employers evaluate employees' disabilities without the support of medication or external aids. The current amendment requires employees' disabilities be considered even if their diseases (such as cancer) are in remission. The ADA legal complaints are ranked third by EEOC, suggesting that there could be a lot of gray areas still unanswered by the law. According to the EEOC, there are about 38.4 million in the workforce that qualify for being disabled under the new ADAAA. Legal attorneys are more convinced that plaintiffs will win as disabilities have a clearer interpretation today.

However, alternate perspectives to this issue are to understand that the word disability per se is disputable. Therefore, policymakers have to frequently evaluate what actually constitutes a physical or mental disability. For instance, traditionally, the workforce viewed only "visible disability" (such as paraplegics, quadriplegics, and visually impaired) as needing special accommodations at work. However, today, health care professionals classify many disabilities that are "invisible" (such as mental disabilities) also requiring special accommodations. Consequently, it is important to reclassify the definitions of disability as the amendment act has done recently to mitigate any misinterpretations or support a dichotomous viewpoint. The ADA is now almost 20 years old, suggesting that this act might require frequent reinterpretations of what comprises physical and mental disabilities. Further the advancements in science and technology allow health care professionals to identify a broader range of diseases.

An international understanding of this act suggests that other countries also provide protection to disabled individuals. The ADA introduced in the 1990s in the United States may have prompted emerging economies like India and Mexico to also introduce disability acts. In 1995, both India and Mexico introduced disability acts (India: The Persons with Disabilities Act; Mexico: The Law for Disabled Persons). The question that remains largely unanswered in these countries is whether these laws are being enforced strictly and who qualifies for being disabled.

Dina Berta

Labor Lawyers: Changes to Americans with Disabilities Act May Lead to More Workplace Discrimination Suits

Employers should expect to see more workplace lawsuits under the newly amended Americans with Disabilities Act, according to labor lawyers who advise restaurant operators.

Unhappy with strict interpretations the U.S. Supreme Court has made since the ADA statute was passed in 1990, Congress acted to expand the law and make it easier for individuals with mental or physical impairments to file discrimination lawsuits. . . .

The law applies to workplaces with 15 or more employees for at least 20 weeks during a year, including part-time and temporary employees.

"The bottom line is that when it comes to ADA litigation, restaurants should now have the same expectation for ADA claims as they do for other discrimination claims, such as gender, race, religion, age and etc.," said Michael Mitchell, a partner in the New Orleans office of Fisher & Phillips and executive editor of the Hospitality Workforce Trends newsletter.

The amended law redefines and expands the definition of a disabled person as someone who is unable to perform a major life activity or is significantly restricted in the duration of a major activity.

Included in the list of major activities are such tasks as walking, standing, lifting, eating and sleeping, and mental tasks such as communicating, reading and thinking. Any major body functions, such as cell growth, digestive and reproductive functions, are also considered major life activities.

"It will no longer be difficult to prove that you have a right to bring such a claim," Mitchell said. "Although employers still have the same ability to argue to a jury that they had a legitimate and non-discriminatory reason to justify an employment action, they can no longer count on being able to defeat such a claim before it gets to that point."

Employers currently are able to avoid litigation by asserting that some employees do not qualify for protection under the law, given the strict interpretations the courts were making, explained attorney David Jordan of the Fulbright & Jaworski employment law firm in Houston.

"But Congress said [the courts] have gone too far," he said. "There were too many people being locked out of protection of the ADA. They wanted more people protected."

After a series of pro-employer decisions by the Supreme Court in 1999, lower courts began applying a "demanding standard" when determining whether a plaintiff was considered sufficiently disabled to advance an ADA lawsuit, Mitchell said.

"Disability advocates reacted angrily to what they considered be an undermining of the act's original intent," he added.

To further broaden the definition of a disability, "mitigating measures" can no longer be considered in determining whether a person is disabled enough for ADA protection, the lawyers said. A mitigation measure, for example, might be a prosthetic leg or hearing aids or medications. Corrective eye glasses or contact lenses were excluded.

"If you have a prosthetic device that enables you to walk just fine, then an employer could argue you were not disabled under the [ADA] act," Jordan said. "The courts said you had to take into account that with such a mitigating measure, you no longer fall under the protection of the ADA. The new legislation removed that."

Mitchell warned that operators, owners and human resources executives will need to update their policies and offer wider accommodations to their workforce. He and Jordan both are encouraging employers to err on the side of caution in considering employee requests for accommodations.

However, "the most prudent and cautious employers are probably already doing enough to protect themselves under the changes of the ADA," Jordan said. His firm is advising clients to be "thorough and seek counsel for close calls. Those who are always making close calls in favor of the employees should be fine."

Victoria Zellers

NO

Make a Resolution: ADA Training

Abstract (Summary)

As the New Year rang in, the Americans with Disabilities Act (ADA) Amendments Act took effect, bringing millions more people within the ADA's protection. The ADA Amendments Act's (ADAAA) vast expansion of disability means that many more applicants and employees are eligible for reasonable accommodations and that employers need a fresh ADA compliance strategy. The ADAAA defines and vastly expands the term major life activities as including caring for oneself, performing manual tasks, seeing, hearing, eating, sleeping, walking, standing, lifting, bending, speaking, breathing, learning, reading, concentrating, thinking, communicating and working. The ADAAA does not require ADA training, but provides a strong business case for it. Sexual harassment training isn't specifically required by Title VII of the Civil Rights Act of 1964 either, but employers recognized the importance of regular sexual harassment training after the US Supreme Court decided Burlington Industries Inc v Ellerth and Faragher v City of Boca Raton.

Now is the time for stand-alone, dedicated coursework.

As the New Year rang in, the Americans with Disabilities Act (ADA) Amendments Act took effect, bringing millions more people within the ADA'S protection. The ADA Amendments Act's (ADAAA) vast expansion of "disability" means that many more applicants and employees are eligible for reasonable accommodations and that employers need a fresh ADA compliance strategy.

In the past, employers often won ADA cases by filing motions for summary judgment and establishing that the plaintiffs were not disabled, avoiding expensive jury trials.

Employers will need to alter their approaches and take a page from what worked in the sexual harassment context. Employers can curb litigation risks through ADA training separate from general equal employment opportunity or nondiscrimination training.

Although training budgets are being squeezed in these tough economic times, training could save employers time and expense in the long run.

The ADAAA broadened the ADA's definition of disability by expanding the term "major life activities," doing away with the "substantially limited" requirement for those regarded as having a disability, and overturning two U.S. Supreme Court decisions that interpreted the ADA'S definition of disability narrowly.

The ADA still covers only qualified individuals with disabilities and provides that to be disabled, an individual must have "a physical or mental impairment that substantially limits one or more major life activities," or must have a record of such an impairment, or must be regarded as having such an impairment.

However, with the ADAAA, the only requirement for the "regarded as" prong is that the impairment must not be minor—a criterion the law does not define—or transitory, defined in the law as lasting less than six months.

The ADAAA also defines and vastly expands the term "major life activities" as including "caring for oneself, performing manual tasks, seeing, hearing, eating, sleeping, walking, standing, lifting, bending, speaking, breathing, learning, reading, concentrating, thinking, communicating and working." The amendment states that major life activities include the operation of a major bodily function, such as "functions of the immune system, normal cell growth, digestive, bowel, bladder, neurological, brain, respiratory, circulatory, endocrine and reproductive functions."

Decisions Overturned

In addition, the ADAAA overturns two U.S. Supreme Court decisions that had limited the ADA'S coverage. One decision let employers consider the ameliorative effects of mitigating measures, such as hearing aids and medication, when determining whether someone has a disability (Sutton v. United Airlines Inc., 527 U.S. 471 (1999)). The ADAAA instead requires that employers evaluate impairments without regard to mitigating measures. Thus, a mental disorder such as depression controlled by medication must be considered in its unmedicated state to determine if it is a disability. The ADAAA does have an exception that permits employers to take into account the effects of eyeglasses and contact lenses.

The ADAAA also overturned a Supreme Court decision that concluded that the term "disability" should be viewed narrowly and that said the ADA requires a demanding standard to prove one is disabled (Toyota Motor Manufacturing, Kentucky Inc. v. Williams, 534 U.S. 184 (2002)). The ADAAA instead provides that disability should be viewed broadly and asks the U.S. Equal Employment Opportunity Commission (EEOC) to issue regulations to further address this issue.

Another important change requires that impairments that are episodic or in remission qualify as disabilities if in their active stage they would substantially limit a major life activity. This revision, along with the one regarding mitigating measures, moves numerous conditions such as cancer, diabetes and epilepsy from a case-by-case determination to almost certain status as ADA disabilities.

The Argument for Training

The ADAAA does not require ADA training, but provides a strong business case for it. . . .

Employers . . . should recognize the value of training HR personnel, managers and supervisors on the ADA and its amendments. While the ADAAA did not alter the ADA'S reasonable accommodation and nondiscrimination requirements, many more individuals will qualify for these protections. So it's essential that key professionals understand what the ADA, as amended, involves.

Training should include review of:

Who is covered. Given the expansion of "major life activities" and the removal of mitigating measures from consideration in disability determinations, almost anyone who has, or is regarded as having, a serious impairment or disease that is not temporary will qualify as disabled. Ensure that training covers any applicable state laws prohibiting disability discrimination.

How hiring policies and practices are affected. Since applicants are covered, re-evaluate hiring processes. Case in point, reading is now a major life activity. Thus, you will need to look at how reading may affect your hiring process. If reading isn't an essential function of the job, such as for a maintenance staff position, and if a candidate can't read, an employer probably will have to provide a reasonable accommodation to help the candidate complete the application process.

However, if reading and/or writing are essential job functions, the employer doesn't need to provide such assistance. The amended ADA does not require employers to change essential job duties. And you are not expected to be a mind reader—you will need to offer assistance only if the applicant requests help.

Employers also should remind those who screen applicants that employers are not allowed to ask whether individuals have disabilities. Interviewers can ask whether someone is able to perform essential job functions with or without accommodation.

The interactive process and its requirements. When someone requests an accommodation, the ADA requires an employer to engage in the interactive process with the person to determine if a reasonable accommodation can be provided to enable that person to perform the requirements of the position. However, many courts have held that an individual does not need to use the magic words, "I'm requesting an accommodation for my disability." Rather, if someone simply states, "I need help or assistance because of my impairment," that triggers the process.

Here are some additional examples of triggers for the interactive process:

- An employee tells his supervisor he is having trouble reading an internal memo because of his poor vision.
- An employee asks her supervisor if she can come to work two hours late because of an appointment with her physical therapist.
- An employee informs his supervisor he cannot work overtime because of his sleep apnea.

Supervisors need to be trained to report statements like these to the HR department.

What accommodations are reasonable. Determining reasonable accommodations varies greatly according to employer and position. It may be unreasonable to require a small construction company to provide a bucket truck to an employee who cannot climb a ladder, but this accommodation may be reasonable for a large utility. Train supervisors to work with HR and corporate counsel to determine reasonable accommodations.

What is prohibited. In addition to providing training on nondiscrimination and reasonable accommodations, teach managers that harassment actions can be brought under the ADA. Of the 27,262 total harassment charges made to the EEOC and state fair employment practices agencies in fiscal 2007, 4,934 were for disability harassment—third after race and sexual harassment and more than the amount for age, national origin or religious harassment. Train all employees to prohibit harassment and to report complaints of impairment-related harassment to HR.

Similarly, retaliation is prohibited. If an individual requests an accommodation, regardless of whether the employer provides the accommodation, that individual is protected from retaliation for making the request.

It's also important for training to cover the interplay between the ADA, as amended, and other laws, including the Family and Medical Leave Act, state nondiscrimination and state family-leave statutes, workers' compensations laws, and Social Security disability.

The amendments will make ADA compliance more complicated and expansive. Now is the time to train the entire HR team and management on the ADA—to minimize mistakes and, should you have to go to trial, aid your defense.

This is one New Year's resolution you need to keep. . . .

EXPLORING THE ISSUE

Will the Americans with Disabilities Act Amendments Act (ADAAA) Be Abused in the U.S. Workplace?

Critical Thinking and Reflection

1. If you were the judge ruling for the *Toyota Motor Manufacturing v. Williams*, how would you have ruled? Why?
2. If you were on the EEOC, would you have supported the amendment of the act (from ADA to ADAAA)? Why? Why not?
3. If you are on the HR team in your organization, what suggestions can you provide to your management to reduce the number of legal complaints filed under this act?
4. Do you think the Sutton sisters had a case that could qualify for ADA?
5. Explain how the disabled in India and Mexico are protected. Are their laws similar to those in the United States or different?

Is There Common Ground?

The Americans with Disabilities Act has been controversial and hence was amended to allow people to understand this law more clearly. The main premise of this act is to integrate physically or mentally disabled individuals equally into our society. The reason that it continues to be contentious could possibly be that the word "disability" has different interpretations for affected groups. Does a person with mental disability need more accommodations than a person with a physical disability? Does disability include only what can be physically observed? What about disabilities that cannot be easily observed? What about individuals whose diseases are in remission?

The other strong argument could also stem from the interpretation of the words "major life activities." For instance, the court ruled against Williams in the Toyota case suggesting that the carpal tunnel syndrome that Ms. Williams had did not impair her from doing her normal household chores. However, she could *not* perform her day-to-day work that provided her main bread and butter—her viewpoint may be that her work is *her* major life activity. What constitutes major life activities in your life?

Additional Resources

Anonymous (2009, September). Revised ADA regs already present challenges. *HR Focus, 86*(9), 2.

Shoskin, J. (2009, June). The ABCs of the NEW ADAAA. *American Agent and Broker, 81*(6), 28–30.

Slobodien, A. and O'Brien, K. (2008, December). The ADA Amendments Act of 2008 and how it will change the workplace. *Employee Relations Law Journal, 34*(3), 32–39.

www.u-s-history.com/pages/h2050.html#: Americans with Disabilities Act.

www.sfgate.com/cgi-bin/article.cgi?f=/g/a/2008/06/13/carollloyd.DTL: ADA Accessibility Lawsuits Causing Headaches for Small Business Owners.

www.arentfox.com/publications/index.cfm?fa=legalUpdateDisp&content_id=1143: Toyota Motor Manufacturing, Kentucky v. Williams.

http://ehssafetynews.wordpress.com/2011/03/25/eeoc-publishes-adaaa-final-regulations-effective-may-24-2011/: EEOC Publishes ADAAA Final Regulations.

www.ideanet.org/content.cfm?id=585970&searchIT=1: International Disability Rights Monitor Publication—Compendium–Mexico.

www.hrhero.com/topics/ada.html: ADA Amendments Act and Americans with Disabilities Act.

http://www.disabilityindia.org/pwdacts.cfm: The Persons with Disabilities Act (1995).

ISSUE 3

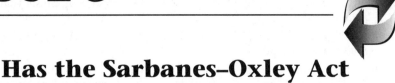

Has the Sarbanes–Oxley Act Helped U.S. Corporations?

YES: Edward Cone, from "Learning to Live with SOX," *CIO Insight, 1*(69), (2006)

NO: C.J. Prince, from "Unintended Consequences," *Chief Executive,* vol. 205, (2005)

Learning Outcomes

After reading this issue, you should be able to:

- Gain an understanding of the Sarbanes–Oxley Act (SOX).
- Understand what happened at the organizations of Enron, Worldcom, and Tyco.
- Define the positive aspects of implementing SOX.
- Understand the negative aspects of SOX.
- Understand alternatives in implementing SOX.

ISSUE SUMMARY

YES: The article offers interesting insights as to why the act is useful in the American corporate world. The article provides several examples to substantiate its points.

NO: C.J. Prince, a writer with 15 years experience, suggests that the Sarbanes–Oxley Act has placed a lot of burden on organizations. Today organizations are more concerned about their ethical rather than their strategic agenda.

The Sarbanes–Oxley Act (also referred to as SOX) was established in 2002 to monitor the accounting and financial standards in publicly held companies. The U.S. corporate world witnessed successive financial scandals in the early 2000s from leading organizations such as Enron, WorldCom, and Tyco.

Enron, a leading energy company, distorted their accounting statements to make the organization look very profitable to investors. Enron filed for bankruptcy in 2001 with billions of dollars in debt. Worldcom, a telecommunication firm, established in 1983, seemed a flourishing company as it acquired almost 65 companies in 6 years. However, they failed to pay adequate attention to their financial statements in terms of investments and expenses, causing their bankruptcy in 2002. The Tyco executives exploited corporate funds for personal expenses, causing immense media attention when they realized Tyco executives had birthday parties costing millions of dollars. The government introduced a federal intervention to make corporate financial accounting practices more transparent.

SOX requires the chief executive officers (CEOs) and chief financial officers (CFOs) to certify that they have provided accurate financial statements. An internal audit committee is also required to confirm the information provided. Further, the financial statements and accounts monitored by internal auditors should also be certified by external auditors also. The act has made sure there are several checks and balances to provide accurate financial records to the public. SOX also wants to guarantee that the chief executives are completely held responsible and accountable for their actions. If executives provide any incorrect financial information, they are liable for high fines and imprisonment.

Professor Prentice, in Learning to Live with SOX, suggests that one of the positives of this act is that it has created an energetic shareholder's environment. The common public has more confidence that organizations will not swindle their money as they are subject to federal regulations. Practitioners have also observed that because of the implementation of SOX companies is taking better efforts to submit accurate financial statements. Scholars suggest such corporate practices will have positive outcomes on the economy. The act also defends whistleblowers or employees who report any wrongdoings in the organization to the concerned. The message of this law is very clear—any unethical acts in the organization should be punished.

However, experts also identify the negative aspects that SOX have created in the U.S. corporate. First, many companies have decided not to go public as they do not need to be SOX compliant if they are privately held. Economists are concerned that this trend could deflate the entrepreneur spirit of the economy. Many companies have become privately held after the act was passed and some public companies have removed their names from the stock exchange list.

Private and public companies differ in specific ways such as their number of investors, disclosure policies, and monetary assets. Generally, private firms are governed by very few investors in comparison to those of public companies, which are completely or partially owned by their shareholders. In addition, public companies are mandated to trade their stocks and also make their annual revenues public. Finally, public companies can raise financial capital by selling any of their stocks or securities to invest in new projects.

Second, the implementation of meeting the prerequisites of SOX is very costly. The average cost for large organizations can range anywhere above

$5 million, making it a very expensive corporate exercise. The costs involve hiring the qualified accounting, legal, and technology expertise to support maintaining accurate records of the organizations' financial statements. This maintenance fee that is required for this act has really squeezed the bottom-line profits for many organizations. Small and mid-sized companies are simply not able to afford the fees associated in complying with SOX. Several financial firms hire specialized software vendors to make sure their technology initiatives for SOX are customized to meet the unique needs of their firms.

Senior executives today are now more concerned about ensuring their organization's ethical status that they are not paying as much attention as they should to the growth and strategy of their firms. They also hesitate to take bold business decisions and have become apprehensive in their expansion plans. Prince, the author of the NO article, suggests this act has crushed the spirit of the nation's free capitalistic model. The United States has established its position as a global leader as its entrepreneurs were willing to take risks in providing a truly spirited marketplace. SOX has made business executives more cautious and vigilant regarding any business ventures. This overall meek corporate attitude will soon become absorbed by their employees also. Also, external boards of directors are extremely concerned to serve on corporate boards as they are worried organizations might not be completely honest with them. The global village is becoming very competitive as countries pursue innovative products and services to stay ahead of the market curve. What will happen to the vibrant entrepreneurial spirit that the United States has always showcased?

Experts provide alternatives in addressing this act as it has created quite a controversy. The choice of becoming a privately held company is still a choice for organizations that do not want to incur the high fees that SOX carries. Organizations can also adopt the strategy of "going dark" which requires organizations to remove their company's name from the stock exchange lists. Organizations need to demonstrate the required number of shareholders to become "dark." Companies that "go dark" do not need to provide any financial reporting statements. Such options provide organizations greater flexibility in their financial management and do not involve any monetary expenses associated with complying to SOX. Finally, organizations can also pursue becoming rigorous in establishing their employees are grounded in ethical standards by frequent training and seminars. Further, they can develop internal controls to maintain high ethical standards in their organizations.

YES 

Edward Cone

Learning to Live with SOX

It seems like a straightforward enough question: is SOX working? Two years after the Sarbanes–Oxley Act (also called the Public Company Accounting Reform and Investor Protection Act of 2002) went into effect, there is a mounting supply of data on hand to throw at the query. But like so many seemingly simple questions, this one isn't. There are a lot of layers to peel back before any serious answer can be reached.

The question invites more questions, such as, "What does 'working' mean?" "Working for whom?"

And to the extent that SOX might be working, are its successes worth the costs? One thing everyone agrees on is that the costs of compliance are much higher than had been estimated. After that, well, define "worth it."

One point of view is represented by Stephen Wagner and Lee Dittmar in their article, "The Unexpected Benefits of Sarbanes–Oxley," published in the April 2006 edition of the Harvard Business Review. They write: "A number of companies have begun to standardize and consolidate key financial processes, eliminate redundant information systems and unify multiple platforms; . . . automate manual processes; . . . better integrate far-flung offices and acquisitions; bring new employees up to speed faster; broaden responsibility for controls; and eliminate unnecessary controls."

Or not, according to a recent paper by Henry Butler and Larry Ribstein for the American Enterprise Institute, called "The Sarbanes–Oxley Debacle: How to Fix It and What We've Learned" (see "True Disbeliever," page 33). It calls SOX "a colossal failure, poorly conceived and hastily enacted during a regulatory panic. . . . SOX supporters are dead wrong in their assessment of SOX—both logic and evidence make it clear that SOX was a costly mistake."

Even quantitative responses, from the number of earnings restatements by public companies since compliance with the law became mandatory (high), to the number of initial public offerings by companies in the U.S. capital markets (low), can be spun in different directions.

And as in so many things, where you stand may depend on where you sit. Groups with particular interests have definite opinions on the question. For audit firms, Sarbanes–Oxley has been called the Full Employment Act of 2002. IT workers with audit skills command a premium in the job market. SOX is working just fine for these folks. But investment bankers who haven't been getting those tasty IPO fees, and small companies forced to pay big dollars to comply? Not so much.

Of course, business and regulation and markets are complex subjects, and in the real world this question is not a binary function with a clear conclusion—on or off, yes or no. But while acknowledging messy, multifactorial reality, and with some caveats and quibbles, we'll venture an answer to the question: Is SOX working?

Yeah, it's working okay. Not perfectly, and not for everyone, but in a broad and measurable sense, the case for SOX is affirmative.

This is a holistic argument. It won't convince the IPO firms or the folks at the American Enterprise Institute. But as Wagner and Dittmar contend, the benefits of SOX go beyond avoiding scandals to rationalizing financial reporting that had grown ragged for a whole laundry list of reasons, including poor integration of merged companies, Y2K fixes, new technology that doesn't play nice with legacy systems, and complex, interconnected supply chains. As high SOX start-up costs are absorbed, the real benefits should accrue to companies with standardized processes and centralized systems that make compliance with regulations of all kinds an integral part of their cultures.

As Senator Paul Sarbanes (D-Md.), one of the bill's cosponsors, said in March, "The benefits of compliance are emerging." He pointed to a CFO Research Services survey of 180 senior finance executives who identified "unexpected benefits from Sarbanes–Oxley compliance." Respondents said Sarbanes–Oxley enables them to manage risk better and uncover weaknesses in financial controls, while boosting operational performance.

Let's walk through some of the pros and cons, the spin and the counter-spin. Your mileage may vary depending on usage.

(I look forward to some full, frank discussion of this issue on my CIO Insight blog, "Know It All," http://blog.eweek.com/blogs/knowitall/ in the weeks to come.)

What Does "Working" Mean?

The Sarbanes–Oxley Act was passed as a response to the financial scandals of the tech-bubble era—the Enrons and WorldComs and Adelphias and Tycos that shook investor confidence and besmirched the reputation of businesses everywhere. In response, Congress decided that the markets need firmer guarantees of corporate compliance with securities law.

If you need any reminders of how grim the situation seemed at the time, consider that the bill sponsored by Sarbanes and Representative Michael Oxley (R-Ohio), passed 423-3 in the House and 99-0 in the Senate. Speaking to a Consumer Federation of America conference in March, Sarbanes said, "Critics who now attempt to minimize the seriousness of the situation should not go unchallenged."

The law demanded several things of public companies, including personal statements by senior executives that their financial statements had been audited and were correct, and statements by internal and external auditors to the same effect. The biggest impact for most companies came from Section 404 of the bill, which details the roles of management and both inside and outside auditors in maintaining a company's internal controls.

Obviously, the markets have rallied (the Dow Jones Industrial Average is up more than 50 percent since its 2002 lows), which, by definition, means that investor confidence is higher. But it doesn't necessarily mean that investors are more confident because of stricter accounting regulations. The overall economy has recovered from recession, the bubble is a distant memory, inflation has been low, and money has been cheap.

The same sort of uncertainty about the value of SOX applies to the lack of big accounting meltdowns. The wave of huge scandals has abated since SOX became law, but it's hard to pin down the role of SOX in preventing the kind of high-dollar chicanery that went on in the recent past. Coincidence is not causality, you can't prove a negative, and so on.

Maybe the scandals stopped for other reasons, and maybe they'll show up again when the economy turns south. As the Wall Street Journal editorial page—no fan of SOX—pointed out in May, all of those famous turn-of-the-millennium miscreants were prosecuted under pre-SOX laws (and that includes Enron Corp.'s Kenneth Lay and Jeffrey Skilling, who went down hard in a Texas courtroom last month). Meanwhile, the showpiece SOX-driven case to date, the trial of HealthSouth Corp. CEO Richard Scrushy, failed to return a conviction.

Robert Prentice, a professor at the University of Texas McCombs School of Business, compares SOX to the expensive and highly annoying Homeland Security regime instituted after Sept. 11, which has seen no further hijackings but has had an unknowable effect on that outcome. "You know how much a metal detector in an airport costs, and how much you pay the people," he says. "But you don't know how much these precautions save. In the same way, we'll never know if SOX prevented a big fraud from happening. And if there is a major case, we won't know if SOX prevented others from occurring at the same time."

Prentice gives Sarbanes–Oxley a cautious thumbs-up, based on things like evidence of decreased earnings management by companies since the law passed, increased investor confidence thanks to CEO certification of results, and improved liquidity. "We're starting to see some interesting stuff in the literature," he says. "These are the things that Congress wanted to do."

Prentice also cites improved accuracy of stock analyst recommendations, and says, "SOX is Congress telling auditors and directors and analysts, for Christ's sake, do your job, take it seriously. That alone is worth something. Do the benefits outweigh the costs? Well, I can say there are a lot of benefits, even if you cannot at this time make a grand conclusion."

By the Numbers

One measure of Sarbanes–Oxley's effectiveness is the rising number of earnings restatements since the law went into effect. Glass, Lewis & Co. LLC is a San Francisco-based firm that tracks the volume of do-overs by public companies. Its March 2006 report, "Getting It Wrong the First Time," shows 1,295 restatements of financial earnings in 2005 for companies listed on U.S. securities markets, almost twice the number for 2004. "That's about one restatement for every 12 public companies—up from one for every 23 in 2004," says the report.

Research analyst Mark Grothe, the study's primary author, sees a direct correlation between Sarbanese–Oxley and the wave of restatements. "It's precisely because of the heightened auditing standards mandated by Sarbanes–Oxley that investors today are getting a true sense, finally, of just how much work remains to be done before they can feel confident about the accuracy of the financial statements prepared by corporate managers," he writes.

"These restatements aren't just about revising subjective judgments or complying with esoteric, complex accounting pronouncements. In hundreds of instances, they stem from basic misapplications of simple rules or critical breakdowns in corporate controls and competencies. . . . Careful scrutiny of these controls, through independent testing and reporting by outside auditors, is what Section 404 of Sarbanes–Oxley mandated. By and large, this testing is what uncovered the weaknesses."

Mike Lofing, another Glass, Lewis analyst, says he believes the number of restatements will drop off over time, although perhaps not to a pre-SOX level. "There was a lot of catch-up going on, and there were probably a lot of controls that should have been in place but were not," he says. "Once those controls are in place, it becomes maintenance."

Are the restatement numbers really such a clear-cut argument for the power of SOX? The Securities and Exchange Commission says that only 12 percent of companies restating their financial reports last year gave SOX Section 404 as the reason for the restatement. But that figure is itself extremely squishy. Just 50 percent of restating companies gave a reason of any sort for their redos, so the overall percentage driven by Section 404 may be much higher. Meanwhile, panelists at an SEC roundtable in May argued that the vast majority of restatements have no material effect, as measured by the response of the stock price, but that the relationship between restatement and "material weakness" in the underlying numbers and process is "almost axiomatic."

Another way of measuring the impact of restatements is by considering the subsequent behavior of the companies involved. Wayne Landsman, a professor of accounting at the University of North Carolina's Kenan–Flagler Business School, has been examining the characteristics of companies that move to different accounting firms, focusing on big audit switches. "Most of the switches by companies are lateral among the Big Four firms," he says. "Auditors aren't dropping companies that restate earnings for being too risky from their client rolls."

Landsman says he has a hard time attributing causality for behavior by companies and investors directly to SOX, and he eschews simple answers. "In economics, it's a social welfare question, like evaluating a tax bill. It hurts some and helps some. Is it having its intended effect? We don't know what we would have observed without it."

Burnt Offerings

Included in that hard-to-attribute category, he says, is the relative dearth of initial public offerings in the SOX era. But critics of the law, from Wall Street to Capitol Hill, have been quite willing to blame SOX for the IPO drought.

Writing in the Wall Street Journal in May, Senator Jim DeMint (R-S.C.) and Representative Tom Feeney (R-Fla.) said that Sarbanes–Oxley is "discouraging U.S. companies from raising capital by going public, which denies them a greater ability to expand and hire new workers. And some businesses that were public when the law was passed have concluded they would rather cut off their access to capital than comply with Sarbox. Since 2002, 75 community banks have gone private, while large companies such as Vivendi have simply de-listed in the U.S."

There are some weaknesses in this analysis, starting with the increasing robustness of the U.S. IPO market. May was the liveliest month for public offerings since the bubble burst, and the first five months of 2006 saw almost 20 percent more IPOs than the comparable period of 2005. But the complexity runs much deeper than this newfound bullishness. The capital markets are awash in an unprecedented amount of private money, providing companies with attractive alternatives to public offerings. Says one partner at a New York City private equity fund, "We are putting good deals on the table, and not coming close because other private investors are so eager to buy these companies. The need to tap the public markets for capital is just not there like it was in the past."

And again, it may be that fewer public offerings represents a successful side of SOX, not a failure. "If you can tie the number of IPOs to SOX, perhaps it shows that firms should have more controls in place before they have access to public markets," says Gregory Bell, a group vice president at CRA International, a Boston-based research and consulting firm that developed a survey of accounting firms and their audit clients.

The Heart of the Problem

At last, an unchallenged fact: SOX implementation is a lot more expensive than the regulators promised it would be. The initial estimates were about $91,000 per company for Section 404 compliance. Not even close: the CRA study showed that the average direct cost of complying with Section 404 at large companies (defined by a market cap of $700 million or more) was $8.5 million in 2004, while companies in the $75 million-to-$700 million range spent an average of $1.2 million. Smaller companies are not yet required to comply with Section 404.

Bell says those costs declined by as much as 44 percent for 2005. "It would not surprise us to see costs continue to decline," he says. "Maybe not as much as between year one and year two, but given the learning curve and the one-time costs, it should become more of a maintenance issue."

None of which changes the fact that SOX compliance is very hard on smaller companies. It not only costs them a relative fortune, but it may solve some problems that don't exist for investors, who already know that smaller companies probably carry greater risks than their larger, more-established counterparts.

Alan Musso is the chief financial officer of Targacept Inc., a development-stage biopharmaceutical firm in Winston-Salem, N.C., that went public on the Nasdaq Stock Exchange earlier this year. Obviously, his company wasn't deterred by the regulatory costs—Targacept won't be required to comply until the end of 2007, a year after issuing its first annual report as a public company—but they are a big deal, nonetheless, for a young company with limited revenues to date. "We're not excited about the compliance costs, but it didn't change our plans," he says. "We would have to spend maybe $250,000 to $400,000 in the first year, and then there's the ongoing cost. That's hard to digest, because we don't see it adding value." He calls the regulations a "distraction that takes money away from developing our products."

It's not that small companies don't need or have strong financial controls, says Musso. Targacept has robust financial and accounting systems from Microsoft Corporation's Great Plains (now Dynamics), he says, but it has not had to spend on the auditing processes. Still, Musso believes that SOX may push some businesses in the right direction. "Companies may be building themselves in a higher quality way around the SOX standards," he says. "But the challenge for companies like ours is the one-size-fits-all solution. We're not as complex as a large company. A lot of what SOX is trying to accomplish at a company our size is done just by having the CEO and CFO certify results, because at a company our size they actually know what's going on."

Relief may be on the way for smaller companies. An SEC advisory committee recommended in late April that companies with revenue of less than $125 million, and a market cap of under $128 million, be exempted from Section 404, and midsize firms exempted in part.

Senator Paul Sarbanes has challenged the recommendations, saying they exempt too many companies, that the committee included too few investor advocates, and that there may not be a statutory basis for the exemptions. "Fortunately, vigorous opponents of the recommendation have stepped forward," he told the Consumer Federation gathering in March.

Sarbanes may be correct that the SEC is suggesting too much of a revision to his namesake law, but it seems a move in the right direction. Such massive regulation is an uncertain science, and even if it is beneficial in general, there is certainly room for improvement.

C.J. Prince

NO

Unintended Consequences

It was meant to help, but Sarbox is wreaking havoc on the bottom line. Will CEOs take it laying down—or push back?

To the architects of the Sarbanes–Oxley Act, the sweeping reform was a quick cure-all for what was ailing Corporate America's moral structure. But as public companies struggled to get their hands around compliance, and particularly onerous Section 404 requirements by the December deadline, they've shelled out millions of dollars to auditors, accountants and consultants. There seems little argument that the pendulum has swung too far.

With chief executives now personally accountable for every uncrossed "t," they've been challenged to design new ways of managing their companies' information flows so that they have a private window into all that goes on. That might be a good thing—assuming it's possible. But while legislation that forces companies to pay more attention to potential malfeasance is certainly positive, most CEOs view Sarbox as a hastily written, poorly conceived law that will have years, if not decades, of unintended consequences for U.S. companies.

The overhaul has proved particularly painful for those CEOs who believe they already had sufficient checks and balances in place, and are now finding that the everyday added compliance demands are draining corporate coffers and CEOs' time, causing U.S. companies to hunker down in defensive, risk-averse mode at the worst possible time. In other words, CEOs agreed at a roundtable, reform is good—but the very legislation that aimed to protect shareholders now stands to harm them. "We're out of balance," said Pat Russo, CEO of Lucent Technologies, "and there is an ultimate price we'll pay for staying out of balance."

Part of that will be the literal price tag—the enormous cost of compliance, which is taking a huge bite out of companies' bottom lines. Eugene McGrath, CEO of New York utility Con Edison, said Sarbox cost $2 million to $3 million to the bottom line "just to pay the extra accountants and all the attorneys to watch over everything we did." He added that, on a more positive note, the company's stakeholders will have assurance that the company is run ethically.

But will that justify the 1 to 2 percent off the bottom line for the investor? Not necessarily, "The costs so far outweigh the benefits. It's unreal," said Robert Ashe, CEO of business intelligence solutions company Cognos, which sponsored the roundtable. "The things that the auditors are doing are just unbelievable."

In the new world of hyper-regulation, it will be auditors, not shareholders, who profit most—and auditors are fully aware of their advantage. "They are gouging," said Al Fasola, director at cable company RCN. "They're getting higher returns from every individual in the firm at a time when they're risk-managing their way out of the accounts that may cause them legal briefs in the future. They're reaping a huge windfall."

Meanwhile, as expenses mount, companies are losing productivity to the compliance grind. "There's the lost opportunity of spending time on doing a deal with a customer so I can generate value versus spending time on internal, process-oriented issues," said Russo, who calculates that she spends at least half a day at each quarter's end with finance specialists, lawyers and binders full of certifications. And that's not counting the unexpected time-draining events, such as one long, drawn out tug-of-war Russo recalled having with Lucent's accounting firm about a matter that should never have been on her calendar. "It was a month's worth of time," she said.

For Con Edison, the focus on compliance is such a strain, it could put future growth at risk. "Prior to Sarbanes–Oxley, our people were working 80 or 100 hours a week," said McGrath. "So Sarbanes–Oxley comes along and I think the big management issue for us is, How do we manage Sarbanes–Oxley and not take our eye off the ball and get into real trouble with the business?"

That is a challenge on multiple fronts. First, the new obsession with rules and regulations is creating a culture more of avoidance and fear than of entrepreneurial ingenuity. "The reason the United States industry has been successful is we've been aggressive," said Donald Nigbor, chief executive of Benchmark Electronics, a service provider and electronics manufacturer. "We've taken risks; we've gone out and promoted new technologies; we've done all these things over the years, and now we're pulling back." That hunker-down mentality, he added, is taking root at the board level, filtering down through the organization, and it will inevitably harm U.S. competitiveness on a global level. "There's a particular danger right now, because the offshore competition American companies are facing is building to a crescendo, a peak, just when we're becoming more timid," Nigbor said. "Sarbanes–Oxley is making every U.S. company more timid, less aggressive."

Sarbox Could Harm Job Growth

Boards in the U.S., in particular, have become risk-averse, in part because of the influence of regulators. "There's an intimidation going on," said Walter LeCroy, chairman of LeCroy Corp., a manufacturer of electronic wave-shape analysis tools. "The boards are being intimidated by the accounting firms, and you just need to attend some of their sessions," he said. "I'll be honest with you, after I attended, I wasn't sure I wanted to be on my own board. They scare the hell out of people."

Wary of doing anything to rouse the ire of an Eliot Spitzer, boards are clamping down on growth moves such as acquisitions. Job growth overall will suffer as a result. "People aren't hiring as many people. They are being more cautious about everything they do," said Nigbor. "So how do you measure that? How do you go in there and ask, 'How many jobs are lost because of Sarbanes–Oxley?'"

And how, for that matter, do you measure the impact on the existing work force? Harold Yoh, CEO of diversified managed services firm Day & Zimmermann, suggested that intense dissatisfaction will plague employees at public companies. "And when you have a frustrated employee, you have one who is not going to be as motivated or as freethinking to come up with a better solution," said Yoh, noting that his private company has been affected because public company customers have stalled projects. "That frustration or de-motivation," he added, "leads to not being in the game as much. If you're frustrated, you're not in the game."

Those frustrated employees may not want to stick around when and if the job market improves. "All of our employees are kind of ready to leave after four years of being frozen, doing extra work and being asked to do more," said Barry Siegel, president of Recruitment Enhancement Services. "Now, all of a sudden, Big Brother is watching them, and they're going to think it's greener on the other side of the street. They're going to look for other positions where they think they won't be watched as much. They can certainly go into the private sector."

Dreaming of Going Private

Rather than wade knee-deep in Sarbox paperwork or languish on the open market, many small or midsize companies already have gone private since the new regulation went into effect. And that's just a taste of what's to come, assuming the current regulations stay in effect, CEOs agreed. "You're just going to see an awful lot of smaller public companies that are going private, point blank and simple," said Maurice Taylor, CEO of wheel-maker Titan International.

Even big companies are fantasizing about the shelter of private life. "I've talked with a number of CFOs from companies listed on the [NYSE] who have said to me, 'If I could easily figure out how to de-list and get off, I'd get off in a heartbeat,'" said Lucent's Russo. "Those are big, reputable companies we want listed on the exchanges in this country."

For those opting to stay in the public market—and a mass exodus seems unlikely—the toll will continue to mount. Some CEOs will attempt to gain a business advantage or a return from the investment so that all is not wasted. For example, Cognos' Ashe noted, one way to leverage more control in terms of management oversight will be to implement more sophisticated tools, such as workflow-based software, document planning systems and transaction controls; those tools will greatly improve CEO visibility into the organization for a number of other purposes.

John Joyce, senior vice president of IBM Global Services and formerly CFO of the computing giant, explained that the company's investment in standardized systems prior to Sarbanes–Oxley made it much easier to comply. "It was painful, as it was for all of us, with 404, but it was not as bad as we thought because we had so many standardized processes," he said. "So now that we've done 404, and we have this information, it's, 'Can we glean business insight from the information that's flowing?' We're obviously going to know more of the details of what's going on at the end of the supply chain. We now have this information, and the question is now, what can we do with it to help run the company better?"

That's a bit rosy for some corporate leaders who feel that in the current climate, CEOs resigning themselves to making lemonade would be a deadly passive move. Even obeying the rules won't keep a CEO out of trouble, they argued. "You get an Eliot Spitzer, and a well-run company, and if the timing is right, the company is just in trouble and becomes a target," said LeCroy. "So I believe that if business just says, 'Well, we've been dealt a tough hand, but we're going to make the best of it'—if that's our whole reaction to this thing, we're in trouble. I think we need to find some way to push back and convey the message that this is not fair; it's not good for the country."

The question remains, How do we get that message across? "How do we collect this experience—what's good about it, what's bad about it, agree on what's bad about it, get into the political process in a way that they understand why correcting it is in their interest," posed McGrath. "If we don't do all of those things, we're going to be sitting here next year and talking about it too."

Some CEOs, like Ashe, believe that with the 404 compliance date having only just passed, it was still too soon to tally the costs and benefits, or to sort out the impact. "There's a lot of learning we're going to accumulate in the next 90 to 120 days, as we find out what the compliance level is," said Ashe, adding that Ernst & Young has estimated a possible 50 percent noncompliance rate for 404. "If it is 50 percent noncompliance, nobody's going to care about 404. If it's 10 percent noncompliance, people are going to care, because those companies are going to be called out."

Regardless of 404 compliance, what shareholders will be crying about is the diminishing rate of return, predicted Patrick Murray, chairman of Dresser. "When people look at the annual reports this year, and the amount of cost that's been loaded into these businesses," he said, "I think it's going to be sooner rather than later that there's a backlash."

One final devilish twist from 404: Auditors have to issue their opinion of a company's internal controls and whether they can anticipate future misdeeds. If the auditors issue a "qualified opinion," meaning they have some concerns about a company's controls, those companies could get pounded in the stock markets or have banks withdraw lines of credit. Depending on how many companies receive qualified opinions, it could be large enough to act as a damper on the overall financial markets.

Add it all up and it's not a reassuring picture: CEOs will take fewer risks and create fewer jobs at the very moment that global competitors are gearing up. They may postpone projects and their share prices could suffer, all while they are reducing their bottom lines to spend on compliance. When the full enormity of the costs of Sarbox sink in, the pendulum may well swing back—if CEOs are willing to give it a good, firm push.

The Hidden Cost of Sarbox

- CEO time is wasted. Forced to spend days on compliance, they spend far less time with customers and looking ahead.
- Boards are scared. Good directors are afraid to serve; those who do are much less likely to approve strategic risk-taking by the CEO.
- Risk-taking is out. Just when companies around the world are becoming more aggressive, U.S. firms are hunkering down. Our timidity is their gain.
- Lower return to stakeholders. As more and more money is poured into compliance, less of it will make it to the bottom line—and even less into shareholder pockets.
- More companies will go private. Even private companies will be hurt by their public company customers' reluctance to engage.
- Bad decisions abound. To avoid auditor scrutiny, managers will take the path of least resistance, and make poor judgment calls in the process.

EXPLORING THE ISSUE

Has the Sarbanes–Oxley Act Helped U.S. Corporations?

Critical Thinking and Reflection

1. Why was SOX introduced in the U.S. corporate?
2. Research and identify the main reasons for the downfall of Enron, Worldcom, and Tyco?
3. What are the positive aspects of implementing SOX in the U.S. corporate world?
4. What are the negatives of implementing SOX in the U.S. corporate world?
5. What are the alternatives to pursuing SOX?

Is There Common Ground?

SOX was implemented to make sure U.S. organizations remain ethical to their shareholders, customers, and investors. Its implementation has helped create increased governance transparency, making executives fully accountable. On the other hand, its implementation is very costly for small and mid-size organizations to manage making them change their investing strategies. The alternatives may be to remain private or "going dark" to avoid paying the high fees associated complying with SOX. Organizations are also instilling a very strong ethical culture to ensue such financial fiascos do not happen again.

Additional Resources

Simon, P. (2009). Why the new systems fail. *Waters, 16*(4), 30–31.

www.investinganswers.com/term/sarbanes-oxley-act-891: Sarbanes–Oxley Act.

www.scu.edu/ethics/dialogue/candc/cases/worldcom.html: Worldcom.

http://www.scu.edu/ethics/publications/ethicalperspectives/enronlessons.html: Lessons from Enron.

http://faculty.mckendree.edu/scholars/2004/stinson.htm: Arthur Andersen and Enron: Positive Influence on the Accounting Industry.

www.msnbc.msn.com/id/9399803/ns/business-corporate_scandals/t/ex-tyco-executives-get-years-prison/: Ex-Tyco Executives Get Up to 25 Years in Prison.

www.usatoday.com/money/industries/manufacturing/2002-12-30-tyco-investigation_x.htm: Tyco Finds Accounting Errors, No Significant Fraud.

www.ehow.com/list_7408953_alternatives-sarbanes_oxley.html: Alternatives to Sarbanes–Oxley.

http://webster.utahbar.org/barjournal/2007/04/going_dark_an_alternative_to_s.html: Going Dark—An Alternative to Sarbanes–Oxley Compliance.

www.investopedia.com/ask/answers/162.asp#axzz1c5uFe3GS: What Is the Difference Between Publicly and Privately-held Companies?

http://securities.stanford.edu/news-archive/2006/20060803_Headline101802_Journal.html: Companies "Go Dark" to Avoid SOX Compliance.

ISSUE 4

Should Employees Be Allowed to Wear Symbols of Faith in the Workplace?

YES: Robert J. Grossman, from "Religion at Work," *HR Magazine* (December 2008)

NO: Robert D. Ramsey, from "When Religion and Work Clash," *Supervision* (September 2007)

Learning Outcomes

After reading this issue, you should be able to:

- Gain an understanding of religious accommodations at the workplace.
- Understand what is reasonable in terms of religious accommodations.
- Describe the three specific court cases of religion at the workplace.
- Gain an international perspective of how other countries view religion at the workplace.

ISSUE SUMMARY

YES: Robert J. Grossman, professor of management, suggests that organizations should adopt a faith-friendly approach and allow employees to wear their symbols of faith. He provides examples of leading companies such as Coca-Cola and Ford Motors that have taken progressive steps regarding wearing symbols of faith and have observed positive HRM outcomes.

NO: Robert D. Ramsey, author and freelance writer, argues that accommodating religious requests might become a never-ending laundry list of requests that could hamper business goals and profits. Organizations should always keep their business interests and objectives as their top priority.

Today's workplace is a rich mosaic of employees from various religious backgrounds. The workforce has Christians, Jews, Muslims, Hindus, Buddhists, among several others. The Title VII that was established in the 1960s dictates that there will be no religious discrimination in the workplace. The question that concerns HRM leaders today is whether employees should be allowed to express or wear external symbols as the workplace is getting increasingly diverse in terms of religion.

In 2008, the SHRM (Society of Human Resource Management) reported that 64 percent of organizations in their study identified they had a diverse religious workforce. In comparison, in 2001, only 36 percent of the organizations in their study identified they had a diverse religious workforce. The results indicate a substantial increase of employees from different religious faiths as immigrants from different faiths become a part of the workforce. In 1970, only 4.5 percent of the population were immigrants and of European Christian descent. However, in 2000, statistics suggest that 12 percent of the population were immigrants, and 16 percent of the immigrants were of European Christian descent. Experts suggest that individuals of other faiths such as Islam, Hindus, and Buddhists are consistently increasing, making the Protestant religion look like a minority.

David Miller, Director of Princeton University Faith and Work Initiative, suggests that diversity initiatives should advocate a free expression of employees' religion also. It seems very unfair to expect employees not to acknowledge their religious values or expressions at the workplace. How can organizations embrace employees' ethnicity without acknowledging their religion?

Several leading organizations such as Coca-Cola and Ford Motors have adopted a very faith-friendly approach. These organizations have allowed employees of different religious faiths to conduct religious meetings at their workplaces. These organizations have also indicated that allowing employees to express their faith has only increased their commitment to the organizations and created a very nurturing environment. For instance, Muslim employees in Ford Motors are allowed to use the on-site prayer rooms for their daily prayers. Such organizational initiatives that support different faiths have only strengthened employee retention. It also has made the workplace more meaningful to these diverse employees. A survey by SHRM indicated that employee morale significantly improved when employees were allowed to wear their symbols of faith or express their religion at the workplace.

On the other hand, Dr. Ramsey suggests that accommodating today's workforce of myriad religions has become a very cumbersome process for HRM professionals. Employees may ask for several religious accommodations to practice their religion (religious holidays, dress accommodations, private space for prayers, and different kinds of food).

The list of religious expressions can become overwhelming and the main challenge for HR professionals is when to draw the line between reasonable and unreasonable requests. The following court cases suggest how organizations might find it difficult to accommodate various religious sentiments about wearing symbols of faith to work. For instance, Sukhbir Channa, of the Sikh faith, was asked to leave Disney World in 2005 as his grooming habits were against the company's dress code policy. Channa's religious faith prohibited him to cut his hair or shave his beard. Disney's employees, referred to as "cast members," are asked to follow a dress code that includes minimum make-up (for females) and clear grooming requirements (for males). Should Disney change their dress code to accommodate certain religious groups?

Another example is that of, Nadia Eweida, a British Airways employee for seven years and a practicing Christian, wore a silver cross to work. The company had a uniform policy that required employees not to wear any visible signs of jewelry. When she refused to remove her silver cross she was suspended from British Airways. Her main contention was that other employees from her company practicing other religious faiths (such as Sikhs and Muslims) were allowed to wear their symbols of faith to work. Was the organization fair in their disciplinary action against Nadia? Another case in 2009 is that of Dr. Zaki, who was refused an employment position in a health clinic in Texas. She was told that she could not wear her headscarf as the clinic policy did not allow employees to wear hats or scarves at work.

Dr. Ramsey suggests that organizations should place their business and corporate strategy as the main criteria for accommodating religious requests. Organizations should not accommodate employees' religious requests that could possibly reduce an organization's business profits. For instance, Somali cab drivers refused to take customers that had liquor or even pet dogs as it was against their religion. Should customers be turned down because of an employee's faith? Dr. Ramsey suggests that it is very important to keep the customer's good interest in mind as that should be the organization's top business priority. Further organizations should not accommodate religious requests that might harm other employees—for instance, Muslim women insisting on wearing religious dress in a manufacturing work environment that could possibly cause harm to themselves or their co-workers.

Some suggestions for alternative perspectives on this may require organizations to explicitly state that some positions might not be able to have any religious accommodations due to business necessities. Organizations can therefore offer employees the choice of whether they would like to follow a dress code policy. For instance, British Airways suggested that Nadia might continue to wear her Christian cross if she would like to work in positions at British Airways that did not require her to wear her uniform. Offering choices will allow the organization to still maintain its image but offer employees the option of wearing their religious symbols or not. These religious policies should be clearly documented and stated initially in the hiring policies so that there is no room for misinterpretation later.

Leading companies such as IBM, GM, and Texas Instruments have gone a step further and created educational seminars or panels so that employees from different faiths may express freely what symbols of faith they would like to wear to work. Such seminars provide two distinct advantages—they allow people from different faiths to express their religious beliefs publicly and permit employees to understand the perspectives of other faiths. Many organizations are also allowing special prayer rooms that employees from different faiths may use to express their religion while at work. Organizations that provide any accommodations will greatly help promote a profile of a workforce that mirrors the global workforce.

An international perspective suggests that wearing or expressing symbols of faith is quite controversial in other countries also. In 2004, France passed a ban on wearing any religious symbols of faith in secondary schools, which included Jewish caps, Christian crosses, and Muslim head scarves. On the other hand, British schools allow students to wear their symbols of faith to their schools in an effort integrate different religions and perspectives.

YES 

Robert J. Grossman

Religion at Work

Abstract (Summary)

The US educational system and other teachings say you should compartmentalize faith, says Bob Pettus, HR veteran, who retired in 2005 as vice chairman of the US' second-largest Coca-Cola bottler. Religion remains integral to life in the US, and religious practices are increasingly diverse. In a 2001 survey conducted by the Society for Human Resource Management (SHRM) and the Tanenbaum Center for Interreligious Understanding in New York, 36% of HR professionals reported an increase in the religious diversity of their employees during the previous five years. While no data are available, many experts say the number of companies that promote or encourage religious expression is trending up. Only half of the 540 HR professionals responding to the SHRM survey said religious issues were part of training for managers and supervisors; 37% said they were part of training for employees. In the end, it seems likely that HR professionals will spend more time with religion and spirituality in the future.

Many employers are weaving religion and spirituality into company cultures. The push may come from bosses or the rank and file—and their motivations vary. Either way, when religion and spirituality cross the threshold, they result in daunting legal and managerial challenges along with perceived benefits.

Bob Pettus spent his entire career with Charlotte, N.C.-based Coca-Cola Bottling Co. Consolidated—all with top-level human resource responsibility. Like an Israelite wandering in the Sinai seeking the Promised Land, he engaged in a quest—to find the keys to attracting and retaining high-performing workers and managers. After decades in the wilderness, he was losing heart.

"Our employees' salaries, benefits and perks were always a little bit ahead of others so we could attract the kinds of employees we needed," recalls the HR veteran, who retired in 2005 as vice chairman of the nation's second-largest Coca-Cola bottler with 5,800 employees in 11 Southeastern states. "I would get all excited about giving everyone a 3.5 percent increase, putting in a new insurance policy, adding a new holiday. But when I made the announcements, there was hardly any response except, 'Hey, that's what everyone else is doing. You guys should have been doing this a long time ago.' We spent all those millions, and all we got for it was 'ho-hum.'"

Then Pettus—who now consults for the company—saw the light. He was meeting the physical and emotional needs of workers, but what about the spiritual? Did it make sense to keep religion under wraps and require people to leave their faith at the doorstep? Equally important, if leaders really believed in running the business in concert with God and religious values, shouldn't they say so?

Pettus knew company leaders who answer affirmatively buck convention: Most business leaders are faith-frosty, convinced that the less religious expression at work, the better. They comply with legal mandates and accommodate individuals who require special arrangements, but go no further.

The U.S. educational system and other teachings "say you should compartmentalize faith," Pettus says. "Folks who are willing to talk about their faith and live it out Monday through Friday often are viewed as fanatical. Someone can go to a football game and scream and holler, throw things in the air and dress like a slob. But at work, if you mention that you should love one another and live right every day—it's like, 'What's wrong with you?'"

Pettus took a stand. Working with the chief executive officer, he drafted a mission and values statement that makes it clear company leaders embrace and honor God. It opens the door to spirituality for all employees and champions stewardship. The statement leads with "Our Values Honor God."

Finally, an initiative that was met with an overwhelming positive reaction. When people learn they can live out their faith, Pettus says, "There's this loyalty, this willingness to go the extra mile."

Faith Focus

Coca-Cola Bottling Co. Consolidated represents one of many faith-focused U.S. companies. These organizations proactively conduct business in a manner that embraces the faiths of leaders or owners. Their faiths provide underlying values that motivate and guide the organizations. A few, such as Coca-Cola Bottling, are publicly traded. Many more—such as Austaco Ltd., a privately owned Taco Bell franchisee with 1,800 workers in Austin, Texas—number among the nation's small and medium-sized and frequently family-owned businesses.

"We classify ourselves as a Christian company—Christ- or God-centered," says Don Barton, Austaco's HR vice president. "We do things like say grace when we have a meal, something a typical company might not do. The employees know that our CEO, Dirk Dozier, is open about sharing his Christian faith in personal testimony. Our motto is to serve, which includes serving our employees on a spiritual basis."

Faith-Friendly

Also welcoming religion are faith-friendly companies. They value inclusion and promote diversity and religious self-expression. They do not align with one religion, but instead invite workers to bring all manners of religious and spiritual expression to the workplace.

At Ford Motor, for example, workers' religious groups have access to facilities after hours for meetings and communicate through newsletters. "Being able to bring your whole self to work is essential to us," says Allison Trawick, global manager in Ford's Office of Diversity and Inclusion in Dearborn, Mich. "That means everyone." At the centerpiece of Ford's religious diversity: the Ford Interfaith Network (FIN), one of eight recognized and supported affiliate groups.

Led by a board of representatives of Buddhism, Catholicism, Church of Jesus Christ of Latter-day Saints, evangelical Christians, Hinduism, Islam, Judaism and Orthodox Christianity, FIN welcomes all religious and spiritual groups. One discovery: "how many values we have in common," says Daniel Dunnigan, manager of worldwide volumes and FIN chairman. "We all value family, integrity [and] personal industriousness and are committed to leading morally upright lives."

Dunnigan says Ford's celebration of religious diversity and the impact it has on culture can't be measured in financial terms alone: The Muslim representative "doesn't have to worry about where he'll go for his midday prayers. He thinks it makes him more loyal. Another man affiliated with the evangelical Christian group told me he wouldn't want to work anywhere else because of Ford's welcoming environment. How do you put a dollar value on this?"

Nation of Believers

Religion remains integral to life in the United States, and religious practices are increasingly diverse. In a 2001 survey conducted by the Society for Human Resource Management (SHRM) and the Tanenbaum Center for Interreligious Understanding in New York, 36 percent of HR professionals reported an increase in the religious diversity of their employees during the previous five years. In SHRM's 2008 Religion and Corporate Culture: Accommodating Religious Diversity in the Workplace survey report, 64 percent said their organizations have some degree of religious or spiritual diversity.

Immigrants affiliated with various religions contribute to these numbers. In 1970, only 4.5 percent of the population was foreign-born; of those, 62 percent came from Europe and were overwhelmingly Christian. By 2000, 12 percent of the population was foreign-born but only 16 percent of that group shared European heritage. Many more came from Asia or Latin America and were Buddhists, Hindus, Muslims, Sikhs or members of other religions. Today, 78.4 percent of U.S. adults are Christian and about 5 percent are members of other religions; 16.1 percent are unaffiliated.

For some, religion and spirituality rest comfortably under the umbrella of "faith." For others, "religion" is a loaded, politically charged word.

"In the business community, many accept the notion that spirituality should be welcome at work, while religion is to be avoided," says Douglas Hicks, associate professor of leadership studies and religion and executive director of the Bonner Center for Civic Engagement at the University of Richmond in Virginia. "They contrast religion as dogmatic, rigid [and] tradition-bound, and spirituality as open, liberating, individualistic and creative."

Diversity's Forgotten Child

To the chagrin of those who favor religious expression, the HR community has been reluctant to champion the cause. "At best, HR has ignored the issues and at worst, it has been hostile," says David Miller, director of the Princeton University Faith & Work Initiative in New Jersey. "How can you say you stand for diversity and inclusion when you limit it to external characteristics and don't extend it to the inclusion of worldviews that include some kind of god or not?"

Until recently, religion and spirituality have been the bête noire of the diversity movement. People who have advocated for diversity in gender, race or sexual orientation have avoided speaking in support of religious expression in the workplace. Hundreds of senior executives are devout but silent, says Miller. "They think it would be career suicide to come forward."

Human resource professionals know that religious expression can lead to litigation or polarization. To avoid problems, "stay away," advises Robert Campbell, senior vice president of HR at NiSource Inc. in Merrillville, Ind., a Fortune 500 company whose 7,600 employees engage in natural gas and electric generation, transmission, storage and distribution.

"HR folks are too busy worrying about where the next lawsuit will come from instead of helping enable people to live the one life they are called to live through a business which has a higher purpose than just to make money," says Don Barefoot, president of C12 Group, a support group for born-again Christian CEOs and business owners, based in Greensboro, N.C. "They're the gatekeepers for society's fears and hang-ups."

But when HR professionals look objectively at the spiritual values of the major religions, they will be less concerned, says Michelle Knox, executive consultant with Novations Group Inc. in Boston. "The values are very similar—integrity, respect for oneself, altruistic behavior, putting others first."

HR professionals are "risk-averse about what can happen from a compliance standpoint, and I was, too," recalls Rod Nagel, senior vice president of human resource operations at Tyson Foods Inc. in Springdale, Ark. But "You'll realize the benefits go well beyond the risks," he says. The publicly traded company's core values literature includes this language: We strive to be a faith-friendly company. . . . We strive to honor God and be respectful of each other, our customers and other stakeholders. . . .

Out of the Shadows

While no data are available, many experts say the number of companies that promote or encourage religious expression is trending up. Georgette Bennett, president and founder of the Tanenbaum Center and a member of SHRM's Workplace Diversity Special Expertise Panel, attributes the trend in part to globalization and the politicization of religion. "With everyone from the [U.S.] president on down wearing their religion on their sleeve, it's not surprising that employers and employees are encouraged to assert their rights."

In fact, "We've reached a tipping point where the conventional wisdom that you keep your spiritual side at home is about to collapse," Miller says, adding that millennials and Gen Xers "want to live a holistic life" and that older workers tend to be interested in religion as well.

The Business Case

Miller says welcoming religious diversity gives recruiters an advantage.

When employers allow spirituality to be expressed, levels of employee commitment and engagement increase, Knox adds. "It allows for greater meaning and reduces stress. Whenever we subjugate something that makes [other people] different, it lessens their ability to be productive and satisfied in their work."

It's no coincidence that in SHRM's Religion and Corporate Culture survey, HR professionals said employee morale was most affected by companies granting religious accommodations, Bennett notes.

To faith-focused executives, byproducts of promoting spiritual expression, such as financial rewards, "are icing on the cake," Pettus concludes. "Don't say you'll get more productivity because people will see it as a ploy to extract more work from them. Do it because it's the right thing to do."

Legal Parameters

Of course, employers are obligated to make reasonable efforts to accommodate the sincerely held religious beliefs of all workers. Accommodation may include opportunities for prayer, respecting holidays—even proselytizing and the distribution of literature. Under Title VII of the Civil Rights Act of 1964, discrimination occurs if an employer fails to reasonably accommodate employees, or if employees are harassed by being required to abandon or adopt, or coerced into abandoning or adopting, a religious practice as a condition of employment (quid pro quo) or subjected to unwelcome statements or conduct based on religion so severe or pervasive that the person finds the work environment hostile or abusive.

Hence, employers must balance the obligation to accommodate religious views of one or more employees—an obligation that legal experts say is becoming more onerous—with the obligation to prevent harassment or creation of a hostile work environment for others. For example, unwelcome words or conduct, whether emanating from a fellow employee or the boss, may be permissible until the target of the communication or conduct objects. Even then, they may not constitute harassment unless considered pervasive or severe.

Navigating this terrain is dicey; hence, most employers opt for a hands-off approach wherever possible.

More Than Meets the Eye?

Religious discrimination charges filed with the U.S. Equal Employment Opportunity Commission (EEOC) more than doubled from 1992 to 2007. Still, the EEOC received just 2,880 charges in 2007, a relatively small number compared to charges filed for other reasons. Of the EEOC claims filed in 2007, the agency found "no reasonable cause" in almost 60 percent. Claims cost businesses $6.4 million that year. Yet, only 2 percent of respondents to SHRM's 2008 Religion and Corporate Culture survey said their organization has been named as a defendant in a lawsuit related to religion in the past 12 months.

But these figures may underrepresent the problem, with many instances unreported or resolved. For example, in a 1999 employee survey by the Tanenbaum Center, 66 percent of respondents said they had seen indications of religious bias at work. Of those who were targets, only 23 percent reported it.

In an April survey of 278 organizations by the Institute for Corporate Productivity (i4cp) in Seattle, nearly one-third of HR executives said they have seen personal clashes in the workplace linked to religion. Thirty-one percent said unsolicited sharing of religious views has been a problem.

In faith-focused organizations, employees sometimes quit, saying they felt "marginalized because the ethos was too Christian," Hicks says. "Many leave without formally complaining, making it difficult to assess the scope of the problem. Workers are vulnerable, unwilling to risk their jobs by coming forward or speaking out. Often, the cultures from which these workers come teach them to 'keep your head low—don't complain.' Also, they don't understand what their rights are."

Frank Manion, senior counsel at the American Center for Law and Justice in Washington, D.C., says people come forward reluctantly; "They don't want to offend anyone."

This can be problematic for employers that run into constructive discharge claims after employees leave. Seemingly, the burden rests on the worker to request that offensive conduct cease, yet Manion envisions scenarios where the conduct is so overt that the burden may rest with the employer. And, don't overlook the possibility that some individuals or groups may set traps that could lead to litigation. "I wouldn't be surprised if people in civil rights groups start sending out 'salts' to test the impartiality of employers," says employment lawyer Michael Homans of Falster/Greenberg PC in Philadelphia. "People aren't required to disclose their religion when they apply, but if the information is volunteered or an applicant displays a cross [or] Star of David or wears the head covering of a Muslim, for example, the potential for a discriminatory response arises."

Almost one-third of 580 HR executives told i4cp researchers that religious discrimination was a workplace concern. "They see it as an issue, but not as one that affects them personally," says Anne Lindberg, i4cp research analyst. "People who have faced discrimination claims have handled it in-house. There's not a lot of news about people being dinged for thousands of dollars in lawsuits. But we're only at the beginning. Once you get some big judgments, the popular media will get on board, and then watch out."

Following Chosen Paths

According to the Pew Forum on Religion & Public Life in Washington, D.C., two-thirds of the population affiliated with a religious tradition hold an inclusionary view, accepting that their chosen path is not the only road to salvation.

One-third think their way is the only way and may be obligated by their beliefs to reach out. For example, data from The Barna Group, a research organization in Ventura, Calif., reveal that three-quarters of the nation's 1 million born-again Christians believe they "personally have a responsibility to tell other people about their religious beliefs."

The challenges presented by proselytizing grow large when supervisors deliver the message.

For instance, Brad Thompson, CEO at Columbia Forest Products in Greensboro, N.C., says leading his company by biblical principles is an opportunity to live his faith. "My goal is that people will sense something different about me. Once they do and want to know where it's coming from, I'll tell them. The best thing I can do is model Christian principles and let people come to me." Thompson identifies a dividing line "between an invitation and a push. I can't see any harm if I invite anyone to attend a religious event or prayer meeting with me. [But] I can't push anyone to the point that I make them uncomfortable."

Although Thompson seems to be within the law, some observers worry. "Because of the unequal power relationship, there should never be a situation where a supervisor is making any kind of religious overtures to a subordinate," Bennett insists.

Managers should not proselytize, agrees Campbell. "You don't want to give anyone the false impression that you'll make a work decision based on your preference. The potential for lawsuits—meritorious or not—is undeniable. If someone has been rewarded or punished for any reason, it's not hard to put a case together attributing the action to religious bias."

Making It Happen

Regardless of the perceived benefits of religious expression in the workplace, employment lawyers counsel caution and following a course that will minimize conflict. That means, regarding religion, less is better. "The suppression by private employers of religious speech at work generally does not create legal exposure for the employer so long as the employer 'reasonably accommodates' religion," Homans says. "Keep references to religious values and God out of written policies and practices; instead, describe your values in the secular language of ethics."

Campbell says even voluntary activities that aren't objectionable under the law—such as joining hands and saying prayers—may prove divisive and stressful, "so the person who is uncomfortable winds up going along."

Still, the growing number of successful faith-friendly and faith-based employers serves as testament that religion and spirituality can flourish in the workplace. Implementation remains key: If it is done carefully, faith-friendly employers may choose to celebrate religious and spiritual inclusiveness even if some people would prefer a secular environment. And faith-focused employers may pursue what critics perceive as "stealth agendas" of conversion, so long as they stick to the law that requires tolerance and equal treatment of all views. "You have to create a culture of openness that says, 'We'll open our conference room or message board on an equal basis to all faith groups; we'll have a brown-bag series where people can talk about their faith.' It should be employee-driven," advises Hicks.

Policies and Training Gap

Whether an employer is faith-friendly, faith-focused or faith-frosty, the issues, rights and responsibilities of workers, supervisors and executives are complicated and call out for detailed policy and training. So far, however, many employers have been slow to act. Of the respondents to SHRM's Religion and Corporate Culture survey, nearly half reported having no policy on religion. Only 2 percent reported having a formal separate policy. The remainder included religion under diversity or antidiscrimination umbrellas.

"The mere inclusion of religion in a list of protected classes in the boilerplate diversity policy does not address the critical issue of accommodation," Bennett argues. The best practice? "Adopt a distinct religious diversity policy," she says.

Miller suggests the following definition of faith-friendly as groundwork for a policy: "As a faith-friendly employer, we recognize the importance of faith to many people, that a spiritual grounding is what makes them tick, and so long as one's practices are compatible with our company's value and mission, we welcome it."

Only half of the 540 HR professionals responding to the SHRM survey said religious issues were part of training for managers and supervisors; 37 percent said they were part of training for employees.

In the end, it seems likely that HR professionals will spend more time with religion and spirituality in the future. Faith-frosty employers will have more accommodations to deal with as workers and managers learn more about the extent of their rights to express their faith. Regardless of motivation, employers who see advantages of actively incorporating faith into the workplace now have advice, guidelines and examples.

But the devil is in the details: "I agree with what the lawyers say about maintaining a nondiscriminatory environment," says Pettus. "Faced with all the do's and don'ts, a normal HR guy would probably hold up his hands and say, 'Golly, if I've got to do all that, I better not do anything and just make sure we don't get into trouble.'" . . .

Robert D. Ramsey

When Religion and Work Clash

Abstract (Summary)

America is known for freedom of religious expression, and most business leaders endorse and support religious tolerance. Increasingly, employers are being asked to make accommodations in the workplace for myriad forms of religious expression, including some controversial and confrontational practices. Accommodating wide-ranging forms of religious expression in the workplace and brokering the resulting conflicts of interest seems to call for divine intervention. The following advice from veteran human resources experts has helped many middle managers resolve problems regarding religion in the workplace. These suggestions will not answer all your questions, but they do provide a framework for developing your own solutions for the issues that occur in your particular work environment: 1. Deal with the rights, needs and attitudes of all workers, not just the ones requesting concessions. 2. Be sure the request is legitimate. 3. Do not make decisions based on personal bias or prejudice or simply what is easiest or the most popular thing to do.

> "What the church should be telling the worker is that the first demand religion makes on him is to be a good workman."
>
> —Dwight D. Eisenhower, US President

America is known for freedom of religious expression, and most business leaders endorse and support religious tolerance. But what happens when the workers' right to practice their religion clashes with the requirements of the job? Who wins? Who loses? Who decides?

These aren't just hypothetical or rhetorical questions. They are real live, in-your-face issues throughout the business world today.

Increasingly, employers are being asked to make accommodations in the workplace for myriad forms of religious expression, including some controversial and confrontational practices. Is there any limit? Is there a line, which should not be crossed? Where is it? Who gets to draw it?

If your answer to the last question was the supervisor or foremen in charge, you are probably right. Often it is up to middle management to define how far the organization will go in permitting religious practices on the job. More than anyone else, supervisors have to reconcile the employee's right to religious expression with the employer's right to get the job done and to meet the needs of customers.

Accommodating wide-ranging forms of religious expression in the workplace and brokering the resulting conflicts of interest seems to call for divine intervention. Yet flesh and blood foremen and managers have to deal with it every day. If you haven't been confronted with such issues in your factory, shop or office, it could happen tomorrow—or even yet today.

A Growing Problem

As the proliferation of diverse religious groups grows in our society, the incidence of conflict between religious practice and job performance becomes stickier, more complex and more challenging for supervisors in all fields. Examples are all around if you're paying attention.

Just within the last year, the media has reported cases where—

- Workers from many minority faiths have asked for time off to observe their religious holidays and special events.
- Islamic women workers have insisted on wearing traditional clothing on the job despite objections regarding safety and security.
- Muslim employees have demanded time and private space to accommodate mandatory prayers during the duty day.
- Jewish workers have lobbied for the addition of kosher food to vending machines and employee cafeteria menus.
- Muslim employees have requested facilities for foot-washing while at work. (At least one Minnesota college has already made this concession.)
- Somali cab drivers have refused to drive fares carrying liquor, which is banned by their religion or fares accompanied by a dog (even a seeing eye or other service dog) because Muslims view dogs as "unclean."
- Some Muslim grocery store cashiers and sackers have refused to handle pork products and have requested that other employees or the customers themselves check and bag these items.

The list could go on. The examples keep piling up and we probably haven't seen anything yet.

It's the Law

Unfortunately, denial is not an option. Making concessions and allowing greater latitude in bringing religious practices into the workplace is not merely a matter of exercising tolerance or simply being nice. It's also a legal requirement.

State and federal anti-discrimination statutes require businesses to make reasonable accommodations for religious practices on the job. "Reasonable" is the operative word.

The law does not require employers to make adjustments that cause undue harm or hardship to the business. Sometimes the workers have to make the allowances or accommodations.

Remaining fair, juggling opposing needs, satisfying the law and maintaining a competitive business edge all at the same time is tricky business. Decisions about mixing religion and work are never easy and each case is different. It's uncharted territory for most managers.

Tips and Guidelines

The good news is that some help is available. The following advice from veteran human resources experts has helped many middle managers resolve problems regarding religion in the workplace. They may assist you as well.

These suggestions won't answer all your questions, but they do provide a framework for developing your own solutions for the issues that occur in your particular work environment:

- Remember that the best and most universal criteria for accepting or rejecting requests to permit certain religious practices in the workplace is still simply, "What would a reasonable person do?"

Model tolerance every day. Building an overall culture of openness and acceptance is the best way to prevent contentious squabbling over isolated religious practices.

- Deal with the rights, needs and attitudes of all workers, not just the ones requesting (or demanding) concessions.
- Weigh the impact of possible accommodations on all employees—and especially on customers.
- Be sure the request is legitimate. Find out if it really is required by the religious doctrine. Some workers may request accommodations that are not considered mandatory by the majority of their faith community.
- Be deliberate. Don't be bullied or stampeded into making a snap decision. Every accommodation granted sets a precedent the organization may have to live with for years to come.
- Don't make decisions based on personal bias or prejudice or simply what's easiest or the most popular thing to do. Always have a bona fide business or legal reason for your action, and always explain your rationale to all those involved or affected by your decision.
- Educate yourself about the practice in question. Learn what it entails, what it means and why it is important to the followers of that particular faith. The greater your understanding, the better your decision will be.
- Find out what others in the industry are doing about similar requests. That's what networks are for. Someone else may have better insight regarding the issue. It's okay to steal good ideas from others—even the competition. There is no copyright on wisdom.
- Be fair and consistent. Anything less sets you up for litigation.
- Always seek the least intrusive or disruptive accommodation.
- When in doubt, don't be afraid to get legal counsel.

- Respect each worker's individual faith or religion even if you have to deny specific requests.
- When all else fails, try praying over the issue. That's one religious practice that not even a supervisor, manager or foreman can deny.

Religious practices and business practices are occasionally at odds with each other. Sometimes business has to bend a little to accommodate personal religious expressions. Sometimes religion has to pull back a bit to allow essential business to be conducted.

And sometimes a compromise can be reached. For example, if excusing employees for a special religious day or event creates a hardship for the employer, an accommodation might be to excuse a limited number of the faithful each year on a rotating basis.

Of course in other cases, no compromise is possible. When Somalian cab drivers in Minneapolis refused to serve paying customers because they were carrying liquor, the employers felt they had no choice but to impose suspensions and to threaten termination for repeated offenses.

I'm reminded of a Board of Directors I once worked for which had a majority of Jewish members and routinely rejected requests from Jewish employees for time off during their holy days. As the Board Chair (a Jew himself) explained, "Sometimes you have to pay a price for your religion."

Granting some accommodations. Refusing others. Compromising when possible. It's all in a day's work for effective supervisors.

The Bottom Line

All Americans are entitled to their personal religious beliefs and to practice and express their faith freely, but they are not necessarily entitled to bring their religious practices to work in someone else's business. Religious freedom is guaranteed by the Constitution. Holding a specific job is not.

If a particular religious practice makes it impossible to fulfill essential job functions or interferes with necessary business transactions, it's probably time for the worker to seek other employment.

As a supervisor and business leader in a democratic society, you are required to make appropriate accommodations to permit individual religious practices by employees. But you are not required to allow employees' religious expressions to drive away customers, to lose business or to go out of business.

Defining when, how or how much to accommodate religious expressions in the workplace involves both decisiveness and flexibility. Different situations demand different solutions. It's not a crapshoot. It's a balancing act. Fortunately, that's what good supervisors and managers do best. . . .

EXPLORING THE ISSUE

Should Employees Be Allowed to Wear Symbols of Faith in the Workplace?

Critical Thinking and Reflection

1. If you were the judge ruling for *Eweida v. British Airways*, how would you have ruled? Why?
2. What HRM policies would you suggest that organizations adopt to make religious expressions more accepting at the workplace?
3. Do you think organizations should provide any religious accommodations in the workplace? Why? Why not?
4. Do you have any symbols of faith that you would like your organization to accommodate?
5. Provide an international perspective as to how other countries accommodate religious expressions at work or school.

Is There Common Ground?

The country is becoming increasingly a nation of immigrants who carry their rich and diverse religious backgrounds. To accommodate this diversity, many organizations are proactively embracing an environment that encourages employees to express or wear their symbols of faith to the workplace. Some organizations are even changing their mission statement to indicate they are accepting of diverse spirituality. Further, increased globalization has made organizations realize that having a diverse religious work environment might possibly enhance business opportunities overseas. On the other hand, opponents of a faith-friendly approach reiterate that business priorities supersede employees' requests for expression of their faiths. They insist that organizations should make sure that their business strategy and business profits are not diminished due to any forms of religious expressions. Organizations should encourage public forums within their organization that can educate other employees and mitigate any religious concerns. Would organizations want to be involved in lengthy courtroom battles like Nadia had with British Airways? Just for a piece of jewelry?

Additional Resources

Flynn, G. (2003). Gray areas in controlling employee lifestyles. *Workforce, 82*(2), 64–65.

Zachary, M. (2005, March). Body piercings and religious discrimination. *SuperVision, 66*(3), 23–26.

http://thedisneyblog.com/2008/06/14/disney-world-sued-over-dress-codereligious-discrimination: Disney World Sued over Dress Code/Religious Discrimination.

www.sikhnet.com/daily-news/sikh-sues-disney-over-worker-dress-code: Sikh Sues Disney over Worker Dress Code.

www.presstv.com/classic/detail.aspx?id=110135§ionid=3510203: US Clinic Denies Muslim Doctor Right to Wear Hijab.

www.msnbc.msn.com/id/4106422/: Debate over Religious Symbols Divides France.

www.personneltoday.com/articles/2008/12/08/48653/eweida-v-british-airways-plc.html: *Eweida v. British Airways* Plc.

http://religions.pewforum.org/reports: The Pew Forum on Public Life—U.S. Religious Landscape Survey.

http://business.timesonline.co.uk/tol/business/law/article7024712.ece: Carey Attacks Judges after Nadia Eweida Loses BA Crucifix Case.

http://news.bbc.co.uk/2/hi/6165368.stm: Woman Loses Her Fight to Wear Cross.

www.america.gov/st/peopleplace-english/2007/November/20071128173019xlrennef0.1781427.html: Religion in the Workplace Is Diversity Issue for U.S. Companies—Many Firms Seek Guidance in Accommodating Employees' Religious Practices.

www.guardian.co.uk/education/2008/jul/29/schools.religion1: Previous Cases: Religious Symbols at School or Work.

Internet References . . .

Top Twenty Five Social Networking Sites

David Wilson, co-owner of Braveheart Design Inc., has transformed social media optimization website by merging traditional media, search engine marketing, and social marketing.

http://social-media-optimization.com/2009/02/top-twenty-five-social-networking-sites-feb-2009/

Social Network Sites: Definition, History, and Scholarship

JCMC is one of the oldest web-based Internet studies journals in existence, having been published quarterly continuously since June 1995. The journal was started by Margaret McLaughlin and Sheizaf Rafaeli in response to the growth of CMC scholarship in the early- to mid-1990s.

http://jcmc.indiana.edu/vol13/issue1/boyd.ellison.html

Pros and Cons of Using Personality Tests in Personnel Assessment

This site is maintained by the international congress on assessment center methods.

http://www.assessmentcenters.org/2004/gen_pros_cons.asp

What Test Should I Use Today? Pros and Cons for Recruiting Managers

HRM Guide publishes articles and news releases about HR surveys, employment law, human resource research, HR books, and careers that bridge the gap between theory and practice.

http://www.hrmguide.co.uk/recruitment/recruiting-assessment.htm

The Pros and Con of a Background Check

EzineArticles.com brings real-world experts and publishers together. Expert authors and writers are able to post their articles to be featured within the site. Our searchable database of hundreds of thousands of quality original articles allows e-mail newsletter publishers hungry for fresh content to find articles that they can use for inclusion within their next newsletter.

http://ezinearticles.com/?The-Pros-and-Cons-of-a-Background-Check&id=1318646

Background Checks: Pros and (Few) Cons

HRhero.com provides legal information, training, and compliance tools on state and federal employment law, supervisor training, and employee management for human resources and other business professionals. HRHero.com is supported by the Employers Counsel Network (ECN), a select group of attorneys from top law firms in all 50 states, Washington, D.C., and Canada.

http://www.hrhero.com/q&a/070105-background.shtml

UNIT 2

Talent Acquisition

Where to hunt for the best talent? How to identify the brightest? Organizations have made recruitment and selection practices their top HRM priority. The quality of any product or service is reflected through the talent of the company's employees. How to ensure the applicants are not lying about their past work accomplishments? This section addresses some critical aspects of staffing practices. The current trend of getting job applicants through social networking sites is examined. Personality tests help identify critical work-related characteristics relevant in today's job market. Background checks have become imperative as society witnesses an increase in delinquent behavior. Can these staffing practices identify qualified talent?

- Are Social Networking Sites Good Recruitment Sources?
- Are Personality Tests Good Predictors of Employee Performance?
- Is Cognitive Ability Testing a Good Predictor of Work Performance?
- Would Mandatory Background Checks for All Employees Reduce Negligent Hiring Lawsuits?

ISSUE 5

Are Social Networking Sites Good Recruitment Sources?

YES: Jamie Vicknair, Dalia Elkersh, Katie Yancey, and Michael C. Budden, from "The Use of Social Networking Websites as a Recruiting Tool for Employers," *American Journal of Business Education*, vol. 3, no. 11, 7–12 (2010)

NO: Daniel J. Solove, from "The End of Privacy?" *Scientific American*, vol. 299, no. 3 (September, 2008)

Learning Outcomes

After reading this issue, you should be able to:

- Gain an understanding of how social networking sites originated.
- Explain how online malice occurs.
- Explain how the SNS approach can be tailored to recruiting needs.
- Gain an international perspective of how other countries adopt SNS at the workplace.

ISSUE SUMMARY

YES: Jamie Vicknair and colleagues suggest most employers use SNS as a preliminary screening tool. They state that though Gen Y applicants are aware of this trend, yet they post a lot of personal information online. This could have powerful consequences on their employment profile.

NO: Daniel J. Solove, a law professor at George Washington University, and also the author on several books on topics related to privacy, asserts that online information is not an accurate and honest source for recruiters. Gen Yers are more likely to post incorrect information when personal and business relationships become unpleasant.

Social networking sites (SNSs) can be defined as Web services that allow individuals to connect with each other and provide information on their social and employment profiles. SNSs allow individuals to network both professionally and socially providing a very strong interactive platform.

A historical background suggests that the first social network site, Six Degrees.com, began in 1997. It was established to allow individuals to connect with classmates and family members. However, this service did not do very well and closed its services in 2000. In 2003, the launching of MySpace revolutionized the online social landscape dramatically. Teenagers flocked to these Web sites to publicly share their personal information and communicate incessantly with their peers. This social site further allowed users to personalize their pages providing their own personal touch. MySpace has more than 100 million members, making it one of the most visited social Web sites.

In 2004, the world witnessed the debut of Facebook, which began primarily as an exclusive Harvard school social networking site. Subsequently, this elitism was expanded to include other university students but yet remained a college-dominated social networking site. In 2005, Facebook expanded its members to include teenagers and professionals, and the global community observed the powerful role social networking had on its members. Facebook provides several marketing and recruiting initiatives for organizations that will allow them to use it both as a recruiting and marketing tool. Facebook is considered the biggest storage of individuals' personal photos on the Internet. In 2003, the introduction of LinkedIn created a social platform exclusively for working individuals. LinkedIn allows professionals to share their education and work expertise, network with relevant professionals, and post any job postings.

The main question is whether these interactive social Web sites are good recruitment sources. Career experts suggest that SNSs are a wonderful way to begin any recruiting dialogue as these sites are used extensively by applicants today. SNSs allow companies to develop a huge applicant data base that HRM departments can potentially contact. SNSs also allow you to identify passive applicants—employees who are not actively looking for a job, and identified as the most qualified talent. A survey conducted by Careerbuilder.com suggests that the percentage of organizations using SNSs as a preliminary or a screening process is increasing every year. This method of recruiting is also very cost-effective, saving organizations several thousands in third-party recruiter's fees.

The Gen Y or Millennials (individuals who are currently between the ages of 18–29) spend an enormous time of their day on the Internet either socializing, working, or chatting. The best way for recruiters to reach out to this target group would be the SNS. The Gen Y group also seems to be very trusting of information they obtain from SNSs compared to that of traditional company Web sites. The research provided by YES article also suggests that Gen Y applicants feel that recruiters can "snoop" on their personal information as it is posted for the entire public. The Gen Y group does not seem to have any qualms about sharing their personal information online.

On the other hand, opponents of SNSs suggest that organizations could be getting inaccurate information about individuals. Online malice occurs consistently as individuals post incorrect information about their peers when personal and business relationships break. Unfortunately, incorrect information posted on the Internet remains perpetually, creating an online reputation that haunts the applicants forever. Further, individuals generally include personal information that is irrelevant to recruiters but would definitely cloud the judgments of the recruiters. Why would organizations want information irrelevant to the job?

Further, HR professionals might run into legal and privacy issues if they recruit applicants based on online information. HRM professionals struggle with how to sift through the deluge of personal and professional information that SNSs offer. Would you hire someone who has a negative online history?

An alternative perspective may be that organizations recruit only through industry-specific social networking sites. This will allow organizations to use a social media but focus only on talent relevant to their organization or industry. For instance, Pfizer, the pharmaceutical giant, has launched its own version of Facebook, called PFacebook, to leverage and identify talent specific to their industry. HP has identified its own SSN with MyCommunity, which allows employees to share positive and negative experiences of their jobs and identify potential jobs within the organization. LinkedIn, a professional SNS, has 8 million global users with organizations scouting for almost 25% of their applicants through their networking resource. LinkedIn International Director suggests that leveraging global talent has been one of their very specific recruiting advantages because of their universal visibility.

Other suggestions for applicants who want to still use SNS may be to strictly limit the personal information they post on their websites. Recruiters even suggest not providing personal data such as date of birth, ethnicity, photographs, or any confidential information as this could definitely dampen recruiters making an objective decision. A study by CareerBuilder.com suggests that a majority (more than 50%) of recruiters do not hire applicants based on what they read or see on social sites. Experts even suggest providing undergraduates with learning seminars on the proper use of "SNS etiquette" so that they may realize early in their careers how damaging inappropriate personal information is for their future employment.

Are individuals from other countries also socially wired like those of the United States? According to a 2010 study, the top three SNS sites are Facebook, Twitter, and LinkedIn based on the range of features and characteristics they offer their members. Facebook is the largest SNS, with approximately about 500 million members. Around the same time the SNSs became prominent in the United States, international SNSs began to emerge. Orkut became synonymous with social networking in Brazil and India. In Japan, Mixi became a household name with more 15 million users, and online customers of Bebo surpassed that of MySpace in the United Kingdom. Facebook provides six different language versions in India to capture the multilingual population. Recruiters in these countries also use these SNSs to connect with potential applicants.

YES 

Jamie Vicknair et al.

The Use of Social Networking Websites as a Recruiting Tool for Employers

Introduction

Employers are increasingly turning to social networking sites as a tool for screening job applicants. According to a survey conducted by Careerbuilder .com (2010), 45% of companies in 2009 used social networking websites as a screening tool for job applicants, a number twice as high as the year before. This statistic indicates the popularity of using these sites as a human resource tool. The use of social networking websites by individuals is a widespread phenomena. The website Facebook.com is currently home to over 400 million users with half of those logging into their account at least once every day (Facebook.com, 2010).

The term "social recruiting" is a buzz phrase used throughout the HR world, which can be defined as "harnessing the evolution of Web 2.0 technologies and social media tools to communicate, engage, inform, and recruit our future talent" (Jacobs, 2009). The use of such social networking websites allows recruiters to connect to a broad array of talented and capable candidates in niche communities (Jacobs, 2009). Reviewing candidates' social networking profiles can be a helpful tool for recruiters looking to hire a candidate. According to an article from HR Focus, a candidates' social networking profile helped a candidate get a job because their profile demonstrated they were well-rounded, creative, had received awards and accolades, and would be a good fit. However, reasons candidates did not receive job offers based on their social networking profiles included the demonstration of poor communication skills, drinking/drug use content, bad mouthing of previous employers/co-workers/clients, and/or posting provocative/inappropriate photographs (HR Focus, 2009).

The use of social networking sites provides socializing outlets and allows users to use their "profile" as a means of self expression and creates a person's social sphere (Hoy and Milne, 2010). The Pew Research Center released a study stating three-quarters of all millennials (those between the ages of 18–29) have created a profile on a social networking site as a means of self expression (Pew Research Center, 2010). According to Budden, Anthony, Budden, and Jones (2007), internet usage for college students has increased and social networking

From *American Journal of Business Education* by J. Vicknair et al. (The Clute Institute, 2010).

online has been growing at an accelerating pace. A recent study indicated that participants spent an average of 6.22 hours per week using Facebook and MySpace (Budden et al., 2007). Many students perceive their profile to be private and only available to be viewed with their consent. Students' unawareness of the unreliable security of social networking profiles can result in negative consequences. Decker (2006) believes users have a relaxed attitude toward personal privacy. For instance, a student was kicked out of his school's honor society because he created a Facebook page that criticized his school (FOXNews.com, 2010). Certain information posted on social networking profiles can have negative implications on college students looking to enter the job market. According to Karl and Peluchette, job offers have been rescinded and internships terminated on the basis of messages and pictures posted on Facebook. One journal notes that using online social networking sites as a tool for recruitment may not provide a true or accurate portrayal of a candidate's personal life or how they may perform on the job (Oleniczak, Pike, Mishra, and Mishra, 2010).

Objectives

An earlier study conducted by Janelle Harrison (2008) investigated student awareness of employer use of social networking websites as a candidate screening tool. Following on the heels of that study, objectives for this study were developed:

- Are students aware that employers have the ability to find information through social networking websites?
- Have students posted information on their social networking profiles they would not want an employer/recruiter to see?
- Do students approve of employers checking social networking profiles as part of the screening effort?
- Are students concerned about the legitimacy of their social networking profile privacy?
- Would students provide potential employees with their social networking profile passwords in order to be considered for a job?

Methodology

A voluntary convenience survey was created to explore research objectives. The questionnaire consisted of nine questions pertaining to the primary objective and four questions designated to respondent demographics. Four open-ended questions encouraged explanations to the nature responses. The survey was emailed and hand-distributed to a random sample of students from all classifications and majors at a state university. Hard copy surveys were distributed to ten classes and upon completion were manually entered by researchers using the online survey. Data from both forms of distribution was recorded using the GoogleDocs application. After the data was combined, it was analyzed using SPSS. The response was 289 students consisting of 39.6% male respondents and 60.4% female respondents. Of the respondents, 32% were freshman, 9.5% sophomores, 13% juniors, 25.7% seniors, and 19.7% graduate students.

Research Statistics

Respondents Using Social Networking Websites

The use of online social networking is a daily occurrence on most college campuses. In order to determine the demographics for the research a survey was distributed regarding the gender, classification, employment status, and organizational involvement of the respondents. Research regarding use of social networking indicated that of the 289 respondents, 91.7% currently use an online social networking site such as Facebook, Twitter, Myspace, or LinkedIn. Of those users 37% reported are male, and 62% are female. There was little variance in usage of online social networking among respondents who were full-time employees, part time employees, or unemployed and the majority of these did claim to use a form of social networking. Of respondents seeking employment, 33% admitted to currently using some form of online social networking. Respondents belonging to an on-campus organization made up 29% of online social networking users.

Are students aware that employers may have the ability to gather recruiting information through social networking websites?

The survey inquired as to whether respondents were aware that employers or recruiters could view their social networking profile even if the account settings were set to private, simply by entering a specific search string into many search engines. The survey found 49.3% of respondents were aware, while 50.7% of respondents were not aware that employers or recruiters could view their social networking profile. Harrison's (2008) study revealed the majority (63.3%) of respondents were not aware of this fact. Of the respondents involved in on-campus organizations 58% believed employers could view their social networking profiles. Of those respondents not involved in on-campus organizations, 55% believed employers could not view their social networking profiles. According to "Managing Accounts Payable," recruiters in companies feel entitled to view a candidate's social networking profile. One quarter of 254 employers surveyed admitted to reviewing an applicant's social networking profile prior to making a job offer (Harrison, 2008, p. 11).

Respondents were asked how often they believed employers viewed social networking profiles. The largest response (45.3%) indicated they believe employers and recruiters look at job candidates social networking profiles all of the time. These results are in contrast to the findings of Harrison's (2008) study where only 15.6% of respondents believed employers did this. Perhaps students are becoming increasingly aware of this potential. Respondents from all educational classifications indicated they believed employers looked at social networking profiles all of the time or some of the time. A majority (65%) of respondents claiming not to be seeking employment indicated they believed employers look at candidates social networking profiles all of the time, while only 31% of those reporting seeking employment believed the same. Many college students believe their social networking profiles are private but are actually being viewed by potential employers (Budden and Budden, 2008).

Do students place or have they ever placed information in social networking profiles they would not want employers/recruiters to see?

According to The HR Specialist (2010), the top three reasons employers reject candidates after online screening are because they posted provocative or inappropriate photos or information, they posted content regarding use of drinking or drugs, and because they bad mouthed a previous employer, co-worker, or client (TheHRSpecialist.com). When asked if there was anything that the respondents did not want a recruiter or employer to see on their profile, 89.6% of respondents claimed no. When asked to expound upon this question most of the respondents responded they had "nothing to hide," but others stated they had "drunk pictures, or pictures with alcohol and cigarettes" they would not want an employer or recruiter to see. One-tenth of respondents claimed they have posted content that they would not want employers to see, while Harrison's study only yielded 3.1% of respondents making that claim. Of freshman respondents, 89% indicated there was nothing they would not want employers or recruiters to see on their social networking profile, while 91% of graduate students said the same thing. These results have an implication for students who are seeking or will eventually be seeking employment. A study conducted by Careerbuilder.com (2010) revealed that recruiters searching the web for information for a possible job candidate used all possible information portals. Of the resources recruiter/employers used, 29% used Facebook as a reference, 26% used LinkedIn, 21% used Myspace, 11% searched blogs, and 7% utilized Twitter (Careerbuilder.com, 2010).

In this study a large majority of respondents (70%) claimed to have removed information from their social networking profile they didn't want others to see while only 29.7% stated they have never removed something from their profile they did not want others to see. The majority of respondents claimed they believed they would not change anything on their profile even if they knew it may be seen by others regardless of the privacy settings on their profile. Only 11.7% said they would change their profile content if they knew it could be seen.

Do students approve of the fact employers may check their social networking profiles?

One survey question asked if respondents thought employers and recruiters have the right to check their social networking profile when evaluating whether or not to hire them. The study found that 69.4% of respondents felt employers or recruiters had the right to check their social networking profile. When the question was cross-tabbed with respondent classification, results revealed that 58.4% of freshman respondents, 70.4% of sophomore respondents, 81.1% of junior respondents, 68.1% of senior respondents, and 80% of graduate respondents agreed employers and recruiters have the right to check their social networking profile when evaluating whether or not to hire them. When compared to job status, the survey showed that 56.8% of unemployed, 76.2% of part-time employed respondents, and 70.7% of full-time employed respondents agreed employers and recruiters have the right to check an applicant's social networking profile before hiring the applicant. The survey indicated 60% of respondents seeking employment and 78.8% of respondents not seeking employment felt employers had the right to check social networking profiles. Respondents were encouraged to explain their answer to the question. These explanations indicated 20% of the respondents felt employers had the right to view social networking pages because the page is public information that anyone can view. Of the respondents 44% felt the company had a right to view the information in order to learn more about the applicant's personality and to ensure the person is not a liability. The explanations indicated that 30% of the respondents felt the information was private or that a person's private life is separate from their professional life and employers did not have a right to view the applicants' social networking page.

Are students concerned about the legitimacy of their social networking profile privacy?

The survey found that 51% of respondents felt their profile was private, while 49% felt their profile was not private. Harrison's (2008) study revealed, 43.8% of respondents felt their MySpace or Facebook profile was private, while 56.3% did not. When this question was compared between genders the survey indicated males and females had a different opinion on the security of profiles. The findings indicated 60.6% of female respondents felt that their social networking profile was private, while 61.6% of male respondents felt that their social networking profile was not private. In a similar study conducted by Hoy and Milne (2010) findings revealed that both men and women were indifferent towards an employer viewing their social networking profile page. The study also indicated that men and women differed in concerns about the privacy of the information posted on Facebook and women respondents were significantly more concerned about the privacy of their social networking profile page than men (Hoy et al., 2010).

Would students give out their social networking profile password in order to be considered for a job?

The majority of the respondents (81%) indicated they were not willing to give out their network profile password to a recruiter in order to qualify for a potential job, while 18.4% were willing. In the city of Bozeman, Montana a hiring policy was implemented that required applicants to provide their user names and passwords for sites including Facebook, Google, Yahoo, YouTube, and MySpace. The issue gained national attention when a local television station learned about the regulations from an anonymous viewer. The city manager reported no one was ever denied a job for failing to disclose user names and passwords on password-protected Internet sites and soon after recalled the policy (Business Insurance, 2009). Respondents seeking employment and those not seeking employment demonstrated no significant variance in willingness to give out passwords to be considered for a job. Among the respondents who were seeking employment, 85% would refuse to reveal passwords to a recruiter for a potential job, while 15% would reveal their passwords.

Of the respondents not currently seeking employment, 81% would refuse to reveal their passwords and 19% would agree to do so. Explanations respondents offered against giving their passwords to potential employers included it would be an invasion of privacy. Some respondents said they did not mind if the employer viewed the main profile page because it is available for the public, but giving away the password would be crossing the line. The respondents who would agree to give out their passwords stated they had nothing to hide, they might really need the job, and they could always change their passwords shortly after the employer checks their profiles.

Recommendations

Further studies may be conducted on employer/recruiter attitudes and use of social networking websites as a screening tool in order to gain a more well-rounded perspective on the subject. Questions regarding how often this practice is used should be addressed as well as which industries in which it may be most prevalent.

Educational programs may use the results of this and future studies to create informational seminars for students regarding proper social networking etiquette. In particular, career services programs may take more initiative to prepare incoming freshman of the implications of posting inappropriate content on social networking profiles. The need for interview etiquette and social networking etiquette is real. It is recommended that a seminar be conducted for incoming freshman on the implications of inappropriate social networking behavior and its impact on future job prospects. A "Keeping it Clean" campaign may help new students understand the consequences of posting negative content.

Lastly, research may be conducted regarding the ethical implications of employers using social networking websites as a tool of discrimination. Many social networking profiles contain information that is usually illegal to inquire about in a job interview.

Conclusion

This topic is becoming important as the use of online social networking sites continues to grow. Respondents are aware employers are looking at social networking profiles at the same time many reported there was nothing posted they would not want employers to see. There was also a resounding consensus that respondents were not willing to give out their social networking profile password in order to be considered for a job. These practices may have implications on the future use of social networking websites as the knowledge of recruiters utilizing the sites may incline users to move towards using them for job searching and professional networking.

Daniel J. Solove

NO

The End of Privacy

Young people share the most intimate details of personal life on social-networking Web sites, portending a realignment of the public and the private.

He has a name, but most people just know him as "the Star Wars Kid." In fact, he is known around the world by tens of millions of people. Unfortunately, his notoriety is for one of the most embarrassing moments in his life.

In 2002, as a 15-year-old, the Star Wars Kid videotaped himself waving around a golf-ball retriever while pretending it was a lightsaber. Without the help of the expert choreographers working on the Star Wars movies, he stumbled around awkwardly in the video.

The video was found by some of the boy's tormentors, who uploaded it to an Internet video site. It became an instant hit with a multitude of fans. All across the blogosphere, people started mocking the boy, making fun of him for being pudgy, awkward and nerdy.

Several remixed videos of the Star Wars Kid started popping up, adorned with special effects. People edited the video to make the golf-ball retriever glow like a lightsaber. They added Star Wars music to the video. Others mashed it up with other movies. Dozens of embellished versions were created. The Star Wars Kid appeared in a video game and on the television shows Family Guy and South Park. It is one thing to be teased by classmates in school, but imagine being ridiculed by masses the world over. The teenager dropped out of school and had to seek counseling. What happened to the Star Wars Kid can happen to anyone, and it can happen in an instant. Today collecting personal information has become second nature. More and more people have cell phone cameras, digital audio recorders, Web cameras and other recording technologies that readily capture details about their lives.

For the first time in history nearly anybody can disseminate information around the world. People do not need to be famous enough to be interviewed by the mainstream media. With the Internet, anybody can reach a global audience.

Technology has led to a generational divide. On one side are high school and college students whose lives virtually revolve around social-networking sites and blogs. On the other side are their parents, for whom recollection of the past often remains locked in fading memories or, at best, in books, photographs and videos. For the current generation, the past is preserved on the Internet, potentially forever. And this change raises the question of how

From *Scientific American*, vol. 299, no. 3, September 2008, pp. 100–106.

much privacy people can expect—or even desire—in an age of ubiquitous networking.

Generation Google

The number of young people using social-networking Web sites such as Facebook and MySpace is staggering. At most college campuses, more than 90 percent of students maintain their own sites. I call the people growing up today "Generation Google." For them, many fragments of personal information will reside on the Internet forever, accessible to this and future generations through a simple Google search.

That openness is both good and bad. People can now spread their ideas everywhere without reliance on publishers, broadcasters or other traditional gatekeepers. But that transformation also creates profound threats to privacy and reputations. The New York Times is not likely to care about the latest gossip at Dubuque Senior High School or Oregon State University. Bloggers and others communicating online may care a great deal. For them, stories and rumors about friends, enemies, family members, bosses, co-workers and others are all prime fodder for Internet postings.

Before the Internet, gossip would spread by word of mouth and remain within the boundaries of that social circle. Private details would be confined to diaries and kept locked in a desk drawer. Social networking spawned by the Internet allows communities worldwide to revert to the close-knit culture of preindustrial society, in which nearly every member of a tribe or a farming hamlet knew everything about the neighbors. Except that now the "villagers" span the globe.

College students have begun to share salacious details about their schoolmates. A Web site called Juicy Campus serves as an electronic bulletin board that allows students nationwide to post anonymously and without verification a sordid array of tidbits about sex, drugs and drunkenness. Another site, Don't Date Him Girl, invites women to post complaints about the men they have dated, along with real names and actual photographs.

Social-networking sites and blogs are not the only threat to privacy. As several articles in this issue of Scientific American have already made clear, companies collect and use our personal information at every turn. Your credit-card company has a record of your purchases. If you shop online, merchants keep tabs on every item you have bought. Your Internet service provider has information about how you surf the Internet. Your cable company has data about which television shows you watch.

The government also compromises privacy by assembling vast databases that can be searched for suspicious patterns of behavior. The National Security Agency listens and examines the records of millions of telephone conversations. Other agencies analyze financial transactions. Thousands of government bodies at the federal and state level have records of personal information, chronicling births, marriages, employment, property ownership and more. The information is often stored in public records, making it readily accessible to anyone—and the trend toward more accessible personal data continues to grow as more records become electronic.

The Future of Reputation

Broad-based exposure of personal information diminishes the ability to protect reputation by shaping the image that is presented to others. Reputation plays an important role in society, and preserving private details of one's life is essential to it. We look to people's reputations to decide whether to make friends, go on a date, hire a new employee or undertake a prospective business deal.

Some would argue that the decline of privacy might allow people to be less inhibited and more honest. But when everybody's transgressions are exposed, people may not judge one another less harshly. Having your personal information may fail to improve my judgment of you. It may, in fact, increase the likelihood that I will hastily condemn you. Moreover, the loss of privacy might inhibit freedom. Elevated visibility that comes with living in a transparent online world means you may never overcome past mistakes.

People want to have the option of "starting over," of reinventing themselves throughout their lives. As American philosopher John Dewey once said, a person is not "something complete, perfect, [or] finished," but is "something moving, changing, discrete, and above all initiating instead of final." In the past, episodes of youthful experimentation and foolishness were eventually forgotten, giving us an opportunity to start anew, to change and to grow. But with so much information online, it is harder to make these moments forgettable. People must now live with the digital baggage of their pasts.

This openness means that the opportunities for members of Generation Google might be limited because of something they did years ago as wild teenagers. Their intimate secrets may be revealed by other people they know. Or they might become the unwitting victim of a false rumor. Like it or not, many people are beginning to get used to having a lot more of their personal information online.

What Is to Be Done?

Can we prevent a future in which so much information about people's private lives circulates beyond their control? Some technologists and legal scholars flatly say no. Privacy, they maintain, is just not compatible with a world in which information flows so freely. As Scott McNealy of Sun Microsystems once famously declared: "You already have zero privacy. Get over it." Countless books and articles have heralded the "end," "death" and "destruction" of privacy.

Those proclamations are wrongheaded at best. It is still possible to protect privacy, but doing so requires that we rethink outdated understandings of the concept. One such view holds that privacy requires total secrecy: once information is revealed to others, it is no longer private. This notion of privacy is unsuited to an online world. The generation of people growing up today understands privacy in a more nuanced way. They know that personal information is routinely shared with countless others, and they also know that they leave a trail of data wherever they go.

The more subtle understanding of privacy embraced by Generation Google recognizes that a person should retain some control over personal information that becomes publicly available. This generation wants a say in how private details of their lives are disseminated.

The issue of control over personal information came to the fore in 2006, when Facebook launched a feature called News Feeds, which sent a notice to people's friends registered with the service when their profile was changed or updated. But to the great surprise of those who run Facebook, many of its users reacted with outrage. Nearly 700,000 of them complained. At first blush, the outcry over News Feeds seems baffling. Many of the users who protested had profiles completely accessible to the public. So why did they think it was a privacy violation to alert their friends to changes in their profiles?

Instead of viewing privacy as secrets hidden away in a dark closet, they considered the issue as a matter of accessibility. They figured that most people would not scrutinize their profiles carefully enough to notice minor changes and updates. They could make changes inconspicuously. But Facebook's News Feeds made information more widely noticeable. The privacy objection, then, was not about secrecy; it was about accessibility.

In 2007 Facebook again encountered another privacy outcry when it launched an advertising system with two parts, called Social Ads and Beacon. With Social Ads, whenever users wrote something positive about a product or a movie, Facebook would use their names, images and words in advertisements sent to friends in the hope that an endorsement would induce other users to purchase a product more than an advertisement might. With Beacon, Facebook made data-sharing deals with a variety of other commercial Web sites. If a person bought a movie ticket on Fandango or an item on another site, that information would pop up in that person's public profile.

Facebook rolled out these programs without adequately informing its users. People unwittingly found themselves shilling products on their friends' Web sites. And some people were shocked to see their private purchases on other Web sites suddenly displayed to the public as part of their profiles that appeared on the Facebook site.

The outcry and an ensuing online petition called for Facebook to reform its practices—a document that quickly attracted tens of thousands of signatures and that ultimately led to several changes. As witnessed in these instances, privacy does not always involve sharing of secrets. Facebook users did not want their identities used to endorse products with Social Ads. It is one thing to write about how much one enjoys a movie or CD; it is another to be used on a billboard to pitch products to others.

Changing the Law

Canada and most European countries have more stringent privacy statutes than the U.S., which has resisted enacting all-encompassing legislation. Privacy laws elsewhere recognize that revealing information to others does not extinguish one's right to privacy. Increasing accessibility of personal information, however, means that U.S. law also should begin recognizing the need to safeguard a degree of privacy in the public realm.

In some areas, U.S. law has a well-developed system of controlling information. Copyright recognizes strong rights for public information, protecting a wide range of works, from movies to software. Procuring copyright protection does not require locking a work of intellect behind closed doors. You can read a copyrighted magazine, make a duplicate for your own use and lend it to others. But you cannot do whatever you want: for instance, photocopying it from cover to cover or selling bootleg copies in the street. Copyright law tries to achieve a balance between freedom and control, even though it still must wrestle with the ongoing controversies in a digital age.

The closest U.S. privacy law comes to a legal doctrine akin to copyright is the appropriation tort, which prevents the use of someone else's name or likeness for financial benefit. Unfortunately, the law has developed in a way that is often ineffective against the type of privacy threats now cropping up. Copyright primarily functions as a form of property right, protecting works of self-expression, such as a song or painting. To cope with increased threats to privacy, the scope of the appropriation tort should be expanded. The broadening might actually embody the original early 20th-century interpretation of this principle of common law, which conceived of privacy as more than a means to protect property: "The right to withdraw from the public gaze at such times as a person may see fit . . . is embraced within the right of personal liberty," declared the Georgia Supreme Court in 1905. Today, however, the tort does not apply when a person's name or image appears in news, art, literature, or on social-networking sites. At the same time the appropriation tort protects against using someone's name or picture without consent to advertise products, it allows these representations to be used in a news story. This limitation is fairly significant. It means that the tort would rarely apply to Internet-related postings.

Any widening of the scope of the appropriation tort must be balanced against the competing need to allow legitimate news gathering and dissemination of public information. The tort should probably apply only when photographs and other personal information are used in ways that are not of public concern—a criterion that will inevitably be subject to ongoing judicial deliberation.

Appropriation is not the only common-law privacy tort that needs an overhaul to become more relevant in an era of networked digital communications. We already have many legal tools to protect privacy, but they are currently crippled by conceptions of privacy that prevent them from working effectively. A broader development of the law should take into account problematic uses of personal information illustrated by the Star Wars Kid or Facebook's Beacon service.

It would be best if these disputes could be resolved without recourse to the courts, but the broad reach of electronic networking will probably necessitate changes in common law. The threats to privacy are formidable, and people are starting to realize how strongly they regard privacy as a basic right. Toward this goal, society must develop a new and more nuanced understanding of public and private life—one that acknowledges that more personal information is going to be available yet also protects some choice over how that information is shared and distributed.

Key Concepts

- Social-networking sites allow seemingly trivial gossip to be distributed to a worldwide audience, sometimes making people the butt of rumors shared by millions of users across the Internet.
- Public sharing of private lives has led to a rethinking of our current conceptions of privacy.
- Existing law should be extended to allow some privacy protection for things that people say and do in what would have previously been considered the public domain.

Fast Facts

- Every day people post more than 65,000 videos on YouTube.
- In 2006 MySpace surpassed [a] million profiles.
- Since 1999 the number of blogs has grown from 50 to 50 million.
- More than 50 percent of blogs are written by children younger than 19. . . .

The Internet Never Forgets

A Public Life

A post on YouTube can provoke global ridicule with the press of a return key. When a young man applied for a job at a U.S. investment firm, he sent along a video with his resume. Called Impossible Is Nothing, it showed the student engaging in a variety of physical feats, from bench-pressing 495 pounds to doing a ski jump to breaking bricks with a karate chop. Throughout the clip, the student bragged about his athletic accomplishments and his overall success in life.

Needless to say, the video was not particularly appropriate for the job he was seeking, and his arrogance was so over the top that the video was quite funny. Apparently, someone at the investment firm leaked the video, and it was posted online. It became an instant hit and has been viewed hundreds of thousands of times. Throughout the Internet, the student has been mocked and parodied. His job prospects have diminished substantially. Although he certainly made a mistake and may have learned a lesson, his youthful bravado and misjudgment are now forever preserved in cyberspace. . . .

EXPLORING THE ISSUE

Are Social Networking Sites Good Recruitment Sources?

Critical Thinking and Reflection

1. Have you experienced anyone posting negative comments about your personality/traits/work ethic? How have you addressed it?
2. What HRM policies/practices do you recommend for organizations that adopt a SNS approach to recruiting?
3. Will you be willing to give your SNS (Facebook, Myspace, etc.) password to a potential recruiter? Why? Why not?
4. If you were in the EEO (Equal Employment Opportunity) policy team, what acts/laws would you introduce to control applicants' online privacy on SNS? Identify a name for the law and provide its main guidelines.
5. How do other countries use SNS specifically for recruiting?

Is There Common Ground?

Social networking sites (SNSs) have provided recruiters a different approach to hiring applicants. Proponents argue that it is very cost-effective, identifies qualified applicants, and allows online dialogues with applicants even before they are hired. Dr. Solove, law professor at George Washington University, indicates that the "Internet never forgets" as there is evidence of applicants who have posted information on YouTube and have had negative consequences in hiring. Would you Google an applicant that you are going to hire? What would you do if you came across negative information about an applicant who looked very promising in the interview? Organizations offer alternatives by providing specific SNS so that they can still recruit specialized talent through social media. Recruiting experts also suggest that the Gen Y group may benefit from SNS seminars right from their schooling years. The city of Bozeman, Montana, created quite a stir when they asked their applicants to provide their SNS passwords. The city suggested their request was only to authenticate applicants' personal and professional information. There was such media uproar that the city suspended this practice very quickly. What would you have done if you were an applicant to the city of Bozeman?

Additional Resources

Anonymous (2007). Using social networking sites for recruitment: Pros & cons. *HR Focus, 84*(4), 8–9.

Anonymous (2009). Social networking: A force for good or evil? *In the Black, 79*(10), 54–55.

Boyd, D. M. and Ellison, N. B. (2007). Social network sites: Definition, history, and scholarship. *Journal of Computer-Mediated Communication, 13*(1), 210–230.

Galagan, P. (2010). Ready or not? *T + D, 64*(5), 29–31.

Leader-Chivée, L., Hamilton, B., and Cowan, E. (2008). Networking the way to success: online social networks for workplace and competitive advantage. *People and Strategy, 31*(4), 40–46.

http://hubpages.com/hub/Pros-and-Cons-of-Social-Networking-Sites: Social Networking Tip: The Pros and Cons of Social Networking Sites.

www.npr.org/templates/story/story.php?storyId=6522523: Social Networking Technology Boosts Job Recruiting.

www.hrworld.com/features/Should-you-012408/: Should You Recruit on Social-Networking Sites?

www.expresscomputeronline.com/20080317/technologylife01.shtml: Using Social Networking Sites for Hiring.

www.workforce.com/section/00/article/26/22/59.php: LinkedIn Skyrockets as Job Losses Mount.

www.huffingtonpost.com/2009/06/19/montana-city-asks-job-app_n_218152.html: Montana City Asks Job Applicants for Facebook Passwords.

http://orangecopper.com/blog/list-of-the-best-social-networking-websites-2011: Review of the List of the Best Social Networking Websites 2011.

ISSUE 6

Are Personality Tests Good Predictors of Employee Performance?

YES: Ira Blank, from "Selecting Employees Based on Emotional Intelligence Competencies: Reap the Rewards and Minimize the Risk," *Employee Relations Law Journal* (December 2008)

NO: Erin White, from "Theory and Practice: Personality Tests Aim to Stop 'Fakers'; Some Say Tool's Accuracy Could Be Improved to Make Misrepresentations Harder," *Wall Street Journal* (Eastern Edition) (November 6, 2006)

Learning Outcomes

After reading this issue, you should be able to:

- Gain an understanding on the Big Five personality characteristics.
- Gain an understanding on the concept of emotional intelligence.
- Understand the main drawbacks in adopting personality tests for hiring.
- Gain an international perspective of how other countries adopt personality tests at the workplace.

ISSUE SUMMARY

YES: Ira Blank, litigation attorney, suggests that personality tests are excellent predictors of job performance because they identify several critical work-related skills needed in today's team and multicultural environment.

NO: Erin White, reporter for the *Wall Street Journal,* cites the studies of Dr. Griffith, which state that students always fake their personality when they realize the outcomes are different. Questions on these tests are so transparent that it is easy to manipulate the answers.

Personality tests help organizations profile personality characteristics. Researchers have identified the "Big Five" personality characteristics: extroversion, adjustment, agreeableness, conscientiousness, and inquisitiveness. Personality traits, such as conscientiousness, have been demonstrated to be good predictors of job performance. About 35 percent of U.S. organizations use personality tests during their hiring process. Daniel Goleman championed the concept of emotional intelligence, which has very similar dimensions to those of the Big Five. The main concepts of emotional intelligence are self-awareness, self-management, social awareness, and relationship management. These dimensions can be measured by personality tests such as the Emotional and Social Competency Inventory (ESCI) or the Emotional Competency Inventory (ECI).

Traditional selection practices usually identify technical competence, work experience, education, and cognitive skills to predict superior job performance. However, organizations are realizing that as employees are increasingly working in a team environment, either domestically or internationally, emotional intelligence plays a very critical role in determining their success. Who will deny that a collaborative work spirit is an asset in organizations today? Emotional intelligence helps identify skills such as leadership, change agent, negotiation, adaptability, and integrity, among several others.

Several studies indicate promising results in the use of emotional intelligence as a predictor of job performance. Retail managers with high emotional intelligence scores have demonstrated superior success in terms of store profits. Further, managers with a higher score of emotional intelligence handled the unpredictable buyers' retail environment much better. Sales employees who received higher scores of emotional intelligence had higher sales records and also lower attrition levels. Superior scores on emotional intelligence also have shown enhanced performance for global executives who constantly need to interact, coordinate, and collaborate among various cultures. Expatriates—employees who work overseas—who score high on emotional stability and openness to experience have shown very positive work results. Studies from the U.S. Army also demonstrate that individuals who score high on personality characteristics were much more successful at their jobs than those who got lower scores on such tests.

Opponents of personality testing suggest that the biggest pitfall of these tests is that applicants can fake their answers. Dr. Griffith of the Florida Institute of Technology suggests that applicants frequently fake their responses on personality tests. Applicants fake answers to get positive scores and also to provide answers that are deemed socially correct. For instance, questions such as "Are you deeply motivated?" will definitely bring out positive responses because the results of such answers are very transparent. Dr. Griffith demonstrated students faking in personality tests in a class study. The first time the students took the test, they were told it was a class-administered personality test. The second time the students took the same test, they were told recruiters were giving the test. The results indicated that 30 percent of the students faked their answers when they thought recruiters were providing the test so that they could get higher scores.

Apart from applicants' honesty about their answers, legal staffing experts are also concerned that some questions in personality tests may be considered invasive. Applicants might question how such questions are related to the job. Therefore, the validity or meaningfulness of such tests is an important concern for organizations while adopting such tests in any hiring process. Organizations should ensure that the questions on the personality tests have a direct relation to the job. Legal experts also suggest that different states have exclusive policies on what kind of questions can be included in personality tests.

Some alternate perspectives to whether personality tests should be used in hiring or not could be to always include personality tests in combination with other hiring practices. Personality tests become controversial when they are provided as the only predictor to the hiring process. Personality tests should be used with other selection practices (such as interviews and job tests) to augment employment information about the applicants. Further, it is very important that organizations do not adopt off-the-shelf or generic personality tests. Organizations should use personality tests that identify KSAs (knowledge, skills, and abilities) relevant to their specific industries. Organizations should use robust tests that have proven to have validity (meaningfulness) and reliability (consistency). The most common personality tests used by organizations are the MMPI (Minnesota Multiphasic Personality Inventory), Myer–Briggs Type Indicator, Hogan Personality Inventory, Personnel Reaction Blank, California Psychological Inventory, and the Employment Inventory. Organizations like Wal-Mart, Target, General Motors, and Universal Studios are among some of the organizations that commonly use personality testing for different employment levels. Human resource professionals should also make sure that personality tests do not demonstrate any adverse impact (unintentional discrimination) or disparate treatment (intentional discrimination) by consulting the required expertise in these fields.

International perspectives suggest personality tests are used predominantly in some cultures because workplace harmony and personal relationships are very important. Kolbe personality tests that identify four distinct categories are increasingly used in the Mexican workplace. Psychometric tests are used by about 25 percent of Indian organizations during the hiring process. Many of the tests that other cultures use are usually adopted from the United States, and HRM experts caution that such tests may not be tapping actual important personal traits relevant to the culture.

Ira Blank

Selecting Employees Based on Emotional Intelligence Competencies: Reap the Rewards and Minimize the Risk

Abstract (Summary)

When evaluating candidates for an open position, an employer has a strategic business decision to make: hire the individual whose skills, work experience, and education most closely match what the employer believes it takes to do the job, or hire the superior performer. Unfortunately, too many employers are confident they can identify and select the former, but they are less confident that they can recognize and hire the latter. Traditionally, employers have looked to work experience, technical skills, cognitive skills, and education as predictors of successful job performance. Testing, moreover, has been met with legal challenges. The most prevalent forms of employment tests have been cognitive tests and personality tests. In recent years, researchers have found that emotional intelligence competencies are predictors of superior job performance. The business case for emotional intelligence is made by numerous studies that show that individuals who have particular emotional intelligence competencies add significant value to their organizations.

> Emotional intelligence is an effective predictor of successful job performance. Emotional intelligence competency-based employee selection can be accomplished in a manner that minimizes legal risk and adds substantial value to the organization.
>
> The ability to make good decisions regarding people represents one of the last reliable sources of competitive advantage, since very few organizations are very good at it.
>
> —Peter Drucker

When evaluating candidates for an open position, an employer has a strategic business decision to make: hire the individual whose skills, work experience, and education most closely match what the employer believes it takes to

From *Employee Relations Law Journal,* vol. 34, no. 3, Winter 2008, pp. 77–85.

do the job, or hire the superior performer. Unfortunately, too many employers are confident they can identify and select the former, but they are less confident that they can recognize and hire the latter.

Traditional Selection Process

Traditionally, employers have looked to work experience, technical skills, cognitive skills, and education as predictors of successful job performance. Employers have used employment applications, resumes, and interviews, and, in some cases, tests to establish those data points. However, although factors such as skills, experience, and education may predict adequate or average performance in a job, they do not identify the outstanding performers.[1]

Testing, moreover, has been met with legal challenges. The most prevalent forms of employment tests have been cognitive tests and personality tests. Cognitive tests are individualized assessment measures of an individual's general mental ability or intelligence. There are generally two forms of cognitive tests: aptitude tests and general intelligence tests.

Aptitude tests are designed to assess an applicant's ability to perform specific tasks.[2] Such tests purport to measure a variety of capabilities, including cognitive skills, verbal skills, and numerical skills.[3] Intelligence tests are designed to measure overall intelligence levels.

However, some standardized general aptitude and intelligence tests have been found to disproportionately disqualify applicants of a particular class (typically race or gender). If the use of any such test or other employment practice has an adverse impact on a segment of the workforce or applicant pool, such as African Americans, women, or individuals who are 40 years of age or older, such use may violate the anti-discrimination laws.[4] There is not a common definition of "disparate impact." The US Supreme Court has spoken of it as substantial disproportionate impact; the Equal Employment Opportunity Commission, on the other hand, defines "adverse impact" as the selection rate for any race, sex, or ethnic group as less than 80 percent of the rate for the group with the highest rate.[5] If the test or other selection procedure has an adverse impact on a particular race, sex, or ethnic group, the employer can justify its use by showing that it is valid.[6]

The law recognizes three types of validation:

1. Criterion-related validation (a statistical demonstration between scores on a selection procedure and the job performance of a sample of workers);
2. Content validation (a demonstration "that the content of [a] selection procedure is representative of important aspects of [job] performance"); and
3. Construct validation (measurement of an underlying human trait or characteristic that is important to job performance).[7]

Criterion-related validation is established when there is a significant positive correlation between comparative success on the test and comparative success on some measure of job performance. Content validation is established when the test itself closely approximates the tasks to be performed on the job. Construct validation is established when there is a significant relationship between the test and the identification of some trait, such as "intelligence" or "leadership," which is required in the performance of the job.[8]

While general aptitude tests and intelligence tests may present the risk of disparate impact claims, tests that require an applicant to perform actual job tasks (such as word processing or typing tests) present a minimal risk of disparate impact.[9]

Personality tests purport to assess an individual's psychological profile. Like other standardized tests such as aptitude and intelligence tests, personality tests present the risk of disparate impact on minority groups.[10] Moreover, when a personality test asks questions that could reveal a mental disability, such as depression, the test could be found to be an unlawful pre-employment medical examination under the Americans With Disabilities Act (ADA).[11] In one such case,[12] a federal appellate court concluded that the Minnesota Multi-Phasic Personality Inventory (MMPI), the most widely used test of adult psychopathology, was a "medical examination" under the ADA that screened out, or had the effect of screening out, job applicants with disabilities. Accordingly, the court held that employers could not lawfully use the MMPI as a pre-employment screening and selection tool.

Emotional Intelligence Competencies

In recent years, researchers have found that emotional intelligence competencies are predictors of superior job performance. Emotional competencies and the emotional intelligence on which they are based became widely recognized as a result of the work of Daniel Goleman.[13] As Goleman points out, intelligence was thought of historically in terms of cognitive skills, such as language and math skills.[14] Emotional intelligence, though, describes noncognitive abilities that are distinct from, but at the same time complementary to, cognitive intelligence.[15]

Emotional intelligence is the capacity for recognizing our own feelings and those of others, for motivating ourselves, and for managing emotions well in ourselves and in our relationships.[16] Intellectual intelligence, measured by IQ, changes little after our teen years.[17] Emotional intelligence, on the other hand, is not fixed genetically, and it does not develop only in our formative years. Rather, emotional intelligence is, for the most part, learned.[18]

An emotional intelligence competency is an individual characteristic (or combination of characteristics) that can be measured reliably and that distinguishes superior from average performers, or effective from ineffective performers, at levels of statistical significance.[19] So what are the emotional intelligence competencies? Goleman's emotional intelligence model identifies four emotional intelligence domains and 19 associated competencies,[20] as follows:

Personal Competence: these capabilities determine how we manage ourselves.

1. Self-Awareness
   - Emotional self-awareness: Reading one's own emotions and recognizing their impact; using "gut sense" to guide decisions;
   - Accurate self-assessment: Knowing one's strengths and limits; and
   - Self-confidence: A sound sense of one's self-worth and capabilities.
2. Self-Management
   - Emotional self-control: Keeping disruptive emotions and impulses under control;
   - Transparency: Displaying honesty and integrity; trustworthiness;
   - Adaptability: Flexibility in adapting to changing situations or overcoming obstacles;
   - Achievement: The drive to improve performance to meet inner standards of excellence;
   - Initiative: Readiness to act and seize opportunities; and
   - Optimism: Seeing the upside in events.
   - Social competence: These capabilities determine how we manage relationships.

1. Social Awareness
   - Empathy: Sensing others' emotions, understanding their perspective, and taking active interest in their concerns;
   - Organizational awareness: Reading the currents, decision networks, and politics at the organization level; and
   - Service: Recognizing and meeting follower, client, or customer needs.
2. Relationship Management
   - Inspirational leadership: Guiding and motivating with a compelling vision;
   - Influence: Wielding a range of tactics for persuasion;
   - Developing others: Bolstering others' abilities through feedback and guidance;
   - Change catalyst: Initiating, managing, and leading in a new direction;
   - Conflict management: Resolving disagreements;
   - Building bonds: Cultivating and maintaining a web of relationships; and
   - Teamwork and collaboration: Cooperation and team building.

While no one individual has strengths in every one of the emotional intelligence competencies, outstanding performers typically are strong in around six such competencies.[21]

The Business Case for Emotional Intelligence Competencies

The business case for emotional intelligence is made by numerous studies that show that individuals who have particular emotional intelligence competencies add significant value to their organizations. For example, the US Air Force found that recruiters who had high scores in the emotional intelligence competencies of assertiveness, empathy, happiness, and emotional self-awareness were three times as successful as the recruiters who did not score well in those competencies.[22] In a retail chain, the ability to handle stress, another emotional competence, was a characteristic of each successful store manager. The most successful store managers—with success measured in net profits, sales per square foot, sales per employee, and per dollar inventory investment—were those best able to handle stress.[23] In another company, sales agents selected on the basis of certain emotional competencies outsold those salespeople selected using the company's old selection procedure.[24] At a national furniture retailer, salespeople hired based on emotional competence had half the dropout rate during their first year.[25] Another study found that the main reasons that executives did not succeed in their careers involves deficits in emotional competencies—specifically, difficulty in handling change, not being able to work well in a team, and poor interpersonal relations.[26]

Measuring Emotional Intelligence Competencies

Because emotional intelligence competencies have been found to be predictive of successful performance in positions in many organizations, the question is: can emotional intelligence be measured? The answer is yes. Several test instruments measure emotional intelligence itself; that is, a person's ability to recognize and use emotion. Other test instruments measure emotionally competent behavior, because it is the emotional competencies of the star performers that add economic value to the organization.[27]

Among the test instruments that measure emotional intelligence are the Multifactor Emotional Intelligence Scale (MEIS) and the Mayer-Salovey-Caruso Emotional Intelligence Test (MSCEIT). The MEIS has evidence of validity and reliability. Cherniss and Goleman conclude that there is no reliability evidence and little validity evidence for the tasks constituting the MSCEIT.[28] Employers who are considering the use of the MSCEIT should, from the standpoint of mitigating legal risk, seek written assurance from the test publisher that the test does not have a disparate impact on minorities or insist upon a written representation as to the test's validity.

The Emotional Quotient Inventory (EQ-i) is a self-report measure of emotionally competent behavior that provides an estimate of the test subject's emotional intelligence. The EQ-i is supported by validity evidence.[29] The Emotional Competence Inventory (ECI) is a 360-degree assessment that develops self, subordinate, peer, and supervisory ratings on 20 emotional and social competencies. The ECI is supported by validity evidence.[30]

A word of caution about using tests to measure emotional intelligence competencies for selection decisions. Emotional intelligence has been described as amounting to something of a rainbow of competencies that may or may not be relevant to a particular job.[31] Accordingly, any test used to measure emotional intelligence for selection purposes should not be a generic measure of emotional intelligence competencies. Rather, the test should be designed to measure the specific competencies that actually predict success in the particular position. When considering whether to use tests of emotional intelligence for selection purposes, attention should be given to whether any particular test or group of tests is sufficiently job related to predict job success.

Implementing an Emotional Intelligence Competency-Based Selection Process

So why should employers use emotional intelligence competencies to recruit, hire, train, and promote employees? For several reasons. First and foremost, numerous studies show that emotional intelligence competencies are predictive of outstanding performance in most jobs. Hiring individuals with higher levels of emotional intelligence and training employees to be more emotionally intelligent adds substantial value to their respective organizations.[32]

Second, emotional intelligence is a matter of risk management. Employees lacking in certain emotional intelligence competencies may present a greater risk of bad behavior, such as theft and sexual harassment.[33] Selecting employees based on emotional intelligence competencies may enhance the likelihood that a "trouble maker" will not be hired.

That said, what are the costs, risks, and benefits of using assessment tools in emotional intelligence competency-based employee selection and development? The cost of an assessment tool, including administration time and any fee paid for using the test instrument may range from $25 to $200 per use.[34]

If and only if an emotional intelligence competency-based test has significant disparate impact based on race or other protected bases, the test must be professionally validated to ensure that the test is predictive of, or significantly correlates with, important elements of the employee's performance.[35] There is little evidence that the more widely used emotional intelligence tests result in adverse selection of minorities.

The Equal Employment Opportunity Commission, as part of its E-RACE initiative, has identified employment and personality tests as an area of concern and has indicated that new guidance on race discrimination in written employment tests will be forthcoming.[36] Therefore, employers should make a point of tracking the results of its emotional intelligence test(s) to ensure that the test(s) do not have an adverse impact, thereby minimizing the risk of a disparate impact claim. In an abundance of caution, the employer should consider going further and ask the test publisher to provide its validity study as evidence of validity. Be aware, though, that the fact that a test is supported by a validity study in itself means little. The validity study should meet the requirements of the Uniform Guidelines on Employee Selection Procedures as they pertain to the professional standards for validity studies. Reputable test publishers will state in writing that the procedures used in validating their particular test were consistent with generally accepted professional standards such as those described in the "Standards for Educational and Psychological Testing."[37] Employers should accept nothing less.

Selection based on interviews without the use of tests necessarily involves the use of subjective criteria to make employment decisions, which in and of itself is not unlawful.[38] However, although a selection process that depends almost entirely on the subjective evaluation of interviewers presents the potential for an adverse impact claim, that risk can be minimized by building objective guidelines into the interview and selection process.[39]

There are advantages to using job-related emotional intelligence tests as part of the selection process. First, when used in tandem with the interview, the test can improve the odds of hiring a superior performer. Second, a test that is validated minimizes the risk of discrimination litigation and liability.

To implement emotional intelligence competency-based selection of employees, with a minimum of risk, an employer can take the following steps:

For each job, perform a job analysis. Identify the job functions, the skills, knowledge, and experience necessary to perform the job, and the competencies that are critical for success.

Develop a job description, incorporating the job functions, the necessary characteristics, and the critical competencies.

Identify the methods that will be used to measure and evaluate applicants' characteristics and competencies and differentiate between the applicants who meet the minimum requirements and those who are likely to be the superior performers. Specifically, decide whether to use emotional intelligence competency tests. If yes, have the test publisher provide you with written confirmation (i.e., the relevant studies) that the test is reliable and valid.

Develop and implement behavioral interviewing using structured interview questions that are valid and relevant. The interview content should be legally defensible. Train the interviewers on accurate, effective, legal interviewing. The interviewer asks the applicant competency-based questions that are designed to elicit detailed information about situations in which the applicant has demonstrated the specific competency in the past. The applicant would typically be asked the following: (a) what was the situation in which you were involved?; (b) what task did you have to accomplish?; (c) what action did you take?; and (d) what results did you achieve?

Select candidates who are strong in the core emotional intelligence competencies that predict successful job performance.

Track and evaluate the economic value added by the superior performers.

Notes

1. Cary Cherniss and Daniel Goleman, The Emotionally Intelligent Workplace, 160 (2001).
2. Herbert G. Heneman and Robert L. Heneman, Staffing Organizations, 358 (1994).
3. Id. at 359.
4. Griggs v. Duke Power Co., 401 U.S. 424 (1971) (disparate impact claim under Title VII of the Civil Rights Act of 1964, 42 U.S.C. § 2000c, et seq. Employer can prevail by showing business necessity and no alternative practices that would not have an adverse impact); Smith v. City of Jackson, 544 U.S. 228 (2005) (disparate impact claim cognizable under Age Discrimination in Employment Act of 1967, 29 U.S.C. § 621, et seq. Employer can prevail by showing that the practice was reasonable); 42 U.S.C. § 12112(b)

(1) ("discriminate" within the meaning of the Americans with Disabilities Act includes actions that cause adverse impact on the disabled).

5. Washington v. Davis, 426 U.S. 229, 246–247 (1976); 29 C.F.R. § 1607.4.
6. 29 C.F.R. Part 1607 (Uniform Guidelines on Employee Selection Procedures).
7. 29 C.F.R. § 1607.5B.
8. Sims v. Montgomery County Comm'n, 890 F. Supp. 1520, 1526, and ns. 8, 9 (M.D. Ala. 1995); see also Gillespie v. Wisconsin, 771 F. 2d 1035, 1040 and n. 103 (7th Cir. 1985).
9. Cynthia D. Fisher, et al., Human Resource Management, 321 (3d ed. 1996).
10. Donald H.J. Hermann, III, "Privacy, the Prospective Employee, and Employment Testing: The Need to Restrict Polygraph and Personality Testing," 47 Wash. L. Rev., 73, 109 (1971).
11. 42 U.S.C. § 12101 et seq.
12. Karraker v. Rent-A-Center, Inc., 411 F.3d 831 (7th Cir. 2005).
13. Daniel Goleman, Emotional Intelligence (1995).
14. Id. at 42.
15. Daniel Goleman, Working with Emotional Intelligence, 317 (1998).
16. Id.
17. Id. at 7, 317.
18. Id. at 7; Daniel Goleman, et al., Primal Leadership, 38 (2002).
19. Gary Cherniss and Daniel Goleman, The Emotionally Intelligent Workplace, 47 (2001).
20. Daniel Goleman, et al., supra at 39.
21. Id. at 38.
22. Cary Cherniss, "The Business Case for Emotional Intelligence.". . .
23. Id.
24. Id.
25. Id.
26. Id.
27. Cary Cherniss and Daniel Goleman, supra at 85.
28. Id. at 100, 106–107.
29. Id. at 114–115.
30. Id. at 92.
31. The Blackwell Handbook of Personnel Selection, 213 (Arne Evers, et al., eds. 2005).
32. The Handbook of Emotional Intelligence, 434 (Reuven Bar-On and James D.A. Parker eds., 2000).
33. "Emotional Intelligence and Employment Practices Liability Part I: The Nature and Importance of Emotional Intelligence.". . .
34. "Emotional Intelligence and Employment Practices Liability Part II: The Legality and Effectiveness of Employee Assessment Tools.". . .

35. See 29 C.F.R. § 1607.3A ("The use of any selection procedure which has an adverse impact on the hiring, promotion, or other employment or membership opportunities of members of any race, sex, or ethnic group will be considered to be discriminatory and inconsistent with these guidelines, unless the procedure has been validated in accordance with these guidelines, or the provisions of section 6 below are satisfied."); 2 EEOC Compliance Manual, § 15-VI.
36. . . .
37. The 1999 Standards for Educational and Psychological Testing are a set of testing standards developed jointly by the American Educational Research Association, the American Psychological Association, and the National Council on Measurement in Education. The 1999 Standards are the third revision of the joint standards. A fourth revision was begun in 2008. The Standards are recognized as sound principles of accepted psychometric practice.
38. See Millbrook v. IBP, Inc., 280 F.3d 1169, 1176 (7th Cir. 2002) (use of subjective criteria for selection decision did not constitute race discrimination).
39. See EEOC v. Rath Packing Co., 787 F.2d 318, 322, 328 (8th Cir. 1986) (hiring practices that lacked selection guidelines but were based on "getting the right person for the job," had an adverse impact on women).

Erin White

NO

Theory and Practice: Personality Tests Aim to Stop "Fakers"; Some Say Tool's Accuracy Could Be Improved to Make Misrepresentations Harder

Abstract (Summary)

About 30% of respondents change their answers to achieve significantly higher scores. Faking "substantially harms the ability of the test to predict" people's performance, Dr. Richard Griffith says. (The students are later told it's a research project.)

Test makers analyze a job for the personality traits that would make workers successful, and then design questions to detect those traits, Dr. Griffith says. The right answer depends on what the employer is looking for; what's good for one job could be bad for another. The tests are designed to reveal an applicant's behavior patterns, not necessarily what someone would do in any particular situation, he adds. "For any given instance, I wouldn't bet a dime" that the assessment would necessarily predict a person's actions, he says.

CraftSystems, Bradenton, Fla., works with Dr. Griffith and has conducted studies to weed out questions that lend themselves to fake answers. Statements such as "I am highly motivated to achieve outstanding results" and "I am more outgoing than shy" were deemed too transparent. Respondents could tell what the question was looking for and answered accordingly.

Psychology Professor Richard Griffith is on a mission to stop "fakers."

To Dr. Griffith, of the Florida Institute of Technology, fakers are people who misrepresent themselves on personality tests increasingly used to screen applicants for entry-level jobs at call centers, retail stores and other customer-service positions. The tests typically ask candidates to agree or disagree with statements about their character and personality traits, hoping to shed light on how the job applicants approach tasks and problems.

Researchers such as Dr. Griffith say it's too easy to lie on some of these tests, because applicants try to predict the "right" answer, which can vary depending on the job. Applicants can also research employment tests on the Web and ask friends who have taken them previously.

In his research, Dr. Griffith collects personality-test responses from community-college students twice, about six weeks apart. The first time, the students' instructor administers the test and tells students to answer honestly. The second time, Dr. Griffith or his graduate assistants pose as recruiters, and distribute tests containing many of the same questions.

About 30% of respondents change their answers to achieve significantly higher scores. Faking "substantially harms the ability of the test to predict" people's performance, Dr. Griffith says. (The students are later told it's a research project.)

Despite the tests' flaws, Dr. Griffith says pre-employment tests are generally more reliable predictors of performance than an interview alone. But he says they could be more accurate.

Test makers analyze a job for the personality traits that would make workers successful, and then design questions to detect those traits, Dr. Griffith says. The right answer depends on what the employer is looking for; what's good for one job could be bad for another. The tests are designed to reveal an applicant's behavior patterns, not necessarily what someone would do in any particular situation, he adds. "For any given instance, I wouldn't bet a dime" that the assessment would necessarily predict a person's actions, he says.

Facing the perennial challenge of hiring the right applicant, more employers have adopted prehire tests in recent years, thanks in part to the Internet making distribution cheaper and easier. About 70% of entry- and midlevel jobs at big companies now include testing, says Scott Erker, a senior vice president at Development Dimensions International, a Bridgeville, Pa., human-resources consultancy.

Sherri Merbach, senior director for organizational development for Orange Lake Resorts, which sells time shares in Florida, says prehire personality tests are especially helpful in hiring salespeople. Sales applicants are usually able to make a good impression—and thus interview well—but sometimes offer answers that don't display great urgency, another quality that Orange Lake is seeking in its sales force.

Ms. Merbach has used bad test scores to dissuade colleagues from offering jobs to some suave candidates. "You're less likely to make a bad hiring decision," she says.

Employers and testing companies are aware that some applicants give misleading answers. So they include questions designed to weed out fakers. But Dr. Griffith says some of these tactics can backfire.

One common question designed to trap fakers asks applicants whether they have or haven't done something common but frowned upon, such as "I have never looked at a dirty book or magazine." In theory, liars are more apt to say they never have, while honest people admit the behavior.

But savvy applicants know to confess. "They fake those in the reverse direction," says Dr. Griffith. Another problem: Applicants who answer truthfully that they've never looked a naughty magazine can be labeled liars.

Ms. Merbach, from the time-share company, says the test she uses, by CraftSystems Inc., is sophisticated enough to reduce the likelihood of faking and is a good predictor of job performance.

CraftSystems, Bradenton, Fla., works with Dr. Griffith and has conducted studies to weed out questions that lend themselves to fake answers. Statements such as "I am highly motivated to achieve outstanding results" and "I am more outgoing than shy" were deemed too transparent. Respondents could tell what the question was looking for and answered accordingly.

Some employers say tests are useful, but need to be used together with other ways of judging applicants. Steve Suggs, president of sales at Sales Manage Solutions LLC, a Knoxville, Tenn., consulting firm, advises clients to use assessments to help make hiring decisions. But he cautions clients not to base hiring decisions solely on the test, because the answers don't always reflect all of an applicant's characteristics.

For example, he says test results may suggest that an applicant is cold and self-centered. In person, though, the applicant may demonstrate that he's learned to control these tendencies and could be effective. In a hiring decision, "there are other factors that come into play," Mr. Suggs says.

EXPLORING THE ISSUE

Are Personality Tests Good Predictors of Employee Performance?

Critical Thinking and Reflection

1. Have you taken any kind of personality test for any job? What has been your experience?
2. Can the Big Five characteristics predict superior job performances? (For instance, a high score on extroversion/adjustment/agreeableness/conscientiousness/inquisitiveness can predict successes at what kind of jobs?)
3. What suggestions do you have for recruiters to minimize "faking" on personality tests?
4. Do you think emotional intelligence is an important predictor of job success?
5. How do other countries adopt personality testing for recruiting?

Is There Common Ground?

Proponents of personality tests suggest that traditional hiring practices might not bring out many personality characteristics that are very critical to the workplace. Relationship management, inspiring leadership, team-building spirit, and adaptability are critical in today's workforce which may not be tapped from conventional hiring practices. Opponents suggest that the possibility of faking responses is the most important drawback of these tests. Further, applicants will usually avoid providing answers that the society holds as ethically wrong regardless of their personal opinions. A middle ground perspective in adopting such a testing approach may be to include personality tests with other hiring practices. This will enable hiring managers to have more employment-related information about applicants to make a sound staffing decision. It is important to ask questions on the test relevant to the job—otherwise court cases such as *Karraker v. Rent-a-Center* may arise. How much weight do you think should be given to personality tests in a staffing process (with other practices such as interviews and skills tests)? Can an introvert fake his or her answers on a personality test to look like an extrovert?

Additional Resources

Adler, I. (2004, March). Workplace referee. *Business Mexico, 14*(3), 15.

Anonymous (2005). Pros and cons of personality tests that employers should consider. *HR Focus, 82*(9), 8–9.

Caruth, D. and Caruth, G., (2009). The reemergence of personality testing as an employee selection procedure. *SuperVision, 70*(3), 9–13.

Knight, V. (2006). Personality tests as hiring tools. *Wall Street Journal* (Eastern Edition), B.3A.

Morrow, E. (2002). Enhance your staff EQ. *Financial Planning, 136.*

Woods, D. and Savino, D. (2007). Do you blush often? Questions on integrity and personality tests that legally embarrass employers. *Employee Relations Law Journal, 33*(1), 3–31.

www.thefreelibrary.com/The+pros+and+cons+of+personality+testing+in+the+workplace.-a0160104861: The Pros and Cons of Personality Testing in the Workplace.

http://articles.techrepublic.com.com/5100-10878_11-5025293.html: Pros and Cons of Psychological Testing.

www.mid-day.com/news/2009/jan/230109-Milind-Joshi-psychometrics-tests-HR-process-Maersk-HR-consultancy-D-G-Deshpande-mental-asylum.htm: Psychometric Tests in India Are Faulty.

www.hrtools.com/hiring/articles/the_pros_and_cons_of_personality_tests.aspx: The Pros and Cons of Personality Testing.

www.ehow.com/list_6887288_pros-cons-personality-testing-employment.html: Pros and Cons of Personality Test for Employment.

http://apps.americanbar.org/buslaw/blt/2006-01-02/caputo.html: When a Test Becomes a Trial.

ISSUE 7

Is Cognitive Ability Testing a Good Predictor of Work Performance?

YES: Martha J. Frase, from "Smart Selections," *HR Magazine* (December 2007)

NO: Rangarajan (Raj) Parthasarathy, from "Emotional Intelligence and the Quality Manager: Beauty and the Beast?" *The Journal for Quality and Participation* (January 2009)

Learning Outcomes

After reading this issue, you should be able to:

- Gain an understanding of the main advantages of cognitive testing for hiring.
- Understand the main drawbacks in adopting cognitive tests for hiring.
- Detail alternate perspectives in adopting cognitive testing.
- Identify an international perspective of how other countries adopt cognitive tests at the workplace.

ISSUE SUMMARY

YES: Martha Frase, freelance writer, suggests that cognitive ability tests are excellent predictors of work performance because they are objective, valid, and reliable. Further, these tests can be administered to a variety of job categories from entry to executive levels.

NO: Raj Parthasarathy, process improvement manager, states that emotional intelligence is the best predictor of job performance because it involves critical components of self and relationship management. Researchers are paying increasing attention to emotional intelligence (EI) as its components have positive consequences on job performance.

Alfred Binet, the French psychologist, introduced cognitive ability testing (CAT) in 1905 to distinguish intelligence levels in school children. Further, over the decades this method of distinguishing intelligence levels became specialized and was adopted at work places also. Today several tests are available and are tailored to specific job environments. The results of cognitive ability testing can be used to identify the intelligence quotient or IQ.

Cognitive ability, referred to as "g" by psychologists, is considered an excellent predictor of job performance for any job occupation. Primarily, people with higher cognitive abilities are able to apply learned information accurately. Second, people with higher "g" levels are able to learn and process information much faster. Therefore, such higher intelligence levels help employees perform much better at the workplace. Further, cognitive ability tests are considered cost-effective as they can be provided to multiple applicants at the same time. Finally, they can be objectively and numerically scored. However, cognitive ability tests create adverse impact or unintentional discrimination against certain ethnic groups. This is considered one of the greatest disadvantages of this testing process as qualified minorities are excluded in the hiring process.

Cognitive ability testing has become very specialized today and can be used to cater to very specific occupational groups. Executive cognitive testing is one such area that has received significant attention as organizations need qualified executives to direct the goals and missions of their organizations. Executives usually have to perform diverse tasks such as integrating information, analyzing critically, and solving business problems. Cognitive ability testing helps identify such higher-order thinking skills. Further, executives are usually expected to perform quickly as organizations expect upper-level talent to "hit the ground running." Therefore, mental ability testing becomes a useful tool to identify talent that will perform at such superior levels.

Practitioners also suggest that "g" testing provides a sense of exclusiveness as to the selected applicants. Many high profile organizations such as Microsoft and Google adopt such cognitive ability testing to identify their most qualified candidate. Organizations that seek such exclusive methods of recruitment also emphasize a performance-driven culture. Bill Gates, founder of Microsoft, made a dramatic statement in the late 1990s when he openly stated that his company uses a lot of cognitive testing as he wanted "brains in his office" (Seligman, 1997). Several researchers share similar thoughts that higher levels of IQ lead to superior levels of job performance.

The most commonly used test is the Wonderlic Cognitive Ability Test, which can be tailored to different organizational environments. This test can be provided as a hard copy or as an online test. There are two kinds of tests: one test involves questions on identifying analogies, antonyms, synonyms, and mathematical solutions among others. The other test includes problem-solving, analyzing, and critical-thinking questions.

On the other hand, practitioners and scholars applaud the concept of emotional or social intelligence (or EI). Daniel Goleman introduced this concept to businesses in the 1990s and it has gained tremendous importance ever since. Emotional intelligence has been identified with self-management and social competence. Self-management includes how well people are aware of their emotions and motivations. Social competence involves how people manage their relationships with others.

People with high emotional intelligence demonstrate high motivation levels, superior team skills, and good stress management. Further in organizational settings high scorers on EI tend to provide inspiring leadership as they are highly self-motivated and also sensitive to listen to their peers. Such people further are able to provide clear rational decisions based on careful and thoughtful decision-making processes. Research suggests that employees with high emotional intelligence are very successful at their jobs and accommodating a work–life balance. Which companies would not hire employees with such profiles?

While researchers debate over the nature versus nurture role (heredity versus environment) in cognitive intelligence, emotional intelligence is considered largely a developed trait. Over the years individuals shape their personal and social competences of EI based on their unique experiences and opportunities they encounter. Developing emotional intelligence is considered as similar to that of building blocks—building one component of emotional intelligence leads to developing another.

Today's business world is replete with global frameworks, intense competition, unrealistic demands, economic downturns, and demanding customers placing a lot of emphasis on qualified talent. Organizations are seeking talent so that they can distinguish themselves in the crowded marketplace. Recruiting and hiring of employees in organizations therefore has become a strategic priority for firms as they navigate in this complex business world.

An alternative perspective to this issue for HRM professionals may be including cognitive testing as one among the battery of selection practices. The mental test should not be used as a sole predictor of applicants' performance. It should be used to supplement information on the applicants so that the managers can make sound hiring decisions. Using interviews, job tests, and resumes to complement cognitive testing can only enhance the KSA (knowledge, skills, and abilities) profile of the applicants. Staffing experts suggest combining these tests with structured interviews (asking applicants relevant job-related questions) will provide one of the best hiring results. Using the tests with other hiring practices will also reduce the controversy associated with cognitive testing.

Cognitive test scores also create adverse impact or demonstrate distinct score differences among the different ethnic groups. Therefore, qualified minorities do not do well as historically these tests result in some ethnic groups scoring lower than others. Consequently, experts suggest alternatives such as developing cognitive tests that do not demonstrate strong racial differences. This could help alleviate many of the concerns associated with these tests creating a skewed representation. While some may argue that one cannot create a test that does not create a racial bias, restaurant industry experts have actually pilot-tested such cognitive ability tests positively.

An international perspective suggests that many countries adopt the method of testing (cognitive and emotional) to identify talent. Scholars also suggest that countries that have a strong uncertainty avoidance (a cultural orientation for procedures and policies) tend to have elaborate kind of staffing procedures in the form of testing.

YES  Martha J. Frase

Smart Selections

Intelligence tests are gaining favor in the recruiting world as reliable predictors of future executive performance.

In the complex process of selecting talent for executive posts, it's common to have candidates take tests designed to measure various characteristics—behavior, for example, or personality, attitudes, integrity or "emotional intelligence."

Lately, a less common type of test—one that measures pure cognitive ability—has been gaining ground among recruiting professionals, particularly those in executive hiring.

"There is a movement to convince companies to do mental ability tests," says Frank L. Schmidt, Ph.D., the Ralph L. Sheets Professor in the Department of Management and Organizations at the University of Iowa in Iowa City. "Academic research is driving this, as evidence is accumulating that mental ability is the best way to measure predicted job performance."

Schmidt has been doing much of that research. His decade-long work suggests that general cognitive ability influences job performance largely through its role in the acquisition and use of information about how to do one's job. People with higher levels of cognitive ability acquire information faster and more easily, and are able to use that information more effectively.

Concerns at the Start

Certainly, some HR professionals question the usefulness and even the fairness of administering intelligence tests in connection with candidate selection. A major concern is that intelligence tests discriminate against certain groups.

Linda Bond has had serious doubts. About 15 years ago, when she was director of human resources at GTE's Management Development Center in Norwalk, Conn., she was concerned that minorities were at a disadvantage because of culturally biased questions and differences in academic exposure, and there was little evidence at the time to prove otherwise.

But in the years since, the science of assessing general cognitive ability—known to psychologists as "g"—has evolved, alongside strong evidence that rigorously designed and executed intelligence tests are not culturally biased.

So Bond has altered her position. "Executive intelligence testing now tends to be more situational, and it has a place and a value," she says. "There appear to be tools to measure and assess critical thinking and leadership skills."

Bond, who left GTE and earned a law degree, represents employers in employment and labor cases for Rumberger, Kirk and Caldwell PA, in Tallahassee, Fla. Now, she says, as she looks at the use of intelligence testing in candidate selection "from a legal perspective, I say, go for it, as long as you can prove it does not have a discriminatory impact and that there is a legitimate business reason for the testing." She adds that in her more than 10 years of legal practice, she has never seen a discrimination case based on intelligence testing.

Qualified Support

Intelligence testing for executive candidates is, for some, a useful tool but not an exclusive one. "In the hiring process, it's important to gather as much information about candidates as possible that relate to the job criteria," says Lori A. LePla, Ph.D., a consultant in organizational development and personnel assessment for Plante & Moran, a global certified public accounting and business advisory firm based in Southfield, Mich.

"G" can be used as a baseline screening at lower levels, she says, but in filling executive-tier posts, "it's another piece of data we have to predict future performance."

In her consulting practice, LePla uses a variety of standardized tests, including intelligence tests. "In general, we find that it's one component of a best-practice selection system that would have several components. As organizations become more progressive, they incorporate more of these best practices."

Not everyone accepts "g" as a necessary selection criterion, however. "It's not wide enough as an indicator to be leaned on really heavily," says Lester Levine, senior director of human capital management for Day & Zimmermann, a Philadelphia-based global provider of engineering, security, and other business services with 23,000 employees. "But if you are looking to have the complete picture—say, trying to select between two really qualified people—it's another arrow in the quiver."

Levine says that while "g" may be "a very good test of potential and has been used that way, people who are selecting senior-level employees are looking for those who have applied that potential."

In other words, why test executive candidates for intelligence when you already know that they are smart? After all, Levine says, "you are picking from people who have been very successful or they wouldn't be on your radar screen. That's fairly good documentation that you have to be pretty smart to get there in the first place."

Justin Menkes, managing director of New York-based Executive Intelligence Group, who provides executive talent assessment to clients, agrees that past performance is the acid test of an executive's potential for success. "But measuring this can be really rough," he says. "It's hard to collect numeric data when you are relying on a candidate's descriptions, truthfulness, and information that is sometimes hard to pull out. An intelligence test makes somebody figure out the right answer in front of you, in the moment, showing their facility for problem-solving."

In fact, intelligence testing can work as a marketing tool for the hiring company, Menkes says. "Executives can't stand the dog-and-pony [show]—the popularity contest of the interviewing process. Anyone at their level can tell a good story, and doing that can be tiresome." But a chance to show their off-the-cuff problem-solving skills in an intelligence test can get them fired up about the job and the company, he says.

Indeed, although it might seem as though senior executives would bristle at a requirement to take tests of their brain power, most candidates actually like such tests, according to industrial and organizational (I/O) psychologists who use cognitive testing. Schmidt says candidates often view the tests as an opportunity to show their mettle. "The job then means more to the successful candidate because not just anyone could have gotten it."

Targeted Applications

Different hiring circumstances lend to the usefulness of intelligence tests, LePla says. "If a candidate has a prior history of on-the-job learning, has had great mentors, has tried-and-tested solutions in his or her toolkit, and is applying for a position that is very similar to previously held positions in which they've had proven success, then intelligence tests will not give us much unique information.

"But if you know the candidate will need to face a steep learning curve or will be making decisions outside of [his or her] area of expertise, the intelligence test can be helpful in predicting how quickly and effectively the candidate will perform."

Schmidt offers another possible reason for intelligence tests for proven executives: the politics of internal hiring. "Sometimes, you are in the position of selecting among internal candidates who are already part of the top management team," he says. "No matter who is chosen, they will have to work together, and it can be a touchy position to have to promote one over another.

"Intelligence testing can provide a more objective, quantifiable way to predict which candidate will be best for this particular job."

Menkes notes that some companies give a classic IQ test to every candidate because "they want to be a culture of academic excellence. They want booksmart people; they don't care if the IQ cutoffs are a turnoff" to candidates.

Beyond the No. 2 Pencil

Intelligence testing was developed by French psychologist Alfred Binet in 1905, initially to identify schoolchildren who needed special instruction. "It was never intended to be a holistic measure of intelligence," says Menkes. "The classical Stanford-Binet IQ test is a powerful predictor of how well someone will do in school, but it becomes less predictive in other applications."

So unless you are promoting a Mensa-type culture, Menkes says, look for an instrument that measures what he calls "executive intelligence." Such instruments can evaluate skills such as the ability to identify flawed assumptions, recognize unintended consequences, evaluate the quality of data, or identify the core issues in a conflict—all in a format that more accurately emulates the real business environment," he says.

There are hundreds of established intelligence tests on the market, so if you are committed to establishing an assessment program, you might want to try a few to find one that fits your business.

Marni Dorman, SPHR, corporate director of human resources at the Scott McRae Group, an automotive sales company based in Jacksonville, Fla., uses both the Hogan Personality Profile and the Watson Glaser Aptitude Assessment. "We use these in the selection process for all levels of management in our auto dealerships and in our Auto Credit Finance Division as well," Dorman says. Test results do not eliminate candidates, she says, "but these assessments seem to be right on target for predicting success in our industry."

The two tests are used together, Dorman explains, to determine both a candidate's leadership style and his or her ability to acquire new skills. Some auto dealership managers have been dictatorial in the past, she says. "We're striving to get away from this, and also to get insights into candidates' capacity to learn." It was the company's in-house I/O psychiatrist, she continues, who decided that "this particular one-two punch is the best for us."

Menkes prefers to sidestep "fill in the bubble" standard instruments; he conducts intelligence tests as structured 30-minute interviews in which candidates consider practical situations that are germane to the position. Usually, the interview is carried out by an HR professional or an I/O psychologist. All interviewees are asked the same questions, and their responses are scored. "You are looking for them to get to one or two 'right' answers," he says, so that results can be measured and compared with those of other candidates.

Deciding on a Test

Most publishers offer off-the-shelf tests and have experts who can tailor a version to your business needs. The advantage of an off-the-shelf test, Menkes says, is that it comes with a large pool of results that you can use to compare your candidates' performances with others who have taken the same test.

Typically, tests are sold as individual units for use by one candidate, starting at $10 for each off-the-shelf test. If you decide to construct your own test or to tailor an off-the-shelf exam to your needs, it's essential that you work with an I/O psychologist to ensure that the test can be validated, say assessment experts such as John W. Jones, Ph.D. While it may seem like a time-consuming step, it's necessary "to avoid test misuse," he explains. "You need to verify your instrument with qualified people. The end product must be properly constructed and validated so there is no impact against protected groups."

Jones, president and senior I/O psychologist for IPAT Inc., a developer of assessment tools and strategies for employee selection and coaching in Savoy Ill., says it is always more complicated to do it yourself than to use an off-the-shelf product, but "a lot of companies have in-house industrial psychologists who can develop a scorable interview that presents intellectual scenarios and hypothetical simulations that skew toward intelligence and mental ability."

If you don't have an in-house expert, Jones suggests, check with the Society for Industrial and Organizational Psychology "to see if there are I/O psychologists in the neighborhood or at the local university, so you can ask them questions about what's appropriate for your selection needs." He also notes that the American Psychological Association "has rigid professional standards that guide testing and use."

In addition, Jones recommends contacting the Association of Test Publishers (ATP), which represents providers of tests and assessment tools and services related to assessment, selection, screening, certification, licensing, and educational or clinical uses. "Their members are committed to only turning out scientific, legally sound instruments," he says.

Jones advises contacting several ATP members, telling them about your business needs and seeing how they respond. Your I/O expert can then evaluate the responses to help you pick the top three publishers so you can ask them to present a formal proposal. "You want to make sure they send you all relevant research on the instruments they use," he says.

Use your I/O expert to help you make a final choice of publisher and test. "It's better when you have a psychologist as a second opinion, but make sure to pick someone without a bias or business relationship with any publishers," Jones says.

Assessing the Results

Once candidate testing is completed, Jones suggests, bring back your I/O expert for a day to do a comprehensive assessment and to compile a short list of about three candidates for review.

"Hiring managers often do see actual scores," says Schmidt, and they can get a lot of information this way. But some companies prefer to mask numeric scores "by using a simple code that puts candidates into a range, like green, yellow, red."

But there is nothing wrong with letting candidates see their own results, Menkes says. "This is a great tool for feedback." He concludes that intelligence testing, "if you do it right, will bring a positive reaction from executive candidates. They get to demonstrate their problem-solving [skills] in a job-relevant way. They respect that, and it leaves an impression of a business culture that cares about excellence. That's not a bad message when you are recruiting."

Online Resources

For more information on intelligence testing in executive hiring, see the online version of this article . . . for links to

- An article on using standardized tests in hiring
- SHRM research on selection tests
- The Society for Industrial and Organizational Psychology
- The Association of Test Publishers
- The American Psychological Association's Testing Information Clearinghouse

Rangarajan (Raj) Parthasarathy

Emotional Intelligence and the Quality Manager: Beauty and the Beast?

The world of quality has undergone several transformations over the years. The 1960s and '70s focused on quality control (a reactive approach) rather than on quality assurance (a proactive approach). A quality manager in this era monitored various metrics and calculations in a bid to correct the process and prevent future problem occurrences.

In the '80s, radical reforms occurred in quality management, and the concept of total quality management gained popularity. During this period, the focus of the quality manager was split between quality control and quality assurance. The quality manager of the '80s was required to focus not just on the current process, but also on the design phase that dictated the process to use and also on planning for quality. Engineering schools began to teach a course titled "design for manufacturability," which emphasized that product design must facilitate manufacturing of parts with acceptable quality.

The '90s saw quality assurance and defect prevention take precedence over quality control. The word "defects" was replaced by "nonconformities." A new viewpoint emerged—by working proactively it was possible to produce products that conform to specifications. The concept of Six Sigma was popularized by Motorola and adopted enthusiastically by GE and other companies. With the goal of Six Sigma set at 3.5 or fewer defects per million opportunities, the role of the quality manager became complex, requiring interaction with all departments of the organization including purchasing, design, production, and fulfillment.

The quality buzzword of the present decade is Lean Six Sigma, a combination of the best practices of Six Sigma and Lean manufacturing. The quality manager of this decade is required to be a dynamic and multi-faceted individual with excellent interpersonal skills and breadth of knowledge. To succeed in this environment, the quality manager of today needs to have not only intelligence, but also emotional intelligence in good measure.

What Is Emotional Intelligence?

The term emotional intelligence was used for the first time by renowned psychologist Daniel Goleman. He emphasized two key domains in emotional intelligence: the personal competence domain (self-awareness and

From *Journal for Quality and Participation,* vol. 31, no. 4, January 2009, pp. 31–34 (refs. omitted).

self-management) and the social competence domain (social awareness and relationships management). Self-awareness includes emotional self-awareness (recognizing the impact of emotions on decision making), self-assessment (knowing the strengths and weaknesses of oneself), and self-confidence (knowledge of self-worth and capabilities). Another important aspect of emotional intelligence is relationship management, which includes traits such as inspirational leadership, conflict resolution capability, and capacity for teamwork.

Carter summarized emotional intelligence as self-awareness, self-motivation, empathy, management of relationships, and management of one's emotions. Craig described emotionally intelligent people as those who can maintain their course and stay calm in the face of pressure and disagreement from the important people in their lives. We may conclude from these definitions that an emotionally intelligent individual does not make decisions based on emotions alone or without considering all the facts of the situation at hand. Instead, he/she makes decisions objectively and dispassionately, with due consideration given to the facts, while emotions based on prejudice and stress are discounted.

An emotionally intelligent quality manager will listen to the viewpoints of representatives from all departments of the company and consider them dispassionately when making decisions impacting product quality and quality assurance. He/she is then able to communicate the rationale behind the decision to personnel at all levels in the organization and work with them to assure product quality without precipitating unnecessary conflicts and without breeding antagonism. In addition, such a manager is able to achieve a good balance between work life and personal life, even in the face of increasing workload and pressures. Last but not the least, such a manager is able to motivate and energize his/her direct reports to achieve optimal outcomes.

Intelligence Versus Emotional Intelligence

Cognitive intelligence (or intelligence as it is normally described) is the ability to perform a task by applying technical or non-technical education acquired using analysis, reasoning, and logic. Clearly, cognitive intelligence does not include relationship management and non-emotion-based decision making in the way emotional intelligence does. Emotional intelligence, by contrast, has very little to do with formal education or analytical skills. Emotional intelligence has everything to do with relationship management and the ability to get along with others, as well as the ability to make sound decisions in an atmosphere of stress, emotions, and pressure.

An individual, therefore, can have a very high level of cognitive intelligence with little or no emotional intelligence and vice-versa. There is no doubt that technical jobs still require a threshold level of cognitive intelligence, whether this is acquired through education or experience; however, all jobs in today's corporate world require emotional intelligence. Cherniss and Goleman emphasized the importance of emotional intelligence in the workplace. Research by Feist and Barron concluded that social and emotional abilities (emotional intelligence) are four times as important as intelligence quotient (a measure of cognitive intelligence) in determining professional success. Singh argues that although cognitive intelligence is important, it is emotional intelligence that decides one's success in the long term.

Emotional Intelligence: Acquired or Developed?

Craig refers to "development spurs" in life, which are transformational in nature. As individuals encounter such development spurs, their behavior and attitudes change; thus, two individuals who start out with identical psychological dispositions will react differently to the same situations based on the specific development spurs they have encountered with the passage of time. We can conclude that emotional intelligence is not acquired overnight, but rather develops over time based on one's experiences and development spurs.

Damasio found that the thinking side of the brain does not work in isolation from the emotional side of the brain. It is believed that human beings developed from monkeys, and monkeys have a well developed emotional brain. The emotional brain seems to be more primitive than the thinking brain and is usually the first to spring into action either for defense or in the face of a stressor. This is consistent with Selye's description of the "fight or flight response" of humans when encountering a stressful situation. The ultimate response to stress in this situation consists of the following phases: alarm reaction, resistance, and exhaustion. It is interesting to note that the final outcome of such a reaction is exhaustion.

An emotionally intelligent individual will not react in either of the above ways to a stressful or an emotionally-charged situation. Instead, an emotionally intelligent individual will have conditioned his/her thinking brain to work in close association with the emotional brain to temper the situational response in the most appropriate way. It is conceivable that such an individual also will apply the same conditioned response in a stressful situation, minimizing or avoiding the fight or flight syndrome referred to by Selye. As emotional intelligence is a conditioned response, it not only can be developed, but also honed, over time to encompass various situational horizons including personal tragedies and shocking situations. The development of emotional intelligence also has an "iterative effect" because as one develops a certain amount of emotional intelligence, this helps the person become more emotionally intelligent, increasing the overall rate of developing emotional intelligence.

Leadership Without Emotional Intelligence

According to Davis and Newstrom, leadership is the process of encouraging and helping others to work enthusiastically toward objectives. Fiedler's contingency model of leadership suggests that the effectiveness of a leader depends on the favorability of a given situation to the leader and states that "leader-member relations," "task structure," and "leader position power" are the three key aspects influencing leadership success. Hersey and Blanchard's situational leadership theory evaluates leadership effectiveness based on compatibility with the maturity level of the employees.

It follows from the above definitions of leadership that a leader needs to be emotionally intelligent to succeed. Stated differently, the leader's degree of success is directly proportional to the level of emotional intelligence attained by the leader. A leader has to work with and influence co-workers. This is nothing more than the relationship management domain of emotional intelligence. Also, as the popular saying goes, "It can be lonely at the top." A leader must be able to make decisions individually as well as in a group setting. Juran and Gryna refer to rewarding individualism as much as rewarding collectivism in an organizational setting as both have their place in the organization.

The buck usually stops at the leader's desk, so leaders should have the ability to make non-emotional and objective decisions, which is possible with emotional intelligence. When a leader has to criticize, it should be through constructive criticism, aimed at bettering an employee or a situation, and never destructive criticism. In the face of opposition, a leader must have the emotional intelligence to hold his/her ground and explain his/her decision objectively. If the outcome proves that the decision was a mistake, a leader must have the humility to accept the mistake and move forward. The leader must learn from the mistake so it is not repeated. Only by displaying these qualities can a leader hope to earn the respect of co-workers and colleagues. Since these leadership traits are part and parcel of emotional intelligence, a leader without emotional intelligence is likely to be a failure in both professional and personal terms.

Achieving Success with Emotional Intelligence

Emotional intelligence helps an individual deal efficiently and effectively with his/her personal and professional life, without getting into emotion-based decision making. The world is becoming increasingly complex due to the social, political, technological, and economic changes. Individuals without emotional intelligence react to pressures from these changes in undesirable ways, producing unpalatable or even illegal outcomes. Such individuals not only bring harm to themselves but also to any professional organization with which they are associated. Organizations naturally seek to hire individuals who possess a high degree of emotional intelligence. These individuals will help their employers in tangible and intangible ways by displaying aspects of emotional intelligence such as unyielding motivation, effective conflict resolution, and dedication to the task at hand.

Charles Darwin's theory of "survival of the fittest" is truer today than ever. Emotional intelligence enables an individual to adapt to the environment at hand without giving up his/her basic principles or losing ground. Emotional intelligence has a lifelong impact on individuals and enables them to face the trials and tribulations of life with self-confidence and realism.

An individual with emotional intelligence definitely will be a part of the fittest of this complex world and will have the ability to survive its ups and downs with dignity and grace, while successfully adding value in his/her professional and personal life.

Conclusion

The lack of emotional intelligence can break or significantly slow a professional's career progression in today's complex world. This is especially true for the quality manager because he/she must interact successfully with employees at all levels in the organization and with suppliers and customers from all cultures. The presence of emotional intelligence in the employees of a company (including the quality manager) will have an impact on improving profitability and productivity. Although today's manufacturing world is complicated, the manufacturing world of the future will be even more so. By developing and utilizing emotional intelligence in work life and in personal life, the quality manager (or for that matter, all employees and managers) will be a "beauty" to his/her environment instead of being the "beast!"

EXPLORING THE ISSUE

Is Cognitive Ability Testing a Good Predictor of Work Performance?

Critical Thinking and Reflection

1. What would you identify as the main advantages of cognitive ability testing?
2. What are some drawbacks of adopting cognitive ability testing?
3. If you were in a staffing team, what suggestions would you have given while including cognitive testing?
4. Do you think emotional intelligence is an important predictor of job success?
5. How do other countries adopt cognitive testing for recruiting?

Is There Common Ground?

Organizations are constantly seeking the best talent and adopting different hiring practices, such as cognitive ability testing, to get the right applicant. Employees with higher levels of intelligence learn work quicker, assimilate information faster, and process ideas better creating a much superior work environment. On the other hand, researchers suggest that higher levels of emotional intelligence (EI) also can create superior work performance. Individuals with higher levels of EI demonstrate a greater understanding of team and project management skills. While the controversy is always whether to use one over the other, experts always recommend using cognitive testing in combination with other hiring practices. This will alleviate much of the concerns and controversies associated with this method of testing. Have you taken a cognitive ability test? Do you think it predicts *your ability* to perform or train at your job? What do you think is *your disadvantage* in taking a cognitive test if it is a part of any hiring process?

Additional Resources

Beaton, E. (2006). Grey matters. *Profit, 25*(6), 62–64.

Berta, D. (2003). HR firm developing unbiased cognitive-ability exam for industry. *Nation's Restaurant News, 37*(43), 4-4,16.

Grensing-Pophal, L. (1998). Plays well with others. . . . *Credit Union Management, 21*(5), 52–54.

Minton-Eversole, T. (2010). Avoiding bias in pre-employment testing. *HR Magazine, 55*(12), 77–88, 80.

Seligman, D. (1997). Brains in the office. *Fortune, 135*(1), 38.

Simms, J. (2003, August). Powered by emotions. *Supply Management, 8*(17), 20–24.

www.eiconsortium.org/reprints/ei_issues_and_common_misunderstandings.html: Emotional Intelligence: Issues and Common Misunderstandings.

http://eqi.org/comp_tab.htm: EI Definitions Comparison Table.

www.opssc.wa.gov.au/recruitment/3_select/tools/cognitive.htm: Cognitive Ability Tests.

http://apps.opm.gov/adt/Content.aspx?page=3-04&AspxAutoDetectCookieSupport=1&JScript=1: Cognitive Ability Tests.

www.wonderlic.com/assessments/ability/cognitive-ability-tests: Wonderlic Cognitive Ability Test Family.

ISSUE 8

Would Mandatory Background Checks for All Employees Reduce Negligent Hiring Lawsuits?

YES: Lessing E. Gold, from "Security and the Law: Get a Background Check," *SDM Magazine* (October 2007)

NO: Chad Terhune, from "The Trouble with Background Checks: Employee Screening Has Become a Big Business, but Not Always an Accurate One," *BusinessWeek* (June 2008)

Learning Outcomes

After reading this issue, you should be able to:

- Gain an understanding on negligent hiring and background checks.
- Gain an understanding of the various court cases highlighted.
- Understand the criteria required for negligent hiring.
- Detail alternate perspectives to conducting background checks.
- Identify an international perspective of how other countries adopt background checks at the workplace.

ISSUE SUMMARY

YES: Lessing Gold, attorney and writer, contends that organizations have a liability in checking the background references of both their permanent or temporary applicants. He indicates how applicants with criminal records emerge back into the work environment with false records, potentially putting customers and coworkers in jeopardy.

NO: Chad Terhune, writer for *SmartMoney,* asserts that information from background checking companies is so inaccurate that it is very unfair to several whose employment records have become blemished. He feels that the unregulated nature of this industry could be one of the main reasons for such employment errors.

Negligent hiring is when an employer hires an applicant without checking his or her background and subsequently the applicant causes harm to their co-workers or customers. The employer would be accused of negligent hiring as the employer failed to take reasonable care to check on an applicant's background, which could have minimized danger or violence at the workplace. Background checks are considered a very critical method in reducing claims of negligent hiring.

Mr. Gold, a legal attorney, suggests that all organizations should conduct thorough background checks on employees whether the position requires it or not. He specifically illustrates a court case of where a customer was kidnapped at gunpoint by a promotional sales representative working for a security company. The representative had a track record of committing felony and kidnapping people. However, the security company had failed to conduct a background check on the applicant which would have definitely brought to light his past criminal track record.

This case was appealed and reversed in the court of law due to definitions specific to the case. The company senior employees argued that background checks were not traditionally performed on promotional sales representatives as they were considered independent contractors. Further, the company's general manager stressed that promotional representatives were not supposed to enter any customers' houses. The representative had done something that was against the norm of the company policies. The company management further refuted that the kidnapping act was not committed during their normal working hours.

Avis, the rental car company, was another case illustrating the importance of background checks. In 1979, Avis was sued for negligent hiring when an employee raped a co-worker. Subsequently it was learned that the employee had a history of violence and also a criminal record. The company had failed to conduct a background check which would have otherwise revealed the employee's criminal past. The female co-worker was rewarded a handsome sum of $750,000. Should organizations not be responsible to provide a safe environment to their customers and co-workers regardless of their employee's status or company policies?

A case for negligent hiring requires the following factors must be proven by the plaintiff (the person who bring the complaint to the court): (1) existence of an employment relationship between the accused and the employer, (2) the accused was not qualified for the job, (3) the employer's awareness of such erroneous hiring, (4) the employer's omission of checking on the accused employee's background.

The main contention in both these cases is that if the organization had exercised reasonable care and performed background checks they would have discovered the employee unlawful histories. Further, performing a background check would save organizations millions of dollars in attorney fees and also reduce any negative reputations. Legal experts contend that employees who meet people (either at homes or in public places) should have thorough background checks. The burden to provide a safe environment rests squarely on organizations.

On the other hand, Mr. Terhune suggests that background checks do not provide authentic information. Organizations that conduct background checks have become a very lucrative business. Several background check companies have mushroomed, creating an unregulated environment. Most of these organizations rely on sources that might not be very accurate and therefore provide incorrect applicant information. Organizations that provide background checks usually provide detailed portfolios describing applicants' work histories, educational backgrounds, credit histories, personal lives, and also drug or alcohol addictions. Usually they charge approximately between $60 and $80 per applicant to conduct background checks.

Several cases point to the inaccuracy of information provided by organizations that provide background checks. Pendergrass, a supervisor at Rite Aid, was fired in 2006 for stealing and improper accounting of store merchandise. The employee denied the allegations and was subsequently proved to be innocent in the court of law. However, Rite Aid submitted the supervisor's complete work record to a background check database including his improper conduct. The supervisor, Pendergrass, was unable to get any jobs at any other retail stores due to his tarnished professional reputation provided by the background check organizations.

Carter, a truck driver who was fired in 2006 for having violated a company policy, is another example that substantiates erroneous information provided by background check organizations. In this case, the truck driver complained about safety issues concerning his vehicle. The company, Martin Transport, viewed his complaints negatively. Though Carter won the court case against the company, his work reputation was completely blemished as no other trucking company would hire him subsequently. The employment database for transport companies, DAC (Drive-A-Check), has a permanent record of his dismissal from Martin Transport. Truck drivers are very apprehensive of getting a negative "DAC" which could completely reduce their potential chances of employment.

An alternative perspective to handle negligent hiring is to begin with a rigorous staffing approach. Many organizations do not require employees to fill out application forms and readily accept applicants' resumes. Usually applicants can easily embellish their resumes, exaggerating their educational or work accomplishments and misleading hiring managers. Legal experts suggest organizations develop detailed application forms that can identify any fallacies in the work or educational accomplishments. The application form also should require applicants to sign and authenticate the information, providing an additional check. In addition, hiring managers should conduct structured interviews thoroughly. They should probe applicants about their past work accomplishments, education, and references in a systematic manner. This will help identify if there have been any yawning gaps or concerns in applicants' employment histories.

Generally hiring interviews are done in such haste that applicants merely share their current work accomplishments, which may also be falsified. The application and interview phases should be followed by background checks that will definitely reveal any problems that applicants may have. This should be complemented by checking on applicants' references diligently. Many organizations have a nondisclosure policy on applicants' performance—experts suggest that there are ways to get around this by asking yes/no questions of whether the current employer will hire the concerned applicant again. Organizations usually avoid conducting reference checks if they feel an applicant has received high scores on his or her resume and the interview. The reference step can only serve to enhance additional applicant information. Many organizations mandate a preemployment drug testing to ensure their applicants do not have any drug history. Firms that adopt such a meticulous approach to their staffing process, especially for jobs that require a lot of public interaction, will greatly reduce the complaints for negligent hiring.

Legal experts also suggest that background checks per se might not help reveal an applicant's mysterious past. A case in point—Natasha Saine sued Comcast as she was raped and almost murdered by a Comcast technician, who visited her house to conduct routine cable work. The company said they were not responsible as they had performed a background check and checked on the references for Frank. Should their hiring process have been more rigorous?

An international perspective suggests that local legal laws and host culture play an important part for completing background checks. In the United Kingdom, it is impossible for background checking firms to get any criminal records from the police without the consent of the recruiting firm and applicant. Further, the process can take as long as 40 days. In China, before conducting background checks, organizations need to get the applicant's employment work number, which the Chinese government assigns to employees. In India, to verify an applicant's educational background, organizations need to have an applicant's "seat number" or admission number for the university to release such records.

YES 

Lessing E. Gold

Security and the Law: Get a Background Check

In a recent case in the State of Georgia, a kidnap victim brought a negligent hiring action against a security company and its authorized dealer after she was kidnapped by the dealer's salesman. The trial court ruled against the plaintiff kidnap victim and granted summary judgment to the security company.

The victim appealed. The victim was kidnapped at gunpoint by a convicted violent felon who had once worked for the alarm company as a "promotions representative" selling home security systems door to door. The alarm company did not perform a background check before hiring the sales person, which would have revealed that he had been convicted of burglary and kidnapping in another state in 1979, sentenced to life in prison, and paroled in 1995. On appeal, the Appellate Court reversed the decision of the trial court.

The president of the defendant security company at deposition testified no background checks were performed on promotions representatives because they were considered independent contractors and not employees.

The general sales manager of the company testified that members of the promotions team were not authorized to enter a prospective buyer's home absent a background check; they were advised that background checks were not required unless the worker was entering a home.

The plaintiff, in her deposition, said she wrote her name, address and telephone number on a form which inquired whether she was interested in having someone contact her about installing a security alarm system. The representative called on the plaintiff on two or three separate occasions. The plaintiff declined to allow the representative into her home. Subsequently, the representative came to the plaintiff's home, where the kidnap occurred.

The issue before the court was whether the alarm company owed a duty to the plaintiff and whether the alarm company breached the duty. The Appeals Court said a jury must decide these questions of fact. The court said the jury must decide whether the defendant has a duty to exercise ordinary care not to hire or retain an employee the employer knew or should have known posed a risk of harm to others, where it is reasonably foreseeable from the employee's "tendencies" or propensities that the employee could cause the type of harm sustained by the plaintiff.

The court further pointed out that the act was not committed within working hours. Therefore, there was an issue as to whether or not the abduction was committed "under the color of employment"—and that also should be determined by the jury, said the court. Therefore, the matter was reversed and remanded to trial.

The bottom line is that companies are advised to obtain a background check on each agent hired to represent the company, whether mandated or not.

Chad Terhune

NO

The Trouble with Background Checks: Employee Screening Has Become a Big Business, but Not Always an Accurate One

Abstract (Summary)

Background screening has become a highly profitable corner of the HR world. At the screening division of First Advantage, profits soared 47% last year, to $29 million; revenue grew 20%, to $233 million. HireRight reported that earnings jumped 44%, to $9 million, last year on revenues of $69 million. Screening often goes far beyond the familiar checking of public criminal records. Just by dint of their heft and permanence, the proprietary data caches they compile can seem authoritative, even though the information sometimes contains errors, innuendos, or outright falsehoods. Lester Rosen, a veteran in the industry and president of Employment Screening Resources, says that, essentially, it's the Wild, Wild West. It's an unregulated industry with easy money and not a huge emphasis on compliance or on hiring quality people to do the screening.

Theodore Pendergrass was shocked in November, 2006, when the Walgreens pharmacy chain rejected his application for a store supervisor job. The company told him a background-screening firm called ChoicePoint reported that a past employer had accused him of "cash register fraud and theft of merchandise" totaling $7,313. "I wanted to cry," Pendergrass says. The $4 billion business of background screening is booming. Companies large and small are sorting mostly mid- and lower-level job applicants based on information compiled by ChoicePoint, its major rivals, and hundreds of smaller competitors. Some employers have grown more vigilant about hiring since the September 11 terrorist attacks. Others like the efficiency of outsourcing tasks once handled by in-house human resources departments or bosses who simply picked up the phone themselves. Whatever their motives, employers are becoming more dependent on mass-produced background reports that rely heavily on anonymous, and sometimes inaccurate or unfair, sources.

Pendergrass' difficulties stemmed from a previous job at Rite Aid. By late 2005, when he was 25 years old, he had reached the first rung of management as a shift supervisor in a Rite Aid store in Philadelphia. His bosses trusted him to oversee cashiers, bank deposits, and merchandise deliveries. Then, in January, 2006, a store official accused him of stealing goods and underpaying for DVDs. He denied the accusations, but the official said police were waiting outside to arrest him if he did not confess. Pendergrass wrote a statement but wouldn't admit to theft. He was soon fired anyway.

Later, at a hearing for unemployment compensation, Pendergrass was vindicated. A state labor referee ruled that Rite Aid had not proved its allegations and awarded him nearly $1,000 in benefits. But Rite Aid had already submitted its theft report to a database used by more than 70 retailers and run by ChoicePoint, the largest screening firm for corporate employers in the U.S. Based in a leafy Atlanta suburb, ChoicePoint says it checks applicants for more than half of the country's 100 biggest companies, including Bank of America, UnitedHealth Group, and United Parcel Service. Because of Pendergrass' tainted ChoicePoint file, retailers CVS Caremark and Target also rejected him for jobs.

Pendergrass, now 27, makes lattes at a Starbucks in Philadelphia. The coffee chain doesn't use a screening firm for entry-level hires. Pendergrass earns $17,000 a year, or 30% less than he did at Rite Aid, and fears his career has been derailed. "I worked hard in that store, and none of this stuff was true," he says. "I would be locked up somewhere if I stole $7,000."

Rite Aid declines to comment. A ChoicePoint spokeswoman says the company's background report merely conveyed information provided by a former employer.

Fat Profits

Background screening has become a highly profitable corner of the HR world. At the screening division of First Advantage, based in Poway, Calif., profits soared 47% last year, to $29 million; revenue grew 20%, to $233 million. HireRight, based in Irvine, Calif., reported that earnings jumped 44%, to $9 million, last year on revenues of $69 million. To grab a piece of this growing market, Reed Elsevier Group, the Anglo-Dutch information provider, agreed to acquire ChoicePoint for $4.1 billion in February—at a 50% premium to its stock price.

Industry surveys show why Reed Elsevier was eager to expand its screening business. In a 2004 study by the Society for Human Resource Management, 96% of personnel executives said their companies conduct background checks on job candidates, up from 51% in 1996. Two-thirds of larger companies say they outsource screening, and many now vet current employees in addition to applicants.

Screening often goes far beyond the familiar checking of public criminal records. For $60 to $80 per applicant, ChoicePoint and its rivals assemble digital dossiers of educational degrees and credit histories as well as interviews with friends, past bosses, and colleagues. Call-center workers wearing headsets inquire about work habits, personal character, and drug or alcohol problems.

Just by dint of their heft and permanence, the proprietary data caches they compile can seem authoritative, even though the information sometimes contains errors, innuendos, or outright falsehoods.

"You won't believe what people tell you," says Mary Beth Gotshall, who has done interviews since 1999 at Employment Background Investigations, a midsize firm in Owings Mills, Md. She and colleagues have collected comments from a father who said he would never rehire his son because he had missed so much work at a family business. Another former boss accused an applicant of stealing and demanded Employment Background help find him. (The firm declined.) "We put everything in there," Gotshall says while juggling employment checks for retailer Ikea, a Pittsburgh medical clinic, and a Texas engineering firm. Her boss, Richard Kurland, chief executive of Employment Background, says the company goes to great lengths to be accurate. "We have a huge responsibility to mankind," he adds.

But Lester Rosen, a veteran in the industry and president of Employment Screening Resources in Novato, Calif., says: "Essentially, it's the Wild, Wild West. It's an unregulated industry with easy money and not a huge emphasis on compliance or on hiring quality people" to do the screening.

Theron Carter, a 61-year-old unemployed truck driver in Middleville, Mich., is waiting for his name to be cleared in a database used widely in the transportation business. In May, 2006, a U.S. Labor Dept. administrative law judge ruled that Carter was wrongly terminated by Marten Transport for making legitimate complaints about the safety of his 18-wheel truck. He had hauled loads for the Mondovi (Wis.) company for only two weeks before being fired in June, 2005. The judge awarded him more than $31,000 in damages and back pay and ordered Marten Transport to delete "any unfavorable work record information" in a report compiled by USIS, a large screening company in Falls Church, Va. Once an arm of the federal Office of Personnel Management, USIS was privatized in 1996. It still screens government workers and runs an employment-history database used by 2,500 transport companies called Drive-A-Check, or DAC.

Despite his legal victory, Carter's DAC report still says Marten Transport dismissed him for "excessive complaints" and a "company policy violation." "No one will hire me," says Carter, who withdrew $50,000 from retirement savings to support his wife and himself. Trucking company J.B. Hunt Transport Services "told me I had excessive complaints and wouldn't hire me. I told them I won my case." Hunt declines to comment.

Marten Transport has appealed the Labor Dept. ruling. A company attorney, Stephen DiTullio, says it would be "fraudulent" for the carrier to remove the reference to excessive grievances from Carter's DAC file. "That was an accurate portrayal of what led to his termination," DiTullio says. Marten Transport has addressed Carter's safety concerns, he adds.

John Griffith, 47, won a similar Labor Dept. ruling in October, 2003, against his former employer, Atlantic Inland Carrier. The administrative law judge ruled that the company wrongly fired Griffith in December, 2001, for complaining about the safety of his truck and ordered Atlantic Inland to remove unfavorable information from his DAC record.

Someone at Atlantic Inland—it's not clear who—had told DAC that Griffith was terminated and not eligible to be rehired because of his grievances. The company eventually deleted that information in January, 2004—more than two years after it was posted. During that time, Griffith says, it was hard to find trucking work. The Aiken (S.C.) resident turned to lower-paying odd jobs, although he recently got back behind the wheel making deliveries for a nursery. "Truck drivers live and die by DAC," he says. "They can ruin a driver's career with a few clicks of their mouse."

Living in Fear

USIS declines to comment on any specific cases. Gripes about its database have made "DAC" a popular verb in the industry, with drivers lamenting they have "been DAC-ed." Responding to the anxiety surrounding the database, USIS officials have defended their methods on radio interview shows aimed at truckers. They argue that screening is legally required, generally accurate, and keeps bad drivers off the road.

But Kristen Turley, director of market development and communications at USIS' commercial-services unit in Tulsa, concedes that no system is immune to mistakes and misuse. "There is a chance somebody who holds a grudge will put negative information in the database," she says. "We are not trying to blackball drivers or ruin their chance to get a job." When a driver disputes a background report, USIS asks its sources for proof supporting negative comments, she says. USIS doesn't seek such evidence up front. "Ideally that would be a good solution," Turley says, but it could dissuade past employers from submitting information in the first place.

The federal Fair Credit Reporting Act covers background screeners, but it hasn't been aggressively enforced. The law says screeners must use "reasonable procedures" to ensure "maximum possible accuracy." It also requires employers to give a copy of background reports to rejected applicants. An applicant can dispute the information, but the Federal Trade Commission has said employers must wait only five business days before hiring someone else, meaning that objections frequently become moot. Lately the agency has focused more on identity theft than on screening, Rebecca Kuehn, assistant director for privacy and identity protection, says.

ChoicePoint has run into trouble because of how it has disseminated personal data. A 1997 spin-off from credit bureau Equifax, the company stumbled in 2004, when it offered a $40 software package at Sam's Club stores that allowed small businesses to obtain personal information on applicants. The company dropped the product after privacy advocates pointed out that it wasn't verifying whether users had a business license and a legitimate purpose for searching, as opposed to snooping on a neighbor or old boyfriend.

Then, in 2005, it came to light that ChoicePoint had given identity thieves pretending to be small business clients seeking background checks access to people's addresses, Social Security numbers, and dates of birth. ChoicePoint agreed in 2006 to pay a $10 million civil penalty to the FTC and $5 million more to compensate 160,000 consumers whose information had been compromised.

Luring Consumers

Today, ChoicePoint bills itself as the gold standard in screening. "The big issue for us is making sure we're doing things as accurately as possible," says Bill Whitford, a senior vice-president. The company conducts 10 million background checks annually and estimates it has about 20% of the U.S. market. "The number of complaints vs. transactions is very low," says Katherine Bryant, vice-president for consumer advocacy. The FTC has logged 695 complaints against ChoicePoint since 2005, some of which related to the identity-theft episode. USIS had the second-highest total, with 89.

ChoicePoint now is trying to draw consumers as clients. It sells a preemployment self-check to people who want a preview of what an employer would learn about them. These reports cost from $24.95 to as much as $75, depending on how customized they are. Savvy consumers can save themselves some money: Under federal law, individuals are entitled to a copy of any background report compiled by a screening company for a minimal fee, generally $10 or less.

Along with price, screening firms compete on speed. HRPLUS, in Evergreen, Colo., offers five reference interviews within 72 hours. At Employment Background Investigations, a whiteboard hanging on a cubicle wall recently celebrated the clearing of 1,025 applicants in one week by a group of about two dozen screeners, a company record.

Screening firms say their services are vital. In many industries, they argue, employers don't seek prosecution of minor infractions but are willing to report them to employment databases. USIS says its retail records have identified more than 30,000 applicants with histories of theft in just the past few years. All theft reports are re-verified with the employer that submitted them before being shared with an inquiring company, USIS says. But mistakes occur, and once a worker is flagged, it can be nearly impossible to work again in retail.

Two screening companies got it wrong in the case of Ingrid Morales. In 2001, Morales, then 26, was fired after only a month as a makeup artist at a Saks Fifth Avenue store in Boca Raton, Fla. Saks cited a report supplied by a retail database, now owned by USIS, and a smaller Florida screening firm, Merchants Security Exchange. The screeners said she had been terminated from a Burdines department store in 1995 for "unauthorized taking of merchandise" valued in the hundreds of dollars. Morales denied the theft allegations. But it wasn't until she sued Burdines and the screening firms in federal court later in 2001 that the information was corrected. USIS deleted the negative reference, and Merchants Security changed her file so that it noted merely a company "policy violation" in connection with her use of an employee-discount card.

A judge dismissed her suit in 2003, ruling that she had not been defamed by Burdines, a part of what is now Macy's, and that the screening firms hadn't violated the law. A spokesman for MAF Background Screening, previously known as Merchants Security, says that "mistakes do happen" and that the Morales case illustrates why applicants should review their background reports. USIS and Macy's decline to comment.

Morales, now 33 and the mother of three children, says that her firing and inability to find work again at store cosmetics counters put her family in a financial bind for several years. Her husband's construction business has since taken off, and she helps manage it from home. But she's still bitter about the background report. "It ruined my whole career, and I felt very humiliated," she says. "They can put whatever they want in your file, and you can't get work." . . .

EXPLORING THE ISSUE

Would Mandatory Background Checks for All Employees Reduce Negligent Hiring Lawsuits?

Critical Thinking and Reflection

1. Do you think the security company was liable? How would you have ruled as the judge?
2. Identify important factors in proving there is a case for negligent hiring?
3. What are the main drawbacks of organizations performing background checks?
4. What are some alternatives for organizations to conducting background checks?
5. How do other countries adopt background checks for recruiting?

Is There Common Ground?

Researchers and practitioners suggest that organizations must use a lot of caution when hiring applicants by thoroughly investigating their backgrounds. Though this process might be an additional step in the hiring process, it can save organizations a lot of liability and most importantly ensure a safe working environment for employees and customers. However, on the other hand, organizations that do conduct background checks have become such an unregulated industry that it is very difficult to verify the accuracy of the information from such sources. Several industry cases report that employees are wrongfully reported while their work records have actually been clean. Experts suggest that organizations follow elaborate recruitment and hiring procedures to supplement background checks. This is even more critical for positions where employees have a lot of interaction with the public. Do you think Comcast was liable in the *Saine v. Comcast* case? What could Comcast have done in their hiring process to avoid such a lengthy lawsuit? Do you think Rite Aid and Martin Transport are legally responsible to Pendergrass and Martin? Why? Why not?

Additional Resources

Babcock, P. and Marino-Nachison, D. (2005). Foreign assignments. *HR Magazine, 50*(10), 91–92, 94, 96, 98.

Greenwald, J. (2007). Employers must exercise caution with background checks. *Business Insurance, 41*(18), 4, 80.

Laitin, J. (2007). Negligent hiring and retention. *Human Resources*, 25–32.

Lashier, R. (2006). Background screening can diminish hiring mistakes. *SDM, 36*(10), 93–94.

Morris, K. (2008, June). Don't forget the background check. *Hotel and Motel Management, 223*(10), 8.

Wells, S. (2008). Ground rules on background checks. *HR Magazine, 53*(2), 47–48, 50, 52, 54.

http://www.illinoislawyerblog.com/2009/02/negligent_hiring_in_illinois_1.html: Negligent Hiring in Illinois.

http://www.apasecurity.net/news.htm; Corporate Liability: Sharing the Blame for Workplace Violence.

http://ezinearticles.com/?How-Reliable-Are-Online-Background-Checks?&id=791570: How Reliable Are Online Background Checks?

http://thecabin.net/stories/070906/bus_0709060003.shtml: Negligent Hiring Liability.

Internet References . . .

Women Face Glass Ceiling in Hiring

About.com is a web property that is part of The New York Times Company and frequently publishes current debatable events. About.com's editorial mission is to help provide practical solutions to the everyday questions and problems faced by millions of readers across a wide variety of topics and interests.

http://careerplanning.about.com/od/forwomenonly/a/glass_ceiling.htm

Are Women Happy Under The Glass Ceiling?

Forbes is an international business magazine that publishes latest business and economic activities.

http://www.forbes.com/2006/03/07/glass-ceiling-opportunities–cx_hc_0308glass.html

Women in Business

About.com is a web property that is part of The New York Times Company and frequently publishes current debatable events. About.com's editorial mission is to help provide practical solutions to the everyday questions and problems faced by our millions of readers across a wide variety of topics and interests.

http://womenshistory.about.com/od/business/tp/women_business_leaders.htm

Women Leaders and Organizational Change

Harvard Business School Working Knowledge is a forum for innovation in business practice, offering readers a first look at cutting-edge thinking and the opportunity to both influence and use these concepts before they enter mainstream management practice.

http://hbswk.hbs.edu/item/3796.html

UNIT 3

Women in Corporate Levels

Have women reached the corporate levels they really want to? Do they enhance business profits? For several decades, women have seemed to struggle for an equal footing in the work place. This section addresses these questions on the role of the women in the American workplace. Women have traditionally faced tacit barriers at the workplace. Scholars and critics have applauded women for their leadership characteristics that could augment or decrease business goals. What does corporate America need to do to enhance the visibility of its female employees?

- Do Women Make Better Business Leaders?
- Does the Glass Ceiling Still Exist in U.S. Organizations?

ISSUE 9

Do Women Make Better Business Leaders?

YES: Ann Pomeroy, from "Cultivating Female Leaders," *HR Magazine* (February 2007)

NO: Herminia Ibarra and Otilia Obodaru, from "Women and the Vision Thing," *Harvard Business Review* (January 2009)

Learning Outcomes

After reading this issue, you should be able to:

- Gain an understanding on what qualities make women better leaders.
- Detail how Safeway's female leadership program helped create female leaders.
- Understand what criteria women may lack to be effective leaders.
- Provide alternate perspectives to the concept that leadership is gender-based.
- Identify an international perspective of how other countries view female leadership.

ISSUE SUMMARY

YES: Ann Pomeroy, who recently served as a senior writer for *HR Magazine,* illustrates with the example of Safeway how organizations have identified that women are better business leaders. She suggests that women have some innate characteristics that serve them well as leaders.

NO: INSEAD Professor Herminia Ibarra and her doctoral student, from their research study, suggest that women demonstrate low visionary skills. These business skills are very important for understanding the dynamic business environment and hence women may not be effective leaders.

The results of a 2004 survey of gender and *Fortune* 500 companies indicated that having female senior leaders contributed to a substantial increase in organizational profits and shareholders' wealth. Safeway, a leading company, demonstrated to the corporate world that having a predominantly female leadership talent pool contributed to increased sales for their grocery stores. The grocery chain has 200,000 employees and is a very profitable $40 billion company in the supermarket industry.

Studies indicate that women have certain personality characteristics that make them natural leaders. Women are basically intuitive, which is considered an excellent trait to determine underlying business problems. They also are very communicative, which can make them more conducive to team and project management. Women are able to multitask several roles very efficiently. Their responsibilities at balancing work and life have helped them prepare to take on different roles efficiently. Female expatriates, employees who are sent overseas on work, demonstrate greater sensitivity to local practices and cultures than men. Therefore these employees are considered a talent asset in multinationals. Women are considered empathetic of employees' and customers' concerns, making them very communicative leaders. They also demonstrate a great sense of tenacity and resilience, which are excellent business traits in a corporate environment known for deadlines and uncertainty. They also tend to be more assertive than men in the workplace, perhaps to minimize any association stereotypical of their gender.

In 2000, Safeway championed a cause to increase female leadership talent through a program called Retail Leadership Development (RLD). The organization has seen wonderful results both in increasing profits and in attracting customers. Realizing that 70 percent of their customers are women, Safeway launched a very proactive program to encourage female talent through development and mentoring. Laree Renda, executive vice-president and one of the 50 most powerful women in the supermarket industry, dedicated her efforts to ensure that top leadership relentlessly supported this gender-based initiative. Today Safeway female managers have increased their representation substantially by 42 percent since the RLD program was launched.

On the other hand, INSEAD Professor Ibarra and her doctoral student emphasize that women still have not made great strides in the corporate ranks because they do not demonstrate a strong sense of visionary skills. Their longitudinal study with 2,816 executives from 149 countries over five years indicated that women performed better than men on several qualities. In this study, women were demonstrated to be more detailed-oriented, interactive, and diligent. However, they did not seem to have high scores on visionary skills—the ability to recognize new business opportunities and promote a strategic orientation. Visionary skills help identify strengths, weaknesses, threats, and opportunities and also navigate effectively in any business environment. Scholars suggest that a lack of envisioning is very detrimental as such leaders cannot foresee potential business strategies and take advantage of good opportunities quickly.

These researchers also offered three possibilities for females to get low scores on visionary skills. Women frequently rely on the opinion and judgment of their peers, making them feel less concerned about opportunities or threats. Women have been observed to rely on hard data and input for making business decisions, while strategic visioning might entail taking a huge leap in the dark. Second, women fail to observe the broader picture of their industry or business environment, though they may be effective leaders within their own organizations. Women fail to articulate clearly their organization's position within the broad picture of their competitors and customers. Finally, women may not view envisioning as a critical leadership competency.

In another global study of 1,000 executives from 9 countries, men were viewed as more effective business leaders. The results of this study indicated the most important quality that male leaders demonstrated was the quality to inspire others successfully. Experts suggest the ability to inspire or persuade others is a very critical competency of leadership that males generally demonstrate. The business world seems to be more aware of the Bill Gates, Warren Buffetts, and Zuckerbergs and that the Laree Rendas (executive vice-president of Safeway), Indra Nooyis (CEO of Pepsi), and Anne Mulcahys (CEO of Xerox) seem to pale in comparison. So the endless debate on which gender makes better leaders continues.

An alternative perspective perhaps is not to view the concept of efficient leadership as gender-based but rather as competency-based. Competencies are the main KSAs (knowledge, skills, and abilities) required to perform a job efficiently. Leadership competencies could include analyzing, delegating, strategizing, inspiring, and coordinating, among others. Leaders also need to manifest being visionary, competitive, knowledgeable, and insightful to make the right business choices. Further leadership positions make special demands on an employee's career. Leadership jobs are usually very demanding, requiring employees to put in more than the average number of hours at work. On average, leaders usually work for about 80 hours or more per week. Leadership jobs may also require employees to make immense sacrifices on their work–life balance schedules. The demands of leadership may actually make individuals self-select whether they can match the high work demands of such positions. This also could be the reason why a majority of women choose not to get into corporate leadership positions early in their lives. Leadership positions may require both "feminine" and "masculine" characteristics with the final answer coming down to not whether *he* or *she* is better, but was *it* a good job done?

Leadership experts also suggest that HRM professionals in organizations establish forums for both male and female leaders to discuss what critical leadership characteristics have helped them become effective leaders. Successful men and women leaders sharing their relevant leadership KSAs may actually help men and women understand and respect each other better as leaders. These forums may also help alleviate stereotypical leadership characteristics associated with either of the genders.

A global perspective suggests that representation of female business leaders in many male-dominated cultures are skewed disproportionately. In India, women comprise a mere 1 percent of the upper-level leadership positions and in Mexico, women represent only 7 percent of the managerial positions. However, a Thunderbird research study of females and leadership positions suggested that Sweden and Switzerland have a predominant participation of females in upper-level positions, suggesting a more egalitarian approach to business leadership.

Ann Pomeroy

Cultivating Female Leaders

Abstract (Summary)

Some companies are making significant progress in stripping away stumbling blocks to gender diversity. One of those companies is Safeway, a Fortune 50 corporation that began focusing a decade ago on ways to identify promote and retain high-potential women. The diversity strategy includes effective communication of the business case for diversity and programs that focus on leadership development, mentoring and work/life balance. Communicating the business case effectively to the entire organization starts with visible leadership at the top. When the women's initiative was implemented in 2000, the Retail Leadership Development program began to focus particularly on women and people of color, and targets were established to increase the number of women and minorities who go through the training. Another resource for women interested in advancing into management is the women's leadership network, established 10 years ago as part of the women's initiative. Since 2000, the number of female store managers has increased by 42%.

Retail grocery giant Safeway is seeing the results from long-standing efforts to help women advance in the company.

The research is clear and dramatic: Female executives can help improve a company's bottom line. According to a 2004 study by Catalyst, a research and advisory organization that focuses on women's issues, Fortune 500 companies with the highest percentages of female corporate officers saw, on average, a 35.1 percent higher return on equity and a 34.0 percent higher return to shareholders than companies with the lowest percentages of female corporate officers.

Yet, despite this correlation, companies don't seem to be doing enough to promote greater gender diversity at the executive level. In fact, progress in this area has essentially ground to a halt.

Catalyst, which has tracked this issue for 10 years, says the results of its latest census, the 2005 Catalyst Census of Women Corporate Officers and Top Earners of the Fortune 500, were disappointing. While the number of women in top positions increased slightly, "the growth rate for the past three years is dramatically lower than the rates we have seen in the past." In other words, Catalyst concludes, "progress has almost come to a standstill."

In spite of these discouraging statistics, some companies are making significant progress in stripping away stumbling blocks to gender diversity. One of those companies is Safeway, a Fortune 50 corporation that began focusing a decade ago on ways to identify, promote and retain high-potential women.

Here is what the company is doing—and how it has prospered as a result.

Helping Women Succeed

Ten years ago, Safeway began facing increasingly stiff competition from upmarket specialty grocers on one end and cut-rate pricing on the other from big box stores such as Walmart and Target. To meet these market challenges, the company began exploring programs to attract, develop and retain its best talent, and to position Safeway as an employer of choice.

Since 70 percent of its customers are women, the retail grocery giant also wanted to broaden the diversity of its workforce to reflect the customer base. The company recognized that a diverse workforce would help it better understand and respond to the needs of its customers, and that would give Safeway a competitive advantage in the marketplace.

Male leadership has long been the norm in the retail grocery industry, so the new programs required a real culture shift. Kim Farnham, director of HR planning, says Safeway took a series of steps aimed at changing the corporate culture to "a culture of development," one that focused on helping women—including women of color—advance into management.

The foundation of today's diversity initiative was laid down in 1997, says Farnham. A diversity workshop to educate managers was designed, balanced workforce goals were created, and a system that holds managers accountable for meeting those goals was developed. Metrics to track their success were put in place.

The goal throughout the planning phase was "to do it right, not to be first on the block," says Farnham. The resulting women's initiative, "Championing Change for Women: An Integrated Strategy," was fully implemented in 2000 as the first piece of Safeway's overall diversity initiative.

The diversity strategy includes effective communication of the business case for diversity and programs that focus on leadership development, mentoring and work/life balance. A rigorous accountability system for measuring and tracking balanced workforce goals alerts the company to any potential problems.

Communicating the Business Case

Larree Renda, executive vice president, chief strategist and administrative officer, says communicating the business case effectively to the entire organization starts with "visible leadership at the top. You need executives who talk the talk and also walk the walk, and I think we've been very good at that."

For example, CEO Steve Burd talks regularly with employees about diversity issues in live discussions and at town hall meetings and conferences.

He also makes a point of discussing diversity via taped satellite broadcasts, part of a program of weekly broadcasts that are sent to store managers and that frequently cover diversity. Managers are expected to make the broadcasts available to their employees. The programs, which can spark discussions at staff meetings in each store, are shown on monitors in the staff break room. In addition, employees can view the broadcasts on their computers, Renda says.

Renda, who was responsible for developing the unique instore broadcast/interactive TV network for training and communication, says the system allows the company to quickly broadcast live or taped programs simultaneously to the approximately 1,800 stores in Safeway's 10 divisions.

When it comes to the taped programs, "diversity is expected to be a regular item on the agenda," she says.

Employees also have access to a series of diversity DVDs featuring interviews with successful Safeway women and people of color.

Developing Future Leaders

Safeway likes to promote from within and has traditionally focused on the retail level as a source of potential managers. Many current executives came up from entry-level positions in Safeway stores through the Retail Leadership Development (RLD) program, a formal, full-time career development program. Farnham estimates that 90 percent of the company's 1,800 store managers moved up through the company ranks this way, and all but one of the 10 division presidents began their Safeway careers working in one of its stores, often as grocery baggers or salesclerks.

When the women's initiative was implemented in 2000, the RLD program began to focus particularly on women and people of color, and targets were established to increase the number of women and minorities who go through the training. Employees who are interested in becoming store managers can apply for the program by taking an entrance exam that tests such basic retail knowledge as understanding gross margins. Applicants also write an essay explaining how they would solve a business problem.

Those who successfully complete the 26-week program are immediately assigned to a store as an assistant manager—a position that can lead to corporate-level jobs.

Safeway's efforts to encourage women to advance don't end there, however. Recognizing that women often need to coordinate work schedules with family responsibilities, the company ensures that all qualified employees—including part-timers and those who work flexible schedules—have the same opportunities for coaching, development and advancement as those who work more traditional hours.

The company also realized that frequent relocations didn't work for some employees, particularly women. As a result, Safeway modified the once-traditional requirement that employees seeking to move up should broaden their experience by doing stints at a variety of company locations. . . .

Development Networks

Another resource for women interested in advancing into management is the women's leadership network, established 10 years ago as part of the women's initiative. The group sponsors such events as the "Women's Road Show," a series of presentations at Safeway locations throughout the country that highlight the success of individual Safeway women and provide learning and networking opportunities.

Wherever the "Road Show" executives speak, they also meet with women in the area who've been identified as likely candidates for management positions and targeted for developmental opportunities in stores. In discussions with these high-potential women about their career interests, the executives suggest potential job opportunities and encourage them to apply for so-called "stretch positions" that can help them advance to the next level.

Today there are five network groups, including groups for blacks, Asians, Hispanics, and lesbian, gay, bisexual and transgendered employees. Each is open to all employees and regularly offers a variety of educational activities and events.

The Diversity Advisory Board, which includes representatives from each major operating and functional area of the organization, also sponsors events and seminars.

In addition to the corporate board, each Safeway geographical area has its own diversity advisory board to address local issues. Today there are 13 advisory boards and 14 network leadership groups throughout the company.

From One Mentor, Many

A strong mentoring program is critical to the success of the company's leadership development efforts. Every Safeway manager, from the CEO on down, is expected to mentor his or her own employees, plus several others.

Because there is a serious lack of female and minority mentors, says Renda, it is expected that a manager's first mentee should be a woman, the next a person of color of either sex, "and then you can have a [white] man, in that order."

Renda, whose responsibilities include retail operations, HR, public affairs, labor relations, government relations, industrial engineering, re-engineering and communications, is the company's top female executive and one of its five highest-paid officers. She's also the company's first—and so far only—female executive vice president, a statistic she would like to see changed. "There should be more of me," she says.

From a 16-year-old, working part time bagging groceries at her local Safeway store, Renda has spent 33 years building a high-powered career at the Fortune 50 company. In 2001 and again in 2002, she was named one of the 50 most influential women in business by Fortune magazine.

As she moved up the ladder, Renda says she was often the first woman to hold each successive new job. As a result, while she always had a mentor, "I've never had a female mentor," she says. She knows how difficult that can be for women, and she feels a special responsibility today to mentor women and to be a role model for the next generation of female leaders. . . .

Jewel Hunt, vice president for corporate deli food service, Starbucks and Jamba Juice, also "believes in mentorship." She has been fortunate to have mentor-managers throughout her career who helped her learn needed job skills as she advanced in the organization. Hunt, who started 25 years ago as a part time bakery salesclerk while she was attending college, recalls when she was promoted to director of marketing for the Northern California division. Her new boss, the chief financial officer at the time, helped her develop the software and complex math skills she would need in her new job.

In turn, Hunt strives to perform the same kinds of services for her mentees. For example, she remembers one mentee who had applied for a director position. Although she was very well qualified, says Hunt, the woman withdrew her application at the last minute. She said she lacked retail skills and was afraid she wasn't ready for the job.

"I knew she was the strongest candidate, so I encouraged her to go ahead and apply," says Hunt. "I promised that I or an associate would personally work with her in the stores if she got the job." The woman agreed, she did get the job, and "today she's a superstar."

Without Hunt's encouragement at the crucial moment, the woman "might have waited a couple of years to apply, and she had so much to add today."

Lori Raya, vice president of retail operations in Safeway's Northern California division, feels a real sense of mission about her responsibility to mentor other women. "My goal is to impact someone's life," she declares. "I love it when I get notes from former mentees who tell me about a promotion and say, 'Thanks for believing in me.'"

Raya says her first mentor at Safeway, who recognized her ability and took steps to keep her when Raya was ready to quit, has had a lasting effect on her life. Raya was in college, working part time and coaching high school girls' basketball, soccer and volleyball in the evening when a new female store manager asked her to change her hours.

Raya explained that the proposed schedule would conflict with her coaching job. "I was ready to walk out the door," she says, when the manager asked, "What would it take to keep you?" Undaunted when Raya said, "Well, your job looks kind of easy!" the woman encouraged her to apply for the RLD program and subsequently became her mentor.

Today Raya is the only female vice president among approximately 19 vice presidents in the retail division, and she is looking ahead toward the next step up—division president. "There is only one female division president today, and I hope to become the second."

Balancing Work and Home Life

Work/life issues tend to affect women more than men, and Safeway seems to have taken this fact into account in its efforts to help all women—regardless of their family status—ensure that they have a healthy work/life balance.

For example, Hunt faced significant work/life challenges as a single mom raising two sons while going to school and working full time.

Her sons, now 22 and 24, were 1 and 3 when she became a single parent. Although her former husband remained involved with the children, he lived in another state and couldn't participate in their day-to-day care. Hunt, who left college before graduation to marry and start a family, now had to raise her sons and finish her degree.

She says she has always had supportive managers at Safeway who helped her juggle school, work and child care. And Safeway's tuition reimbursement program helped pay for her degree.

"I've always been grateful that Safeway helped me with work/life balance" during that difficult time, she says.

In turn, she tries to do the same for the women she mentors today. She makes a point of working with them on the kinds of problems that are particularly relevant to women—the need to work flexible hours during some periods, for example, or to deal with child care or elder care responsibilities.

Safeway also makes a point of ensuring work/life balance for those who do not have children. For example, Dianne Lamendola, group vice president for information technology, has no children and does not plan to have any. She does, however, have an active life outside of work.

Lamendola spends many hours training for competitions in adventure racing, a demanding sport that combines running, kayaking, mountain hiking, navigation and orienteering. When Lamendola is in training, she does not hesitate to say she can't work late on a particular night. Since she throws herself into her work with the same kind of energy she devotes to adventure racing, Safeway knows she's a high performer for the company too.

In addition to her outdoor activities, Lamendola serves on the board of the San Francisco Bay Area Girl Scouts, participates in a book club, and enjoys spending time with her sister and her nieces and nephews.

Because she has so many outside interests, Lamendola says work/life balance has always been important to her. At Safeway, she has been able to pursue those interests while holding a very demanding job.

Accountability

Managers are responsible for driving the company's diversity efforts throughout the organization, so education and training begins with them. All new managers, starting at the top, attend the Managing Diversity Workshop, an eight-hour session cofacilitated by a line manager and HR. Farnham says she intentionally involves line managers to avoid the perception that the workshop is "just an HR program. It's integrated into the business," she says.

While each manager attends the workshop only once, "we recognize that diversity education is not complete in one eight hour session." Farnham says the education continues through events sponsored by the network groups and diversity advisory boards, through video productions such as a "Women in Management" DVD, and through regular diversity discussions in staff meetings. A toolkit designed to guide managers in incorporating diversity discussions into their staff meetings is available on the company intranet.

"Safeway is a data-driven company," says Farnham. "We track census data to identify the demographics of each geographic area," and this data is used to set each manager's specific targets for developing women.

Managers are evaluated on their success in meeting the diversity goals via balanced scorecard data and performance evaluations from their supervisors, employees and customers. And there are big incentives for managers to reach their diversity targets: High marks all around can increase a manager's bonus by up to 10 percent, and consistently high ratings are critical to advancement in the company.

Conversely, those who have trouble meeting their goals will be coached by senior leaders, and their bonuses can be reduced.

The Proof Is in the Pudding

The following metrics offer mounting proof of the success of the women's initiative programs. Since 2000, says Farnham, the number of female store managers has increased by 42 percent. Within that group, the number of white females rose 31 percent and the number of women of color shot up a whopping 92 percent.

She cites another statistic to corroborate the connection between these increases and the women's initiative strategies. During the past five years, says Farnham, the number of women who have qualified for and completed the RLD program rose 37 percent.

There is external validation of the initiative's success as well. Last year, Safeway's "Championing Change for Women: An Integrated Strategy" was honored with the highly coveted Catalyst Award, which is presented annually by the nonprofit research organization to outstanding companies that promote the career advancement of women and minorities.

In addition, Safeway's diversity efforts have garnered praise from global investment bank Lehman Brothers. A research report prepared by the bank's independent analysts points out that Safeway's diversity programs have not only "led to substantial advancement for women and minorities both at the stores and at the corporate office," but also increased the company's sales and earnings. (In an industry with razor-thin margins, Safeway today is a highly profitable $40 billion company with 200,000 employees throughout the United States and Canada.) "Diversity is good for business," concludes the report.

CEO Burd is fully aware of the value a diverse workforce brings to the company. In his acceptance speech at the Catalyst Award ceremonies last year, Burd told the audience that Safeway had approached the subject of diversity as a business issue, "just like we do any other important objective."

In fact, he said, "all we did was act in our own best self interest."

Herminia Ibarra and Otilia Obodaru

Women and the Vision Thing

Many believe that bias against women lingers in the business world, particularly when it comes to evaluating their leadership ability. Recently, we had a chance to see whether that assumption was true. In a study of thousands of 360-degree assessments collected by Insead's executive education program over the past five years, we looked at whether women actually received lower ratings than men. To our surprise, we found the opposite: As a group, women outshone men in most of the leadership dimensions measured. There was one exception, however, and it was a big one: Women scored lower on "envisioning"—the ability to recognize new opportunities and trends in the environment and develop a new strategic direction for an enterprise.

But was this weakness a perception or a reality? How much did it matter to women's ability to lead? And how could someone not perceived as visionary acquire the right capabilities? As we explored these issues with successful female executives, we arrived at another question: Was a reputation for vision even something many of them wanted to achieve?

A Brilliant Career

A leading services company CEO we'll call Anne Dumas typified in many ways the women we spoke with. The pillar of her leadership style was a principle taught to her 20 years ago by her first boss: Always stay close to the details. As she explained it: "I think strategy comes naturally from knowing your business and the forces that influence your market, clients, and suppliers—not at a high level but at a detailed level. Intermediaries kill your insight. You obviously can't monitor everything, but nothing should keep you from knowing in detail the processes on which your company runs—not supervising everything but understanding at a detailed level what is going on. Otherwise, you are hostage to people who will play politics. At best you don't have full information; at worst you're vulnerable to hidden agendas. My job is to go to the relevant detail level."

In her four years as CEO, Dumas had achieved some impressive results. She had doubled revenues and operating margins, given the company a new strategic direction, and undertaken a fundamental reorganization of the company's core processes and structures. More recently, she had turned her attention to developing her leadership team.

IDEA IN BRIEF

- Women outshine men in many areas measured by 360-degree assessments but score low on one key leadership capability: envisioning.
- Three theories could explain why. Women might use different processes than men for shaping the future. They might perceive that they have less license to go out on a limb. Or they might not buy into the value of being seen as visionary.
- Vision is a must-have for enterprise leadership, regardless of gender. Luckily, it's a capability that can be learned.

Yet Dumas knew she should somehow improve her communication effectiveness, particularly in her role as an executive member of her parent company's board. One challenge was her stylistic mismatch with her chairman, a broad-brush, big-picture thinker who often balked at what he perceived as excessive attention to detail. She found herself reluctant to favor "form over substance." She told us, "I always wonder what people mean when they say, 'He's not much of a manager but is a good leader.' Leader of what? You have to do things to be a leader." She went on to imply that so-called visionary behaviors might even be harmful. "We are in danger today of being mesmerized by people who play with our reptilian brain. For me, it is manipulation. I can do the storytelling too, but I refuse to play on people's emotions. If the string pulling is too obvious, I can't make myself do it."

Dumas's reluctance is not unusual. One of the biggest developmental hurdles that aspiring leaders, male and female alike, must clear is learning to sell their ideas—their vision of the future—to numerous stakeholders. Presenting an inspiring story about the future is very different from generating a brilliant strategic analysis or crafting a logical implementation plan, competencies on which managers like Dumas have built their careers.

Indeed, a whole generation of women now entering the C-suite owe their success to a strong command of the technical elements of their jobs and a nose-to-the-grindstone focus on accomplishing quantifiable objectives. But as they step into bigger leadership roles—or are assessed on their potential to do so—the rules of the game change, and a different set of skills comes to the fore.

Vision Impaired

Our research drew on 360-degree evaluations of 2,816 executives from 149 countries enrolled in executive education courses at Insead. As with most 360-degree exercises, these managers filled out self-assessments and invited subordinates, peers, supervisors, and other people they dealt with in a professional context, such as suppliers and customers, to evaluate them on a set of leadership dimensions. In total 22,244 observers participated. (See the sidebar "Critical Components of Leadership" for a description of the Global Executive Leadership Inventory, or GELI.)

As we looked for patterns within this data set, we focused on differences between the male and female leaders, both in terms of how they saw themselves and in terms of how the observers evaluated them. Certainly, there were plenty of data to work with, since 20% of the executives assessed and 27% of the evaluating observers were women. When analyzing the data, we controlled for the effects of the executives' age and level.

The first surprise for us, given prior published research, was that we found no evidence of a female "modesty effect." Quite the opposite: Women rated themselves significantly higher than men rated themselves on four of the 10 GELI dimensions we analyzed. And on the remaining dimensions, the women and men gave themselves ratings that were about the same.

Our analyses of how leaders were rated by their male and female associates—bosses, peers, and subordinates—also challenged the common wisdom. Again based on prior research, we'd expected gender stereotypes to lower the ratings of female leaders, particularly those given by men. That was not the case. If there was a gender bias, it favored female leaders: Male observers scored female leaders significantly higher than they scored male leaders on seven dimensions, and female observers scored them significantly higher on eight. (See the exhibit "Comparing the Ratings of Male and Female Leaders.")

Ratings on one dimension, however, defied this pattern. Female leaders were rated lower by their male observers (but not by women) on their capabilities in "envisioning." That deficit casts a large shadow over what would otherwise be an extremely favorable picture of female executives. The GELI instrument does not claim that the different dimensions of leadership are equal in importance, and as other research has shown, some do matter more than others to people's idea of what makes a leader. In particular, the envisioning dimension is, for most observers, a must-have capability.

Intrigued by this one apparent weakness, we looked more closely at the observers' ratings. Was a particular group responsible for bringing the envisioning scores down? Indeed one was. As shown in the exhibit "Who Says Women Aren't Visionary?" the male peers (who represented the majority of peers in our sample) rated women lower on envisioning. Interestingly, female peers did not downgrade women, contrary to the frequently heard claim that women compete rather than cooperate with one another. Our data suggest it's the men who might feel most competitive toward their female peers. Male superiors and subordinates rated male and female leaders about the same.

What It Means to Be Visionary

George H.W. Bush famously responded to the suggestion that he look up from the short-term goals of his campaign and start focusing on the longer term by saying, "Oh—the vision thing." His answer underlines vision's ambiguity. Just what do we mean when we say a person is visionary?

The distinction between management and leadership has long been recognized. Most agree that managing for continuous improvement to the status quo is different from being a force for change that compels a group to innovate and depart from routine. And if leadership is essentially about realizing

IDEA IN PRACTICE

When taking on more-strategic leadership roles, both men and women must come to grips with the vision thing. Here's a high-level plan for making that happen.

- **1. Get a vision test.** Undergo a 360-degree evaluation to explore the differences between how you see yourself and how others see you. Find out whether you have a vision gap to close and who perceives it. As Insead coaches say, if one person tells you that you have donkey ears, don't listen; if two people tell you, go buy yourself a saddle.
- **2. Gain a new respect.** Learn to appreciate vision as a matter of not just style but substance. It's not about meaningless mission statements but about strategic acumen and positioning know-how. Respect the size of the challenge you may face. If you pride yourself on your people skills, establishing the distance needed for a helicopter view may require reinventing your identity as a leader.
- **3. Leverage (or build) your network.** Strategic analysis demands a solid grasp of what is happening outside your group and firm. A good external network is the first line of defense against insular thinking. If you're like most executives we've studied, your network probably isn't strong enough to take you to the next level.
- **4. Learn the craft.** Much of envisioning can be learned the old-fashioned way: at the elbow of a master. Find role models and study how they develop and communicate strategic ideas. Then work with your leadership development organization or a good executive coach to identify training and tools to build your capabilities.
- **5. Beware of identity traps.** When you are very good at a needed task, the whole organization will conspire to keep you at it. Stop being so hands-on. Even if delivering on the details has always been your ticket to advancement, staying in the weeds is risky now.
- **6. Constantly communicate.** As your vision develops, find opportunities to articulate it. Don't wait until it's perfect. Try out draft versions along the way and even after the vision is mature. You'll never be seen as visionary if you don't get the word out.
- **7. Step up to the plate.** A vision doesn't come only from the outside; it comes from greater self-confidence. It is an internal presumption of competence: giving yourself latitude, believing in your ability, and assuming responsibility for creating a future for others.

change, then crafting and articulating a vision of a better future is a leadership prerequisite. No vision, no leadership.

But just as leadership is a question of what one does rather than what one is, so too is vision. It encompasses the abilities to frame the current practices as inadequate, to generate ideas for new strategies, and to communicate possibilities in inspiring ways to others. Being visionary, therefore, is not the same as being charismatic. It entails "naming" broad-stroke patterns and setting strategy based on those patterns. (See the sidebar "What Does It Mean to Have Vision?")

Visionary leaders don't answer the question "Where are we going?" simply for themselves; they make sure that those around them understand the direction as well. As they search for new paths, they conduct a vigorous exchange with an array of people inside and outside their organizations, knowing that great visions rarely emerge from solitary analysis. As "practical futurists," leaders also test new ideas pragmatically against current resources (money, people, organizational capabilities) and work with others to figure out how to realize the desired future. True strategists offer much more than the generic vision statements that companies hang on their walls; they articulate a clear point of view about what will transpire and position their organizations to respond to it. All of this adds up to a tall order for anyone in a leadership role. It's not obvious, however, why it should be a particular challenge for women.

Perception or Reality?

As we sought to understand why women fail to impress with their vision, research findings from prior studies were not much help. To begin with, most attempts to compare men's and women's styles have focused on how leaders are rated by subordinates. Yet, as we all know, leaders play a key role in managing stakeholders above, across, and outside their units. Moreover, the vast majority of studies ask participants either to rate hypothetical male and female leaders or to evaluate "the majority" of male or female leaders they know, rather than the actual, specific leaders they know well. Empirical studies of gender differences in leadership styles have often used populations of students, members of diverse associations, and nonmanagers, rather than the midlevel to senior business managers we are actually trying to understand.

We turned therefore to the experts who were living this reality every day: the women participating in our executive education programs. When we asked

---

CRITICAL COMPONENTS OF LEADERSHIP

The Global Executive Leadership Inventory (GELI) is a 360-degree feedback instrument developed at Insead's Global Leadership Center by Manfred Kets de Vries, Pierre Vrignaud, and Elizabeth Florent-Treacy. To identify significant dimensions of exemplary leadership, they interviewed more than 300 senior executives over the course of three years. The emerging questionnaire was then validated on an international sample of more than 300 senior executives and MBA students. The result, GELI, measures degrees of competency in these dimensions of global leadership, which it defines as follows[1]:

Envisioning
Articulating a compelling vision, mission, and strategy that incorporate a multicultural and diverse perspective and connect employees, shareholders, suppliers, and customers on a global scale.

Empowering
Empowering followers at all levels of the organization by delegating and sharing information.

Energizing
Energizing and motivating employees to achieve the organization's goals.

Designing and aligning
Creating world-class organizational design and control systems and using them to align the behavior of employees with the organization's values and goals.

Rewarding and feedback
Setting up the appropriate reward structures and giving constructive feedback.

Team building
Creating team players and focusing on team effectiveness by instilling a cooperative atmosphere, promoting collaboration, and encouraging constructive conflict.

Outside orientation
Making employees aware of outside constituencies, such as customers, suppliers, shareholders, and other interest groups, including local communities affected by the organization.

Global mind-set
Inculcating a global mentality, instilling values that act as a glue between the regional or national cultures represented in the organization.

Tenacity
Encouraging tenacity and courage in employees by setting a personal example in taking reasonable risks.

Emotional intelligence
Fostering trust in the organization by creating—primarily by setting an example—an emotionally intelligent workforce whose members are self-aware and treat others with respect and understanding.

1. GELI contains two additional dimensions, life balance and resilience to stress, which we did not analyze in our study, since many observers were unable to provide evaluations on them.

how they would interpret our data, we heard three explanations. First, several women noted that they tended to set strategy via processes that differed from those used by their male counterparts. This suggests that what may in fact be visionary leadership is not perceived that way because it takes a different path. Second, we heard that women often find it risky to stray away from concrete facts, analyses, and details. And third, many women betrayed negative attitudes toward visionary leadership. Because they thought of themselves as grounded, concrete, and no-nonsense, and had seen many so-called visionary ideas founder in execution, they tended to eye envisioning behaviors with some suspicion. Each of these interpretations invited serious consideration.

THEORY 1: Women are equally visionary but in a different way. Several of the women who had taken the GELI survey argued that it is not that women

COMPARING THE RATINGS OF MALE AND FEMALE LEADERS

In the 360-degree assessments of participants in Insead's executive education program, female leaders received higher ratings than male leaders in most dimensions of leadership. But in one dimension—envisioning—women were rated lower than men.

	Which leaders rated themselves higher?	Which leaders did male observers rate higher?	Which leaders did female observers rate higher?
Envisioning	Neither	**Men**	**Women**
Empowering	Neither	Neither	Neither
Energizing	**Women**	**Women**	**Women**
Designing and aligning	**Women**	**Women**	**Women**
Rewarding and feedback	Neither	**Women**	**Women**
Team building	Neither	**Women**	**Women**
Outside orientation	**Women**	**Women**	**Women**
Global mind-set	Neither	Neither	Neither
Tenacity	Neither	**Women**	**Women**
Emotional intelligence	**Women**	**Women**	**Women**

lack vision but that they come to their visions in a less directive way than men do. One executive put it like this: "Many women tend to be quite collaborative in forming their vision. They take into account the input of many and then describe the result as the group's vision rather than their own." Another said, "I don't see myself as particularly visionary in the creative sense. I see myself as pulling and putting together abstract pieces of information or observations that lead to possible strategies and future opportunities."

Vivienne Cox, CEO of BP Alternative Energy, is known for having an "organic" leadership style. She led a team that crafted a strategy for moving BP into alternative energy in a more unified and substantial way, by combining a set of peripheral businesses such as solar, wind, and hydrogen-fired power plants into one new low-carbon-powered unit that BP would invest billions in. Ask those involved how the new strategy came about, and the answer always involves multiple players working collaboratively. One of her key lieutenants described Cox's approach like this: "She thinks about how to create incentives or objectives so that the organization will naturally find its own solutions and structures. It encourages people to be thoughtful, innovative, and self-regulating." Cox herself claims that her role is to be a "catalyst." She consistently articulates a management philosophy in which the leader does not drive change but, rather, allows potential to emerge.

Interestingly, the processes these women describe do not hinge just on a collaborative style. They also rely on diverse and external inputs and alliances. At BP Alternative Energy, Cox spent much of her time talking to key people outside her business group and the company in order to develop a strategic perspective on opportunities and sell the idea of low-carbon power to her CEO and peers. Her ideas were informed by a wide network that included thought leaders in a range of sectors. She brought in outsiders who could transcend a parochial view to fill key roles and invited potential adversaries into the process early on to make sure her team was also informed by those who had a different view of the world. Our results hint at an interesting hypothesis: By involving their male peers in the process of creating a vision, female leaders may get less credit for the result.

THEORY 2: Women hesitate to go out on a limb. Some women responded to our findings by noting that they need to base their marching orders on concrete facts and irrefutable analysis, not unprovable assertions about how the future will take shape. Here, two Democratic candidates for the 2008 U.S. presidential race offer an interesting parallel. Barack Obama was viewed as a visionary, a charismatic communicator offering a more hopeful if undetailed future. Hillary Clinton was viewed as a competent executor with an impressive if uninspiring grasp of policy detail. According to a recent *New Yorker* article by George Packer, Clinton as much as admitted that she does not inspire through rhetoric and emotion. She said: "A President, no matter how rhetorically inspiring, still has to show strength and effectiveness in the day-to-day handling of the job, because people are counting on that. So, yes, words are critically important, but they're not enough. You have to act. In my own experience, sometimes it's putting one foot in front of the other day after day."

Might women feel they have to choose between being seen as competent and in control or being visionary? Recall Anne Dumas, our services executive, and her pride in having a vast, detailed knowledge of what is happening in her firm. Often, she told us, she'd called on that reservoir of data to defend her position against challenges. The same attitude comes through in the observation of a management consultant who told us, "Men speak more confidently and boldly on an issue, with very little data to back it up. Women want to have a lot of data and feel confident that they can back up what they are saying."

A common obstacle for female leaders is that they often lack the presumption of competence accorded to their male peers. As a result, women are less likely to go out on a limb, extrapolating from facts and figures to interpretations that are more easily challenged. When a situation is rife with threat—when people, male or female, expect that they are "guilty until proven innocent"—they adopt a defensive, often rigid, posture, relying less on their imagination and creativity and sticking to safe choices.

The presumption-of-competence effect is compounded by gender stereotypes that lead us to expect emotional, collaborative women and rational, directive men. When men communicate from the heart or manage participatively, it's taken as evidence of range, an added plus. Women's emotional communication or inclusive process, by contrast, is implicitly viewed as proof of an incapacity or unwillingness to do otherwise, even if the situation calls for it.

THEORY 3: Women don't put much stock in vision. Do men and women really have different leadership styles? Certainly a lot of ink has been spilled on the question, but the answer provided by hundreds of studies, subjected to meta-analysis, is no. When other factors (such as title, role, and salary) are held constant, similarities in style vastly outweigh the differences. The occasional finding that women are slightly more people oriented and participative tends not to hold up in settings where there are few women—that is, in line positions and upper management. But put aside the science and ask individuals for their opinion on whether men and women have different leadership styles, and most women (and men) answer yes.

This can only complicate the solution to the vision deficit. It's one thing for a woman who suspects she is wrongly perceived to resolve to change certain behaviors in order to convey the competence and substance she has to offer. It's quite another thing when her own self-conception has become colored by the same biases.

Our interviews with female executives highlighted one potential difference in attitude between the genders that could explain women's lower ratings on envisioning. We suspect women may not value envisioning as a critical leadership competency to the same extent that men do or may have a more skeptical view of envisioning's part in achieving results. Over and over again in our discussions with women, we heard them take pride in their concrete, no-nonsense attitude and practical orientation toward everyday work problems. We were reminded of a comment made by Margaret Thatcher: "If you want anything said, ask a man; if you want anything done, ask a woman." Many of the women we interviewed similarly expressed the opinion that women were more thorough, had a better command of detail, and were less prone to self-promotion than men. Like Anne Dumas, they valued substance over form as a means of gaining credibility with key stakeholders. A pharmaceutical executive elaborated further: "I see women as more practical. Although the women in my organization are very strategic, they are also often the ones who ground the organization in what is possible, what can or cannot be done from the human dimension."

Making the Leadership Transition

Women may dismiss the importance of vision—and they may be reassured by the many claims made over the years about their superior emotional intelligence—but the fact remains that women are a minority in the top ranks of business organizations. Our findings suggest to us that the shortfall is in no small part due to women's perceived lack of vision.

The findings of a 2008 study by Catalyst researchers Jeanine Prime and Nancy Carter and IMD professors Karsten Jonsen and Martha Maznevski

WHAT DOES IT MEAN TO HAVE VISION?

Across studies and research traditions, vision has been found to be the central component in charismatic leadership and the essence of the oft-noted distinction between management and leadership. But what does it look like in action? As detailed by the Global Executive Leadership Inventory, behaving in a visionary way is a matter of doing three things well:

Sensing opportunities and threats in the environment

- simplifying complex situations
- foreseeing events that will affect the organization

Setting strategic direction

- encouraging new business
- defining new strategies
- making decisions with an eye toward the big picture

Inspiring constituents

- challenging the status quo
- being open to new ways of doing things
- inspiring others to look beyond limitations

concur. In it, more than 1,000 executives from nine countries (all alumni of executive education programs) were asked for their impressions of men and women in general as leaders. Both men and women tended to believe that the two genders have distinct leadership strengths, with women outscoring men on some behaviors, and men outscoring women on others. But here's the catch: When people were asked to rate the behaviors' relative importance to overall leadership effectiveness, the "male" behaviors had the edge. Across countries, "inspiring others"—a component of our envisioning dimension—landed at the top of the rankings as most important to overall leadership effectiveness. And what of the areas of leadership where men agreed that women were stronger? Let's take women's standout advantage: their much greater skill at "supporting others." That one ranked at the bottom of the list. As a component of overall leadership effectiveness, it was clearly not critical but merely nice to have.

We've seen how these priorities play out at close hand, in the personal stories of women we study. Particularly at midcareer, when senior management sizes up the leadership potential of competent managers, they take their toll. A manager we'll call Susan offers a cautionary tale. A strong performer, Susan rose through the functional ranks in logistics and distribution, thanks to her superior technical and people skills and belief in running a tight ship.

As a manager she prided herself on her efficient planning and organizing and her success in building a loyal, high-performing team. But her boss saw her capabilities differently. By this point in her career, he expected her to sense emerging trends or unexploited opportunities in the business environment, to craft strategy based on a view of the business as opposed to a view of her function, and to actively work to identify and bring on board stakeholders. Eventually a proposal came from outside her division calling for a radical reorganization of it. Still focused on making continuous improvement to the existing operation, Susan lacked the networks that would have helped her spot shifting priorities in the wider market and was blindsided by the idea.

It's often observed that the very talents that bring managers success in midlevel roles can be obstacles to their taking on bigger leadership roles. That was Susan's situation, and it's possible that it is a common trap for women. Having had the message drummed into their heads that they must be rational, nonemotional, and hyperefficient, they might actually place a higher value than men on knowing the details cold and getting the job done. That, in turn, makes their leadership transition more difficult, because they stick with what they know longer. Another woman we interviewed, this one an investment banker, captured the scale of the challenge. "It's like my whole basis for existence is taken away from me," she told us, "if I can't rely on the facts." Her words reminded us that an executive's accustomed approach and style define who she is as a leader. To walk away from them is to be left without a clear sense of identity.

The challenge facing women, then, is to stop dismissing the vision thing and make vision one of the things they are known for. In a senior leadership role, it's the best use of their time and attention. It's a set of competencies that can be developed. And of all the leadership dimensions we measured, it's the only thing holding women back.

EXPLORING THE ISSUE

Do Women Make Better Business Leaders?

Critical Thinking and Reflection

1. Do you think women make better leaders? Provide specific business examples.
2. Do you think industries that cater predominantly to female customers would perform better under female leaders and vice-versa? Why? Why not?
3. Why do you think women do not display high visionary skills? What do people who have high visionary skills demonstrate?
4. What are some alternate perspectives that HRM professionals may explore when thinking of effective leaders?
5. Identify and describe women in leadership positions in other countries? Has their trajectory been similar of different to the female leaders in the US?

Is There Common Ground?

Women have shown to have some innate characteristics that help them navigate very well in leadership positions. Personal characteristics such as intuitiveness, interpersonal skills, multi-tasking, feeling of empathy, and determination are identified as some excellent leadership qualities that women generally demonstrate. As women have been traditionally underrepresented at the workforce, it is only aggressive organizational initiatives, such as the RLD of Safeway, that can make women climb up the corporate ranks. Women make up 50% of the managerial positions in the US workforce and hold 14.6% of the corporate Fortune 500 positions. On the other hand, scholars suggest that women may lack visionary skills that help business leaders provide the big picture, generate new ideas, inspire new opportunities, and foresee strategically. Leadership experts suggest that not to view this concept as male or female but consider the gamut of competencies required for such positions. What leadership characteristics does Indra Nooyi, the CEO of Pepsi, demonstrate that makes her so successful? Are they similar to those of Bill Gates, founder of Microsoft? How? What characteristics are similar and what are different?

Additional Resources

Anonymous (2008). Power of women: Or should that be Women of Power? Business Today, 10–15.

Frauenheim, E. (2007). Bias study sees few gains for female leaders. Workforce Management, *86*(15), 12,14.

Houlihan, A. (2008). It's A Woman's World: How Women Can Thrive in Any Industry. Cost Engineering, *50*(8), 8–9.

http://womensissues.about.com/od/intheworkplace/a/WomenLeaders.htm: Qualities of Women Leaders; The Unique Leadership Characteristics of Women.

http://sbinformation.about.com/cs/development/a/womenbiz.htm: Inspirational Women in Business.

http://knowledgenetwork.thunderbird.edu/research/2009/07/10/women/: Women as business leaders: Where does your country rank?

http://mindbodypolitic.com/2008/08/06/795/: Women Business Leaders in India.

http://money.cnn.com/magazines/fortune/fortune500/2007/womenceos/: Women CEO for Fortune 500 companies.

www.notjustthekitchen.com/money-finance/one-more-time-do-women-make-better-leaders-than-men: One more time- do women make better leaders than men.

www.catalyst.org/publication/94/women-take-care-men-take-charge-stereotyping-of-us-business-leaders-exposed. Women "Take Care," Men "Take Charge:" Stereotyping of U.S. Business Leaders Exposed.

www.forbes.com/2008/05/28/gender-strategy-behavior-lead-manage-cx_mk_0528sexes.html: Women Vs. Men: Who's Better At Business?

www.usnews.com/news/best-leaders/articles/2008/11/19/americas-best-leaders-indra-nooyi-pepsico-ceo: America's Best Leaders: Indra Nooyi, PepsiCo CEO.

Hymowitz, C. (2007). Women Get Better At Forming Networks To Help Their Climb. Wall Street Journal (Eastern Edition), p. B.1.

Zabludovsky, G. (2001). Women managers and diversity programs in Mexico. The Journal of Management Development, *20*(4), 354–370.

ISSUE 10

Does the Glass Ceiling Still Exist in U.S. Organizations?

YES: Jessica Marquez, from "Gender Bias Found to Start Early in Career," *Workforce Management* (June 2009)

NO: Anonymous, from "Women in the Economy (A Special Report)—Tales from the Front Lines: On How They Did What They Did," *Wall Street Journal* (p. R.6, 2011)

Learning Outcomes

After reading this issue, you should be able to:

- Gain an understanding on the concept of glass ceiling.
- Detail why women experience the glass-ceiling effect.
- Understand how successful women have achieved their successes.
- Provide alternate perspectives to the concept of the glass ceiling.
- Identify an international perspective of how other countries view the glass-ceiling concept.

ISSUE SUMMARY

YES: Jessica Marquez, journalist at *Workforce Management,* suggests that women face the glass ceiling possibly because their careers begin much later and they have more career interruptions due to family commitments.

NO: The article provides examples of leading women in the corporate world. These professional women share their work stories and corporate recipes with the readers.

The term glass ceiling first appeared in *Wall Street Journal* in 1986 in a discussion on corporate women with respect to their career growth. The *glass-ceiling* concept can be defined as any barriers women face in attaining higher positions or salaries in their organizations. Women traditionally have a difficult time trying to get to the upper corporate levels as these positions have been conventionally held by men. However, federal acts such as Title VII, affirmative action, and also the Equal Pay Act have provided women a sense of equality at the work place.

In 1970, women were 38 percent of the workforce but today represent almost 47 percent of the workforce. More than half of the college graduate degrees today awarded are to women. Women in the United States compete for the highest political positions and also hold Supreme Court positions. Yet the path to the top seems to be a road less traveled by women.

Proponents suggest that statistics are misleading as women still face invisible barriers to become leaders in their fields. Women are consistently underrepresented at every management level, with the distinction becoming very apparent in upper echelons. A gender study indicated that women began to feel the discrimination even at the first level of management where the representation of the men exceeded women by 28 percent. This difference in gender representation increased to 50 percent at upper levels. Generally men hold executive-level positions twice as often as women do. A study on *Fortune* 500 companies suggest that women hold just 16 percent of corporate executive positions and constitute about 6 percent of top earners at *Fortune* 500 companies. Discriminatory pay patterns continue as women are still paid lower than men, though federal interventions may try to offer gender equality at the workplace. In 2002, male CEOs of nonprofit organizations earned $147,085, while their female counterparts earned $98,108. Why is there such a difference in pay? We will let readers make their own judgments regarding these salary figures.

The reasons why women face such invisible barriers are due to several reasons. Generally family obligations impede women from pursuing a linear career path as they tend to be the main caregivers for their families. Women generally take career breaks to raise their children and support other family responsibilities. At the workplace, women usually do not participate in the old boys' network, an informal method of socializing, which enhances employees' corporate visibility. Women are also not asked to frequently relocate as often as men are, possibly due to family commitments. Such opportunities, whether domestic or international, usually provide promotional or developmental opportunities. An international study "Holding Women Back" based on 12,800 leaders in 76 countries found that women had 9 percent expatriate (working overseas) opportunities in comparison with 21 percent for men. Further, many organizations do not offer work–life balance programs and a supportive environment which is very conducive to women's professional success.

On the other hand, others feel corporate success is dependent on a variety of factors. Many women have made a tremendous mark in corporate boardrooms. A *Wall Street Journal* journalist, Ms. Blumenstein, interviews four successful women and shares their recipes of corporate successes. The article suggests that achieving any high career positions require individuals to be passionate about their jobs, network aggressively, and demonstrate creativity. Mellody Hobson, president of Ariel Investments, suggests that being passionate about the job was her first step to become very successful at her job. She also insists on working with male employees who believe in and encourage the success of their female peers as another step in her in being successful. She also networked ardently with other leaders opening several doors to other leadership opportunities. Dr. Gerberding, president of Merck, the pharmaceutical giant, suggests that some innate female characteristics may make women effective corporate leaders. For instance, she refers to "horizontal leadership"—a characteristic that requires leaders to form collaborative networks outside their own hierarchy. Women naturally possess these interpersonal qualities that can be effectively leveraged for businesses. She also suggests networking with other leaders in other industries to understand the flavors of effective leadership. Marissa Mayer, the first female engineer at Google, also underscores passion for the job as one of the most important predictors of job success. She also states that women do not need to demonstrate masculine characteristics to prove any accomplishments. Debra Lee, chairman and CEO of BET Networks, implies that women may also have to be very aggressive in their industries to achieve the positions they want.

What are some alternate perspectives to the glass-ceiling effect? Women suggest their way to the top can be achieved through organizations that actively recruit female applicants, colleges that promote minorities, and support networks that endorse career planning. Organizations, such as Macy's and Kellogg's, promote corporate diversity by having women in visible leadership positions. For instance, more than three-fourths of the Macy's workforce is women, with about two-thirds of the women holding supervisory positions. Kellogg's, an industry leader, promotes the employee resource groups such as women of Kellogg's (WOK) that actively helps women reach their highest professional levels through internal networking. Dell has women representing about one-third of its global employees and actively promotes women into leadership positions by encouraging their managers to be informal mentors to women. Colleges that actively promote protected groups (such as women and African Americans) help students find the best transition to organizations that would promote their careers. Further, women find they are able to develop their careers better if they are a part of support groups that proactively mentor how to make the journey to the top. Women are also becoming entrepreneurs and therefore business leaders in their field. In a study of women and business types, women choose to launch their businesses as sole proprietorship instead of corporations, suggesting they want to be their own bosses. This is another alternative that women may pursue to completely avoid the "glass-ceiling" path that might be difficult to ascend.

The glass-ceiling experience exists in other countries also and is usually exacerbated by cultural and traditional gender stereotypes. For instance, in India, less than 15 percent of the scientists are women. Several cultures do not accept female business leaders, making the glass-ceiling concept even more obvious. However, in politics, women create great strides and frequently make the news headlines. New Zealand appointed its first woman prime minister in 2000, WHO (World Health Organization) appointed its first female director-general in 2002, and Mexico appointed its first female governor for the state of Yucatán in 2007. Brazil, regarded as a very powerful emerging economy, elected a female president in 2010. Dilma Rousseff was chosen as the first female president, providing an immense change to a culture that is considered traditionally masculine.

Jessica Marquez

Gender Bias Found to Start Early in Career

Abstract (Summary)

Despite discussion regarding women hitting the glass ceiling once they reach the executive level, discrimination starts much earlier in their careers, according to a recent paper by Development Dimensions International (DDI). Their data suggests that when you look at the things that would help people develop in their careers, women wouldn't get the same opportunities as men did, says Ann Howard, DDI's chief scientist. Many companies don't track how many women participate in high-potential programs, which also adds to this problem, says Jan Combopiano, VP and chief knowledge officer at Catalyst, a New York-based organization dedicated to helping businesses build inclusive workplaces for women.

Discrimination

Despite discussion regarding women hitting the glass ceiling once they reach the executive level, discrimination starts much earlier in their careers, according to a recent paper by Development Dimensions International.

"Holding Women Back," which is based on responses from 12,800 leaders in 76 countries, found that women face gender discrimination from the very beginning of their careers.

"Our data suggests that when you look at the things that would help people develop in their careers, women wouldn't get the same opportunities as men did," says Ann Howard, DDI's chief scientist.

One of the main areas where employers fail to include women is in their high-potential programs, where they identify those employees who managers believe could make strong leaders someday.

According to the study, there were 28 percent more men than women in high-potential programs at the first level of management and 50 percent more men than women in such programs at the executive level.

The problem with many companies' high-potential programs is that there is often no standard procedure to identify candidates, Howard says. Usually it is up to the managers to choose candidates, she adds.

"I'm not saying that there is some evil plot here," Howard says. "It's just that managers might think about future executives as men because that is the traditional norm at the company."

Many companies don't track how many women participate in high-potential programs, which also adds to this problem, says Jan Combopiano, vice president and chief knowledge officer at Catalyst, a New York-based organization dedicated to helping businesses build inclusive workplaces for women.

"It's really important that there is accountability tied to these programs," Combopiano says. "It's critical for overcoming gender stereotyping."

Another way to make sure that women have the same opportunities as men to advance their careers is by having a formal succession planning program in place, Howard says.

"It sets the same objective standards for everyone," she says.

Companies need to pay attention to all leadership development programs and make sure gender stereotypes don't get in the way of advancing women, Howard says.

"Employers need to have objective performance management standards in place," she says.

Too often a company will say that there aren't women in management roles because they took time off to have babies, but that often doesn't explain the issue, Howard says.

"The bottom line is that women are just as capable as men and if you have objective standards in place, women can show their stuff," she says.

Anonymous

NO

Women in the Economy: Tales From the Front Lines. Mellody Hobson, Julie Louise Gerberding, Marissa Mayer and Debra L. Lee on How They Did What They Did

The challenges women face often cut across industries. But some are also unique to specific sectors. Women who have risen high in four industries—finance, health, technology, and media—sought to illuminate these issues by recounting their own experiences and assessing how women generally have fared in their fields.

Mellody Hobson, president of Ariel Investments in Chicago, spoke with *The Wall Street Journal*'s Rebecca Blumenstein. Julie Louise Gerberding, president of Merck & Co.'s Merck Vaccines unit, sat down with the Journal's Laura Landro. Marissa Mayer, Google Inc.'s vice president, consumer products, talked with the Journal's Julia Angwin. And Debra L. Lee, chairman and chief executive of BET Networks, a unit of Viacom Inc., spoke with the Journal's Alessandra Galloni.

Here are edited excerpts of their conversations.

MS. BLUMENSTEIN: Mellody, you played such a major role in building Ariel up. Could you describe how you did it? There's a stereotype that women don't know how to manage money and don't know how to take risks.

MS. HOBSON: I was an intern at my firm. I fell in love with the investment business, and from the very beginning I knew this was where I was going to work for my career. So I could think very long term about how to build our company. That ultimately allowed us to accomplish quite a bit.

MS. BLUMENSTEIN: Did you have more freedom as a woman, less of a hindrance from some of the structural barriers that might have come up at a big company?

MS. HOBSON: There's no question about it. My business partner, John Rogers, who started our firm, was very used to strong women. His mother was the first black woman to graduate from the University of Chicago law school, in the '40s.

So John was always very happy for me to be out and about representing Ariel.

MS. BLUMENSTEIN: You have very strong ties politically in Chicago. You appear on "Good Morning America." You're very involved in your community and things outside of work. Could you talk about the importance of reaching out and almost building your own persona?

MS. HOBSON: With some women, even in my own firm, you have to sort of push them out because they think, "I've got to do a really good job, which means staying very focused." I learned very early that I can do a better job if I have other stimuli that give me a broader perspective.

And what people with that focused mind-set don't realize is how important those outside relationships can be. I helped Bill Bradley when he ran for president in 2000. I worked as hard on his campaign as I worked on my job every single day. Obviously, we were unsuccessful. But then one day, Bill calls and says, "I'm on the board of Starbucks, and I'm taking you with me." He recommended me to Howard Schultz. I never imagined that was possible—I'm like this pipsqueak in Chicago.

So I get to be in the room with one of the most successful brands in the world, with a front-row seat to all the things that are going on around the world. And, ultimately, I get to bring those ideas and knowledge back to our firm as it relates to all the other investing that we are doing.

So I always say to people in terms of going out and being of this world—be it business, politics, nonprofit or whatever—it actually makes you a better businessperson.

MS. LANDRO: For those of you who aren't familiar with Dr. Gerberding's many accomplishments, she started out as a physician and was in academia for some years before she went into public service and ran the Centers for Disease Control, where she was basically on the front lines protecting us from all of the horrible things out there—bioterrorism, SARS, anthrax. After leaving public service, she went to head a large business, Merck Vaccines.

You've said you think women have certain characteristics that make it easier for them to be good managers. Can you elaborate on that?

DR. GERBERDING: In a word, meta leadership. Which is not just knowing yourself and being able to lead within your organization, in a vertical way, but it's the horizontal leadership: the ability to lead networks of people who are not in your own power domain. That horizontal leadership takes different skills than vertical leadership. And it requires people to know how to negotiate, to be able to be true and effective partners and collaborators, to find that third path, to be able to walk in someone else's shoes with emotional intelligence and empathy.

And while men and women possess those skills, I think some of them are attributes that women are naturally inclined or more socialized to excel in. And in this very complicated world in which we live, that horizontal leadership probably is one of the key success factors for any organization.

MS. LANDRO: Tell us about how you wound up at the CDC and reorganized some things there.

DR. GERBERDING: I was asked to come there to lead the Patient Safety Hospital Infections Group. Then, by an amazing set of coincidences, I was involved in the response to the anthrax attacks.

And I think that's what prompted the secretary to ask me to take on the leadership of the agency. Having been an emergency-room doctor and an ICU attending, I think I was naturally better at making decisions in those kinds of situations than people who hadn't been used to crisis management.

I think the CDC is the finest government agency there is. And yet it was not an agency designed for public-health preparedness or for emergency response. And suddenly our nation found itself in a situation where those were really important public-health imperatives. We had anthrax, we had SARS, we had avian influenza, we had monkey pox, we had West Nile marching across the U.S.

We had one public-health crisis after another. And so I felt that the public-health agency needed to evolve another set of capabilities and another set of strengths.

I went to the CEOs of the business leaders in Atlanta like Bernie Marcus from Home Depot, Oz Nelson, the former CEO of UPS, the CEO of Delta. I went and consulted with people who had to have faced organizational transformation in their own organizations and asked for their advice and consultation. I also went to the military because I have learned that our military probably does the best job of any organization in investing in leadership development. I hired some retired military personnel to come and help us with the preparedness planning for influenza pandemic.

AUDIENCE QUESTION: At the CDC you had an opportunity during a time of crisis that gave you greater leadership. In your career or others, have you seen where women have stepped up to take jobs where others were reluctant to go because there's great opportunity for failure? And yet by taking those risky situations, those turnaround situations, they really did add to their toolbox.

DR. GERBERDING: I certainly have seen women accept challenges that would be considered high-risk challenges. I don't know whether or not women or men are preferentially more suitable to those kinds of crises.

But what I do notice in crises is that women are more likely to reach to each other for support. So it was very natural for me when I was leading the CDC to find other women in government that I could connect to or confer with or talk to who would help me. And I in turn would try to support and help them.

I didn't observe much of that among the men that I encountered. I think men want to be perceived as more competent and more independently effective. And it may be harder to acknowledge that they need help or that you can create a whole that's greater than the sum of the parts.

MS. ANGWIN: Marissa, you joined Google in '99 as the first female engineer. You've been a manager at Google since. . . .

MS. MAYER: Probably since about 2002.

MS. ANGWIN: And so you manage a lot of male engineers, right? How is that for you?

MS. MAYER: People ask me a lot about what it's like to be a woman at Google, but I'm not really a woman at Google—I'm a geek at Google. I'm surrounded by people who love technology and love to try out the latest gadgets and love to see what can you do with this piece of code or that piece of code. We're excited about all the same things, and that's our common ground.

MS. ANGWIN: One thing that's interesting about your generation is that in the past women in business tried to maybe keep some of their femaleness in check, whereas you celebrate your love of fashion, your love of cupcakes. These are two things the brand Marissa stands for. How has that helped or hurt you within the organization?

[Google's VP of new products Marissa Mayer tells WSJ's Julia Angwin that even in the male-dominated field of technology, she's less aware of her status as a woman, than her status as a geek.]

MS. MAYER: I think it's just something that's separate. One of the things that's really important to me is getting more young women into science and technology. One of the trade-offs that often happens for girls is they think, "I like art. I like fashion. And I'm going to have to hide that or dial that back in order to get taken seriously." I don't think that's necessarily the case. In a lot of issues of fashion and things like that, there is also just an engineering problem that has to do with material strength and how something moves, how something works. A lot of times it's very engineered, so there are commonalities there.

I think it's important to send the message that you don't have to give up your femininity in order to be in a male-dominated space like the Internet.

MS. ANGWIN: The McKinsey report did say tech and finance are lagging behind other industries in terms of women's success.

MS. MAYER: I personally am very optimistic. I think that one of the things that really helps is the idea of, one, role models, but two, actually getting to see how technology applies in your everyday life. For me, growing up, I knew one woman computer scientist, and she worked at J.C. Penney on the catalog system. That wasn't something that I got to touch and feel every day.

Now, with the pervasiveness of the Internet, videogames, technology just being all around us, I hope a lot more young women get interested in how can you build that and how can you build the next great thing that really helps people.

MS. GALLONI: Debra Lee, chairman and CEO of BET Networks, is the woman behind famous shows like "The Game" and "The Mo'Nique Show."

You started at BET in 1986 as general counsel. And then 10 years later you were promoted to chief operating officer. And you say many people below you tried to sort of trick you. They figured, "She doesn't know my business, so I'm not going to tell her things."

Can you tell us a little bit about how that happened? And how much do you think that that had to do with the fact that you were a woman?

MS. LEE: It was a small, entrepreneurial company. I had been part of a peer group of probably seven or eight other executives. All except two were male. I went from being part of the peer group to being the boss. And I found out all the other men had asked for the COO position, so they were not happy when I was given it.

So there was a lot of "hide the ball" going on. They didn't feel like they should educate me and give me insight into their divisions. They thought the more they could just run their divisions and keep them away from me, that I would be unsuccessful. Little by little, I had to change that team and hire people who were loyal to me, who wanted to see me succeed and weren't there to see my demise.

MS. GALLONI: How long did it take you to complete the process?

MS. LEE: It took about six years before I felt very comfortable that it was my own team. And that's longer than it should have taken.

I don't want to generalize about women, but I was trying the "nice girl" approach. So I didn't come in, as some men do, and fire everyone and start all over. I tried to work with them. I tried to support them. I tried to show them that I was a good person. And then when I saw it wasn't going to work, I eventually had to fire most of them.

If I had to do it over again, I would come in day one and make changes.

MS. GALLONI: As we'll see in the media breakout session and part of the McKinsey report, the media actually do quite badly in terms of the advancement of women. But media also are very influential in terms of perception. Do you think the image of women in media does not help the advancement of women?

MS. LEE: It probably does not help. But I just think it's so important to have women in the rooms making decisions about programming and images, because that's the only we'll ever be at parity and ever really change the way we're going.

When I became CEO of BET, it was right after the Don Imus incident with Rutgers women's basketball. And people were looking at hip-hop and saying, "If Don Imus was wrong, then all these young hip-hop artists must be wrong, too, for calling women names and everything."

And all of a sudden one day I had protesters outside my house. And I'm like, "How does this happen? I'm doing the right thing, I care about women, I care about the images of African-Americans. And now I have protesters outside my house?"

But it really made me sit back and think about BET, BET as a brand, what I wanted my legacy to be, what I wanted to leave in terms of programming. And that's really influenced my approach to original programming and really has turned BET around in the past couple of years. I'm very proud of that.

EXPLORING THE ISSUE

Does the Glass Ceiling Still Exist in U.S. Organizations?

Critical Thinking and Reflection

1. Do you think the glass-ceiling effect still exists in organizations today?
2. Why do you think women experience the glass-ceiling effect?
3. What are the most common recipes for upper-level corporate success?
4. What are some alternate perspectives that HRM professionals may explore when considering the glass-ceiling effect?
5. Research and explain the glass-ceiling concept in three other countries?

Is There Common Ground?

Advocates of the glass-ceiling concept suggest that such underrepresentation begins quite early in women's careers and becomes pronounced at executive levels. The possible reasons could be that women generally prefer to take a hiatus to fulfill either maternal or caregiver obligations. On the other hand, successful women suggest career success depends on demonstrating true passion for the job and exhibiting excellent leadership qualities. The alternate perspectives are that women may pursue their path to upper-level positions by joining corporate or academic institutions that endorse and promote female leadership. As of 2011, only 12 females hold CEO positions at *Fortune* 500 companies. How did Carol Bartz and Ursula Burns become the CEO of Yahoo and Xerox? Did they experience any "glass ceiling" to climb to the summit? Did they join any special support groups? What was their recipe to get to the top?

Additional Resources

Anonymous. (2007). Women to watch (A special report); The Journal Report Online. *Wall Street Journal* (Eastern Edition), R.2.

Anonymous. (2009). Breaking the glass ceiling. *Black Enterprise, 39*(7), 121–123. Retrieved September 3, 2009, from ABI/INFORM Global. (Document ID: 1631636591).

Brusino, J. (2009). Women entrepreneurs choose a different path. *T + D, 63*(9), 21.

Connolly, J. (2004). Real transparency will break the glass ceiling. *Personnel Today*, 17–19.

Donnellon, A. and Langowitz, N. (2009). Leveraging women's networks for strategic value. *Strategy & Leadership, 37*(3), 29–36.

Gilgoff, D. (2009). Investing in diversity: American corporations have long lacked minorities and women at the top. But more employers, recruiters, and business schools are working on it. *U.S. News & World Report, 146*(10), 72.

Lockwood, N. (2004). The glass ceiling: Domestic and international perspectives. *HR Magazine, 49*(6), R2–R9.

Nancherla, A. (2009). One step forward, two steps back. *T + D, 63*(7), 24.

Woodard, T. (2006). Developing women leaders. *Leadership Excellence, 23*(9), 10.

http://www.livemint.com/2009/06/01002900/Bureaucracy-glass-ceiling-que.html?pg=3: Bureaucracy, Glass Ceiling Queer Pitch for India's Women Scientists.

http://www.woopidoo.com/profession/women/index.htm: Women Business Leaders.

http://jantucker.suite101.com/the-glass-ceiling-a29187: The Glass Ceiling—Does It Still Exist?

http://money.cnn.com/magazines/fortune/fortune500/2011/womenceos/: Women CEOs.

http://www.bbc.co.uk/news/world-latin-america-11662623: Brazil Elects Dilma Rousseff as the First Female President.

Internet References . . .

History of e-Learning

E-learning Web site is a comprehensive resource and information guide on e-learning, online learning, and programs in different areas of study, including instructional design, accredited online distance education, online degrees, and colleges and universities in the United States of America and Canada.

http://www.about-elearning.com/history-of-e-learning.html

The High Impact Learning Organization

This Web site provides research, guides, case studies, and vendor analyses filled with practical best practices in enterprise learning and talent management. The research is based on detailed discussions with hundreds of companies implementing real-world learning and talent management solutions.

http://store.bersinassociates.com/governance.html

Electronic Gadgets Like Apple iPod—A Boon or Bane?

The Articlesbase Internet Web site has established itself as one of the Internet's leading article directories and offers custom articles written by expert authors.

http://www.articlesbase.com/technology-articles/electronic-gadgets-like-apple-ipod-a-boon-or-bane-513360.html

Some Advice for Handling Information Overload

Law Professor Blogs is a network of Web logs ("blogs") designed to assist law professors in their scholarship and teaching. Each site focuses on a particular area of law and combines both (1) regularly updated permanent resources and links and (2) daily news and information of interest to law professors. The editors of this network are leading scholars and teachers who are committed to providing *the* web destination for law professors in their fields.

http://lawprofessors.typepad.com/law_librarian_blog/2009/11/some-advice-for-handling-information-overload.html

Fedgazette: Business News from the Federal Reserve

Fedgazette is a regional business and economic newspaper providing information on the latest business and economic news. This is a publication of the Federal Reserve Bank of Minneapolis and provides this Web site as a convenience to its customers, depository institutions, and the public.

http://www.minneapolisfed.org/publications_papers/pub_display.cfm?id=2154

Do Unions Work?

The pros and cons of labor unions are presented here. eHow.com is an online community dedicated to providing visitors the ability to research, share, and discuss instructional solutions that help complete day-to-day tasks and projects. It combines the experiential knowledge of certified experts with the practical knowledge of everyday people to help discuss, plan, and complete things.

http://www.ehow.com/about_5097523_pros-cons-labor-unions.html

UNIT 4

Employee Performance and Organizational Productivity

What HRM practices will enhance employees' performance? Do certain HRM practices dissuade employee performance? Organizations are constantly seeking practices to enhance employee performance and therefore increase their business profits. The digitized world today allows for continuous learning, which organizations are taking advantage of to enhance knowledge capital. The information overload that employees experience with increased dependence on technology has brought such practices into question. The collaborative efforts of unions are seen both in the positive and negative light. Can these HRM practices augment organizational performance?

- Does Increased Dependence on Laptops, Cell Phones, and PDAs Hurt Employee Productivity?
- Do Unions Help Organizational Productivity?

ISSUE 11

Does Increased Dependence on Laptops, Cell Phones, and PDAs Hurt Employee Productivity?

YES: Paul Hemp, from "Death by Information Overload," *Harvard Business Review* (September 2009)

NO: Michelle LaBrosse, from "Working Successfully in a Virtual World," *Employment Relations Today* (2007)

Learning Outcomes

After reading this issue, you should be able to:

- Gain an understanding on the concept of information overload.
- Understand how information overload impacts the quality of work and life.
- Identify the advantages of working in a virtual environment.
- Provide alternate perspectives to overcoming the problems of information overload at work.

ISSUE SUMMARY

YES: Paul Hemp, a Harvard Law School graduate and editor of the *Harvard Business Review*, argues that our current society is facing loss of productivity due to excessive dependence on technology (such as BlackBerrys, cell phones, etc.), blurring boundaries between home and work.

NO: Michelle LaBrosse, one of the 25 Most Influential Women in Project Management, contends that modern technological devices allow employees to be connected to form virtual teams.

Psychologists suggest that the current workplace promotes and encourages the attention deficit trait syndrome. Employees are prone to make a lot of mistakes as they are constantly connected to different methods of telecommunication, creating an "information overload" environment. This phrase first appeared in 1970 as Alvin Toffler suggested that too much information could create problems at work. At work and at home, employees are inundated with messages from emails, BlackBerrys, and cell phones, not allowing them to give their complete attention to any single task on hand. Hence employees are more likely to make errors and also demonstrate reduced attention.

A 2008 AOL study on e-mail users and their personal habits indicated that individuals had a compulsion to check their e-mails constantly, with 60 percent of individuals checking their e-mails even in their bathrooms. Employees today lead lives that rob their members of having even a single private moment! Further, a tremendous reliance on such external devices has completely blurred the boundaries between work and home. Studies have shown that children feel neglected with their parents' continuous interaction with their BlackBerrys, which has made them feel, in extreme cases, almost like orphans.

How does "information overload" create decreased employee productivity? Primarily, employees are not able to process the information they receive as quickly as it arrives. Second, they have to prioritize quickly the information they receive and decide which demands their immediate attention. Is it a co-worker's text, a boss's e-mail, or a spouse's call that will get their immediate attention? Employees are constantly in a state of partial attention as they are communicating with one person (co-worker) and thinking of what to say in their next medium of communication (boss's e-mail). Therefore employees do not provide undivided attention to their work tasks in hand as information is coming rapidly from different directions.

How does "information overload" impact organizations? Productive work time is lost with employees trying to compulsively stay connected with work and home via different forms of communication. In a study of 2,300 Intel employees, employees said that one-third of the e-mails they receive are not important. Employees also indicated they spend 2 hours a day reading and responding to their e-mails, wasting enormous corporate time. Microsoft researchers have determined that it takes employees about 25 minutes to revert back to their work-related tasks after they are interrupted by any external method of communication (such as BlackBerry, IMs, e-mails, Facebook, Twitter).

A Harvard Business study demonstrated that an average employee spends 40 percent of his or her time handling information received on such devices (laptops, cell phones, and PDAs) and spends only 60 percent of work time on value creation activities related to work. Research also suggests that the average employee changes what he or she is doing online once in every 3 minutes. This concept has caught the attention of practitioners and researchers alike and a Web site dedicated to understand and remedy this problem has been established (Information Overload Research Group; http://iorgforum.org/).

Proponents of adopting technological devices at work suggest that they help employees balance their work and life agenda better. Employees spend less time commuting and therefore can stay connected with their organizations from their homes. Further, in a globalized workplace such devices help employees stay connected with their international peers enhancing knowledge and learning significantly. Michelle LaBrosse, founder of a successful virtual company, insists that such technology was instrumental for the success of her global organization. However, she suggests employees should develop ground rules in using these external technological devices. LaBrosse suggests that such devices should be used to enhance team-building and internal employee communication. Every work project should have clear deadlines with frequent updates on employees' progress as a "distance working" comes with many disguised distractions. As e-mail management is very time-consuming, the author advises employees to learn to write effective e-mails with very meaningful subject headers. These headers should indicate what and who needs to take the action. Usually many e-mail communications involve a "daisy-chain" approach where employees spend hours reading e-mails they do not need to provide any definitive inputs. Further, employees should be given a digital protocol—how quickly are they expected to respond to e-mails, BlackBerry messages, and cell phones? This will reduce a lot of anxiety for those employees who feel a need to be constantly wired when working remotely. Organizations can use Wikis, an online collaborative environment, very effectively to enhance the productivity of their work environment. Such an online dialogue allows employees to coordinate and plan their work schedules strategically.

An alternative perspective is to establish some ground rules and restrictions at the workplace so that employees are ensured they are not addicted to any technological devices. Morgan Stanley, the financial service giant, has proactively taken efforts to reduce their employees' technology addiction. Employees are encouraged to use software filters to distinguish important and non-important e-mail messages so that they can give priority to the important tasks. Microsoft and IBM are working on futuristic software applications such as Priorities and IM savvy that allow employees to be interrupted less so that they can have a productive work environment. IBM also has established specific days (Think Fridays) to allow employees to get away from the Internet clutter and experience quiet time reflecting on work. The management at Intel constantly advises its employees on how to send e-mails efficiently and not to overcrowd employees' inboxes if not required. Experts also suggest employees set times to check their e-mails (for instance, from 9 am to 11 am) so that other employees may also know about their online work schedule. They also should make time to get away from their work desk to a "quiet spot" to work without any online interruptions.

Employers are also beginning to also regulate employees' Internet usage while at work. Many organizations monitor their employees' time on the Internet and in addition have a policy of not allowing employees use the Internet for personal reasons. This greatly helps control the hours the employees actually spend their time working without any personal interruptions. Several employee monitoring software (such as SurfWatch and Little Brother) are available in the market, allowing organizations to target exactly what they want to monitor (Web-surfing by employees, sharing of valuable company information, checking personal e-mail). While introducing any monitoring software, organizations should inform employees of such practices due to privacy laws. Organizations will benefit to inform employees the reason for monitoring is to enhance employees' productivity and not preview their personal lives.

YES 

Paul Hemp

Death by Information Overload

The value of information in the knowledge economy is indisputable, but so is its capacity to overwhelm consumers of it. HBR contributing editor Hemp reports on practical ways for individuals and organizations to avoid getting too much of a good thing. Ready access to useful information comes at a cost: As the volume increases, the line between the worthwhile and the distracting starts to blur. And ready access to you—via e-mail, social networking, and so on—exacerbates the situation: On average, Intel executives get 300 e-mails a day, and Microsoft workers need 24 minutes to return to work after each e-mail interruption. Clearly, productivity is taking a hit. Technological aids can help, such as e-mail management software for you, a message-volume regulation system for your organization, or even more-sophisticated solutions being developed by Microsoft, IBM, and others. Yet, battling technological interruptions on their own turf only goes so far. You also need to change your mind-set, perhaps by seeking help from personal-productivity experts or by simply accepting that you can't respond to every distraction that flits across your screen. Similarly, organizations must change their cultures, for instance by establishing clear e-communication protocols. In the end, only a multipronged approach will help you and your organization subdue the multiheaded monster of information overload. The secret is to manage the beast while still respecting it for the beautiful creature it is.

New research and novel techniques offer a lifeline to you and your organization. Can everyone just stop whining about information overload? I mean, in the knowledge economy, information is our most valuable commodity. And these days it's available in almost infinite abundance, delivered automatically to our electronic devices or accessible with a few mouse clicks. So buck up, already!

Wait a second: Can I just stop whining about information overload?

The flood of information that swamps me daily seems to produce more pain than gain. And it's not just the incoming tidal wave of e-mail messages and RSS feeds that causes me grief. It's also the vast ocean of information I feel compelled to go out and explore in order to keep up in my job.

From *Harvard Business Review,* vol. 87, no. 9, September 2009, pp. 82–89.

Current research suggests that the surging volume of available information—and its interruption of people's work—can adversely affect not only personal well-being but also decision making, innovation, and productivity. In one study, for example, people took an average of nearly 25 minutes to return to a work task after an e-mail interruption. That's bad news for both individuals and their organizations.

There's hope, though. Innovative tools and techniques promise relief for those of us struggling with information inundation. Some are technological solutions—software that automatically sorts and prioritizes incoming e-mail, for instance—designed to regulate or divert the deluge. Others prevent people from drowning by getting them to change the way they behave and think. Who knows: Maybe someday even I will enjoy swimming in the powerful currents of information that now threaten to pull me under.

The Problem for Individuals

Information overload, of course, dates back to Gutenberg. The invention of movable type led to a proliferation of printed matter that quickly exceeded what a single human mind could absorb in a lifetime. Later technologies—from carbon paper to the photocopier—made replicating existing information even easier. And once information was digitized, documents could be copied in limitless numbers at virtually no cost.

Digitizing content also removed barriers to another activity first made possible by the printing press: publishing new information. No longer restricted by centuries-old production and distribution costs, anyone can be a publisher today. (The internet, with its far-reaching and free distribution channels, wasn't the only enabler. Consider how the word processor eliminated the need for a stenopad-equipped secretary, with ready access to typewriter and Wite-Out, who could help an executive bring a memo into the world.) In fact, a lot of new information—personalized purchase recommendations from Amazon, for instance—is "published" and distributed without any active human input.

With the information floodgates open, content rushes at us in countless formats: Text messages and Twitter tweets on our cell phones. Facebook friend alerts and voice mail on our BlackBerrys. Instant messages and direct-marketing sales pitches (no longer limited by the cost of postage) on our desktop computers. Not to mention the ultimate killer app: e-mail. (I, for one, have nearly expired during futile efforts to keep up with it.)

Meanwhile, we're drawn toward information that in the past didn't exist or that we didn't have access to but, now that it's available, we dare not ignore. Online research reports and industry data. Blogs written by colleagues or by executives at rival companies. Wikis and discussion forums on topics we're following. The corporate intranet. The latest banal musings of friends in our social networks.

So it's a lot of stuff—but what precisely is the problem? Well, the chorus of whining (punctuated by my own discordant moans) apparently has some validity. Researchers say that the stress of not being able to process information as fast as it arrives—combined with the personal and social expectation that, say, you will answer every e-mail message—can deplete and demoralize you. Edward Hallowell, a psychiatrist and expert on attention-deficit disorders, argues that the modern workplace induces what he calls "attention deficit trait," with characteristics similar to those of the genetically based disorder. Author Linda Stone, who coined the term "continuous partial attention" to describe the mental state of today's knowledge workers, says she's now noticing—get this—"e-mail apnea": the unconscious suspension of regular and steady breathing when people tackle their e-mail.

There are even claims that the relentless cascade of information lowers people's intelligence. A few years ago, a study commissioned by Hewlett-Packard reported that the IQ scores of knowledge workers distracted by e-mail and phone calls fell from their normal level by an average of 10 points—twice the decline recorded for those smoking marijuana, several commentators wryly noted.

Of course, not everyone feels overwhelmed by the torrent of information. Some are stimulated by it. But that raises the specter of . . . [cue scary music] . . . information addiction. According to a 2008 AOL survey of 4,000 e-mail users in the United States, 46% were "hooked" on e-mail. Nearly 60% of everyone surveyed checked e-mail in the bathroom, 15% checked it in church, and 11% had hidden the fact that they were checking it from a spouse or other family member.

The tendency of always-available information to blur the boundaries between work and home can affect our personal lives in unexpected ways. Consider the recently reported phenomenon of . . . [cue really scary music] . . . BlackBerry orphans: children who desperately fight to regain their parents' attention from the devices—in at least one reported case, by flushing a BlackBerry down the toilet.

The Problem for Companies

Most organizations unknowingly pay a high price as individuals struggle to manage the information glut. For one thing, productive time is lost as employees deal with information of limited value. In the case of e-mail, effective spam filters have reduced this problem. Still, a survey of 2,300 Intel employees revealed that people judge nearly one-third of the messages they receive to be unnecessary.

Given that those same employees spend about two hours a day processing e-mail (employees surveyed received an average of 350 messages a week, executives up to 300 a day), a serious amount of time is clearly being wasted.

"Many companies are still in denial about the problem," says Nathan Zeldes, a former Intel senior engineer, who oversaw the study. "And though people suffer, they don't fight back, because communication is supposed to be good for you." Zeldes is now the president of the Information Overload Research Group, a consortium of academics and executives.

Another set of problems involves the constant interruptions we face, whatever the value of the content. When you respond to an e-mail alert that pops up on your screen or to the vibration of your BlackBerry when you're "poked" by a Facebook friend, you do more than spend time reading the message. You also have to recover from the interruption and refocus your attention. A study by Microsoft researchers tracking the e-mail habits of coworkers found that once their work had been interrupted by an e-mail notification, people took, on average, 24 minutes to return to the suspended task.

The scenario the researchers described was unsettlingly familiar. Dealing with the message that had prompted the alert represented only a portion of the time off task. People often used the interruption as an opportunity to read other unopened e-mail messages—or to engage in such unrelated activities as text-messaging a friend or surfing the web. Surprisingly, more than half the time was spent after people were ready to return to their work: cycling through open applications on their computers to determine what they'd been doing when interrupted; getting distracted by some other work in progress as they moved from one window to another; and reestablishing their state of mind once they finally arrived at the application they'd abandoned nearly a half hour earlier.

Distractions created by incoming e-mail and other types of information also have more-subtle consequences. Research by Teresa M. Amabile of Harvard Business School has identified reduced creative activity on days when work is fragmented by interruptions. And we know from other research that even young workers, who have lots of experience frequently switching from one device or application to another, need uninterrupted periods during which to successfully tackle particularly demanding tasks.

Another eerily familiar, if rarely articulated, consequence of information overload is receiving attention from researchers: the delay in decision making when you don't know whether or when someone will answer an e-mail message. If you don't hear back in a timely fashion, you're left wondering: Was your message willfully ignored by the recipient because it ticked him off? Automatically diverted to his junk mail folder? Left for later response? Or is it simply languishing unnoticed because he's swamped by e-mail? (Some of these questions would be answered if more e-mail recipients—though don't count me among them—would click on those annoying confirmation-of-receipt requests that some senders activate.)

The ambiguity created by this online silence can sometimes be worse than a delayed response, according to Northwestern University researcher Yoram Kalman. Our minds go through a series of semiconscious calculations based on past experience: How long does this person usually take to answer e-mail? Should I bother her with a follow-up? Should I escalate my efforts by leaving a voice mail message, and at which number? Should I walk over to Building D to see whether she's at her desk? Shout out the window at the top of my lungs? Meanwhile, you may have to put a project on hold for an indefinite period while you await a response that the recipient could provide in no more than a minute or two.

What does all this add up to? It's not easy to quantify the costs of these and other consequences of information overload. But one calculation by Nathan Zeldes and two other researchers put Intel's annual cost of reduced efficiency, in the form of time lost to handling unnecessary e-mail and recovering from information interruptions, at nearly $1 billion. He says organizations ignore that kind of number at their peril.

Help for Individuals: TECHNOLOGY

During a recent brainstorming session about cutting-edge management ideas, Jerry Michalski was, well, the birdbrain of the group. As recounted in a recent blog post by my colleague Lew McCreary, who was sitting next to him, Michalski would hear something particularly intriguing—and immediately "tweet" to his Twitter network requesting further information. He'd often get a quick response, sometimes with a link to an article or a blog.

If there seemed to be value in the concept—first generated in the room, then enriched by the external commentary of his Twitter flock—he'd share it with others and then add it and relevant links to a software application, called TheBrain, on his laptop. He uses this tool, which visually associates related pieces of information on a computer screen, to save and categorize newly acquired knowledge.

Wow! Michalski, an independent consultant who advises companies on the use of social media, isn't drowning in a cascade of information. He's not even trying to ride it out in a barrel. He's surfing Niagara Falls. So what's his secret?

"You have to be Zen-like," he patiently explained to me. "You have to let go of the need to know everything completely."

Michalski can afford to let go a bit, because he has at his disposal a set of powerful and personalized filters: social networks that gather, select, and value information for him. One of these consists of his friends on Twitter. Another is Twine, a collaborative bookmarking tool that keeps you up-to-date on selected topics of interest, or twines, by channeling to you online content that fellow idea junkies who subscribe to your twines have found useful. The software tool also scans other twines and automatically recommends items that seem relevant to your interests.

"I hardly read blog posts anymore unless someone tweets me about it or I get the link in my feed," says Michalski, who is an adviser to Twine. "Trust your community to filter and flow the right things to you when you need them."

Somewhat less ambitious technologies exist to help those of us who are more enervated than enlivened by the flood of information, especially e-mail. New software tools offer an array of ways to better manage your inbox. Some prioritize Outlook messages by importance, as determined by your history with particular senders; sort e-mail threads according to the work project they relate to; or filter out e-mail that is no longer relevant because, for example, someone else has provided specific information sought by the sender. Others automatically turn e-mail messages into tasks or appointments; let you know how much time you spend responding to messages; and even fetch information from blogs and internet news feeds about people you e-mail, so that you can, for example, congratulate a customer on a recent success (though this, of course, adds to your inflow of information).

If you're more e-mail addict than victim (a semantic difference, perhaps), a Google engineer has devised something to fight your need for a fix. It's an optional link on your Gmail page that, when you click it, turns your screen gray and displays the message "Break time! Take a walk, get some real work done, or have a snack. We'll be back in 15 minutes"—and then counts down the time until you're able to resume checking messages.

Help for Individuals: A NEW MIND-SET

It may be true that people can't overcome an addiction without help, whether support group or technology. But in the end it's up to you to take control of your information problem. And that means modifying your thinking and behavior.

One approach is to religiously adopt one of the disciplines advocated by personal-productivity gurus—for example, David Allen's "getting things done" method (breezily referred to as GTD by the enlightened). But you had better know yourself well enough to determine whether a particular creed is right for you. For example, the familiar advice to check your inbox no more than several times a day won't help if you are someone who is racked by anxiety as you imagine the growing glut of ignored messages.

Or what about a simple mantra? Maybe "inbox zero," Merlin Mann's imperative to never let e-mail accumulate. Or "five.sentenc.es," the address of a single-page website that challenges people to adopt, as an antidote to procrastination in answering e-mail, "a personal policy that all email responses regardless of recipient or subject will be five sentences or less."

Regaining some productivity may require you to shed feelings of guilt and inadequacy about not promptly answering e-mail. Adopt Jerry Michalski's Zen-like attitude. Or follow author Clay Shirky's advice and abandon any hope of keeping up, accepting that you simply cannot read, never mind respond to, all your messages, even those from people you know. The aforementioned AOL survey reported that 26% of e-mail users have either declared or are considering "e-mail bankruptcy." The rash act of deleting all of your messages will leave your e-mail creditors unsatisfied, but it may be just the fresh start you need. (I haven't resorted to this—yet.)

Help for Companies: TECHNOLOGY

Max Christoff is wary of the eye-popping estimates of information overload's cost—one puts the total negative impact on the U.S. economy at nearly $1 trillion—because they often fail to consider the value of information, including that conveyed by the much-maligned e-mail. But Christoff, executive director of information technology at Morgan Stanley, knows the challenges individuals face in managing masses of information. So he's experimenting with ways to ameliorate the problem for employees at the financial services firm.

For example, his team has developed software designed to mediate e-mail interruptions by distinguishing urgent messages from those that may be important but don't require immediate attention. It takes into account a variety of factors, including whether the sender is a client or someone else the recipient has flagged. The software could be tailored to a particular user's behavior—for example, classifying as urgent messages those from senders whose e-mail the recipient typically turns to first. But that makes the classification criteria less transparent, which tends to make users anxious. "If people don't trust the system, they'll interrupt themselves and go check their non-urgent messages to be sure mistakes weren't made," Christoff says.

Christoff's modest efforts to tackle information overload at Morgan Stanley are unusual. Although nearly everyone acknowledges that individuals, to varying degrees, pay a personal price in their struggles to manage e-mail and other types of information, few businesses have viewed the challenge as a corporate issue.

Organizations are increasingly realizing, though, that they stand to benefit from helping people get a better handle on the problem. Besides enabling individuals to process information more efficiently, companies should also encourage them to be more selective and intelligent about creating and distributing information in the first place.

Several new technologies focus on regulating e-mail volume within an organization. A pilot software tool called Postware requires employees to affix a noncash "stamp" to each internal e-mail they send, drawing from a fixed daily allotment. A market-based system known as Attent, developed by a company called Seriosity, allots users equal amounts of a virtual currency, which they use to attach a value to each message as a signal of importance. Recipients can then prioritize their inboxes on the basis of the value assigned to individual messages. The currency on incoming messages is deposited in the recipient's account for use on later outgoing e-mails. Of course, "wealthy" e-mail users, who receive lots of currency from senders seeking their attention, will have more to spend on outgoing e-mail, possibly skewing the apparent importance of messages from them.

Other, more futuristic tools under development aim to sense our work patterns and determine when we don't want to be bothered. Microsoft researchers are developing a set of applications, dubbed Priorities, that might, for example, delay someone's e-mail alerts by gauging not only a message's urgency but also the recipient's receptiveness to an interruption. The software would automatically assess the message (Does it include a phrase like "as soon as you can"?), the user's activity (Are you in a scheduled meeting with someone from your client contact list?), and the user's mental state (Have you been actively working on a document that has led you to ignore other alerts in the past few days?).

IBM is working on a program called IM Savvy, an instant-messaging "answering machine." It senses when you are busy—by, for example, detecting your typing or mouse patterns—and tells would-be interrupters that you aren't available. But the tool gives senders the option of interrupting you anyway if they must. "The problem with intelligent [software] agents that stand between you and interruptions is that if they get it wrong and don't interrupt you, even just once, there may be a high price to pay," says Jennifer Lai, the leader of the IM Savvy team.

Help for Companies: CULTURE CHANGE

A company's responses to information overload will invariably require not only technology but also a change in collective behavior. That can begin with education. Nathan Zeldes, the former Intel engineer, combined technology and education in a real-time software tool called the Intel Email Effectiveness Coach, designed to help users achieve productive e-mail behavior. When the user clicks on Send, but before the message is transmitted, the program gently warns about potential e-mail blunders and breaches of etiquette—for instance, a "Reply to All" that will send the message to everyone on the distribution list.

Companies also need to establish organizational norms for electronic communication, either explicit or implicit. If a standard is implicit, senior executives should set an example. No employee wants to be the first to abandon a practice that contributes to e-mail overload, such as sending weekly reports to all division heads simply to maintain visibility.

A firm might create a weekly "e-mail–free morning": a ban on in-house, though not external, e-mail (and possibly phone calls, instant messages, and drop-in chats). The aim would be to carve out an extended stretch of relatively uninterrupted time.

Or a manager might identify for her direct reports situations in which an in-person exchange or a phone call should replace an e-mail—not so much to foster face-to-face interactions as to speed decision making. When three or four e-mails have bounced around a group, someone may simply need to pick up the phone and settle the issue at hand.

The IT department could come up with guidelines specifying the preferred communication channels for different types of information. For example, e-mail could be reduced significantly if group newsletters and announcements were posted on a company intranet or wiki, which pulls in people seeking the information instead of pushing it at them. A rule of thumb: If the information in an e-mail you're about to send, even if potentially important in the future, is not urgent, post rather than push.

The IT folks could also replace those irksome confirmation-of-receipt requests from senders with auto-responses from recipients. Such responses would alert senders to your personal schedule for answering e-mail and urge them to phone if something needs attention sooner than you are likely to respond. That could reduce confusion stemming from differences in people's unspoken expectations. If I think of an e-mail as something to be answered within the business day and you think of it as something to be answered upon receipt, ill will and bungled decisions may ensue. If you escalate the contacts—instant message, voice mail, a huffy visit to my cubicle—you'll end up increasing the total volume of information related to a single request.

When suggested norms, such as not sending e-mails to colleagues after 10 PM, fail to stick, encouragement can become enforcement—shutting down e-mail servers at 10:01. (In what some saw as a draconian move, an exasperated CIO at ratings firm Nielsen Media Research recently ordered the e-mail system's "Reply to All" function to be disabled.)

Strict measures may ultimately be necessary because information overload has an ethical dimension. One person's urgent e-mail request for information, of unquestioned value to the sender, usually comes at a significant price for the interrupted recipient, for whom the request may be neither urgent nor important. (The down arrow in Outlook, indicating to the recipient that the message is of low importance, has always intrigued me: Even when it is used, which is rarely, many people open the message immediately, curious to see what content warranted the designation.)

In looking for ways to reduce the burden of information overload, an organization must strive to balance sender benefits against recipient costs. And leaders need to ensure that a solution doesn't simply shift the burden from one group to another, whose shouldering of it will come at a net cost to the organization.

The transfer of burdens: Now there's an appealing notion. Let me seize upon it as an opportunity to shift, once and for all, my burden of recipient's guilt—for failing to promptly answer e-mail—onto the shoulders of those selfish senders of the messages in my inbox.

Ahhh, that's better. Maybe information overload isn't so bad after all.

10 Ways to Reduce E-mail Overload

AN OVERWHELMING VOLUME OF ADVICE is available on how to manage e-mail more effectively. Here are some favorite tips I've gleaned from websites such as Lifehacker, 43folders, and Davidco—plus a few that grew out of personal mishaps.

As a Recipient

1. To avoid constant distractions, turn off automatic notifications of incoming e-mail. Then establish specific times during the day when you check and take action on messages.
2. Don't waste time sorting messages into folders; inbox search engines make that unnecessary. (One possible exception: Create an "urgent action" folder—but don't forget to check it.)
3. Don't highlight messages you intend to deal with later by marking them as "unread." In Microsoft Outlook, accidentally typing in the wrong keyboard shortcut will irrevocably designate every item in your inbox as "read." ("Undo" isn't an option, it turns out.)
4. If you won't be able to respond to an e-mail for several days, acknowledge receipt and tell the sender when you're likely to get to it.

As a Sender

5. Make messages easy to digest by writing a clear subject line and starting the body with the key point. Use boldface headings, bullet points, or numbering to highlight action items—and to note who's responsible for each one.
6. To eliminate the need for recipients to open very short messages, put the entire contents in the subject line, followed by "eom" (end of message).

7. Whenever possible, paste the contents of an attachment into the body of the message.
8. Minimize e-mail ping pong by making suggestions ("Should we meet at 10?") rather than asking open-ended questions ("When should we meet?").
9. Before you choose "reply to all," stop and consider the e-mail burden that your choice places on each recipient. If you wouldn't be able to justify that burden, remove the recipient from the send list.
10. For your own sake, send less e-mail: An outgoing message generates, on average, roughly two responses.

Michelle LaBrosse

NO

Working Successfully in a Virtual World

Remember when the word *virtual* sounded futuristic? At a time in the not-too-distant past, corporations and managers tried to imagine a world where they couldn't physically see their employees every day. Today, working virtually is a normal part of our workplace. According to a 2005 report by iGillottResearch Inc., the U.S. mobile workforce stood at 56.6 million in 2004, and that figure will rise to more than 61 million by 2009. (The firm defines a mobile employee as anyone who is out of the office more than 20 percent of the week but is still working.)

Although working virtually is part of the norm, often teams and companies still struggle with how to manage virtual teams and virtual projects. I'm passionate about the virtual workplace because it has been the backbone of the growth of my business. My company has over 20 full-time employees and over 50 contractors who work virtually. It is common for them to go several months without face-to-face meetings—and in some cases they may never meet. A virtual model has allowed us to grow globally, with licensee programs in Europe, Australia, Canada, the Far East, South Africa, and South America. This kind of global growth is possible for companies of all sizes because of virtual teams and the technology that fuels the possibilities of the virtual workplace.

Virtual team members can be working in a variety of environments. They can be working from home offices, or telecommuting centers that their employer operates; they can be sharing offices or desks based on travel and work schedules; or they can be road warriors who spend most of their workday traveling.

Regardless of where employees are working from, building a virtual model provides benefits for the employer and employees, including:

- **A larger talent pool.** Working virtually means you have access to the best employees, because you can recruit from anywhere in the world.
- **Flexibility.** Flexibility is not only attractive to prospective employees, but also a competitive advantage that allows you to respond quickly to changes in your market.
- **Increased productivity.** Employees spend less time commuting, creating less stress and wear and tear from traveling, and affording more time to balance work and family life. The time employees gain to

spend on business tasks can be more focused; often, working outside a traditional office can be more fluid, with fewer interruptions.

- **Opportunities for globalization.** Globalization is no longer for the big guys. It's really about having access. With a global team, the workday can be 24 hours instead of eight.
- **Fewer expenses.** Both travel and real estate expenses are decreased substantially in a virtual model.
- **Less environmental impact.** Virtual workplaces have an eco-friendly benefit—as they decrease commuting, they also decrease both traffic congestion and air pollution.
- **More inclusive workforce.** Virtual work environments also give workers with physical challenges more opportunities.

Who Works Well in a Virtual Environment?

In his book *Good to Great,*[1] Jim Collins told us to put the "right people on the bus." That's even more important in a virtual environment. You not only have to hire the right people for the job, but also hire people who can succeed virtually.

Who are the best candidates for working in a virtual workplace? People who are self-starters and who don't need to be micromanaged or heavily monitored are more likely to succeed in a virtual workplace. They need to be comfortable running projects and responsible for completing the deliverables of their projects.

People who love what they're doing work well virtually. It's difficult to keep people engaged when they don't have a passion for what they're doing. So, when I hire, I look for passion.

If the individuals don't like to carry a BlackBerry and a cell phone or work across multiple time zones and aren't very technically literate to start with, it makes it incredibly difficult to thrive in a virtual environment. We conduct a capability assessment as part of the hiring process to ensure that candidates will fit in this environment. This assessment looks at their current skill level, analyzes their strengths and weaknesses, and maps this information to their job descriptions. Time and again, we see that being highly technically literate is a primary prerequisite for success.

The New Water Cooler

Leaders used to worry about the loss of the water cooler, but I think the virtual world has become the new water cooler—even in physical locations. When you go into companies these days, they are often very quiet—because everyone is communicating via e-mail and instant messaging (IM). E-mail, IM, conference calls, and Webinars can connect teams and create community.

The Tools and the Rules

Once you have the right team members, you need to give them the right tools and some ground rules for success.

The right tools are easy enough to find. Most of us already have them or have access to them: e-mail, instant messaging, conferencing (both video- and tele-), cell phones, BlackBerries, Webinars, and collaborative work tools like the Wiki.

Ground Rules

Once the tools are in place for your organization, the biggest barriers are often around communications and work culture. Ground rules that focus on them can increase your team's productivity and let you reap the rewards of the virtual workforce.

- **Build trust.** In order for people to work effectively virtually, there has to be trust. Trust doesn't happen magically. It is built when you bring your team together for training or team building, and it continues to grow with clear expectations consistently set by leaders and met by the team. Launching the project with a face-to-face meeting is a great way to kick off a virtual project. If you can't meet in person, you can do virtual team-building activities. For example, you can have everyone on the team create a profile on Facebook or MySpace—with the objective of having team members give more of a sense of who they are as people.

  A team builder that we've had great success with when we bring our people together is building kayaks. Our project-management techniques are embedded into the activity, and it's very revealing from a team-building perspective. I often learn a lot as the leader watching the activity, and it gives me insight about people's leadership skills and their ability to follow a process.
- **Set expectations with a project agreement.** Project agreements help to eliminate unnecessary conflict because objectives, expectations, time lines, and roles and responsibilities are clearly defined. In a virtual environment, it's important to regularly update the project agreement and post it to the collaborative work environment or e-mail it out to the team.
- **Manage results, not activity.** In the physical office environment, "busy work" often gets mistaken for real work. In the virtual environment, when you can't see what people are doing, the key is to manage results. Monitor and measure the results, and be clear about the goals.
- **Schedule regular communication.** It's important that there is a regular time for reporting both progress and potential pitfalls to the team. This keeps people on track and gives everyone the discipline of a team check-in. It's ideal if there is a standing time every week or every month—depending on your project milestones. Remember to build in time for feedback, coaching, and support.
- **Create communication that saves time.** Have you created an e-mail culture that wastes time with endless "daisy-chain" conversations that take several hours to read? Does your team spend hours trying to solve an issue with an e-mail conversation that could have been solved with a 30-minute conference call? Because e-mail is such a critical tool in our work environments, it's important to create a new

culture of effectiveness around it. Train employees to write meaningful subject lines that communicate what the e-mail is about. Also, make sure they lead with what is important and who needs to take action on what. Many deadlines can be missed when the action is buried in paragraph 12.

- **Create standards that build a cohesive culture.** What are your standards of quality? How do you define excellence? What does your brand mean to each employee? Making sure everyone knows the answers to those three questions is even more important when people are scattered geographically. Virtually, you need to create cohesion with excellence and a sense of pride in what your company stands for.
- **Define rules of responsiveness.** When people are working remotely, it's important that you define what the rules of responsiveness are for your culture. How quickly are people expected to return an e-mail, an instant message, or a phone call? What is your protocol when people are out of the office or on vacation? If you're in a customer service environment, it's important to have clear expectations regarding how to respond to all customer inquiries.
- **Use collaborative tools like the Wiki:** Working virtually is *not* about platitudes. It is about systems—creating the systems that enable people to do their work from anywhere and everywhere. There has to be a very strong commitment to giving people the tools they need to help run the business and serve the customers. If they have to go somewhere to answer the phone to serve the customers, they cannot work virtually.

We use a Wiki—an online work environment—as a central hub for our work. This allows us to coordinate our projects and processes in one place and easily see the progress we're making. It's a living memory for our organization, capturing our intellectual capital. We started this for the marketing group to reduce the e-mail and to better capture the various marketing initiatives and decisions. Within one week, it was adopted by all the other people in the company: IT projects, facilities to coordinate facility work, accounting to coordinate budgeting with the different parts of the business, and course development to keep track of course upgrades. It has increased our productivity and also created a central "memory" for all of our work.

- **Pay attention to cultural cues and time zones.** When you're working on a global team, you need to be sensitive to the time zones that in which you are working. For example, in which time zone are the deadlines relevant? Are you scheduling calls at a time that works best for all time zones? Also, remember that cross-cultural communication becomes even more of an issue in e-mail. Pay attention to how your colleagues communicate in e-mail. How formal are they? How are they addressing each other? Don't automatically assume an informal tone until you have gained the trust and respect of your team.
- **Create an attitude of gratitude.** Reward people when they do well. Especially when people are working virtually, they need to know when they've made a difference. We created a program called "The Attitude of Gratitude" where people have 2,000 points every month

to distribute to their coworkers to thank them for whatever they did during the month. The top three people with the most points at the end of the month win. First place is something worth $500, second place is worth $300, and third place is worth $200. It's a companywide employee-recognition program that everyone participates in, and it creates both buzz and community.

Working virtually is not a trend. It's a way of life today. So, focus on what you can do to be a better manager or team member. These tips are a good starting point as you build your own best practices for effective project management in the virtual world. Enjoy the journey and invite your team to help you create a powerful work culture.

Note

1. Collins, J. (2001). *Good to great: Why some companies make the leap . . . and others don't*. London: Random House.

EXPLORING THE ISSUE

Does Increased Dependence on Laptops, Cell Phones, and PDAs Hurt Employee Productivity?

Critical Thinking and Reflection

1. What suggestions do you have to mitigate the information overload syndrome in organizations today?
2. How does information overload rob an employee's quality of work/life?
3. What do you see as the advantages of working in a 24/7 virtual environment?
4. What are some alternate perspectives that HRM professionals may pursue to reduce the problems of information overload?
5. What would you suggest to reduce employees' usage of the Internet for personal reasons?

Is There Common Ground?

Organizations are now truly concerned that increased dependence on external devices that are supposed to make employees more productive are having negative consequences. Employees frequently want to check their technological devices during work creating terms such as infomania, infoglut, and click syndrome, among several others. Intel, a leading hardware company, suggests that employees lose almost $1 billion in terms of reduced work efficiency and employee work distractions due to their immense dependence on their technological devices. Are such technology devices a boon or a bane? Proponents suggest that current technology is a boon and a blessing for employees as it helps employees to balance work and life and allows them to communicate effortlessly with their global counterparts. HR experts also suggest organizations will benefit by introducing an Internet monitoring system. This could be definitely met with employee resistance but finally will help toward the organization's goals. Will you like to work in an environment that has Internet monitoring? Why? Why not?

Additional Resources

Craig, T. (2008). How to avoid information overload. *Personnel Today, 31.*

Firoz, N. M., Taghi, R., and Souckova, J. (2006). E-mails in the workplace: The electronic equivalent of "DNA" evidence. *Journal of American Academy of Business, Cambridge, 8*(2), 71–78.

Hornung, M. S. (2005). Think before you type: A look at email privacy in the workplace. *Fordham Journal of Corporate & Financial Law, 11*(1), 115–160.

Rubel, S. (2008). Too much infotechnology can lead to brain overload. *Advertising Age, 79*(7), 18.

Spira, J. (2007). From knowledge to distraction. *KM World, 16*(3), 1, 32.

Sweetnam, S. (2006). Email tactics. *T + D, 60*(1), 13.

Totty, M. (2007). Office technology; operation overload: Software tools allow people to manage the clutter that threatens to overwhelm their daily lives. *Wall Street Journal* (Eastern Edition).

www.refresher.com/mindfulnetwork/articlelive/articles/35/1/Information-Overload/Page1.html: Information Overload.

http://online.wsj.com/article/SB124683648696297965.html: Information Overload? Relax.

www.marketwatch.com/story/information-overload-deal-with-it: Are We Overwhelmed Yet?

www.infogineering.net/understanding-information-overload.htm: Understanding Information Overload.

www.nypost.com/p/news/business/jobs/going_under_CYfNjDpebuvcfWpSPfV4VJ: Going Under: Information Overload Is Drowning Office Workers.

ISSUE 12

Do Unions Help Organizational Productivity?

YES: AFL-CIO, from "Unions Are Good for Business, Productivity, and the Economy," http://www.aflcio.org/joinaunion/why/uniondifference/uniondiff8.cfm (2009)

NO: Dennis K. Berman, from "The Game—Dr. Z's Chrysler Predicament: Selling Unions on Sacrifice," *Wall Street Journal* (Eastern Edition) (April 24, 2007)

Learning Outcomes

After reading this issue, you should be able to:

- Define collective bargaining and the various types of unions.
- Gain an understanding on the positive HRM outcomes of unionized workforces.
- Describe the disadvantages of an unionized workforce.
- Provide alternate perspectives that HRM professionals can pursue to labor unions.
- Describe how organizations use labor unions in European and Latin American countries.

ISSUE SUMMARY

YES: The American Federation of Labor and Congress of Industrial Organizations (AFL-CIO) Web site identifies the work of Professor Harley Shaiken, from the University of California–Berkeley, who states the positive impact of unions on HRM outcomes.

NO: Dennis Berman, *Wall Street Journal* journalist and 2003 Pulitzer Prize winner, argues that the current state of the auto industry is mainly due to excessive demands of the unions. The high cost of maintaining labor is passed on to the consumers and reduces organizational profit margins.

Unions are labor organizations that allow employees to negotiate with their employers about areas of employment such as pay and benefits, employee grievances, hours of employment, labor disputes, and conditions of work, among others. Employees work together as an entity to collectively bargain for their interests with the management. The mutual agreement between employers and employees is called the collective bargaining agreement, which identifies comprehensively the work-related interests of any union. In 1935, the National Labor Relations Act was established to provide a mechanism to settle any problems between the management and the labor.

Unions can be local, national, or international. Local unions usually represent employees of a local organization or plant. National unions usually represent employees from a particular craft or industry from any part of the nation (United Auto Workers, United Steelworkers). International unions represent employees from a particular craft or industry on a global scale. In the 1970s, approximately 27 percent of the workforce was unionized in the United States, while in 2011 only about 12 percent of the workforce is unionized. Federal employees are five times more likely to be unionized than private employees. The membership in unions slowly declined over the years as unionized workforces were considered to be very contentious. Further, the economy has been moving slowly from a manufacturing to a service environment which is characterized as being less unionized.

Professor Harley Shaiken, from the University of California–Berkeley, suggests that unionized workforces provide several positive organizational outcomes. They include higher productivity, lower employee turnover, improved workplace communication, and a better-trained workforce. Studies also suggest that because of such positive HRM outcomes unionized workforces are 22 percent more productive than nonunionized workforces. Organizations that have unions seem to provide increased quality of products or services. The classic example of a unionized workforce producing excellent products is Saturn Corporation, the automobile corporation that produces excellent cars. Unionized workforces are more likely to demand for training which results in higher quality of products and services. Organizations with unions also have demonstrated reduced employee turnovers because of opportunities available through collective bargaining to improve their work conditions. Members of labor unions also display a very collaborative approach to any problem solving as they are unified in their broader causes. Such positive HRM outcomes have shown to contribute to the bottom-line profits of any organization.

On the other hand, a Wall Street journalist suggests that unions have tremendous negative effects on organizations. A contemporary example is that of the auto industry that has filed for bankruptcy due to excessive labor union demands. As unions increase their demands excessively, the effects are seen substantially on the increased prices of the final products and services. This generally squeezes into the profit levels of organizations. The filing of bankruptcy by the automobile companies has shown the business world the negative effects that labor unions may have.

The current debacle of the auto industry seems to make scholars and practitioners very distrustful of their existence. The United Auto Workers (UAW) has a very tight hold over the operation of the auto industry. The UAW are also identified for some of their unreasonable demands—a case in point: JOBS bank, an excessive labor benefit. This benefit, an agreement between the auto industry and the UAW, allowed the employees to receive 85 percent of their wages even if they are laid off or absent from work. This benefit was referred to as the corporate jet perk of the auto industry unions as it seemed ridiculous and unreasonable. The whole nation witnessed the financial debacle when the auto industries sought a bailout from the government as they were struggling to remain profitable. UAW workers are more expensive to maintain than Japanese or European auto workers. For instance, UAW employees receive on an average $18 more per hour than Toyota employees.

The ability to strike is the other biggest weapon that unions have that can potentially hamper organizational productivity. Strikes are when an entire group of employees refuse to come to work unless their work demands are met. The word "strike" appeared first in the 1700s when workers in Philadelphia print factories stopped coming to work because they wanted an increase in their wages. The trend to use strikes to meet work demands was frequently used by labor unions over the decades. A classic example of the power of strikes was that of air traffic controllers in 1981 when thousands of employees demonstrated a strike demanding for better wages, work, and benefits. The former President Reagan intervened as the entire air industry came to an absolute standstill. Professor Peter Morici, an authority on unions, indicates that the unions' power to bring any work to an absolute standstill is what makes the model of labor unions completely flawed.

Unions being controversial have made several occupation groups reconsider alternatives they may pursue. The teachers' unions are an example of how several states have established their own educators' organizations to handle any labor grievances. Membership into these organizations is voluntary and not mandatorily imposed. Several states have their own independent teacher organizations to protect the rights of their members. The national teachers' organization, Association of American Educators, offers several benefits to teachers who do not want to belong to a union. Similarly other trade occupations have established their own professional organizations to represent their rights without the contentious agenda of labor unions.

Other alternative organizations are choosing to reduce their reliance on unionized workers are to outsource, to adopt nonunionized policies, and to introduce progressive human resource management practices. GM decided to outsource its core and noncore manufacturing to external vendors to diminish its dependence on unionized labor. Walmart, the retail giant, is able to provide its low cost to customers and avoid unionized labor through targeted outsourcing. GM, the automobile leader, recently introduced a nonunion policy in one of their plants in Michigan, though it has historically been unionized. This might be just a new beginning for a company that has been traditionally exploited and dependent on their unions. Experts also suggest providing progressive human resource management practices will greatly reduce the dependence on labor unions. These practices provide employees empowerment and job satisfaction creating a work environment of high performance. For instance, the BMW plant in South Carolina has invested tremendously in its employees that they feel a deep sense of loyalty and commitment to the company.

An international perspective suggests that European workforces are much more unionized with countries such as the Netherlands, Denmark, and Sweden having almost 80 percent of their workforce unionized. In countries like Germany, institutional practices such as codetermination and work councils are very powerful expressions of the labor unions. These labor practices allow board representation of labor members, making employers and employees negotiate for work-related benefits at the same board level. In several Latin American countries, labor unions are considered more as political platforms, with unions and political parties working very closely toward mutual causes.

YES 

AFL-CIO

Unions Are Good for Business, Productivity and the Economy

According to Professor Harley Shaiken of the University of California-Berkeley, unions are associated with higher productivity, lower employee turnover, improved workplace communication, and a better-trained workforce. Prof. Shaiken is not alone. There is a substantial amount of academic literature on the following benefits of unions and unionization to employers and the economy:

- Economic Growth
- Productivity
- Competitiveness
- Product or service delivery and quality
- Training
- Turnover
- Solvency of the firm
- Workplace health and safety
- Economic development

Economic Growth

During the period 1945–1973, when a high percentage of workers had unions, wages kept pace with rising productivity, prosperity was widely shared, and economic growth was strong. Since 1973, union density and collective bargaining have declined, causing real wages to stagnate despite rising productivity. This decline in union density and bargaining contributed to the current financial crisis and severe recession, as unsustainable asset appreciation and easy credit took the place of wage increases most workers were not getting.

Productivity

According to a recent survey of 73 independent studies on unions and productivity: "The available evidence points to a positive and statistically significant association between unions and productivity in the U.S. manufacturing and education sectors, of around 10 and 7 percent, respectively."

Some scholars have found an even larger positive relationship between unions and productivity. According to Brown and Medoff, "unionized establishments are about 22 percent more productive than those that are not."

Product/Service Delivery and Quality

According to Professors Michael Ash and Jean Ann Seago heart attack recovery rates are higher in hospitals where nurses are unionized than in non-union hospitals. According to Professor Paul Clark, nurse unions improve patient care by raising staff-to-patient ratios, limiting excessive overtime, and improving nurse training.

Another study looked at the relationship between unionization and product quality in the auto industry. According to a summary of this study prepared by American Rights at Work:

> The author examines the system of co-management created through the General Motors-United Auto Workers partnership at the Saturn Corporation. . . . The author credits the union with building a dense communications network throughout Saturn's management system. Compared to non-represented advisors, union advisors showed greater levels of lateral communication and coordination, which had a significant positive impact on quality performance.

Training

Several studies have found a positive association between unionization and the amount and quality of workforce training. Unionized establishments are more likely to offer formal training. This is especially true for small firms. There are a number of reasons for this: less turnover among union workers, making the employer more likely to offer training; collective bargaining agreements that require employers to provide training; and finally, unions often conduct their own training.

Turnover

Professor Shaiken also finds that unions reduce turnover. He cites Freeman and Medoff's finding that "about one fifth of the union productivity effect stemmed from lower worker turnover. Unions improve communication channels giving workers the ability to improve their conditions short of 'exiting.'"

Solvency

Labor's enemies assert that unions drive employers out of business, but academic research refutes this claim. According to Professors Richard Freeman and Morris Kleiner, unionism has a statistically insignificant effect (meaning no effect) on firm solvency. Freeman and Kleiner conclude "unions do not, on average, drive firms or business lines out of business or produce high displacement rates for unionized workers."

Workplace Health and Safety

Employers should be concerned about workplace health and safety as a matter of enlightened self-interest. According to an American Rights at Work summary of a study by John E. Baugher and J. Timmons Roberts:

> Only one factor effectively moves workers who are in subordinate positions to actively cope with hazards: membership in an independent labor union. These findings suggest that union growth could indirectly reduce job stress by giving workers the voice to cope effectively with job hazards.

The benefits of unions in terms of safer workplaces are hardly new. According to one most recent study, unions reduced fatalities in coal mining by an estimated 40 percent between 1897 and 1929.

Economic Development

Unions also play a positive role in economic development. One good example is the Wisconsin Regional Training Partnership, "an association of 125 employers and unions dedicated to family-supporting jobs in a competitive business environment. WRTP members have stabilized manufacturing employment in the Milwaukee metro area, and contributed about 6,000 additional industrial jobs to it over the past five years. Among member firms, productivity is way up—exceeding productivity growth in nonmember firms."

Dennis K. Berman

NO

The Game—Dr. Z's Chrysler Predicament: Selling Unions on Sacrifice

Abstract (Summary)

"They clearly have to do something different than what they're doing now," says Paul Walser, owner of the Walser Chrysler Jeep dealership in Hopkins, Minn. "It's not working."

Piled on when the U.S auto industry was far more dominant, these costs erode what little profit the company can turn. In the past five years, Chrysler's $2.7 billion in operating profit actually morphed into a $1.75 billion loss when factoring in these payments. It is why many bankers say the company's value is a fraction of the $39 billion price Daimler originally paid. In fact, they say this bundle of liabilities is worth zero. Things could well turn around, but Daimler has made it clear it doesn't have the patience. It wants a sale. Fast.

"We're not interested in equity," Mr. [Buzz Hargrove] said. "We've met the test in terms of quality productivity and are not about to give. It ain't going to happen with our union."

Forget about making better cars. Or even about the rise of private equity. The best way to understand the sale of Chrysler Group is as blood sport between parent DaimlerChrysler and its North American unions.

Is DaimlerChrysler willing to get fully ruthless with its employees, in spite of its well-hewn image as loveable corporate citizen? The answer will make for some gripping theater in the months ahead. That is because this deal really is about persuading the company's unions to roll back their own health and pension benefits.

The stock market already is acting like an agreement is nigh, having added $20 billion in value to Daimler since the auto maker said it was considering a sale. But the market underestimates just what rough business this separation is going to be.

"If people buying it think they're going to get concessions out of us, it's not going to happen," said Buzz Hargrove, head of the Canadian Auto Workers union, in an interview.

To first approach the problem, it is best to consider the 82-year-old Chrysler Group less like a car company and more like a hard-luck case. The company carries an estimated $18 billion in unfunded health-care and other benefit costs, all of which weigh heavily on the business.

"They clearly have to do something different than what they're doing now," says Paul Walser, owner of the Walser Chrysler Jeep dealership in Hopkins, Minn. "It's not working."

Piled on when the U.S auto industry was far more dominant, these costs erode what little profit the company can turn. In the past five years, Chrysler's $2.7 billion in operating profit actually morphed into a $1.75 billion loss when factoring in these payments. It is why many bankers say the company's value is a fraction of the $39 billion price Daimler originally paid. In fact, they say this bundle of liabilities is worth zero. Things could well turn around, but Daimler has made it clear it doesn't have the patience. It wants a sale. Fast.

"Unless the [United Auto Workers] is willing to modernize the workplace and abandon its class-warfare labor negotiations, it's impossible to run the company," argues Peter Morici, a University of Maryland business professor and longtime critic of the auto unions.

Daimler suffers from a rich man's conundrum. The profits at its other divisions continue to subsidize Chrysler. The UAW did grant some historic concessions to General Motors and Ford Motor last year. But those were for companies that were truly on the brink. DaimlerChrysler simply isn't. So why should the unions sacrifice?

Daimler's answer is clear: To scare the heck out of the union, by separating it from Daimler. The very idea of separation—any separation—already has proved a windfall for Daimler's stock. There is no turning back now.

But for this gambit to work, DaimlerChrysler's chief executive, Dieter Zetsche, will have to prove exactly the opposite of the affable, avuncular character he played in his company's own television commercials.

Consider his predicament. A buyer isn't going to take on Chrysler without some guarantees of reduced worker costs. Either Daimler can hang on to those costs, invalidating the purpose of the whole exercise, or the new buyers have to coax the workers into giving something up.

Prospective private-equity bidders Blackstone Group, Centerbridge Capital Partners and Ceberus Capital Management are considering trading workers' hard benefit checks for much murkier stock of a newly split Chrysler. That has yet to inspire much joy, and who can blame them. The unions typically value such equity at zero, according to a person who has worked with their bargaining committees in the past. The best bet might come from Canadian car-parts concern Magna International Inc., which at least has a tradeable stock that is easy to value and is said to be the preferred option for the unions.

"We're not interested in equity," Mr. Hargrove said. "We've met the test in terms of quality productivity and are not about to give. It ain't going to happen with our union."

Expect the unions to be especially resistant once the personal wealth of Blackstone founder Stephen A. Schwarzman is revealed when that firm files more detailed initial public offering documents. That number could top a flabbergasting $20 billion—not exactly an owner who compels one to accept a smaller paycheck.

This is where Dr. Zetsche's ruthlessness will be put to the test. If the unions won't budge, he might have to ratchet up the threats to get them to the bargaining table. These threats could be everything from a piecemeal break-up to closing large parts of the company or even a bankruptcy filing.

Whether reasonable or not, such threats ring hollow coming from a company with the both the profits and imprimatur of Mercedes-Benz. No one feels sorry for the guy in the S600 sedan.

This will make it very hard for Dr. Zetsche to really pressure the company's U.S. unions—and run the risk of alienating the company's German workers, too.

Daimler probably will find a willing buyer for Chrysler. But doing so will likely mean it taking on the bulk of the liabilities it thought it was shedding in the first place. C'est la guerre, Dr. Z.

EXPLORING THE ISSUE

Do Unions Help Organizational Productivity?

Critical Thinking and Reflection

1. Define collective bargaining and the different types of unions?
2. What are the most important advantages of having a unionized workforce?
3. What are some negative outcomes of having labor unions?
4. Do you think the JOBS bank perk was reasonable? Why? Why not?
5. What are some alternate perspectives that HRM professionals may pursue to reduce the dependence on labor unions?
6. How do other countries perceive the role of labor unions in their workforce?

Is There Common Ground?

Labor unions were formed initially to ensure that employees have a powerful voice at the workplace and also to maintain a balance of power between employers and employees. On the positive side, unionized organizations have demonstrated several positive results such as increased productivity, reduced turnover, and increased internal communication. On the other side, critics of labor unions suggest they are only an expense and do not have any positive effects. In 2008, unionized workforces received 21 percent higher wages and also 40 percent more benefits than nonunionized labor forces. HRM professionals offer several alternatives to unions such as outsourcing, nonunion strategies, and effective HRM practices. What do you think will be effective in reducing the role of unions? What are some practices that the BMW plant offers its employees to enhance their engagement and commitment? Is outsourcing a good strategy to avoid the reliance on labor unions?

Additional Resources

Anonymous. (2008). Reasons to oppose a union. *Management Report, 27*(11), 7–8.

Vaughan, M. (2009). High state taxes hit union workers harder. *Wall Street Journal* (Eastern Edition), A.5.

http://www.ehow.com/about_5097523_pros-cons-labor-unions.html: The Pros and Cons of Labor Unions.

http://www.edubook.com/pros-and-cons-of-labor-unions/9111/: Pros and Cons of Labor Unions.

http://www.epi.org/economic_snapshots/entry/webfeatures_snapshots_20070620/: Strong Unions, Strong Productivity.

http://www3.signonsandiego.com/stories/2009/sep/07/labor-day-reverence-lost-say-historians/: Labor Day Reverence Is Lost, Say Historians.

http://money.howstuffworks.com/strike1.htm: How Strikes Work.

http://www.npr.org/templates/story/story.php?storyId=5604656: 1981 Strike Leaves Legacy for American Workers.

http://crossroadsmag.eu/2009/07/dutch-labour-participation-rate-one-of-the-highest-in-the-eu/: Dutch Labour Participation Rate One of the Highest in the EU.

http://www.psrf.org/issues/teachers.jsp: Teachers, Unions and Professional Alternatives: A Question of Choice.

http://news.heartland.org/newspaper-article/1999/07/01/teachers-find-alternatives-national-unions: Teachers Find Alternatives to National Unions.

http://labornotes.org/blogs/2010/02/gm%E2%80%99s-%E2%80%9Cnorthern-strategy%E2%80%9D-go-non-union: GM's "Northern Strategy": Go Non-Union.

http://www.uri.edu/research/lrc/research/papers/Carter_Union_Avoidance.pdf: Union Avoidance Practices: Differential Effects of Three Strategies.

Internet References . . .

The Good and Bad of Teacher Merit Pay

This site is filled with relevant educator's information about San Benito and their schools, faculty, and the students. It also provides a link for additional research on teacher merit pay.

http://www.sanbenito.k12.tx.us/Hot%20News/042604hotnews.html

How Should Pay Be Linked to Performance?

Harvard Business School Working Knowledge is a forum for innovation in business practices, such as pay for performance. The information here offers readers a first look at cutting-edge thinking and the opportunity to both influence and use these concepts before they enter mainstream management practice.

http://hbswk.hbs.edu/item/5703.html

Forced Ranking: Pros and Cons

AllBusiness.com is an online media and e-commerce company that operates one of the premier business sites on the Web. This site addresses real-world business questions and presents practical solutions. Here you will find discussions on, and see both the positive and negative aspects of, forced ranking.

http://www.allbusiness.com/services/educational-services/4283450-1.html

Effects of Excessive CEO Pay on U.S. Society

This award winning article discusses U.S. executive pay from various perspectives.

www.svsu.edu/emplibrary/Whelton%20article.pdf

A Brief History of CEO Pay

This Web link provides an insightful timeline analysis of executive pay over several decades.

www.c-suiteinsight.com/index.php/2011/06/a-brief-history-of-ceo-pay/

UNIT 5

Compensation and Performance Appraisal

Should organizations promote mediocre work performances? Do employees have preferences in the type of rewards they get? Organizations are striving to compensate employees in a way that will help to retain them. Most organizations reward employees a merit pay regardless of their work performance. Firms are debating best methods to attract, acquire, and retain employees. Employers also want to ensure that performance appraisals actually evaluate employee performance. Can organizations compensate and reward employees truly based on their performance?

- Has Merit Pay Lost Its Meaning in the Workplace?
- Is Forced Ranking an Effective Performance Management Approach?
- Is the U.S. Executive Pay Model Flawed?

ISSUE 13

Has Merit Pay Lost Its Meaning in the Workplace?

YES: Fay Hansen, from "Merit-Pay Payoff?" *Workforce Management* (November 2008)

NO: Susan J. Wells, from "No Results, No Raise." *HR Magazine* (vol. 50, no. 5, pp. 76–80, 2005)

Learning Outcomes

After reading this issue, you should be able to:

- Define merit pay as it applies to organizations.
- Gain an understanding of the challenges of adopting merit-pay systems.
- Describe how to establish a system that pays only for merit.
- Identify alternatives of merit-pay systems that HRM professionals may provide.
- Understand international perspectives on the subject.

ISSUE SUMMARY

YES: Fay Hansen, contributing editor for *Workforce Management*, provides studies of leading professors from Stanford and MIT which suggest that merit pay has lost its meaning because employees are not being actually rewarded for performance. They assert that this compensation system is not distinguishing between success and failure and hence has lost its meaning in the workplace.

NO: S. J. Wells, a writer for *HR Magazine*, contends that organizations should become rigorous in establishing a pay-for-performance culture. She provides examples of organizations that have established such practices successfully.

Merit pay can be defined as providing increases in an employee's pay based on his or her job performance. A 2009 study suggests that U.S. human resource leaders will decide how to distribute their organizations' $200 billion in merit increases for their employees. While the amount seems huge, the most contentious piece of the merit pay is that employees are rewarded merit increases regardless of their job performances. On an average, organizations usually provide employees merit increases of approximately 3.6–3.8 percent on their base salaries. Should employees receive merit increases in pay when their performance is mediocre?

Professor Pfeffer of Stanford University suggests that organizations have debated how to reward employees effectively for their performances. Many organizations, such as Hewlett-Packard and Verizon, struggle to identify the best methods to compensate and reward high performers. Organizations vacillate on whether they should provide high bonuses or merit increases for their employees. The main question that remains to be answered is which form of compensation will lead to higher organizational productivity? However, some organizations suggest that when they adopted pay initiatives that identified and rewarded their star performers (such as employee of the month or star of the quarter), it has resulted in dysfunctional practices. Employees have observed a reduced collaborative spirit and a sense of negativity among employees when such reward systems are introduced. Hence, organizations continue to use the traditional merit-pay systems that award a minimum percentage raises regardless of the performance levels. Therefore, employees receive different performance ratings of superior, average, or low yet they obtain the same merit increases. This pay practice may contribute and promote a work culture of mediocrity and consequently to reduced firm performances. Therefore, what is the meaning or value of a merit increase?

Emilio Castilla, assistant professor of MIT, in a study of technically skilled employees, identifies that the main problem of the merit-pay system is establishing a consistent procedure between performance evaluations and merit increases. Organizations should make it very clear to employees that their annual performances will be their defining criteria for their merit-pay increases. Therefore, organizations should adopt rigorous performance ratings that can justify such annual raises. This should be a transparent system so as not to create any complications that are associated with pay and rewards. Further, he adds that the profits of any business experiences should also be included as a component of the merit increases. For instance, if a business unit makes significant profits, employees in that unit should therefore get higher merit increases. A significant negative HR outcome of the traditional merit-pay method is that superior performers feel demoralized as all employees receive the same pay increases. Hence, such star performers leave organizations in hope for better remuneration systems for their work. Why should organizations lose their star performers because of a traditional pay system that does not distinguish the good, the better, and the best well?

Wells, a journalist for the *HR Magazine*, suggests that organizations should proactively establish a rigorous compensation system based on employee performance. He refers to this concept as "tough love," implying a zero tolerance policy for rewarding low performers. Organizations should establish a reward system clearly, communicate the goals frequently, and evaluate employees' performance regularly. Most often organizations have these practices in place but do not enforce them strictly in their organizations. Experts are confident that if the top management reiterates the theme that poor performers will not get the merit increase, a pay-for-performance culture can be instilled.

The NO article also shares how a technology-based company has implemented such a "tough-love" policy and has seen positive organizational outcomes. The management has ensured that employees get the clear message that their base salary increases are completely dependent on their annual performances. The company has also tied the cost-of-living raises to be based on employees' performances. The firm noticed reduced turnover and also exiting of employees who did not like the new performance culture. Another financial organization rewarded its star performers 20 percent increases and did not award any raises to its poor performers. The company noticed a doubling of its stock prices as firm performance increased substantially.

Managers should also know how to provide effective performance reviews to employees. Usually mangers do not provide realistic performance reviews in fear that they might lose their employees. Therefore, it might be imperative that organizations provide additional training so that managers actually provide authentic feedback. Management should also make managers understand what a critical role performance management plays in deciding the quality of their products and services.

An alternative perspective to this issue might be to provide employees another opportunity for appraising their performances. This might give employees a second chance to turn around their inferior performance levels. Experts suggest that employees who have not performed to receive the annual merit increase should be provided additional time so that they may meet job expectations. This might also make employees perceive organizations to be developmental in their approach rather than punitive. Also, it may suggest that employees are at different learning levels and some employees take a longer time to learn some skills and vice versa.

Scholars suggest alternatives to the merit-pay system could be providing lump-sum bonuses. Employees who perform at superior levels should be recognized and rewarded in special ways. These bonus rewards should be provided when employees achieve specific organizational goals. This could alleviate the main problem associated with the annual merit-pay system as superior performers do not feel distinguished from the average or the low performers. Every employee receives the same percent raise regardless of his or her performance. This is a fatal flaw in the merit-pay and performance system of the U.S. corporate world. Several companies are replacing merit-pay systems with pay-for-performance plans to ensure their tops performers are justly rewarded.

An international perspective suggests that merit-pay practices are followed by organizations in other countries also. In the United Kingdom, merit pay is referred to as PRP (performance-related pay). It follows a model similar to that of the U.S. corporate culture of providing annual increases of around 3 percent. In Japan, merit pay was introduced in the early 1990s to diminish the practices of seniority pay. It has been received with mixed reactions as the traditional Japanese school of thought perceives it might disturb the concept of group harmony, which is very important to their collective culture. In 2009, China announced that it would implement merit pay in its public sector services such as teaching and health care to increase productivity in these sectors.

Fay Hansen

Merit-Pay Payoff?

Abstract (Summary)

Human resources executives help manage the $4.5 trillion that US corporations are spending on wages and salaries in 2008 and determine how to distribute the $200 billion increase in wage and salary spending for 2009. Most of this increase will take the form of merit pay, the nearly universal method for distributing wage and salary raises across the US and, increasingly, around the world. The seemingly self-evident premise underlying merit pay and other individual performance-based pay plans is that they produce higher employee and organizational performance. Most companies, however, do not test the actual impact of performance-based rewards on employee behaviors and financial results. Survey reports show years of flat merit increase budgets that barely meet inflation rates and bear no relationship to productivity growth or profitability trends. Emilio Castilla, assistant professor at MIT's Sloan School of Management and a visiting professor at New York University, advises HR executives to pursue collaboration with academic researchers.

It doesn't exist, several recognized experts say. The issue for companies is not whether they should be paying more for performance compensation programs, but whether they should be paying less.

When Verizon Business announced the completion of the first next-generation trans-Pacific undersea optical cable system in September, senior vice president for human resources Robert Toohey was buried in budget decisions. "A big struggle is deciding whether you invest more in merit pay or short-term incentives," he says. "Am I going to get more out of higher bonuses or a 2 percent increase in fixed pay through merit increases? Which will drive employees to perform better?"

Verizon Business, based in Basking Ridge, New Jersey, is one of the three operating units of Verizon Communications. The unit generated $21.2 billion in revenue in 2007 and employs 32,000 workers worldwide. Pay decisions carry huge consequences. "You can't walk into finance and tell them you want to spend another $50 million on merit pay without a business case," Toohey says.

Human resources executives help manage the $4.5 trillion that U.S. corporations are spending on wages and salaries in 2008 and determine how to distribute the $200 billion increase in wage and salary spending for 2009. Most of this increase will take the form of merit pay, the nearly universal method for distributing wage and salary raises across the U.S. and, increasingly, around the world.

A large part of the remainder will go to a complex array of incentive plans. Spending on variable pay plans for salaried exempt employees as a percentage of payroll will reach 10.6 percent in 2009, with 90 percent of all organizations using at least one variable plan, Hewitt Associates says.

The seemingly self-evident premise underlying merit pay and other individual performance-based pay plans is that they produce higher employee and organizational performance. Most companies, however, do not test the actual impact of performance-based rewards on employee behaviors and financial results. The most comprehensive empirical studies flow from the academic world, where evidence is mounting that the assumptions underlying individual performance-based pay programs are wrong.

With the drive for evidence-based management now moving across all corporate functions, the sheer force of intuitive practices and the shortage of obvious alternatives no longer suffice as justifications for rewards programs that tear into corporate resources. The real question posed by the best research is not whether companies should be spending more for individual performance pay programs, but whether they should be spending less.

Meritless Pay

One of the most forceful advocates for evidence-based management is Jeffrey Pfeffer, the Thomas D. Dee II professor of organizational behavior at Stanford University's Graduate School of Business. Drawing from his own work and citing three decades of empirical studies, Pfeffer testified before a 2007 congressional hearing on federal personnel reform that the idea that individual pay for performance will enhance organizational performance rests on a set of assumptions that do not hold in the vast majority of organizations.

Pfeffer, with the full support of other recognized experts, continues to sharpen the challenge that now sits squarely before human resources executives and compensation directors.

"The evidence is overwhelming that individual pay for performance does not improve organizational performance except in very limited cases," he says. "Why do people, when confronted with the facts, turn their backs on them?"

Given the lack of evidence that merit pay boosts employee performance and organizational results, should companies abandon it?

"We've already abandoned merit pay," Pfeffer says. "Merit pay is not based on merit. Performance evaluations are biased; overwhelming studies show this. Even if merit pay was based on merit, the pay increases are not enough to motivate employees, but they are enough to irritate them."

Survey reports show years of flat merit increase budgets that barely meet inflation rates and bear no relationship to productivity growth or profitability trends. The major salary budget surveys point to 2009 merit increases averaging 3.6 to 3.8 percent, with the highest performers receiving 5.6 to 6 percent. In effect, for the vast majority of employees, merit increases are unevenly distributed cost-of-living and market-adjustment increases couched in the language of performance rewards.

Even when companies create seemingly significant pay differentiation between low and high performers, the actual cash increase is insufficient to sustain performance—or it drives the wrong behaviors, Pfeffer says. And, as many studies show, high levels of differentiation destroy engagement, breed distrust and undermine teamwork.

A series of experiments conducted by Hewlett-Packard in the 1990s verified longstanding academic studies demonstrating that high incentives for top performers adversely affect organizational performance. Despite the deluge of consultants calling for companies to boost pay differentiation, Pfeffer cites dozens of studies showing that more dispersed pay distributions generate higher turnover, lower quality and a vast array of unintended results, including serious ethical breaches and business-killing behaviors.

"Individual performance pay plans cost a lot of money and upset everyone," Pfeffer says. Perhaps more important, when companies overestimate the power of financial rewards to affect behaviors, they neglect critical skills development and strong leadership, which Pfeffer and other experts agree play a more central role in raising organizational performance.

"Effective management is a system, not a pay plan," Pfeffer notes. "The mistake is that companies try to solve all their problems with pay."

At Verizon Business, Toohey takes a more holistic view. "I take it beyond pay," he says. "When an employee leaves, does he leave for more money? Managers will say that the employee had a better offer. But why did the employee pick up the phone and call the headhunter in the first place? Was the employee trained and developed? Was there proper management? Are you spending the appropriate amounts on training and do employees know how much you are spending? You must have the right data to determine any of this."

Building the Evidence

At the heart of the performance pay problem sits the assumption that correlation implies causation. That assumption continues to pervade decision making in human resources and pay plan design.

"There is the inferential issue," Pfeffer says. "The CEO drank Wild Turkey; the company performed well; ergo, all CEOs should drink more Wild Turkey. The company uses individual incentives; the company performs well; ergo all companies should use more incentives."

Toohey encounters the difficulty of separating correlation and causation at Verizon Business. "I can look at training dollars for a sales channel and the performance of that sales channel. But does that tell me the training improved performance, or does it mean that the channel had really talented people to begin with?" Without the necessary data collected over time, the actual determinants of performance cannot be verified.

Distinguishing correlation from causation is a substantial part of the evidence-based approach to workforce management and pay plan design. "The first step is to know what the evidence says," Pfeffer says. "Know the research literature that pertains to your business. Diffusion and persistence do not prove effectiveness."

The second step is to run experiments. In companies with multiple sites or divisions, HB executives and compensation directors can take the opportunity to learn by doing. Pfeffer advises executives to run performance pay programs in specific units and test the results. "It's not that hard to do," he says. "Many organizations do not run one consistent pay plan throughout the company, and no law says you have to."

"Treat the organization as a prototype," Pfeffer says. For research models, HR executives can look to marketing, particularly Internet-based marketing, where departments are constantly researching, testing and redesigning. It is critical, he emphasizes, to collect data in a way that does not simply confirm existing biases about pay and behavior.

The objective is to move away from the assumptions that continue to shape pay plan design but are inconsistent with logic and empirical studies. "Evidence-based management is a way of thinking and being open to learning, as opposed to assuming that we already know, which is the ideological view supported by casual benchmarking," Pfeffer says.

"It comes down to how we educate people as executives and HR executives. The goal is to transform human resources into the R&D department for the human system, which is the most important system in almost all organizations," Pfeffer says. "HR executives have to change how they think about their jobs."

"In R&D, you go into the laboratory, you experiment and you keep up with the research that others do. You are not involved in rule enforcement but in value creation for the organization through learning and experimentation. Can you imagine walking into the R&D lab at a pharmaceutical company, asking the chief chemist about an important new study and having him respond that they don't keep up with the literature in chemistry?"

Clearing the Obstacles

"In the whole area of pay for performance, HR has been deficient," says Mark Ubelhart, principal in Hewitt Associates' Human Capital Foresight practice. "When companies look at performance pay design, they look at their business strategy and prevalent practices and best practices, but you have to go beyond benchmarking."

"Improved employee performance may or may not lead to better business performance," Ubelhart says. "Hewitt studies show that when companies pay more, business performance is better. But you have to spend time to determine if this is predictive and causal. And if you have a good company, spending more on performance pay has to make it an even better company for there to be a causal relationship."

The obstacles to building an evidence-based approach are substantial, but not insurmountable. "The first problem is talent," Ubelhart says. "You have to apply rigorous academic techniques to the performance pay issue. A lot of companies have talented professionals in human resources, but to migrate to a decision science, you have to have the in-house talent or tap it from outside. Companies are now trying to bring in analytical expertise."

The second problem is data. "The company has to access its own data on human capital and use it," Ubelhart says. "We are absolutely seeing signs that this is changing. And investors want data on human capital. Not long ago, investors only looked at executive compensation, but now they are looking at human capital."

The third problem is the need for a common language. "You need standardized metrics for reporting, and this is beginning to emerge," Ubelhart says. "Once one or two companies disclose human capital metrics in specific terms, CEOs will demand that their HB departments disclose human capital data as well. In two to three years, we will see HB migrate to analytics for broader disclosure, but for people with a classic HB background, it's quite challenging."

Emilio Castilla, assistant professor at MIT's Sloan School of Management and a visiting professor at New York University, advises HB executives to pursue collaboration with academic researchers. "HB has tended not to be open to collaboration or research or even to understanding the tools involved," he says.

"The very top executives at companies are more open to collaboration," Castilla says. "HB is more resistant at companies where the HB function is viewed as an administrative function and the HB executive is not part of the top executive team. Where they are part of the top executive team, they are more open to collaboration."

Castilla reports that some HB executives are closing the knowledge gap between practitioners and academics through two methods. First, they follow the curricula at the top business schools and participate in university seminars and colloquia. Second, they call in academic experts to collaborate on research work. Both methods can produce a knowledge transfer that builds data for evaluating pay plans.

Pfeffer notes the existing evidence points to group bonuses, profit sharing and gain sharing, which is a form of profit sharing, as more effective forms of performance-based pay than merit pay or individual incentives. "Group plans are more collective and recognize the interdependent nature of work today," he says. "Most employees look at their total compensation and want to see that they share in the success of the organization."

Whether a pay plan is individual or group-based, the point is to put evidence behind the assumption that it improves organizational performance, or if the evidence is not affirmative, to make the appropriate business decision. "We've seen finance and marketing migrate to a decision science on spending issues," Ubelhart says. "Now it's HB's turn."

Susan J. Wells

NO

No Results, No Raise

Denying poor performers merit increases can pay off.

The term "merit increase" should mean that an employee is getting a pay increase based on merit. All too often, however, employees get salary increases regardless of whether their performance over the previous year was meritorious. In fact, many employees who don't meet the minimum requirements of their job collect "merit" increases year after year.

Even if those increases are marginal, experts say, giving them to all employees regardless of their results sends the wrong message—both to poor performers who are being rewarded for less-than-stellar achievement and to top performers who get a smaller piece of the salary-budget pie.

Culturally, however, managers may not be ready to stomach the seemingly harsh practice of giving poor performers no merit increase at all. They may find it is easier to spread rewards around to all employees to avoid the conflict that withholding pay increases from some workers could unleash. Or, HR may view withholding merit increases as unfair to employees who may be held back from reaching their full potential by circumstances beyond their control.

It's clear that employers' compensation systems aren't making the grade. Only 10 percent of organizations describe their merit pay programs as "very effective," according to an employee attitude survey conducted in 2002 of 335 companies by Hay Insight (the research and survey arm of Philadelphia-based HR consulting firm The Hay Group), WorldatWork and Loyola University of Chicago.

By contrast, adopting and enforcing—the get-tough approach to merit pay has clear advantages: It doesn't waste increasingly precious salary-budget dollars, it sends the right message that improvement is imperative, and it doesn't fund underperformers at the expense of high-performing employees. . . .

Making "Tough Love" Work

The problem for many organizations is that the budget for pay increases is small—on average 3.5 percent, according to research by Hewitt Associates. That leaves little room to differentiate pay between top performers and mid-level performers—much less bottom performers.

And that's not an effective way to spur performance. "You cannot get entrepreneurial results from a communistic approach—that socialistic feeling that everybody gets something," says Chuck Coonradt, founder and CEO of The Game of Work, a management consulting company in Park City, Utah. "In my opinion, it's a practice we ought to scrap."

Coonradt believes a lot of what he calls "merit fear" comes from lack of courage on the part of managers to deny rewards to the undeserving.

But, when companies spread pay **raises** around to all employees, something unintentional happens, says Larry Reissman, New England practice leader for The Hay Group. "Long-tenured low performers penetrate the top portions of salary ranges, while high performers change jobs so often that they never get to those ranges at all," he says.

This wouldn't happen at one investment firm Reissman worked with that gives new meaning to the term "tough love." There, merit dollars are given to eligible employees who consistently year after year exhibit exceptional performance. In general, top performers are funded at the expense of lower performers and nonperformers.

In fact, even average performers at the company generally get less than the average salary increase budget number, which can pose a communication challenge for managers, he says.

Communicating Your Policy

The trick to making a compensation system like this work is to combine clearly defined goals, good communication, and a fair and frequent performance review system.

"It's futile to try to establish a pay-for-performance culture without openly discussing goals, how to accomplish them and what it means to an employee's pocketbook," says Paul Shafer, business leader in the broad-based pay practice for Hewitt Associates in Lincolnshire, Ill.

Employees also need to know what the consequences are for not meeting performance expectations, including a clear statement in the employee handbook and at performance reviews that they're not automatically entitled to an annual merit increase.

Regardless of whether times are flush, that statement alone can send a powerful signal from management that the company is serious about everyone's performance. The top performers get more. Those holding back the organization get less . . . or nothing.

That's exactly the message employees hear at SecureWorks Inc., where the company's CEO gets involved in every employee's compensation review, says Kerry Solomon, vice president of HR at the 103-employee Internet security services provider in Atlanta.

After an employee self-evaluation, manager assessment and input from Solomon, a proposed evaluation and pay recommendation is presented to the CEO. "The CEO reviews and blesses" the recommendation on whether the employee should or should not receive a pay increase.

And when the company implemented a new pay-for-performance plan in 2002, it was communicated in writing, in person—and over and over again throughout the year. "Our CEO and department heads repeat the message continually," Solomon says.

"It's human nature not to hear or understand something new. People hear what they want to hear. You must clearly, consistently and frequently repeat your message. Saying it once is simply not enough," she says.

Constant pay raises helps employees get the message that the company compensates on the basis of **results**, not simply effort. "Your base salary is about meeting your base job requirements," Solomon says. "Employees know that if they're not meeting or exceeding or learning or growing, they're not going to get a regular increase."

That includes cost-of-living adjustments. At SecureWorks, cost-of-living increases are considered at the same time as annual reviews. If an employee is performing and excelling, he's granted a base increase. But if a merit **raise** isn't called for, the company also doesn't automatically grant a cost-of-living increase.

Employees have at least two other chances to earn other compensation throughout the year—either a stock option grant or restricted stock and a bonus. If performance improves, one or both of these rewards are available to the employee, which usually more than accounts for any loss of a cost-of-living **raise.** But if the employee's performance still lags requirements, Solomon says, "it's safe to assume they've self-selected out" of the company "and will no longer be a member of our team by the next annual performance review."

The payoff? Since the new pay plan was implemented, voluntary employee turnover has stayed at less than 5 percent. "After year one of the program, there was a lot of jubilation," Solomon says. "Those who weren't happy virtually self-selected out."

Goals

At SecureWorks, goals are set at the beginning of each year. Company goals are set by the management team and are printed and framed on the walls of the company's offices, break rooms and rest rooms. "Repeat it, distribute it, post it and re-emphasize it in person," Solomon stresses.

Department goals, which support the corporate goals, are set by managers and their teams. Individual goals, which support company and department goals, are set by each employee together with their manager. All goals must be achievable, measurable and aligned with the corporate strategy.

Individual goals have to be based on a realistic view of the future and connected to what the company needs to achieve.

Getting Managers on Board

The hardest part of a system that withholds merit increases from poor performers is giving the bad news to the employee who isn't getting a **raise** that year. Managers fear delivering the news, and HR fears the backlash.

Experts say the best way to fend off a bad reaction is to make sure no one is surprised by the news. If your organization does a good job of continually communicating throughout the year that poor performers don't receive a merit increase, and managers do a good job of communicating how their employees are doing on their performance throughout the year, there should be no surprises. Offering feedback throughout the year also should give employees a chance to improve their performance.

To help managers give good feedback, provide them with tools and talking points about topics such as what "superior" and "unacceptable" performance looks like, how merit raises should link to employee achievement and growth on the job, and how to deal with the tough questions likely to come from less-than-stellar performers. Take managers through role-playing exercises, for example, that guide them on having the difficult conversations.

Reissman cites the example of a financial services company whose culture was very accepting of speeding through performance reviews and not wanting to deliver bad news to anybody. When a new CEO joined the company, however, he brought in a new pay plan with highly differentiated rewards. Under the new system, there is no limit to what star performers can earn in merit increases—and some go as high as 20 percent. Poor performers get nothing, Reissman says. Managers who have to make the tough decisions during performance conversations get coaching to boost their skills.

The company credits its tougher merit system with helping it to achieve a doubling of its stock price two years after going public. The tougher system weeded out poor performers voluntarily—a "good" kind of turnover. Plus, high performers reached even higher because they were more accurately rewarded with dollars they deserved. All of this led to better overall company profitability and performance.

To add some checks and balances to your organizations performance review system, Shafer says, HR must establish organization-wide consistency in divvying up the merit money. He suggests the creative use of peer pressure by sharing information with all managers on how each one of them distributed their pay increase budgets.

"You can see who stayed within the [compensation strategy] guidelines and who didn't," he says. "It can work very well to get people to conform to your rules."

Explore Alternatives

If withholding pay seems like harsh punishment for an employee with promise, consider delaying the merit increase. "Sometimes, giving the employee three to six months to turn it around can help achieve performance worthy of reward," Reissman says.

Another strategy is to offer lump-sum payments instead of a base-salary increase. For example, instead of giving a 3 percent salary jump, give a 3 percent payout in one lump sum. "It looks like a bonus, comes out of the merit budget pool, but doesn't have the effect of raising salary" or hourly wages, Reissman notes. Distributing rewards this way helps stretch merit budgets while over time slowing down salary growth—an attractive goal for many compensation managers. "The biggest challenge is getting managers to not overuse it," Reissman says.

Above all, keep it simple.

"If you differentiate pay, you need to do a good job of assessing performance," he says. "That means everyone should know who's doing the job, who's outstanding and who's not doing the job. Don't micromanage shades of gray; get managers to really think about who it is in the company who deserves more—and who doesn't."

Brad Hill, principal of Tandehill Human Capital, a consulting firm in Warrenville, Ill., says HR and managers need to remember that base pay or merit increases "are forever and an annual event" that raises salary from that point on. "So over time," he says, "you want to absolutely make sure those increases meant something."

EXPLORING THE ISSUE

Has Merit Pay Lost Its Meaning in the Workplace?

Critical Thinking and Reflection

1. What is your understanding of merit pay?
2. Why is merit pay so challenging for organizations?
3. Do you think having practices such as the "Employee of the Month" is effective or not?
4. What are alternatives that HRM professionals may consider to reward their superior performers?
5. How do other countries perceive pay for performance?

Is There Common Ground?

Organizations need to take a different approach to develop compensation practices that will actually reward true performance. Managers fear if they isolate star performers, they might lose their average-performing employees. Consequently, they follow a merit-pay system—unfortunately which is not tied to merit—therefore, they make many high-performing employees extremely dissatisfied. A Watson/Wyatt 2009/2010 pay survey of 235 companies suggests that U.S. companies continue to pay their employees an average merit pay increase of 3.5 percent. However, making their pay directly related to their performance will greatly contribute to increased productivity. It might also help attract quality talent as superior performers like to see rewards for their hard work. President Obama has taken a proactive stand on merit pay for the national teachers as he feels the nation should not promote a pay system that rewards failure. The alternate perspectives to this issue suggest allowing employees a second chance to perform to prove their merit and also providing superior performers lump-sum bonuses to differentiate their work. How do you think "star" employees should be rewarded? Should organizations eliminate the merit-pay system completely? Would lump-sum bonuses be the answer to merit pay? Should organizations provide employees another chance to evaluate their performances?

Additional Resources

Anonymous (2009). 2010 Pay outlook: Raises are back, though they will be small. *HR Focus, 86*(9), 5–7.

Fox, J. B. and Donohue, J. M. (2004). When changing from merit pay to variable/bonus pay: What do employees want? *Performance Improvement Quarterly, 17*(4), 5–17.

Meckler, L. (2009, March 11). U.S. news: Obama seeks to expand merit pay for teachers. *Wall Street Journal* (Eastern Edition), p. A.6.

Risher, H. (2008). Adding merit to pay for performance. *Compensation and Benefits Review, 40*(6), 22.

http://k6educators.about.com/od/assessmentandtesting/a/meritypay.htm: Pros and Cons of Merit Pay For Teachers.

http://blogs.edweek.org/edweek/Bridging-Differences/merit_pay/: Does Merit Pay Make Sense?

http://www.nytimes.com/2000/01/28/nyregion/unions-call-merit-pay-proposal-unacceptable.html: Unions Call Merit Pay Proposal Unacceptable.

http://www.nytimes.com/1993/10/02/world/japanese-starting-to-link-pay-to-performance-not-tenure.html: Japanese Starting to Link Pay To Performance, Not Tenure.

http://english.people.com.cn/90001/90776/90785/6746707.html: China to Promote Merit Pay System.

ISSUE 14

Is Forced Ranking an Effective Performance Management Approach?

YES: Alex Blyth, from "Cull or Cure?" *Personnel Today* (May 2007)

NO: Gail Johnson, from "Forced Ranking: The Good, the Bad, and the Alternative," *Training* (May 2004)

Learning Outcomes

After reading this issue, you should be able to:

- Define forced ranking as it applies to organizations.
- Distinguish between forced ranking and forced distribution.
- Gain an understanding of the advantages and disadvantages of the forced-rank system.
- Identify alternatives that HRM professionals may provide to the forced-ranking systems.
- Understand international perspectives on the subject.

ISSUE SUMMARY

YES: Alex Blyth reiterates the thoughts of Microsoft leaders on forced ranking. This performance approach is very good at identifying the underperformers and rewarding the stars.

NO: Gail Johnson, former editor of *Training* magazine, suggests this method is flawed because it encourages a very competitive and dysfunctional work environment.

Forced ranking is a performance management approach that ranks employees in predetermined groups of performance. Former CEO of GE Jack Welch championed this performance approach in the 1980s. He perceived the best approach to performance management was to rank the high performers and yank the poor performers. This method also came to be referred as the "rank and yank" method. The advantages of this approach are that it rewards top performers, identifies employees with developmental needs, and dismisses underperformers. The traditional forced ranking rates employees in three groups: the top 10 percent, the middle 70 percent, and the bottom 20 percent.

GE was one of the first companies to adopt this method. It was very successful in adopting this performance approach and also observed it enhance their business profits. Today about 20 percent of the *Fortune* 500 companies adopt this performance management method with very positive firm results. High-profile organizations, such as Microsoft, also applaud this method as it instills a very performance-driven work culture. Microsoft executives believe that 15 percent of their employees should be dismissed annually. This kind of system would definitely make sure that the performance system rewards success and penalizes failure. With other methods of performance appraisals, frequently, the stars or high performers carry the load of the work of their mediocre and underperformers. Why should organizations promote a performance management system that rewards mediocrity?

Richard Grote, another champion of forced ranking, provides a distinction between forced ranking and forced distribution. Forced ranking is a method of ranking leadership and upper-level talent numerically. Forced distribution is grouping of employees in different performance groups. He also suggests that forced ranking produces best results when adopted for short time frames (3 years) as it helps dismiss the underperformers that will contribute to enhance their bottom-line profits. Such an approach will allow organizations to slowly reduce its number of underperformers.

The other point of view suggests that this method is completely flawed and promotes dysfunctional organizational behaviors. First, when employees are made to compete with another it results in a very competitive work environment that promotes negativity. Employees might think twice about helping their peers in work-related issues as they are constantly focused on their rank and performance. On the other hand, high-performing employees might feel disillusioned as their peers view their accomplishments and star status negatively. Experts also suggest that an appraisal system that publicly acknowledges performance might be intimidating to many.

Further, in today's team-oriented work environment such an appraisal system does not contribute to a collaborative corporate spirit. Moreover, employees ranked in the lowest rung could file for lawsuits as they may perceive the system to be unfair and discriminatory. Ford Motor got into a lawsuit as it classified its employees into three performance categories (A, B, and C). The organization mandated 10 percent of the employees to be placed in the lowest category. This created a lot of disillusionment among the employees, who subsequently filed for a class action suit. Consequently, the Ford Motor Company had to modify this method of appraisal.

There are many alternative perspectives that could identify employee performance effectively and minimize the use of forced ranking. The most important aspects of a performance management process are to ensure managers are accountable and honest with their employees regarding their performance. Often managers are not candid about their employees' performance problems in fear of employees' retaliation and turnover. Many organizations do not train their supervisors to rate their employees effectively, which could contribute to their not being able to identify performance problems well enough. The performance management approach should include a developmental component that allows employees to receive any corrective training to improve their performance.

Organizations will benefit tremendously in managing performance if they clearly identify the KSAs (knowledge, skills, and abilities) required of their employees for their TDRs (tasks, duties, and responsibilities). Usually, organizations do not provide their managers sufficient training in managing the performance management process, which requires managers to provide honest evaluations, timely coaching, and constant feedback. The ranking approach that distinguishes superior performers can also be substituted by providing compensation to employees that are performing at higher levels. Rewarding high performers with lump-sum bonuses will encourage and motivate them to perform better. It is also important when instituting bonus plans that the decision-making mangers collaborate with their HRM professionals to ensure they are making objective pay decisions.

Several organizations have adopted effective performance management systems without adopting a ranking method. Lockheed Martin, a major player in the aerospace industry, has implemented a very successful appraisal system that has been very successful. Employees are differentiated on the basis of five categories (exceptional, high contributor, successful contributor, basic contributor, and unsatisfactory). The definitions of each of these categories are provided by the managers to their employees so that employees clearly understand the performance levels expected in each category. Most employees at Lockheed Martin receive the successful contributor category ratings and the extreme category ratings are used with great caution.

In another instance, McKesson Information Solutions, a health-care software company of 6,000 employees, adopted a rigorous performance management approach without adopting the ranking method. They introduced the management by approach (MBA) method which consists of identifying goals, measuring performance, and providing feedback. The most important emphasis in this method is providing consistent feedback and adopting corrective actions early.

An international perspective suggests that performance appraisal management is a very sensitive topic in many cultures. The paternalistic management approach adopted in many Asian and Latin American cultures make an objective appraisal method quite difficult. Superiors and subordinates form a very close relationship that goes beyond the definitions of the job. Further, dismissal of employees due to poor performance is considered a social stigma and used minimally. Therefore, hard core practices like forced ranking and forced distribution will definitely be frowned upon in various cultures.

YES 

Alex Blyth

Cull or Cure?

Abstract (Summary)

Microsoft chief executive Steve Ballmer caused a stir last year when he announced to the Institute of Directors conference that he culls one in every 15 employees every year. He suggested that all business, large and small, would benefit from such an approach. His views received support from a recent survey by global talent management consultancy Hudson, which found that 77% of 562 executives and senior managers in the UK believe that a fixed quota for annual staff dismissal would boost financial performance and productivity. Yet despite these many alleged benefits, only 4% of companies surveyed dismiss a proportion of their staff. Many critics of the culling approach believe that companies should instead focus on re-engaging underperforming employees. Tom Barry, BlessingWhite Europe managing director, says it is not good practice to search out the disengaged simply to cull them. However, Ballmer does have some supporters. If a company is to conduct a cull, it needs to ensure it is done properly.

Should HR advise managers to cull less-effective staff, or work with them to improve performance? Alex Blyth considers the arguments.

Microsoft chief executive Steve Ballmer caused a stir last year when he announced to the Institute of Directors conference that he culls one in every 15 employees every year. He suggested that all businesses, large and small, would benefit from such an approach.

His views received support from a recent survey by global talent management consultancy Hudson, which found that 77% [of] 562 executives and senior managers in the UK believe that a fixed quota for annual staff dismissal would boost financial performance and productivity.

The advantages of pursuing this policy were described in Hudson's research as ensuring strong team members are not carrying weaker ones, allowing underperforming staff to pursue a fresh challenge more suited to their abilities, and increasing productivity overall.

Yet, despite these many alleged benefits, only 4% of companies surveyed dismiss a proportion of their staff. The remaining 96% might well be looking at these results and wondering if they should follow suit.

Opposition to Culling

Most companies are quick to dismiss the idea. Cathy Monaghan, head of HR at reward consultancy PES, says: "This is a great idea if you want to manage through fear, retribution and paranoia, and create a general air of unease.

"This sort of culling makes people focus on appearing productive, leads to short-termism, and attracts the wrong sort employees. It's also expensive, as you incur recruitment costs to replace the staff you have culled."

Others raise issues with the practical implementation of the idea. "What is the right percentage?" asks Chris Howe, director of ChangeMaker, an HR and change management consultancy. "If you pick an arbitrary number such as 15%, how do you know that is right? What if you have only 7% of underachievers, and you are therefore throwing out 8% of good people?"

Nearly one-quarter (24%) of respondents to the Hudson survey believe that deliberately dismissing underperforming staff increases morale among the rest of the team. But for Hamish Cameron Blackie, partner at accountancy firm and UK200Group member Barlow Robbins, this is a poor way of motivating staff.

"Culling the bottom performers will only ever motivate those on the cusp of success or failure. Those who are at the bottom of the performance table will be demotivated and will not care about their performance any longer. Those in the middle ground, but comfortably distant from the danger of being dismissed, won't care about the policy either," he says.

Finally, there are concerns about the legality of culls. "How would this be explained to an employment tribunal?" points out Nadia Motraghi, a barrister specialising in employment law at Old Square Chambers. "It doesn't appear to be a genuine redundancy situation, because the workforce cull appears unrelated to the level of work that needs to be carried out and the number of employees needed to do that work. From a legal perspective, regular staff culls are likely to require employers to get their chequebooks out."

Alternative Approaches

Many of these critics of the culling approach believe that companies should instead focus on re-engaging underperforming employees. Tom Barry, managing director of leadership consultancy BlessingWhite Europe, says: "It's not good practice to search out the disengaged simply to cull them. It may not be their fault. Companies should try to ensure that the activity of all employees is aligned to strategic goals."

For others, it is more important to focus on the high performers in an organisation. Mike Penny, director of executive search consultancy Warren Partners, says: "Companies often spend so much time on underperformers that they forget to stretch the top performers intellectually and support their development needs. Instead, they can inadvertently punish great performance by overloading them with extra work."

These critics of the culling strategy all agree that it is far better to hire the right people in the first place. Dave Millner, consultancy director of recruitment consultancy Kenexa Europe, says: "If companies have to cull one in 15 staff every year to maintain performance standards, then they are failing to hire the right staff in the first place."

And 72% of respondents to the Hudson survey agreed, admitting there would be less need to release staff deliberately if recruitment processes were more rigorous.

The Case for Culling

However, Ballmer does have some supporters. Stuart Duff, head of development at occupational psychologists Pearn Kandola, believes that the culling approach is simply the logical conclusion of performance management. "Why bother to have a performance management system if you don't act at both ends? Most companies, however, just reward the top performers and ignore the poor performers," he says.

"The reason for this is that it is difficult to manage performance to the extent that you can be confident enough to fire someone. Few managers have the time to do this. Paradoxically, they're too busy to manage their staff properly. However, those organisations that do set their staff clear goals, and manage their progress towards the achievement of those goals over a long period of time, can then act on the results and reap the rewards."

He points to a major IT consultancy that does this. "The HR department sits down once a year with line managers and asks them who are the high performers they want to promote, and who are the poor performers dragging them down, who they want to fire," says Duff.

"Because the company vigorously executes its performance management system, line managers can answer these questions confidently and the organisation can make the right decisions."

This may sound heartless, and Duff says this approach is likely to promote a culture of internal competition and destroy employee loyalty. However, Chris Welford, director of talent and assessment at HR consultancy Penna, believes that culling can even be good for those who get fired.

"The initial reaction to this idea is horror. However, if you think it through, it's more sensible than it sounds. Most people have skills, but they're not always used in the right way," he says.

"In any organisation, there are about 10% of people who are in the wrong job. It makes sense to have adult conversations with them about their future and then to help them find work that will use their skills. It's much better to do that than to hide behind procedures and rules-based management."

All in the Implementation

If a company is to conduct a cull, it needs to ensure it is done properly.

Andy Cook, managing director of HR consultancy Marshall James, advises: "Any systems in place to measure staff performance must be objective and non-discriminatory. Communication of company policy must be robust, so that employees are not surprised if they find themselves in the bottom percentile and action is taken to dismiss them. Policies and procedures must always be transparent and, most importantly, legal."

Gail Johnson

NO

Forced Ranking: The Good, the Bad, and the Alternative

Abstract (Summary)

Whether they call it rank or yank, the vitality curve or top grading, as many as one-third of employers use forced ranking on at least some members of their workforce. Although there is no one specific way to conduct forced ranking, the most common model is to rank employees on a bell curve, designating 20% of employees as superstars, the middle 70% as the average but vital backbone of the company, and the remaining 10% as weakest links. Despite all of the exposure forced ranking has received, corporate America remains fuzzy about the issues surrounding this workforce performance tool. Executives often mandate a forced ranking system because it's the easiest and fairest way to make necessary cuts in a down economy. But Bob Rogers says forced ranking is a poor way to manage poor performers. Rogers, who is the president of Development Dimensions International, a human resource consulting company based in Pittsburgh, has managed and worked under forced ranking systems throughout his career. He claims that forced ranking sends a negative signal to employees and has a tremendous downside in terms of teamwork, culture, competitiveness and legal problems.

One out of five Fortune 500 companies use forced ranking as a workforce management tool to determine whether employees will receive rewards or hit the trail. But is forced ranking the best way to weed out the low-potentials in your organization?

Whether you call it rank or yank, the vitality curve or top grading, as many as one-third of employers use forced ranking on at least some members of their workforce. Forced ranking became all the rage during the tenure of former General Electric CEO Jack Welch. Each year, 10 percent of GE managers are assigned the bottom grade, and if they don't improve they are asked to leave the company. When GE launched forced ranking and the company's profits started to soar, a number of high-profile companies adopted the GE model of forced ranking, among them Pepsico, Conoco, and notoriously, Enron. Today, as many as 20 percent of Fortune 500 companies now apply forced ranking.

Forced ranking is based on the idea that in order to grow, a company must identify its best and worst performers, then reward top performers with bonuses and development opportunities—while showing the bottom-feeders the door, or at least encouraging them to leave.

Although there is no one specific way to conduct forced ranking, the most common model is to rank employees on a bell curve, designating 20 percent of employees as superstars, the middle 70 percent as the average but vital backbone of the company, and the remaining 10 percent as weakest links. Some companies use quintiling, where managers rank the employees they supervise into five groups, from the top 20 percent to the bottom 20 percent. Others take the totem pole approach, ranking employees one on top of the other.

Despite all of the exposure forced ranking has received, corporate America remains fuzzy about the issues surrounding this workforce performance tool. Dick Grote, a former GE executive, is president of Grote Consulting, Addison, Texas, and helps companies launch forced ranking systems. He says people often confuse forced ranking with forced distribution. By definition, forced distribution is part of the performance appraisal process and requires that at least 5 percent of employees be placed in the bottom category, 15 percent in the next category, and no more than 10 percent in the top category.

Forced ranking, on the other hand, is conducted independently of the performance appraisal process and usually only senior executives and managers are ranked to groom and identify potential leaders. "Most people think everyone is ranked from top to bottom," Grote says. "That's a common misconception."

Grote believes that forced ranking works best when used as a short-term fix, not an ongoing process, and he recommends using the approach for a maximum of three years. "The first year you are getting a huge payoff because you identify the 10 percent who are not strong contributors," he says. "By the second year you have narrowed it down. By the third year, you have cut the organizational fat and are getting down to bone and muscle. The job is done and it's time to move on to other processes to manage people."

Executives often mandate a forced ranking system because it's the easiest and fairest way to make necessary cuts in a down economy. "The alternative to forced ranking is promoting people who aren't the stars and retaining poor performers," Grote says.

Robert Rogers says forced ranking is a poor way to manage poor performers. Rogers, who is the president of Development Dimensions International (DDI), a human resource consulting company based in Pittsburgh, has managed and worked under forced ranking systems throughout his career. He claims that forced ranking sends a negative signal to employees and has a tremendous downside in terms of teamwork, culture, competitiveness and legal problems. "Forced ranking is all the rage, but it's also seriously flawed," he says.

When Rogers worked under a forced ranking system in the U.S. Air Force he saw an immediate change in the attitude of his peers. "Our entire division requested to work for the highest ranking commander because we knew that a general wasn't going to let his direct reports get a low rating, as compared to a colonel," he says. "We found ways to work around the system real fast."

Throughout his career, Rogers has come across horror stories of how employees abuse the forced ranking system. "Some managers hire low potential employees from the start," he says. "I met a manager who hired someone he knew was not a top performer, but he needed to fill his quota of C-performers so he offered that employee up."

Eventually, says Rogers, employees under a forced ranking system begin to doubt their abilities to do a good job. "They believe that their continued employment rests not on what they do but on who supports them and how well they can articulate that," he says.

Differentiation or Discrimination?

There is, perhaps, no subject that managers are more reluctant to talk about than forced ranking. "Companies see forced ranking as a competitive advantage," Grote says. "They don't want to share. What's to be gained by going public? Absolutely nothing."

And "nothing" was what we heard after requesting interviews with several corporate giants to discuss their forced ranking systems, including Intel ("we would like to pass on this opportunity"), Capital One ("not able to participate in the story at this time"), EDS ("no comment"), and Microsoft ("not available for interview at this time").

GE declined an interview, but a company spokesperson provided the following comment: "GE believes in rating people, and we have used a ranking system for decades. It's very much part of GE's performance-based culture as well as being part of a holistic process of being continuously assessed. As a result, employees always know where they stand and how they can perform better."

Grote admits to being a vocal, but lonely advocate of forced ranking. "It's very easy to point out flaws and problems with forced ranking because it makes people uncomfortable and there has been so much negative publicity."

Most of the negative publicity stems from a flurry of class action lawsuits by workers who were given low ranks. Take Ford Motor Co.'s experience as an example. Ford's system graded employees A, B, or C, and required 10 percent of employees to get a C. "Their intent was to remove poor performers, but instead the automaker landed in court," says Rogers. "Eventually, after six lawsuits were filed against Ford by disgruntled workers, former CEO Jacques Nasser announced that this unpopular grading system was being modified."

But what many call discrimination is simply a company's way of differentiating their employees, according to Grote. He says that although lower ranked employees might believe that the ranking procedure produces illegally discriminatory results, these lawsuits stem from the fact that managers have not done a good job of telling the truth about how people are doing, "if an employee has always been told he is doing well, and then all of the sudden a forced ranking process comes along and he is told he is in the bottom 10 percent, the employee says, 'This can't be right. I wonder if the reason is because I am elderly, black, female, homosexual . . . take your pick.' That's where the lawsuits stem from."

Grote says it's difficult for managers who have always been told not to discriminate to change their way of thinking, because they have to get used to the idea of discriminating on the basis of talent and ability. "Now they are being forced into a process that does exactly the opposite," Grote says. "It forces them to say Mary is better than George but not as good as Sally—and that's tough. That's why there is so much bad press and unhappiness because forced ranking is necessarily discriminatory."

Alternatives to Forced Ranking

Discriminatory or not, DDI's Rogers says there is a better way to get managers to manage all employees—high and low performers alike—than to resort to forced distribution or forced ranking. He says if a company wants to retain the best employees, it must use a performance management system that holds employees accountable for results, encourages open and honest feedback between employees at all levels, provides a convenient way to develop talent, and features a compensation process that is based on performance and pays the higher performers more than it pays substandard performers.

An example of this type of performance management system is used at McKesson Information Solutions, a healthcare software and services company in Alpharetta, Ga., and a division of McKesson Corp. "We don't believe in forced ranking, we don't think it's right or useful," says Terry Geraghty, senior vice president of human resources for the company's Information Solutions division. Instead, the company uses a traditional performance management system to track and manage the performance of its 6,000 employees. But the solution took years to develop.

When Geraghty was hired four years ago, he walked into a company with an employee turnover rate of 23 percent, dreadful employee satisfaction surveys, low morale and customer service problems "From an HR perspective, we were in crisis mode," he says.

The company had just completed nearly 20 acquisitions to become the largest healthcare IT company in the industry. As a result, there were at least seven formal performance management systems and another 10 hybrid versions floating around. "Our first attack strategy was to use performance management to address morale and bring the different business units together," he says. "We knew that building a single performance management system was the glue that was going to hold the company together."

Geraghty and his team consolidated the company's performance management systems into one common system from San Mateo, Calif.-based SuccessFactors, then sent 600 managers to a full-day training program offered by DDI in just three months.

The company's performance-based system requires employees to have six to 10 objectives that relate to their individual job and the requirements of their department. The employee and manager agree on the top three or four that will have the greatest impact on the employee's success during the year. Managers measure and track those objectives and provide coaching throughout the year.

Geraghty admits that the performance management system is nothing radical, it's just executed very well. The Web-based system tracks the development of 5,000 employees. In addition to 24/7 access, managers can also access Web-based development guides and competency behavior guides used to help set objectives.

An Employee-Driven Solution

While some companies launch performance management systems in response to CEO demand, Lockheed Martin Corp., a Bethesda, Md., advanced technology company, developed its performance recognition system in response to employee demand. That demand came in the form of survey responses in which employees revealed their desire for more feedback from their managers and that the company needed to improve how it recognized and measured performance.

Lockheed had a cultural challenge on its hands. As the result of numerous mergers and acquisitions in the 1990s, Lockheed grew to become the major player of the aerospace industry, bringing together more than 17 companies. But the mergers also brought 17 different company heritages—including dozens of approaches to performance management.

The company needed a single way to differentiate employees and pay for performance. Michael Hopp, director of leadership and employee development, and his team walked a tightrope of trying to balance Lockheed's need with the needs of its employees and managers—and they didn't take this challenge lightly. They formed a best practices team that took two years to research and learn the best ways companies were managing employee performance.

Then Lockheed formed a team of managers to develop its performance recognition system. "We didn't want this process to be developed in a vacuum," Hopp says. "We needed our managers to give us their recommendations and solutions that worked for them as well as supported Lockheed's needs."

Once the managers' recommendations were approved, the HR implementation team rolled out the paper-based performance recognition system in 2002 while simultaneously building a Web-enabled system.

The result was a three-phase process for managers that included setting employee expectations in the first quarter of the year; ensuring that employees were performing to expectations throughout the year with interim reviews, ongoing feedback and coaching; and finally completing an assessment during the first quarter of the second year.

After a three-year planning and implementation process, Lockheed rolled out the Web-based performance recognition system in each of its business units last year and built training around a one-day course. Lockheed trained 15,000 managers to use the system to track and manage the performance of 100,000 employees. The Web-enabled system provides a common process to recognize employee contributions, features a common rating scale, aligns with Lockheed's core values, links to compensation and provides management and employee training.

Distribution Guidelines

Now that the performance recognition system was launched, Hopp and his team faced the challenge of training managers on how to assess employees. Lockheed had a high skew, with 80 percent of employees rated in the top categories of performance. "That information was not very useful because we were telling everyone that they were superior," he says.

Hopp again turned to Lockheed's managers, but this time they developed a distribution scale with definitions and guidelines for the categories of exceptional, high contributor, successful contributor, basic contributor and unsatisfactory.

The rating system uses words rather than numbers or letters. "At first glance it looks like a five-category scale, but it's really three because there is a large, highly successful middle category," Hopp says. "These are the people who are doing everything we want them to do and are doing it well. We want them to do this forever."

Employee differentiation is expected based on their performance relative to the definitions that are written by the managers. The system is unique because managers increment from the middle, not from the top or bottom. Rather than starting with a blank slate for each employee, managers read the definition for "successful contributor" first because most employees fall into this category. The manager reviews the definitions for the "exceptional" and "unsatisfactory" categories, but must have clear evidence to place employees into these categories.

"Part of the philosophy of this system is to make employees feel good because they are successful contributors," he says. "The challenge is that every employee thinks they are above average. So in response, we have defined this category as above average and tell them 'You're doing everything right.'"

Less than 1 percent of employees fall into the unsatisfactory category, and they receive a performance improvement plan instead of a pink slip. Managers are trained not to be rigid when it comes to percentage guidelines. "Many employees look at this as a forced distribution, but we are skittish about calling it that," Hopp says. "These are simply guidelines."

Similar to Lockheed Martin, the first year McKesson Information Solutions rolled out its new system Geraghty noticed a very skewed distribution with more than 70 percent of employees receiving a rating of 1 or 2 on a 5-point scale. Receiving a 1 meant that most employees were significantly exceeding expectations. "Roughly two-thirds of our employees were exceeding expectations in terms of performance," Geraghty says. "That looks great on paper, but our business results didn't line up with the individual performance results."

Geraghty and his team determined they would have to hold managers accountable to accurately rate performance as well as set up challenging objectives. As a result, the company published the following distribution guidelines and holds its managers accountable to them:

1 = Significantly exceeds expectations (7 percent)
2 = Exceeds expectations (23 percent)
3 = Expectations fully met (55 percent)
4 = Met some, but not all expectations (10 percent)
5 = Did not meet expectations (5 percent)

Geraghty is passionate about measuring performance. "McKesson Corp. is a Fortune 20 company in a highly competitive growth business, so it's a good thing when an employee fully meets expectations."

The distribution guidelines are used as a discussion point between managers. "If a manager has business results and can demonstrate that his team has exceeded these guidelines, we allow that," he says. "But if a business unit is struggling and has inflated ratings, managers have to justify why the business results do not coincide with the high percentage of employees ranked superior."

Training's Critical Role

Whether a company chooses to launch forced ranking or a performance management system, experts agree that training plays a critical role in whether the system sinks or swims. Forced ranking advocate Grote refuses to work with any company that will not invest in the training of its managers as part of the forced ranking process. "People's careers are so affected by this, managers better know what they are doing," he says.

Although McKesson Information Solutions' performance management system is successful, Geraghty admits the first year was rocky. "We're into our third year, and it is a much different place," he says. "The process goes smoother, and people understand they have to be trained."

McKesson requires that its managers attend an annual training program where they role play, practice, and learn about the new features and functions of the Web-based system. Managers also go through scenarios on how to rate performance accurately. This increased role of training has been part of a big culture change at the company. "It's now part of our culture that employees must do very well at the company to exceed expectations, and the training emphasizes that message," Geraghty says.

Training also ensures that managers know how to rate people accurately. "Because managers don't like to deliver bad news, most have not been effective raters of performance," says Geraghty. "Our managers must have the guts to sit down with someone and tell them that they did not meet all of their expectations and here's what they need to do. We train them how to do that."

Lockheed's Hopp agrees that teaching managers how to assess employees is vital to the success of any performance management system. "The idea of performance recognition was new for many employees," he says. "Some parts of the company didn't even use the concept of individual employee objectives."

Hopp and his team created a one-day training program to teach managers the Web-based system as well as how to assess performance and communicate the results to employees. Lockheed also provides additional training using modules from Harvard ManageMentor, an online performance support tool from Boston-based Harvard Business School Publishing's e-learning division.

The results of the additional training speak volumes. After a five-year planning and implementation deadline, Lockheed has achieved most of its goals for the system. "We have successfully linked performance ratings to salary increases for all of our exempt employees and most of our non-exempt employees," Hopp says. In addition, Lockheed's individual business units have achieved their performance differentiation guidelines.

Results of a recent employee survey found improvements in the perceived link between individual and organizational objectives. Employees said their performance had improved due to ongoing feedback and differentiation. High performers felt they were getting the appropriate amounts of recognition and reward. "I think we are about 60 percent there," Hopp says. "I want to continue to enhance the ability of managers to really use this and to really make those connections."

Three years into McKesson's performance management system the company has gone from crisis to celebration, experiencing 31 consecutive months of declining turnover. This transformation has resulted in the company being ranked #52 in *Computerworld's* top 100 places to work in information technology, as well as being ranked the second best place to work in Atlanta by the *Atlanta Chronicle*.

Recent employee survey results also verify the system's success. The company used Chicago-based global survey firm ISR to survey its employees, and 79 percent of employees said that they understood how their performance is evaluated, compared to an industry norm of 67 percent. Seventy-seven percent of McKesson's employees say that performance reviews are conducted regularly, compared to an industry norm of 60 percent.

Geraghty feels good about these results. "It's been a long road, but McKesson is a different place to work," he says. "Thanks to our performance management system we have a very motivated and engaged workforce."

EXPLORING THE ISSUE

Is Forced Ranking an Effective Performance Management Approach?

Critical Thinking and Reflection

1. What is your understanding of forced ranking and forced distribution?
2. Which organization introduced this method first and why is it so successful?
3. What are the disadvantages of this performance management approach?
4. What are some alternatives that HRM professionals may consider instead of adopting forced ranking?
5. How do other countries perceive using forced ranking method to measure performance?

Is There Common Ground?

Any performance management process should identify the high, the mediocre, and the underperformers. Leading organizations, such as Microsoft, GE, and Pepsico, are among the *Fortune* 500 companies that have successfully adopted the forced ranking method. Experts maintain the underpinning emphasis of this approach is rewarding superior employee performances. This will enhance the competitive advantage of the firm as superior performers get motivated to perform better. Which CEO would not want such a win–win situation? Opponents of the forced ranking system suggest it is fundamentally flawed. They also question how to implement the system if employees do not fall into a traditional performance curve of superior, mediocre, and underperformers. With a forced ranking method a collective team spirit is lost as employees contest with each other for the winner's cup. There are other alternatives to the forced ranking method such as providing a thorough job analysis (KSAs and TDRs) or following an MBA approach. These methods can help identify any errors in employees' performance early without any punitive consequences. Would you like to work in an environment that ranks employees? Why? Why not? What do you recommend as some best approaches to train mangers to become more effective in the performance management process? Why do you think managers are not honest with their employees in the appraisal process?

Additional Resources

Anonymous (2007). Forced rankings of employees bad for business. *Machine Design, 79*(18), 30.

Boehle, S. (2008). Keeping forced ranking out of court. *Training, 45*(5), 40, 42, 44, 46.

Hazels, B. and Sasse, C. (2008). Forced ranking: A review. *S.A.M. Advanced Management Journal, 73*(2), 35–39.

http://www.allbusiness.com/services/educational-services/4283450-1.html: Forced Ranking Pros and Cons.

http://hbswk.hbs.edu/archive/5091.html: Forced Ranking: Making Performance Management Work.

http://news.cnet.com/The-folly-of-forced-rankings/2009-1069_3-950200.html: The Folly of Forced Rankings.

www.gibbonslaw.com/news_publications/articles.php?action=display_publication&publication_id=790: Forced Rankings: The Latest Target of Plaintiff's Employment Lawyers.

www.ddiworld.com/DDIWorld/media/white-papers/forcedrankingalternatives_wp_ddi.pdf?ext=.pdf: Managing the "C" Performer: An Alternative to Forced Ranking.

ISSUE 15

Is the U.S. Executive Pay Model Flawed?

YES: Sarah Anderson, John Cavanagh, Chuck Collins, Mike Lapham, Sam Pizzigati, from "Executive Excess 2007," at the Institute for Policy Studies, http://www.ips-dc.org/reports/#84 (2007)

NO: Robert B. Reich, from "The Economic Argument for CEO Pay," *Wall Street Journal* (Eastern Edition) (September 14, 2007)

Learning Outcomes

After reading this issue, you should be able to:

- Understand why the U.S. executive pay model is flawed.
- Define golden parachutes and executive perquisites.
- Gain an understanding of why executives should be paid highly.
- Describe how to establish alternatives to the executive compensation system.
- Understand international perspectives on the subject.

ISSUE SUMMARY

YES: Compensation expert and IPS Fellow Sarah Anderson and her colleagues argue that U.S. CEOs are substantially overpaid in a 2008 study conducted for the Institute for Policy Studies.

NO: Professor Reich from Berkeley states that the capitalistic system promotes a principle of supply and demand. There are very few qualified executives, so they are in high demand. Executives have distinguished educational and work records that result in their elaborate pay levels.

U.S. corporate executives' salaries usually include their base salaries, bonuses, stock options, stock grants, executive benefits, and executive perquisites. In the 1960s, the CEO salary was 41 times more than that of the average employee.

In the 1980s, the CEO salary was 40 times that of the average worker. But in 2009, the average CEO made 400 times more than that of the average employee. The average pay of these executives has become 10 times larger over the decades while the other employee levels have not seen such magnificent increases in their pay levels. The topic of executive pay has created national debates and recently caused the government to introduce even federal interventions.

There are several points contributing to the U.S. executive pay model being flawed. First, the "average employees" (nonexecutives) do not experience similar percentage increases in compensation levels as their executives do. Economists observe that the American economy has abundant salaries to offer their top executives but fail to pay their "average employees" in the same lavish manner. During any decade, the minimum wages and average wages for employees rise by barely 7 percent, while in contrast CEOs salaries rise almost 45 percent. Further, frequent media attention to executives' annual salaries makes this a much discussed issue.

Second, the U.S. culture, with its emphasis on individualism, likes to lavish a celebrity status on their executives. U.S. executives make more than their overseas professional counterparts. CEOs from other countries make only 10–12 times more than of their average employees. In 2006, European CEOs made one-third of what the U.S. CEOs made annually. In 2008, CEOs in Japan and Europe made 1.5 and 6.6 million in comparison to the U.S. executives' average pay of 13.3 million. Further, in the European and Asian economies, executives have shown to take a financial cut in their salaries if their companies were not performing well.

Third, usually the salaries executives negotiate and receive are not related to the performance of the firms. Many executives quit failing companies, negotiating an exorbitant golden parachute package (severance package, which is usually four–five times their annual salary, plus stock options and pension plans). Research suggests that the average departing executive in the United States receives a golden parachute package of almost $16.5 million. Thus, underperforming executives actually leave the companies rest assured that they will be well compensated for their entire lives. U.S. executives seem to be the only level of employees that are paid even for their mediocre performance. Which "average employee" from any industry can negotiate to leave his or her job with a high pay albeit with a track record of poor performance? Finally, executive employees negotiate substantial money even for their retirement plans. On an average, CEOs bargain for almost 10 million in their retirement benefits. In contrast, in 2004, only 36.3 percent of individuals 65 and older had any retirement plans.

Executive perquisites or perks, a component of executive compensation packages, are quite controversial and also get the frequent attention of media journalists. Perks are additional rewards that are provided to executives to enhance their professional images and statuses. Perks can be any luxury items such as corporate jets, lavish apartments, exclusive memberships, shopping trips, and vacation packages. For instance, in 2008, the biggest earner of perks was Johnson & Johnson CEO William Weldon, who received about $154,000 for personal travel. It is when the perks become unreasonable, such as when

Tyco's top executive spent an extravagant $6,000 for shower curtains, that it leaves the "average employee" bewildered.

On the other hand, advocates of high executive pay suggest that executives rightly deserve their high pay. Primarily, the argument is that executives are completely responsible for managing their organizations. Such jobs are extremely stressful and ruthlessly demanding. It requires long hours at work completely distorting their work–life balance schedules. Therefore, executive employees need to be compensated more than adequately for their very challenging positions. Second, executives are fully responsible for the goals and mission of their organizations. They analyze, direct, and coordinate employees and also are fully accountable to their customers. The top executives have to ultimately answer their customers even if their employees make any corporate blunders. Why should corporate executives not receive elaborate salaries? Third, the market economy works on the principle of pure supply and demand. Recruiting and hiring such top talent is very difficult and therefore when such talent is identified it carries a very high price. Many of these executives have distinguished college degrees and several years of professional experience. Customers are willing to pay a very high price for exclusive brands based on the same economic principle. Why would organizations not pay high salaries for the unique KSAs (knowledge, skills, and abilities) that executives have?

Further, advocates of high executive pay also argue that such talent is required to perform very well right from day one. Most jobs usually provide probations or trial periods, but executive jobs do not allow time for such luxury. Therefore, such talent needs to be compensated at superior levels to provide these employees the required motivation to perform at high levels. The market economy works on the simple principle that products high in demand come with a lofty price. Experts suggest that this seems to be the storyline of hiring U.S. executives.

There are several alternatives that HRM professionals may pursue in addressing this issue. Experts suggest that several interventions should be adopted to keep the executive pay in check. First, an executive cap should be imposed so that U.S. executives are not getting paid so exorbitantly. Second, any form of extra compensation, such as stocks and bonuses, provided should be strongly related to the firm's performance. For instance, AIG, the leading insurance company, stated that most of its executives will receive bonuses based on their firm's performance. Third, professionals also suggest providing executives deferred compensation that will compensate executives based once again on maintaining the firm's performance for a specific time period (3 or 5 years).

Finally, the federal government can provide interventions to make executive pay more reasonable. The president has taken a bold step in putting a cap on executive salaries ($500,000) for those organizations receiving bailouts from the government. He further states that compensation committees should strongly monitor the elements of the compensation packages to minimize unreasonable compensation demands. He has also stipulated several executive pay policies for organizations seeking government assistance. This might be a first step by the government that may keep executives' salaries in check about their unfair compensation packages.

An international perspective suggests that in other countries top executives do not get lavish compensation packages that U.S. executives do. In 2008 in China, the chairman and president of the top Chinese banks were paid approximately $230,000 annually in comparison to the $19.6 million awarded to J.P. Morgan's CEO. In 2008 in India, the chairman of Reliance (textile industry), received $10 million amidst vociferous critics that executive compensation should be capped. In many of these emerging economies, the governments mandate a cap on executive compensation packages which is calculated as a percentage of the net profits.

YES 

Sarah Anderson et al.

Executive Excess 2007: The Staggering Social Cost of U.S. Business Leadership

I. Introduction

What's the "going rate" for leadership in the United States today?

This question would once have made little sense. Years ago, we didn't treat "leadership" as a marketable skills set. Today we do. We have academic centers that teach leadership, headhunters who search for it.

Our grand enterprises and institutions still sometimes hire their top leaders from within. But they feel no pressure to hire someone already deeply steeped in the specific work they do. They seek, or at least claim to seek, proven leadership ability, from individuals who have demonstrated a capacity to innovate and inspire, analyze and imagine.

A good leader, we have come to believe, can perform successfully almost anywhere. The CEO of Home Depot can become the head of Chrysler. A military general can become a school superintendent. You need not know how a particular industry operates to play a leadership role within it. You need only know how to lead. Leadership skills, and leadership skills alone, can make you eminently marketable.

Every market, of course, sports a "going rate." Try to collect significantly above that "going rate," if your skill be computer programming or selling real estate, and you'll likely get nowhere quick.

But the market for leadership doesn't seem to work that way. Some individuals with leadership skills in our contemporary United States—those individuals who sit atop America's business enterprises—are capturing far more compensation for their labors than individual leaders in other fields who appear to hold the same exact leadership skill set.

Indeed, our current pay gap between American business leaders and their leadership counterparts in other walks of American life today runs wider, often far wider, than the pay gap a generation ago between business leaders and average American workers.

Back around 1980, big-time corporate CEOs in the United States took home just over 40 times the pay of average American workers. Today's average

American CEO from a *Fortune* 500 company makes 364 times an average worker's pay and over 70 times the pay of a four-star Army general.

Another example of this growing leadership pay gap: Last year, the top 20 earners in the most lucrative corner of America's business sector, the private equity and hedge fund world, pocketed 680 times more in rewards for their labors than the nation's 20 highest-paid leaders of nonprofit institutions pocketed for theirs.

Most Americans, over recent years, have become aware that business leaders make enormously more than the workers they employ. The gap between business leaders and other leaders in our society has received considerably less attention. This report, our 14th annual examination of executive excess, seeks to remedy that situation.

But we will begin this year's report on more familiar ground, with a review of the current status of the gap between business leaders and their workers. That gap remains at unconscionably wide levels.

The CEOs of major American corporations, the data show, once again last year made as much in a day as average workers took in over the entire year. The 20 top kingpins of the private equity and hedge fund industry last year made more than average worker annual pay *every ten minutes.*

These numbers shock but do not surprise. We have come, as a society, to expect—and even accept—such phenomenally wide pay differentials between workers and business leaders. These differentials have come to appear as a given of modern economic life.

But modern economies, in reality, do not require excessive business executive pay to function. If they did, then the business executives that American executives compete against in the global marketplace would be just as excessively compensated as American executives. They aren't. Top executives of major European corporations, we show in this latest edition of *Executive Excess,* last year earned three times *less* than their American counterparts.

The vast rewards that go to business leaders in the United States represent, in short, not an inevitable unfolding of marketplace dynamics, but a marketplace failure.

Markets that fail need to be corrected, and, in generations past, Americans organized politically to make sure needed corrective action took place. These Americans broke up monopolies. They established a minimum wage. They regulated business behavior. *Executive Excess 2007* spotlights, in this historic spirit, a series of corrective initiatives we here today can take to restore a modicum of balance to modern American economic life.

We ignore initiatives like these at our peril. The outrageously massive rewards now attainable at the top of our economic ladder do our society no good. They ravage the enterprise teamwork that true leaders strive to nurture. They discourage individuals with leadership talent from entering less lucrative fields where their skills could make an important contribution to our common well-being.

In a democracy, we don't depend on leaders to fix problems like these. We citizens take leadership responsibilities onto ourselves. This year's *Executive Excess* aims to help this process along.

II. CEOs v. Workers

The CEO-Worker Pay Gap

Last year, CEOs of major U.S. companies collected as much money from one day on the job as average workers made over the entire year. These CEOs averaged $10.8 million in total compensation, according to an Associated Press survey of 386 *Fortune* 500 companies, the equivalent of over 364 times the pay of an average American worker.

Meanwhile, the private equity boom has pushed the pay ceiling for American business leaders further into the economic stratosphere. Pay data for the chiefs of these privately held firms remain difficult to obtain, but *Forbes* magazine estimates that the top 20 private equity and hedge fund managers, on average, took in $657.5 million last year, or 22,255 times the pay of the average U.S. worker.

These massive private equity take-homes have an enormous impact on inequality in the United States, at both ends of the economic ladder. Private equity managers, to extract such massive personal rewards out of the companies that sit in their portfolios, typically make decisions—on matters ranging from job cuts to pensions—that place steady downward pressure on U.S. working standards.

Astronomical pay packages for managing partners at privately held investment companies also serve to bump up the already overly ample pay of CEOs at publicly traded corporations. CEOs are now routinely leaving their corporate perches to take on far more remunerative leadership slots in the private equity world. Those who remain within publicly traded corporations, meanwhile, use the threat of exit to bargain even higher pay for their executive services.

To retain leadership talent, the argument goes, publicly traded companies must simply pay more. This past March, at a House Financial Services Committee hearing, one business professor cited massive private equity payoffs as evidence that CEOs "may even be underpaid at public companies."

Minimum Wage

This Labor Day, American workers can celebrate the first raise in the federal minimum wage in ten years. But the minimum wage increase that went into effect July 24 makes barely a dent in the gap between pay rates at the American economy's top and bottom. In the decade that ended in 2006, CEO pay rose roughly 45 percent, adjusted for inflation. The real value of the minimum wage, with this year's increase from $5.15 to $5.85, now stands 7 percent below the minimum wage's value in 1996.

Average worker pay has, over the past decade, also lagged far behind CEO compensation. In 2006, average American workers earned $29,544 per year, up 7 percent from 1996.

The Pension Gap

New federal corporate disclosure rules are shining a brighter light on the stark disparity between CEO and worker pensions. According to data available in proxy statements for the first time this year, large company CEOs last year enjoyed a $1.3 million average increase in the value of their pensions. The biggest CEO increase in pension account value—$10.7 million—went to Textron's Lewis B. Campbell. By contrast, the share of ordinary U.S. workers with any type of retirement account has declined in recent years.

According to the most recent Federal Reserve Board survey, only 58.5 percent of households headed by 45-to-54-year-olds had any type of retirement account in 2004, down from 64.3 percent in 2001. Of those in that age bracket who did have such funds, the average account value grew by only $11,325 over those same three years, or roughly $3,775 per year.

According to the Corporate Library, CEOs of S&P 500 companies retire with an average of $10.1 million in their Supplemental Executive Retirement Plan, just one type of special account large American companies regularly set up for their top executives. To place that number in perspective: In 2004, only 36.3 percent of American households headed by an individual 65 years or older held any type of retirement account at all.

Those over-65 households *with* pension protection in 2004, according to the Congressional Research Service, held an average of $173,552 in their retirement accounts, a miniscule 1.7 percent of the dollars in the supplemental accounts set aside for America's top CEOs. Looking at all American households, regardless of age, slightly more than half had retirement accounts in 2004. The average value of these accounts: $129,310.

Among the king-sized supplemental CEO pension stashes accumulated by the end of 2006: $91.3 million for William McGuire of the UnitedHealth Group. Edward Whitacre of AT&T followed closely behind with $84.7 million. Pfizer CEO Hank McKinnell accumulated $77.1 million in his supplemental retirement account before his ouster last year.

With even financially healthy U.S. companies, including IBM, Verizon, Motorola, Hewlett-Packard and Sears, slashing their worker pension benefits, the CEO-worker pension gap is likely to grow even wider.

III. U.S. Business Leaders vs. Other U.S. Leaders

Healthy democracies and dynamic economies require strong leadership, in every sector of society. But current pay practices in the United States send a quite different message: that only for-profit business leadership really matters.

Business leaders, our compensation patterns proclaim, add tens, hundreds, and even thousands of times more value to our society than the leaders we hold responsible for educating our youth, protecting our national security, providing essential public services, or crafting the laws that govern us.

Such extreme pay gaps undermine our future. These gaps siphon off talent from public service and create a nonstop revolving door between government and the business world that breeds conflict of interest and corruption and distorts our democracy.

Top leaders in non-business sectors of our society already earn comfortable incomes. These incomes do not need to be raised. To limit leadership pay gaps, we need to address the problem of excessive pay in the for-profit sector.

Private Equity and Hedge Funds

The top 20 highest-earning leaders of private equity and hedge funds collected an average of $657.5 million in 2006. The top four each pocketed over $1 billion. These men—and they are all white men—are leading a revival of the 1980s leveraged buyout phenomenon that hollowed out a variety of once-venerable companies, while enriching a precious few. Last year saw more than 1,000 corporate buyouts worldwide, with a total value estimated between $500 and $700 billion. Hedge funds now account for 30 to 60 percent of daily global turnover in financial markets.

Unlike companies that are publicly traded on Wall Street, private equity and hedge funds are not required to report executive compensation to the federal Securities and Exchange Commission. These funds also rely on different forms of compensation. Investment managers reap their rewards primarily from management fees and a share of the profits from fund investments, rather than from stock options, salary, and bonuses.

Private equity and hedge fund managing partners typically receive 20 percent of the profits their funds generate and an annual fee that equals 2 percent of the assets they manage. Some managers demand even higher rewards. For example, James Simons commands 44 percent of profits and 5 percent of assets from investors in his two hedge funds, Medallion and Renaissance Institutional. Last year, he raked in $1.1 billion from Medallion and $395 million from Renaissance. His total earnings: nearly $1.5 billion.

After Simons, Steven Cohen of SAC Capital scored the second-highest Wall Street investment fund windfall, with $1.2 billion. Cohen's wealth has proved a boon to art dealers. He recently acquired an Andy Warhol image of Marilyn Monroe, "Turquoise Marilyn," for an estimated $80 million, nearly three times the price garnered for a similar painting by the pop artist.

Cohen shared second place on the investment fund payday list with Kenneth Griffin, head of Citadel Investment Group. The 38-year-old Griffin has also made a name for himself as an art collector and will soon have his name etched on a section of the Art Institute of Chicago. For the site of his second wedding in 2003, Griffin chose Versailles, where the ill-fated King Louis XVI and Marie Antoinette also tied the knot.

Two of last year's 20 highest-paid hedge fund managers first became public figures as 1980s-era corporate raiders. T. Boone Pickens, for example, made a fortune two decades ago bidding for Gulf Oil and other big oil companies. His current hedge fund, BP Capital, invests almost exclusively in the energy industry and last year generated $1.1 billion in earnings for Pickens.

Another icon of the "greed is good" 1980s, Carl Icahn, cleared $350 million in 2006. Most notorious for his 1986 takeover of TWA, a company he left in bankruptcy, Icahn today heads the Icahn Partners fund, a two-year-old venture that manages about $2.5 billion in assets.

Publicly Traded Companies

The top 20 highest-paid executives of U.S. publicly traded companies raked in an average $36.4 million in 2006. The top earner: Yahoo's Terry Semel, whose $71.7 million in annual earnings consisted almost entirely of options grants estimated to be worth $71.4 million. The Internet services chief also cashed in $19 million in options last year. Semel stepped down as CEO in June, amid widespread shareholder concern over the company's sluggish performance.

The second- and third-highest-paid U.S. CEOs last year both hailed from the oil industry, a sector that continues to benefit from record-high world crude oil prices. Bob Simpson of Texas-based XTO Energy took in $59.5 million, including a $31 million cash bonus and $27 million worth of new options grants. He cleared another $39.8 million exercising previously awarded options.

XTO Energy last year also donated $6.8 million to Baylor University, Simpson's alma mater, for the construction of a sports complex. In exchange, the XTO proxy explains, the university will name the new athletic complex after Simpson—and provide him "access to certain sporting events."

The sixth-highest-paid CEO in 2006 was Angelo Mozilo of Countrywide Financial, with $42.9 million. In July 2007, the company's sub-prime mortgage woes drove its foreclosure rates to the highest level in more than five years and contributed to a global liquidity crisis.

Non-Profits

In 2005, the most current year with data available, the 20 highest-paid nonprofit leaders in the United States averaged $965,698 in compensation. The highest-paid—Harold Varmus, the chief executive of the Memorial Sloan-Kettering Cancer Center in New York—earned $2,491,450. Varmus won the 1989 Nobel Prize for his research on the genetic basis of cancer.

The lowest-paid of the 20 top nonprofit leaders, University of Pennsylvania President Amy Gutmann, collected $675,000 for her labors overseeing a school with nearly 24,000 students and 5,000 faculty members. UPenn's budget last year totaled $4.87 billion, more than the revenues of XTO Energy, whose CEO gathered up nearly $60 million in 2006. Five university presidents, besides Gutmann, appear on the top 20 nonprofit pay list.

Over the last several years, several scandals have taken down nonprofit leaders who seem to have yearned to live the same imperial lifestyles as their corporate counterparts. Lawrence Small, a former banker, stepped down as head of the Smithsonian Institution in early 2007 after reports that his lavish leadership style required $2 million worth of spending on chauffeured cars, private jets, and exclusive hotels. Benjamin Ladner lost his job as American University president in 2005 after news reports revealed he had spent university money on personal chefs, limousines, and extravagant family parties.

Federal Executive Branch

By law, the President of the United States earns the highest salary in the federal government, $400,000 last year. Vice President Richard Cheney, who accumulated enormous wealth in the private sector before entering the Bush White House, made a government salary of $208,575 in 2006. Rounding out the 20 highest-paid federal executive branch officials: 15 cabinet secretaries and other cabinet-level government executives who earn the top executive pay grade of $186,600.

Military Service

In 2006, 15 top brass earned $187,390, the highest military pay rate. These included the chair and vice chair of the Joint Chiefs of Staff, the heads of each branch of the military, as well as the chiefs of various specialized commands, such as John Abizaid, who retired this year as head of the Central Command. Abizaid oversaw some 250,000 U.S. troops in 27 countries, including Iraq and Afghanistan. High-ranking generals round out last year's military top 20. Their base pay: $152,000.

All these generals are operating in an increasingly privatized war-time environment where many basic operations that used to be direct Pentagon responsibilities have been contracted out to powerhouse defense industry corporations. The CEOs of the top six defense contractors last year each pulled in between $12 million and $24 million. These included the chief executives of Lockheed Martin ($24.4 million), Boeing ($13.8 million), Northrop Grumman ($18.6 million), General Dynamics ($15.7 million), Raytheon ($11.9 million), and Halliburton ($16.5 million). Each of these six business leaders last year made more in a week than any of the generals made in a year.

U.S. Congress

The two highest-paid members of the U.S. Congress—the House speaker and Senate majority leader—each earned $212,100 salaries in 2006. The minority leaders in both chambers earned $183,500. All rank-and-file senators and representatives received $165,200 in paychecks last year.

The lowest-paid corporate executive on last year's list of the 20 highest-paid CEOs in America—Viacom's Philippe Dauman—personally pocketed over seven times more compensation for his leadership labors than the 20 top leaders in Congress together.

The huge gaps between congressional and business pay levels keep the revolving door spinning between Capitol Hill and K Street lobby groups. According to Public Citizen, 43 percent of the members of Congress who left office between 1998 and mid-2005 eligible to lobby actually became lobbyists.

This revolving door threatens government integrity in two ways:

- Members of Congress who are hoping to land lucrative private sector jobs have an incentive to shape public policy to please potential future employers or clients.
- Lawmakers-turned-lobbyists have privileged access to their former colleagues that can give them undue influence to advance their clients' interests.

In late July, the House of Representatives passed new ethics legislation that chooses not to extend the ban on lobbying by former House members from one to two years after their congressional service ends.

IV. U.S. Business Leaders vs. European Business Leaders

American executives continue to leave their European counterparts in the compensation dust, even after recent increases in European executive pay levels. In 2006, the 20 highest-paid European managers made an average of $12.5 million, only one third as much as the 20 highest-earning U.S. executives. The Europeans earned less, despite leading larger firms. On average, the 20 European firms with the highest-paid executives on the continent had sales of $65.5 billion, compared to $46.5 billion for the 20 U.S. firms.

The gap between U.S. and European executives is actually running wider than the dollar-equivalence figures below suggest. The drastic fall in the value of the dollar against the euro serves to inflate the compensation European executives received last year.

French executives dominated the list, making up 10 of the 20 highest-paid European executives. The top-earning French executive, Carlos Ghosn of Renault, took in $45.5 million, mostly in stock options. This total does not include Ghosn's compensation from Nissan. Ghosn has been CEO of both Renault and Nissan since 2005. Once considered a hero of the auto industry for resuscitating the Japanese automaker, Ghosn has had to face angry shareholders of late as both firms have performed sluggishly. Ghosn recently gave up his post as head of Nissan's North American operations.

The top-ranked German executive, Josef Ackermann of Deutsche Bank, collected $12.4 million. Ackermann became a lightning rod figure in Germany's ongoing executive pay debate when he faced criminal charges for having helped approve, as a board member, massive bonuses for executives at another German company. Ackermann and five other board members at this company were charged with "breach of fiduciary trust." Ackermann's unapologetic defense of both the bonuses and his own massive paycheck provoked charges that the Swiss-born banker was injecting a more ruthless style of American capitalism into a relatively egalitarian German society. The former head of the German Social Democratic Party called Ackermann's behavior "disastrous to the image of democracy."

V. Proposals for Change

This section highlights six practical initiatives that can rein in excessive executive pay. Five involve more equitable taxation, while one would use government contracting dollars to encourage more reasonable pay.

Recent polls suggest that these reforms would enjoy broad public support. The same July 2007 *Financial Times*/Harris poll that found widespread European support for capping executive pay found that 77 percent of Americans feel that corporate executives "earn too much." Only 11 percent admire "those who run" America's "largest companies" either "a great deal" or "quite a bit."

On top of that, Americans—by an overwhelming margin—want to see their nation's top income-earners pay more in taxes. Just 12 percent of Americans feel their country "correctly taxes those who earn the highest incomes." Five times that number, 61 percent, feel wealthy Americans "should be taxed more."

Proposals

Eliminate Tax Subsidies for Excessive CEO Pay

Under current law, corporations can deduct, as a "business expense," whatever excessive pay packages they hand their top executives, simply by defining that excess as a "performance incentive." This tax loophole essentially operates as an incentive for excessive compensation. The more corporations shell out in executive compensation, the less they pay in taxes. And the rest of us taxpayers wind up paying the bill.

Rep. Barbara Lee (D-Calif.) is promoting a reform that would cap the amount of executive compensation corporations are permitted to deduct to 25 times the pay of a company's lowest paid worker. Corporate boards would still be allowed to pay their executives as much as they wanted. They just wouldn't be able to deduct excessive amounts from their taxes.

If such a deductibility cap had been in place last year, the 386 companies included in the Associated Press pay survey would have paid as much as $1.4 billion more in 2006 taxes—just on their CEOs' compensation alone. That additional revenue, if earmarked for reducing class sizes in overcrowded schools, would have been enough to pay the annual salaries of 29,218 elementary school teachers.

And that's just the amount that would have been generated by capping the deductibility of CEO pay at these 386 firms. Rep. Lee's proposal, if enacted, would apply to all top management compensation within a company that exceeds the 25-to-1 ratio.

Down through the years, many noted figures in the business world have argued for reasonable ratios between executive and worker pay. A century ago, financier J. P. Morgan insisted on 20-to-1 ratios, a theme picked up in more recent times by Peter Drucker, the founder of modern management science.

End the Preferential Tax Treatment of Private Investment Company Executive Income

Rep. Sander Levin (D-Michigan) has introduced legislation that would plug the tax loophole that allows managers of the nation's private equity and hedge funds, individuals who often make hundreds of millions of dollars a year, to pay taxes at lower rates than average Americans.

These managers currently pay taxes on a substantial portion of their personal income at the 15 percent capital gains rate, not the 35 percent rate that would apply if their earnings were treated as ordinary income. Private investment managers earn an annual administrative fee (usually 2 percent) and carried interest on profits (usually 20 percent), often called a "carry." The tax code treats the carry portion of pay as capital gains, even though the investment manager is providing a professional service.

A recent Economic Policy Institute paper estimates that this loophole costs the federal treasury about $12.6 billion a year. This lost revenue, EPI notes, would be enough to fully fund a five-year, $35 billion expansion of SCHIP, the public health insurance program for America's low-income children.

Cap Tax-Free 'Deferred' Executive Pay

Most major corporations in the United States today—85 percent of the companies in the S&P 500—have created special "deferred pay" accounts for their top executives. Dollars in these accounts earn guaranteed interest, compounding on a tax-free basis, until the executives retire. Last year, according to an analysis by Equilar, a compensation analytics firm based in California, the median major company CEO deferred pay account held $3.7 million.

But this median understates the vast sums that some top executives have accumulated. The chief executive at retail giant Target, Robert Ulrich, held $133.5 million in his deferred pay account at year's end, all of this over and beyond the dollars in Ulrich's regular pension and 401 (k).

Standard 401 (k) plans, the only tax-deferral tool available to rank-and-file corporate employees, carry strict deferral limits. Workers under age 50 can this year defer from their taxes no more than $15,500 in 401 (k) contributions. Corporate executive deferred pay plans allow unlimited deferrals.

Senate Finance Committee chairman Max Baucus (D-Montana) and the panel's ranking minority member, Senator Charles Grassley (R-Iowa), earlier this year pushed all the way to a House-Senate conference committee legislation that would have limited annual executive pay deferrals to $1 million. The proposal, attacked fiercely by corporate interests, did not survive the conference committee deliberations. But Senator Baucus has pledged to revisit the initiative.

Eliminate the Tax Reporting Loophole on CEO Stock Options

Corporations are currently allowed to report one set of executive stock option compensation figures to investors on their financial statements and a completely different set of figures to the Internal Revenue Service (IRS) on their tax returns.

Corporations deduct the value of executive stock options, greatly reducing their taxes. At the same time, they often report a significantly lower stock option expense to their shareholders. The IRS examined corporate tax returns filed between December 2004 and June 2005 and identified a $43 billion discrepancy between deductions claimed to the IRS and option expenses reported to shareholders.

The U.S. Senate Permanent Subcommittee on Investigations examined the stock option tax deductions claimed by nine companies over five years. The deductions exceeded their reported stock option expenses by a total of more than $1 billion, or 575 percent. For example, of the 12 million stock options the Occidental Petroleum CEO exercised during the five-year period, the company claimed a $353 million tax deduction—12 times as much as the book expense that, under current accounting rules, would have totaled just $29 million.

This creative bookkeeping is not currently illegal. Senator Carl Levin, chairman of the U.S. Senate Permanent Subcommittee on Investigations, feels these companies "are benefiting from an outdated and overly generous stock option tax rule that produces tax deductions that often far exceed the companies' reported expenses."

Link Government Procurement to Executive Pay

Some of the most excessive executive pay packages over recent years have gone to CEOs whose companies take in much of their revenue from government contracts. Most of these contracts involve the defense industry.

Federal procurement law already limits the amount of pay that a company with a government contract can bill the government for executive compensation. But this "cap" only applies to direct federal dollars. Corporations whose profits or share prices soar after receiving a federal contract remain free to pay their top executives whatever company boards please.

A simple change could end these executive windfalls. The federal government could deny procurement contracts—or economic development subsidies or tax breaks—to all firms that pay their top executives over 25, 50, or even 100 times what their lowest-paid workers receive.

The federal government currently denies contracts to companies that increase, through discriminatory employment practices, racial or gender inequality in the United States. The same principle could be invoked to deny contracts to companies that, through excessive executive compensation, increase the nation's economic inequality.

Increase the Top Marginal Tax Rate on High Incomes

In 2006, not one of the compensation dollars collected by the business leaders discussed in this report faced a federal income tax rate higher than 35 percent.

Back in the 1950s, by contrast, earned income over $400,000—the equivalent of less than $3 million today—faced a top marginal tax rate of 91 percent.

These steeply graduated tax rates, in place for most of the mid-20th century, served to actively discourage excessive compensation. They sent a powerful cultural message that compensation beyond a certain lofty level serves no useful societal purpose.

Our contemporary CEO pay explosion began in the early 1980s, shortly after the Reagan administration sped through Congress legislation that dropped the top marginal tax rate from 70 percent, its level since 1964, down to 50 percent. The top rate has since dropped even lower. These lower rates may not have "caused" the executive pay cascade. But they opened the floodgates.

Any move to restore mid-20th century top marginal tax rates would raise substantial revenue for investments in education and other social programs that could significantly broaden economic opportunity. If the federal income tax rate on all annual income above $10 million were raised to 70 percent—and the tax rate on all income between $5 million and $10 million were raised to 50 percent—federal revenues in 2008 would increase by a stunning $105 billion.

Robert B. Reich

The Economic Argument for CEO Pay

According to research published recently by the Washington-based Institute for Policy Studies, the 20 highest-paid corporate executives earned on average $36 million in total compensation last year. The typical CEO of a Fortune 500 company didn't do quite as well, but at $10.8 million didn't do so badly—that's more than 364 times the pay of an average employee. Forty years ago, top CEOs earned 20 to 30 times what average workers earned.

The trend has ignited a flurry of attention in Washington. Last year the Securities and Exchange Commission ordered companies to reveal more detail about executive pay, but it's still hard for investors to decipher what companies disclose. SEC chairman Christopher Cox recently complained that a typical remuneration report is "as tough to read as a Ph.D. dissertation." In April, the House approved a proposal for a mandatory "say on pay" vote by shareholders. Although the White House opposes it and it has little chance of becoming law, expect Democrats to hammer away at the theme this election year.

Hold on.

There's an economic case for the stratospheric level of CEO pay which suggests shareholders—even if they had full say—would not reduce it. In fact, they're likely to let CEO pay continue to soar. That's because of a fundamental shift in the structure of the economy over the last four decades, from oligopolistic capitalism to super-competitive capitalism. CEO pay has risen astronomically over the interval, but so have investor returns.

The CEO of a big corporation 40 years ago was mostly a bureaucrat in charge of a large, high-volume production system whose rules were standardized and whose competitors were docile. It was the era of stable oligopolies, big unions, predictable markets and lackluster share performance. The CEO of a modern company is in a different situation. Oligopolies are mostly gone and entry barriers are low. Rivals are impinging all the time—threatening to lure away consumers all too willing to be lured away, and threatening to hijack investors eager to jump ship at the slightest hint of an upturn in a rival's share price.

Worse yet, any given company's rivals can plug into similar global supply and distribution chains. They have access to low-cost suppliers from all over the world and can outsource jobs abroad as readily as their competitors. They can streamline their operations with equally efficient software culled from many of the same vendors. They can get capital for new investment on much the same terms. And they can gain access to distribution channels that are no less efficient, some of them even identical.

So how does the modern corporation attract and keep consumers and investors (who also have better and better comparative information)? How does it distinguish itself? More and more, that depends on its CEO—who has to be sufficiently clever, ruthless and driven to find and pull the levers that will deliver competitive advantage.

There are no standard textbook moves, no well-established strategies to draw upon. If there were, rivals would already be using them. The pool of proven talent is small because so few executives have been tested and succeeded. And the boards of major companies do not want to risk error. The cost of recruiting the wrong person can be very large—and readily apparent in the deteriorating value of a company's shares. Boards are willing to pay more and more for CEOs and other top executives because their rivals are paying more and more for them. Former Home Depot CEO Robert Nardelli to the contrary notwithstanding, the pay is usually worth it to investors.

The proof is in the numbers. Between 1980 and 2003, the average CEO in America's 500 largest companies rose sixfold, adjusted for inflation. Outrageous? Not to investors. The average value of those 500 companies also rose by a factor of six, adjusted for inflation. In 2005, for example, Exxon Mobil reported $36 billion in profits. Its former chairman, Lee R. Raymond, retired that year with a compensation package totaling almost $400 million, including stock, stock options and long-term compensation. Too much? Not to Exxon's investors, who enjoyed a 223% return over the interval, compared to the average 205% return received by shareholders of other oil companies, a premium of about $16 billion. Raymond took home just 4% of that $16 billion.

As the economy has shifted toward supercapitalism, CEOs have become less like top bureaucrats and more like Hollywood celebrities who get a share of the house. Hollywood's most popular celebrities now pull in around 15% of whatever the studios take in at the box office. Clark Gable earned $100,000 a picture in the 1940s, roughly $800,000 in present dollars. But that was when Hollywood was dominated by big-studio oligopolies. Today, Tom Hanks makes closer to $20 million per film.

Movie studios—now competing intensely not only with one another but with every other form of entertainment—willingly pay these sums because they're still small compared to the money these stars bring in and the profits they generate. Today's big companies are paying their CEOs mammoth sums for much the same reason.

If you assume shareholders would rein in CEO pay, take a look at the United Kingdom. Since 2003, changes in British securities law have given investors more say over what British CEOs are paid. Nonetheless, executive pay there has continued to skyrocket, on the way to matching the pay of American CEOs.

Companies listed on the London stock market have done sufficiently well that British investors don't care what CEOs are paid. Full disclosure with shareholder approval might make it harder for a CEO to claim to be worth it if his company's shares have lost ground during his tenure or risen no more than the average share prices of other companies in the same industry. But given the intensity of competition for star performers, disclosure and approval might cause CEO pay to soar even higher.

This economic explanation for sky-high CEO pay does not justify it socially or morally. It only means that investors think CEOs are worth it. As citizens, though, most of us disapprove. About 80% of Americans polled by the Los Angeles Times and Bloomberg in early 2006 said CEOs are overpaid. The reaction was roughly the same regardless of the respondent's income or political affiliation. But if America wants to rein in executive pay, the answer isn't more shareholder rights. Just as with the compensation of Hollywood celebrities or private-equity and hedge fund managers, the answer—for anyone truly concerned—is a higher marginal tax rate on the super pay of those in super demand.

EXPLORING THE ISSUE

Is the U.S. Executive Pay Model Flawed?

Critical Thinking and Reflection

1. What are the main flaws of the U.S. executive pay model?
2. Explain the terms perquisites and golden parachutes.
3. What points would you argue to support that executives should receive high salaries?
4. What are some alternatives that HRM professionals may consider in executive pay?
5. How do other countries perceive their executive pay salaries?

Is There Common Ground?

U.S. executives are frequently criticized for getting very unreasonable total pay packages. Critics do not fail to comment that these executives seem to be affluent even with a poor and failing economy. The irony of the Detroit automakers flying in their private jets to Washington, D.C., to appeal for their federal bailout did not escape any viewer's attention. However, proponents of high executive pay levels suggest that making comparisons of executive pay to that of other professional levels seem quite inappropriate. The analogy made by journalists, politicians, and economists of executive pay levels to those of the "average worker" seems meaningless. Do you compare the salary of a software professional to that of an administrative assistant? Why? Why not? Each profession carries the burden of their own specialized skills making such comparisons pointless. The alternative perspectives suggest making compensation solely based on the executive performance. Do you think the government should stipulate a cap on executive pay? Why? Why not?

Additional Resources

Anonymous. (2009). Compensation paid to CEO/shareholder was reasonable. *Practical Tax Strategies, 82*(5), 298–300.

Krell, E. (2003). Getting a grip on executive compensation. *Workforce, 82*(2), 30–34.

Marquez, J. (2007). 5 questions: In defense of CEO pay. *Workforce Management, 86*(16), 8.

Welch, J. and Welch, S. (2008). CEO pay: No easy answer: the free market may at times overcompensate. But there's not a better system. *BusinessWeek* (4092), 106.

http://bulletin.aarp.org/states/fl/2009/17/articles/overall_ceo_pay_falls_but_top_executives_still.html: Overall CEO Pay Falls, But Top Executives Still Get Lavish Perks Like Tax Prep and Chauffeurs.

www.wsws.org/articles/2009/apr2009/ceos-a04.shtml: Wall Street Journal Report: US Executive Perks "Flourished" in 2008.

http://currents.westlawbusiness.com/Articles/2009/08/20090803_0011.aspx?cid=&src=WBSignon: Cutting the Perks: Execs Lose Jets, Jetco's Lose Execs.

www.compensationresources.com/press-room/executive-perks—What's Appropriate Today.

www.reuters.com/article/idUSTRE58M2QU20090923: Study Shows U.S. Bank CEO Pay Dwarfs Rest of World.

http://online.wsj.com/article/SB10001424052748704500604574482560792145116.html: Indian CEOs Get What They Deserve.

www.voxeu.org/index.php?q=node/5292: New Thinking on Executive Compensation; Pay CEOs with Debt.

www.allbusiness.com/human-resources/compensation/1386-1.html: Executive Compensation and Benefits.

www.msnbc.msn.com/id/29003620/ns/business-us_business/t/obama-imposes-limits-executive-pay/: Obama Imposes Limits on Executive Pay.

Internet References . . .

Mixing and Matching Four Generations of Employees

FDU Magazine is published by Fairleigh Dickinson University, which is the largest private university in New Jersey. This article discusses generational differences and how these differences effect the dynamics within the workplace.

http://www.fdu.edu/newspubs/magazine/05ws/generations.htm

Different Generations in the Workplace Can Collaborate Successfully

This Web site provides a column by generational expert and internationally known consultant, coach, writer, and speaker Phyllis Weiss Haserot on intergenerational relations and navigating the challenges of the multigenerational workplace for better productivity, retention, succession planning, and business development results. This site provides accounting news, information, tips, tools, resources, and insight—everything you need to help you prosper and enjoy the accounting profession even more.

http://www.accountingweb.com/topic/education-careers/different-generations-workplace-can-collaborate-successfully

High Performance Work Practices and Human Resource Management Effectiveness: Substitutes or Complements?

AllBusiness.com is an online media and e-commerce company that operates one of the premier business sites on the Web. The site has received critical acclaim from *The Wall Street Journal, Forbes, Business 2.0, Fortune, The New York Times, US News and World Report, USA Today,* and other publications. AllBusiness.com helps business professionals save time and money by addressing real-world business questions and presenting practical solutions.

http://www.allbusiness.com/business_planning/business_structures/3501627-1.html

Best HR Practices for Today's Innovation Management (The Human Side)

This Web site hosts a number of articles and literature on HR management. Here you will find an article that provides the best HR practices and innovation management techniques.

http://www.allbusiness.com/human-resources/108204-1.html

UNIT 6

The Effect of HRM Practices

Can different generations work harmoniously together at the workplace? Do elaborate HRM practices provide strategic advantages? The current workforce has employees from different generations working together that HRM professionals are concerned might require different HRM practices. On the other hand, both practitioners and scholars applaud the results of effective HRM practices on firm performance with many blue-chip examples from U.S. corporations. Can HRM practices be different and rewarding at the same time?

- Does Attracting, Developing, and Retaining the Millennial Generation Require Significant Changes to Current HRM Practices?
- Do Human Resource Management (HRM) Practices (Such as Selection, Training, Performance Management, and Compensation) Contribute to Increased Firm Performance?

ISSUE 16

Does Attracting, Developing, and Retaining the Millennial Generation Require Significant Changes to Current HRM Practices?

YES: Charles Woodruffe, from "Generation Y," *Training Journal* (July 2009)

NO: Dana Kyles, from "Managing Your Multigenerational Workforce," *Strategic Finance* (2005)

Learning Outcomes

After reading this issue, you should be able to:

- Understand the different terms for the various generations.
- Identify work-related characteristics of the different generations.
- Gain an understanding of the positive work-related characteristics of the millennials.
- Recognize the negative work-related characteristics of the millennials.
- Provide some alternatives in understanding this concept.

ISSUE SUMMARY

YES: Charles Woodruffe is an author and CEO of a company that focuses on managing winning talent. He states that Gen Yers might need a new set of management practices as the current practices might not be very congruent with their personality needs and characteristics. This generation has experienced accomplishments and rewards right through their lives and will have the same expectations at the workplace.

NO: Dana Kyles, freelance writer for *BusinessWeek* and *Strategic Finance* magazines, informs readers that it is possible for multiple generations to work harmoniously together. Several HRM practices appeal to all the generations unanimously and organizations should try and identify these common practices.

The American corporate is witnessing a new kind of workforce diversity. Four generations born in different time periods are currently working together; the Pre-Boomers or Matures (1900–1945), Baby Boomers (1946–1964), Generation Xers (1965–1979), and Generation Y or millennials (1980–1999). Researchers suggest that each generation carries their unique work-related characteristics shaped inimitably by their historical, economical, and cultural ties. The Pre-Boomers are considered loyal and conforming, the Baby Boomers are known to be competitive and hardworking, the Gen Xers are individualistic and tech-savvy, and millennials are considered multitasking and high-achieving. By 2014, the workforce will have a third of its employees being 50 years and older. As of 2011, the millennials constitute almost 25 percent of the workforce.

Organizations are concerned that the millennials may need a new set of management practices. The positive characteristics they bring to the workplace are that they are very competent technically. They have used technology all their lives right from their school through their college years. They also have a strong need to achieve and are willing to work even on the weekends to get their jobs done. Their boundaries between work and life seem blurred as they are constantly using technology to either connect socially or professionally. Thus, they do not mind taking work to complete at home and talking to personal friends while at work. They are very comfortable working in teams as they have been exposed very well to team activities in their schools and colleges. Further, this generation is considered the champion of multitasking, shaped again by the unique technological innovations of their times. The cell phones, BlackBerrys, iPhones, iPads, and many other technological devices have been introduced during their generation.

On the other hand, the negative side of the Gen Y is that they have been used to receiving predominantly only positive feedback. Therefore, they do not to take criticism very well, whether it is from management or co-workers. Further, they do not like to show deference to hierarchy as their generation has always demonstrated a casual approach to authority. They are fiercely competitive as they have excelled in both their core and extracurricular activities very well. They have generally been successful academically such that they do not accept failures very well. They feel they should be able to socially network and do not hesitate to use Facebook or MySpace from their work. They also do not mind staying connected with their supervisors from the privacy of their homes.

What kind of different HRM practices would the millennial generation need? First, as Gen Yers have generally experienced more comfort in their lives, attractive compensation packages are very important for them. Further, this generation desires materialistic things as they strive to maintain similar living standards to those of their parents. Second, they will seek training and development opportunities as they cherish learning experiences. Third, their high sense of achievement will also make them seek for professional titles and corporate visibility. Finally, they have grown up with brand names that they will strongly prefer to work for organizations that are branded as the employers of choice.

On the other hand, Diane Kyles suggests that it is possible to have similar management practices with diverse generations at the workplace. It requires a thorough understanding of each generation's core work-related values and personality traits. Research suggest that the Matures are loyal and motivated by public recognition, the Boomers are competitive and good at networking, Gen Xers crave for opportunity and autonomy, and Gen Yers need to stay connected socially with their peers through technology. Organizations can provide an excellent workplace for multi-generations by creating work projects that appeal to all generations. For instance, any work project can be redesigned to cater to different generations' perspectives. For instance, the Boomers might want to lead the project while the Gen Yers might want to be the technical experts. It is also important to acknowledge each generation's strengths so that it helps design appropriate work projects.

Scholars suggest that HRM practices can be maintained status quo as different generations may like some practices unanimously. Despite their age differences the four generations would like some form of flexibility in their work schedule whether it is in flexible scheduling, job sharing, or telework. Gen Xers might want the extra time to spend with their school-going children, while the Boomers might want that time to spend with their aging parents. Organizations can provide cafeteria benefits that would provide flexibility in choosing benefits relevant to the different generations. The Matures and Xers would definitely prefer more money in their retirement package, while the Xers would want more money toward college tuition reimbursement and Gen Yers definitely would want more hard cash to build their personal lives. A recent study of WorldatWork said organizations should consider generational differences by offering flexibility in the same core practices.

Professionals suggest several alternative perspectives for organizations in addressing this concept. First, it is important to instill a corporate culture that supports and understands generational differences rather than highlighting their differences. Each generation can learn from the other—organizations can offer seminars or forums to enhance this understanding. As organizations uphold diversity, they should also endorse hiring and retaining multigenerational talent. This can become a tremendous competitive advantage for firms as their generational workforce caters to diverse customers and introduces new markets.

Second, firms should focus on acquiring employees with superior KSAs regardless of what generations they represent. This will send a message loud and clear that acquiring qualified talent is paramount. Therefore, organizations should spread a wide recruiting net so that they attract qualified applicants from various backgrounds. Third, organizations should provide work places that keep employees engaged and absorbed—experts suggest that employee disengagement is consistently on the rise and its negative outcomes are very costly to organizations. Organizations that have engaging practices can retain employees from different generations. Firms that have different generations in their workforce should definitely offer choices in their benefits as this is one area in which the different generations may have varied perspectives. It is possible for the different generations to work together harmoniously if HRM practitioners provide progressive human resource management practices that can attract, develop, and retain a diverse talent capital.

YES  Charles Woodruffe

Generation Y

Abstract (Summary)

Finally, a survey last year by the CIPD and Penna came out with findings that run counter to the Generation Y stereotype. It found that Generation Y members were less concerned about CSR than Baby Boomers and also "far less likely to rapidly change jobs than was thought." Maybe another Generation Y quality is the ability to pick up on, and adapt rapidly to, changing economic circumstances.

Charles Woodruffe asks why?

In the run-up to the recession, there was a plethora of articles and conferences claiming to unlock the perplexing nature of Generation Y.

They are the pipeline of new talent available for employers but their values, needs—indeed, demands—were seen as different to those of their forebears. Employers were trying hard to understand them in order to attract and retain them. They were presented with a stereotype of very demanding, "want it all now" young people who were difficult to recruit but easy to lose. Generation Whine was rather cruelly applied as an alternative epithet.

The Generation Y stereotype has a logical basis in the way in which members of that generation were parented. In talking about Generation Y, we are talking about people brought up by active parents Although, somewhat irritatingly, every writer seems to date the generation differently, Generation Y is broadly the group of people born in the early 1980s and runs through to those still in secondary school. Their parents are broadly from the group known as the Baby Boomers—those born between the end of World War Two and the mid 1960s.

The key feature of Generation Y's upbringing is that their Baby Boomer parents have been heavily involved in it. We are talking about the huggy parents who ferry their children from event to event, do their homework for them, help them with their applications and, most importantly, have given them a high sense of self-worth.

Nor has the active parenting ended. The Americans have conjured the marvellous term 'helicopter parents' to describe the ongoing vigilance of the parents of Generation Y. This vigilance extends to a willingness to take issue with HR managers who do not recruit their progeny!

So where has all this left the children? Supposedly, members of Generation Y are marked out by their self-belief. They have had a history of positive feedback, understanding and parents answering their every need. They have little track record of frustration and having to wait. They have tended to be able to obtain what they want when they want it—be it a lift to a party or the latest Game Boy/Xbox etc. And the members of Generation Y that you are seeking to recruit and train will, almost by definition, have had a history of academic success.

As if having doting parents was not enough, members of Generation Y came to the labour market—until last autumn—at a time of plenty. But autumn 2008 might, of course, be where the story ends. In summer 2009, we need to take stock. Firstly, we were only ever talking about a caricature. Secondly, we need to decide whether the caricature still applies and matters.

The Caricature

If you follow Maslow's Hierarchy of Needs, with basic survival and security needs at the bottom and self-actualisation at the top, the parenting and background economy were said to have resulted in Generation Y being able to move directly to address higher-order needs. By the caricature, they are self-actualisers. In the workplace, they are painted as a high-maintenance generation, marked out by:

- High ambition
- Sense of entitlement
- Outspoken—they show a high willingness to challenge managers and are undeterred by traditional hierarchy, giving off an air of over-confidence
- Inability to take criticism
- Wanting work-life balance and flexibility. One survey suggests that 85 percent want to spend 30–70 percent of their time working from home
- Wanting attentive management from supervisors and regular appreciative feedback.

Generation Y is also said to:

- Struggle with processing failure and criticism
- Unable to internalise lessons
- Have difficulty with unclear guidelines or minimal management—yet not want to be told what to do
- Be ready to resign if their jobs are not fulfilling and fun, with decent holidays and the opportunity for career breaks and time off for charity work.

At the same time, Generation Y offers several positives, including:

- A complete at-oneness with IT—they have been brought up with it
- Team-working skills
- Self-belief to achieve

- A high level of drive. Seemingly in contradiction with the emphasis of Generation Y on work-life balance, people comment on their willingness to work after hours and at weekends to get a job done.

That was the caricature of Generation Y up to the recession—a time when Generation Y did not fear unemployment, having every belief in its ability to secure alternative employment. What is the status of the caricature now?

Firstly, like all caricatures, it would be foolish to apply it without thought or inspection to everyone born in the decade and a half from the early 1980s. Secondly, there is probably a germ of truth in it that it would be equally foolish for managers to deny.

On one hand, the caricature is an exaggeration and shorthand for a particular type of person. On the other hand, it recognises changes that have taken place in people's expectations at work that have spread beyond people born in those specific years.

Dealing first with the characteristics of the Y generation, you should clearly not think that everyone born within their timeslot will embody all their characteristics—good or bad. Their stereotypical behaviour was generally an unrealistic and irritating way for people to approach employers (I recall hearing of a person in their mid twenties throwing a strop because their bonus was merely half a million pounds); nowadays it is just plain ludicrous.

Of course, there will be some who, recession or not, continue to live out the caricature to its extreme. It seems to me that you do not have to adapt to their shortcomings, which—taken to an extreme—might stop them being seen as talent in the first place. Instead, your selection systems need to pick out the ones who will adapt to work life in your organisation.

However, and returning to the germ of truth in the caricature, there has to be some mutual adaptation. You will choose members of Generation Y who seem the most productive people or the best investments. They will choose you if you have recognised that the centre of gravity of what you offer people has changed.

This change has also spread outside the confines of Generation Y, just as Facebook and iPods are not the monopoly of a particular generation. It is a change from which it will be hard to turn away, even in a recession, though, of course, people might well have retraced their steps down Maslow's hierarchy. Everyone might be concerned with job security, but that does not mean they will be positively engaged if their other needs are ignored.

So how do you engage people who have become used to the new generation of employment? Essentially, you have to get alongside their needs and values and make sure you address their priorities. For several years, I have used a needs triangle to try to summarise what people nowadays are looking for in work. This is not perfect science but it does offer a way of ordering people's needs.

1. The package

Generation Y—particularly males—are said to be quite focused on their salary. This has been put down to their student debt burden and the need for a good salary to join the property ladder. However, although the package is a vital component of being an employer of choice, few people flock to an otherwise bad employer purely because it pays well. Generally, the package is the least sure way of retaining people for it is the inducement that is most easily matched by another employer.

2. Employability

We do not go to work just to earn today's money, but tomorrow's also. People are concerned with an income stream rather than just immediate money. There are four major factors that affect employability:

- *Being developed* People nowadays demand development. They recognise that the future is uncertain and that even a committed employer cannot guarantee a job. They want to be ready with a passport to alternative employment. Organisations must give a high priority to people's development in order to attract and retain them. Development must cover professional and managerial/leadersip skills. The most powerful development comes from providing people with new experiences, particularly experiences that challenge them.
- *Involvement with prestige projects* Ambitious people, notably today's Generation Y graduates, like visibility. They relish the opportunity to tackle prestigious projects, particularly those that will give them exposure to people with power within the organisation. Assuming their contribution is a positive one, such exposure enhances employability.
- *Career advancement* Drive and motivation is part of what makes people talented. Advancement feeds their goal of securing and maintaining an income stream. Part of being an employer of choice comes from letting good people get ahead quickly.
- *Being part of a prestigious organisation* There is an advantage to the employee in working for a prestigious organisation that is at the leading edge of its sector. It has a currency on the job market that will generate future income. The importance of this factor is clear from organisations' thirst to be among the list of Top 100 employers (e.g., The Times Top 100 Graduate Employers).

3. Job satisfaction

If people go out to work to generate the income for a style of life, they also want to be happy while doing so. Six components of job satisfaction can be separated:

- *Achievement* To be an employer of choice, you want your staff to be telling their friends about the tremendous achievements they have notched up, not how they are bored out of their brains and underutilised. Generation Y puts great store by using its strengths.
- *Respect and recognition* People are less tolerant than in the past of status distinctions and barriers. They want to be trusted with information and to have their hard work noticed. Members of Generation Y are also said to be intolerant of status barriers: they expect to be able to email

senior people and might well extend this to those at the top of their employing organisations. Raising managers' skill levels is vital to being an employer of choice. Indeed, they need to lead rather than manage. Generation Y is also described as in particular need of regular feedback, having grown used to regular testing at school and university.

- *Autonomy* People enjoy a sense of autonomy and of being trusted to get on and deliver. They can be frustrated if they do not feel a sense of ownership over their projects or if they lack real responsibility. It was partly satisfying this sense of autonomy that made 'dot coms' so attractive.
- *Balance between work and private life* Generation Y is said to be particularly intolerant of a lack of integration between work and private life. It is not so much a sense of balance as a blurring of the two that matters. Members expect to come to work and be logged into Facebook or MSN at the same time as doing their work. At university, they are used to mixing work (study) and their private life and would see it as restrictive to have boundaries at work. They are the permanently connected generation.
- *Congruent values* People want to work in an organisation with values that are congruent with their own. By definition, values are something on which we differ. However, at any period of time there is a dominant value system with which employers would be better off being congruent than discordant. For example, nowadays, organisations strive to parade their CSR credentials and this must be for their staff to witness as much as their customers. But it is vital that this is authentic: Generation Y is vigilant to a lack of integrity. Generation Y is also said to be particularly vigilant to identity and intolerant of working towards something that does not reflect its own sense of identity.
- *A sense of fun in a good working environment* Many people prefer to work in an informal and fun atmosphere. Organisations have sought to meet this in all sorts of ways, such as by having trendy office environments, 'dress-down' days and team-building events of various sorts. A lack of teamwork/cooperation was cited as a turnover driver by 19 percent of leavers in a survey by TalentDrain.

Individual Focus

Perhaps more important than any of the above needs is the requirement to treat people as individuals. In response, organisations are doing their best to customise what is provided to employees, ensuring as far as possible that each person's particular needs are met.

But They'll Leave Anyway

However, the image of Generation Y is that you can meet its members' needs as much as you like but they'll leave anyway to build their CVs. They do not have staying with their first employer as their game plan, so what is the point of bothering with them?

There are two responses to this. Firstly, will they all leave? The answer, surely, is of course not, especially in the current economic circumstances. If you can offer them the chance to build their employability, some will stay, some will go with the possibility of coming back and some will be lost forever.

Secondly, the ability to build employability is, in truth, probably greater for large organisations than others. Certainly, small firms would be naïve to think they can readily take on graduates who will stay to lead their organisation in the future. It is simply not in the Generation Y blueprint. Quite realistically, they will see that they need to move around and build their CVs. On the other hand, large multinationals can offer a series of employments akin to moving between organisations.

This is fortunate because opting out of employing Generation Y is only realistic for smaller organisations. Large volume recruiters like retailers, the civil service, law firms and accountants have to keep topping up their talent pipeline. Other organisations could consider leaving their recruitment of future leaders until people have matured into the ways of work. That is not to say that they should boycott Generation Y: it is just that the relationship is likely to be an affair rather than a marriage.

Conclusions

Generation Y makes up approximately 20 percent of the workforce and is vital to our economic future. Some of them will behave in line with their caricature. In a recession, one hopes for their sake, many will not. However, it is also the case that what people expect from work has evolved and this evolution extends beyond Generation Y.

The task of employers is to separate the employable from the unemployable but also to adapt to the changing demands of each generation in just the same way that they adapt to the changing expectations of their customers.

Finally, a survey last year by the CIPD and Penna came out with findings that run counter to the Generation Y stereotype. It found that Generation Y members were less concerned about CSR than Baby Boomers and also "far less likely to rapidly change jobs than was thought." Maybe another Generation Y quality is the ability to pick up on, and adapt rapidly to, changing economic circumstances.

Dana Kyles

Managing Your Multigenerational Workforce

Abstract (Summary)

For the first time in American history, corporations are challenged with managing four generations of employees at once, each with different values, expectations, and attitudes. The old models of who works and what they work for are steadily changing, but this new workplace diversity does not have to wreak havoc on productivity or retention. If leveraged properly, it can actually increase efficiency and employee satisfaction. The four groups are Matures, Baby Boomers, Generation Xers, and Nexters. Regardless of what group you are in or what group you manage, success can be achieved through understanding. Consider the following strategies: 1. Create both function- and project-oriented assignments. 2. Watch your mouth. 3. Acknowledge strengths and commonalities. 4. Listen. 5. Look beyond appearances. 6. Keep an open mind. The main thing to keep in mind is that each generation has something valuable to add to the workplace, and managers need to make sure that happens.

It takes time, talent, tact, and perseverance—but the end product can be a great place to work with a wonderful talent pool.

What happens when multiple generations work together in a department or on a team but they don't know or understand the generational values of their colleagues? BAMU!!! Sparks fly, and production may implode. For the first time in American history, corporations are challenged with managing four generations of employees at once, each with different values, expectations, and attitudes. The old models of who works and what they work for are steadily changing, but this new workplace diversity doesn't have to wreak havoc on productivity or retention. If leveraged properly, it can actually increase efficiency and employee satisfaction.

The four groups are Matures, Baby Boomers, Generation Xers, and Nexters. After describing them, I'll suggest some effective ways to manage them.

Name: Matures (aka Pre-Boomers, Silents, Traditionalists, Veterans)
Age: Born between 1900 and 1945
Population: 75 million in workforce
Characteristics: Loyal, consistent, conforming

Matures, the oldest group, aren't known to go against the grain or challenge authority. They are structure-loving, abide-by-the-rules-type folks who came of age during the Great Depression and World War II. Influenced by war times and military backgrounds, most are comfortable with conformity and a top-down management style. Their values are based on respect for authority, integrity, and delayed gratification. Often motivated by verbal or written recognition, awards, and public acknowledgment for a job well done, this segment is most loyal to their employer and doesn't believe in job switching. They often prefer being an "expert" in their function, and employers enjoy the consistency that comes with that preference.

Name: Baby Boomers

Age: Born between 1946 and 1964

Population: 80 million in workforce

Characteristics: Competitive, political, hardworking

The influence of their stay-at-home moms, Western heroes, and hopes of post-war prosperity weren't enough to counter influences from "free love" societies, civil rights protests, and Vietnam. This free-spirited generation rebelled against conformity and everything that resembled it. In doing so, they redefined traditional family roles, changed social norms, raised the divorce rate, and accumulated unprecedented amounts of credit card debt. Known for their workaholic ethic, Boomers will do whatever it takes to get the job done and get ahead, and they expect to be rewarded with status symbols such as advanced titles, more money, special parking spaces, and large private offices. They outnumber all other generations and hold a majority of management-level positions in the workforce. Baby Boomers are master networkers who rank relationship building higher than most other work virtues. They are also approaching retirement and are heavily concerned with financial and job security.

Name: Generation Xers

Age: Born between 1965 and 1979

Population: 46 million in workforce

Characteristics: Individualistic, disloyal, techno literate

Generation Xers are considered the most challenging group to manage. Often viewing corporate relationship building as a degree of "bootlicking," they, unlike the former generation, could care less about titles or hierarchies and prefer to stay out of corporate politics. This computer-savvy generation finds security in their own skills. If they can't continue to learn and develop in their work environment, they will leave it. Their values aren't hard to understand considering they entered the job market during a period of massive corporate layoffs and a brutal economic recession. It's quite logical that they are skeptical of authority and don't trust corporate America. Being the first generation reared in single-parent/nontraditional homes where their "caretaking" duties were critical to the family's survival also makes their strong belief in work/life balance understandable. Opportunity and autonomy are the ultimate corporate rewards for this generation. Not only is it a reward—it's a requirement for them to be happy and productive in the workplace.

Name: Nexters (aka Generation Y, Millennial)

Age: Born between 1980 and 1999
Population: 75 million just entering the workforce
Characteristics: Techno literate, purposed, multitasking

Generation Next is coming of age during a time of technological sophistication, extreme economic swings, individual/entrepreneurial prosperity, terrorism, and HIV/AIDS. Also products of nontraditional families, they are developing the self-resiliency of the previous generation. Nexters are looking for purpose and fulfillment in their careers. Not so much concerned with the American Dream as defined by the Baby Boomers or the individuality of the Xers, Nexters want meaningful jobs that allow them to cater to the greater good of society. They want their managers to relate to them and value their contributions. If they aren't valued or feel they aren't contributing, they will leave. Their greatest reward is internal, not external.

Getting Along

Regardless of what group you are in or what group you manage, success can be achieved through understanding. Consider the following strategies:

- Create both function- and project-oriented assignments. Creating a mixture of function- and project-oriented assignments appeals to all generations. The Matures get to be experts within their function, Boomers can lead a project or function and satisfy their need for status, Xers can continue to develop/acquire new skills by jumping from project to project to project, and Nexters can fit in the slot they deem most valuable to them.
- Watch your mouth. Generational clashes typically stem from miscommunication. Choose a communication style suitable for the audience and that is considerate of their work drivers. For example, using the work-hard/play-hard motto and bragging about working evenings and/or weekends during a job interview as a description of a work culture is more likely to repel the younger generations and attract the Boomers. Also, knowing that Matures may feel a little anxious about computer technology, other generations should seek understanding of Matures' competency levels when implementing new technology instead of assuming they know as much as everyone else, and they should offer the appropriate technology training.
- Acknowledge strengths and commonalities. Acknowledging the strengths of each generation provides a strategic edge in workforce planning or team formulation. For example, if a department wants to establish a new activity-based management (ABM) system, a Mature can provide functional knowledge and expertise about drivers and metrics, a Boomer can act as coordinator using his/her network to gather necessary support and cooperation, and the Xers and Nexters can determine or develop the technology for tracking and rolling out a training and implementation plan.
- Listen. When a Mature tells a Nexter she is shooting herself in the foot, she should take heed and learn from the wisdom. If an Xer requests a month to create a new decision model that proposes to do in one

mouse click what it takes two clerks eight hours a week to do, let him. It probably works.
- Look beyond appearances. Diversity is difficult to manage if the mere sight of someone automatically puts them into a category. Get to know employees and their backgrounds before making judgments. For example, if Mr. Boomer's idea of business casual is a blazer, starched blue shirt, and creased slacks but the Xers dress in Polos, khakis, nose rings, and boots, he shouldn't assume they aren't serious about their careers.
- Keep on open mind. It's a must!

Obviously, I've just touched on a few main points here so you can get a quick overview of the groups. Remember, though, that not every person fits all of the characteristics of his/her generation's description. For example, the older Baby Boomers may reflect more characteristics of the Matures, and the younger Baby Boomers may be more like GenXers. And the Nexters may reflect a number of the values of the Matures.

The main thing to keep in mind is that each generation has something valuable to add to the workplace, and we, as managers, need to make sure that happens.

EXPLORING THE ISSUE

Does Attracting, Developing, and Retaining the Millennial Generation Require Significant Changes to Current HRM Practices?

Critical Thinking and Reflection

1. Define Pre-Boomers, Baby Boomers, Gen X, and Gen Y.
2. What are some positive and negative work-related characteristics of Gen Y?
3. Should HRM practices be modified to cater to Gen Y?
4. What are some alternatives that HRM professionals may consider in managing a multigenerational workforce?

Is There Common Ground?

The millennials have experienced a life of comfort in comparison to that of the other generations. Further, their generational times have seen some of the best technological revolutions. For instance, the Internet, cell phones, BlackBerrys, iPhones, and other innovations have mostly been introduced in their times, making this generation extremely confident about using technological devices. Experts suggest that organizations may have to modify their current HRM practices to accommodate the Gen Yers. However, opponents suggest that no changes are required to the HRM practices other than providing policies and procedures that might appeal to all the generations. HRM professionals need to establish practices that have the flexibility to be tailored to the different generations. Experts also suggest developing organizational cultures that support generational differences and take advantage of the differences to their business needs. Have you experienced working with Pre-Boomers, Gen Xers, or Baby Boomers? What has your experience been? What suggestions do you have for organizations to handle this new labor trend? Why do you think experts suggest that Gen Yers will need new management practices?

Additional Resources

http://www.primacy.com/primetimes/200804/featured_article.html: Gen X vs. Gen Y: Nike Compares the Two.

http://www.andersonperformance.com/News/Articles/ToEngageGenYWorkersAdoptNewApproaches.htm: To Engage Gen Y Workers, Adopt New Approaches.

http://assets.aarp.org/www.aarp.org_/cs/misc/leading_a_multigenerational_workforce.pdf: Leading a Multigenerational Workforce.

http://legalcareers.about.com/od/practicetips/a/multigeneration.htm: The Multigenerational Workforce.

ISSUE 17

Do Human Resource Management (HRM) Practices (Such as Selection, Training, Performance Management, and Compensation) Contribute to Increased Firm Performance?

YES: Anonymous, from "Google's Lessons for Employers: Put Your Employees First," *HR Focus* (vol. 85, no. 9, pp. 8–9, September 2008)

NO: Keith H. Hammonds, from "Why We Hate HR," *Fast Company* (vol. 97, pp. 41–47, 2005)

Learning Outcomes

After reading this issue, you should be able to:

- Understand the resource-based theory of organizations.
- Detail the best HRM practices at Google Inc.
- Understand why HRM departments cannot contribute to firm performance.
- Provide some alternatives in understanding this concept.

ISSUE SUMMARY

YES: This article interviews the senior HRM leader in Google Inc. to identify how HRM practices have contributed to their phenomenal success and growth of the organization. Lazlo Bock, HRM leader of Google, insists that it is his HRM practices and the Google employees that make his organization outstanding.

NO: Keith Hammonds, former executive editor of *Fast Company* magazine, suggests that HRM leaders are never in the forefront in most organizations. Hence, HRM departments do not provide any substantial profits or growth in organizations.

HRM includes a wide range of practices, right from an employee's entrance into an organization to his or her final exit. In the early 1990s, the concept of strategic human resource management or the adoption of effective HRM practices to enhance a firm's competitive advantage began to emerge. Until then, organizations competed with one another mainly on the basis of their products or services. Organizations soon realized that competitors could easily imitate their products or services, outdoing any competitive advantages. However, Professor Jay Barney provided a revolutionary theory, the resource-based view, suggesting firms can enhance their sustainable competitive advantage by adopting strategic HRM practices. He suggested that organizations look for their competitive advantages within their own organizations by developing unique practices and investing in their employees. He stated that such advantages cannot be easily mimicked by competitors and will sustain organizations in the marketplace. Therefore, an increased awareness that employees and their HRM practices can provide organizations with sustainable competitive advantages became entrenched.

Google Inc. is a classic example of a company that has adopted strategic HRM practices very effectively to enhance their firm performance. This 12-year-old company, with about 20,000 employees, had annual revenues of $19 billion in 2009. They have a major share of the market with 50.8 percent of the Web-service market. How have they achieved such a phenomenal growth in such a short time? Is it their effective strategic HRM practices?

The HRM department at Google is called People Operations and comprises employees from three different fields: traditional HRM, consulting, and psychology backgrounds. This multidisciplinary approach in managing human resource management practices has produced a classic people operations model. They recruit mainly from elite colleges, headhunters, or employee referrals as these forms of recruitment ensure a very qualified applicant pool. Their hiring practices are very elaborate with the goal of hiring the most qualified. It involves multiple behavioral interviews and cognitive ability tests. Behavioral interviews allow employers to ask very specific job-related questions based on applicants' past experience. Cognitive ability tests are considered to be one of the best predictors of job performance. The company provides extensive opportunities for training such as self-directed (e-learning), on-the-job learning (from other team members), and external presentation (subject matter experts), rendering for a very well-developed workforce.

Their performance appraisal system follows a format of 70 percent (main work), 20 percent (any Google project that interests employees), and 10 percent (any extracurricular class or learning) work policy as the company insists that a variety of work-related activities can tremendously enhance employees' creativity and innovative spirits. The company offers breakfast, lunch, and dinner free for their employees or "Googlers" at their 15 ethnic restaurants on their corporate campus. The new employees or "Nooglers" are also made welcome with presents and lunches with potential managers. In addition, employees can claim $8,000 annually for tuition reimbursements and new parents get $500 for 4 weeks so that they can care for their newborns.

Keith Hammonds, an MBA graduate from Harvard, suggests in his very forthcoming article that HRM practices do not contribute to enhanced firm profits. He supports his information with statistics suggesting that organizations neither seek qualified talent nor do they develop their internal talent. He adds that graduates from top schools do not pursue HRM careers as they do not consider such professions rewarding. He argues HRM departments are not strategic partners and will not become involved in organizations' long-term planning initiatives. He emphasizes this statement with the fact that employees who become HRM professionals do not have sufficient academic background in business courses (such as finance or strategy) that can contribute to the firms' bottom profits. He adds expert comments from Professor Ulrich, considered a leader in human resource management, who suggests that only when HRM professionals contribute value to the main players in the organization can they be considered strategic partners.

Further, HRM professionals are constantly wary of the myriad federal laws that make them concerned more about lawsuits rather than about firm performances or business profits. In the present dynamic and flexible business landscape, while most departments are constantly trying to innovate, HRM departments are trying to standardize to stay attentive to the federal laws. He provides merit pay as an example to prove his point, which is a standard procedure adopted even though everyone knows that it does not reward superior performers. He also provides input from Professor Grattton, a leading international HRM expert, that HRM professionals are struggling to become strategic partners as businesses change their strategies rapidly, which HRM departments simply cannot understand. Further, many organizations today are outsourcing HRM functions—so what do HRM departments actually do?

An alternate perspective to this prompt is to make sure that HRM professionals adopt financial metrics for their HRM practices. For instance, if they provide a corporate training program, they need to measure if the participants of the training program contributed to or enhanced the firm's profits. In other words, HRM members have to constantly measure how their practices contribute or add value to the firm's revenue. The HRM departments have to become accountable for recruitment, selection, training, performance appraisal, and compensation practices. Most often HRM departments merely deliver the required practices without measuring its financial results. HRM professionals should measure how their practices distinguish their products and services in the marketplace to increase the firm's revenues. It also means HRM departments have to radically change some of their current mediocre practices of merit pay and annual performance appraisals that really do not augment or add value to the firm. The HRM leaders should also get involved with the top leaders in developing the mission or goals and understanding how their roles can enhance the corporate strategy. The HRM departments can also be cost-effective by staying ahead on legal issues so that their organization may not face undue liabilities. Generally, organizations lose millions of dollars in court cases due to negligent behavior of their employees.

An international perspective suggests that emerging economies like China and India are adopting strategic HRM practices as it has proven to increase firm performance. These economies now provide elaborate training and development, careful selection, and unusual benefits that they did not provide a decade ago. Further, an increased presence of multinationals in these countries has prompted the local Chinese and Indian organizations to mimic international HRM practices also.

Anonymous

Google's Lessons for Employers: Put Your Employees First

Abstract (Summary)

Freedom and curiosity are what popular employer Google is all about, Laszlo Bock told attendees at a session at SHRM's annual conference and exhibition in Chicago. Bock is VP in charge of people operations, a key role in an organization that focuses on hiring and developing the right people. Being open to ideas from employees is really what's central to Google's success as a workplace, Bock maintained, although people may assume it has more to do with the fact that employees can bring their pets to work or the availability of onsite car washes.

Freedom and curiosity are what popular employer Google is all about, Laszlo Bock told attendees at a session at SHRM's annual conference and exhibition in Chicago. Bock is vice president in charge of people operations, a key role in an organization that focuses on hiring and developing the right people.

Being open to ideas from employees is really what's central to Google's success as a workplace, Bock maintained, although people may assume it has more to do with the fact that employees can bring their pets to work or the availability of onsite car washes.

Google's People Ops group includes hundreds of employees with experience in three key areas: "classical" HR people, people from business consulting with good problem-solving skills, and detail-oriented experts in areas such as statistics and psychology. The group has developed an efficient list of questions to ask job applicants that helps predict success within the organization. And a "self-nomination" system is used for promoting people: When they feel they are ready, the company conducts an extensive evaluation, relying heavily on input from peers.

Google's rules of engagement with employees, according to Bock:

- Hire learners. They are inquisitive, and when they fail, they will ask how they can do better.
- Give people the tools and resources to succeed; then let them.

- Work on small projects in small teams.
- Keep structures flat. Especially as the company gets big, information needs to flow up.
- Discuss everything you can publicly.
- Give performance-driven raises. This is helpful in controlling turnover and enhancing retention.
- Reward success, don't penalize failure. "If you don't fail, you're not doing your job well." Quarterly goals are set and performance evaluations are based on these; the company aims for a 70 percent success rate.

Keith H. Hammonds

Why We Hate HR

In a knowledge economy, companies with the best talent win. And finding, nurturing, and developing that talent should be one of the most important tasks in a corporation. So why does human resources do such a bad job—and how can we fix it?

Well, here's a rockin' party: a gathering of several hundred midlevel human-resources executives in Las Vegas. (Yo, Wayne Newton! How's the 401(k)?) They are here, ensconced for two days at faux-glam Caesars Palace, to confer on "strategic HR leadership," a conceit that sounds, to the lay observer, at once frightening and self-contradictory. If not plain laughable.

Because let's face it: After close to 20 years of hopeful rhetoric about becoming "strategic partners" with a "seat at the table" where the business decisions that matter are made, most human-resources professionals aren't nearly there. They have no seat, and the table is locked inside a conference room to which they have no key. HR people are, for most practical purposes, neither strategic nor leaders.

I don't care for Las Vegas. And if it's not clear already, I don't like HR, either, which is why I'm here. The human-resources trade long ago proved itself, at best, a necessary evil—and at worst, a dark bureaucratic force that blindly enforces nonsensical rules, resists creativity, and impedes constructive change. HR is the corporate function with the greatest potential—the key driver, in theory, of business performance—and also the one that most consistently underdelivers. And I am here to find out why.

Why are annual performance appraisals so time-consuming—and so routinely useless? Why is HR so often a henchman for the chief financial officer, finding ever-more ingenious ways to cut benefits and hack at payroll? Why do its communications—when we can understand them at all—so often flout reality? Why are so many people processes duplicative and wasteful, creating a forest of paperwork for every minor transaction? And why does HR insist on sameness as a proxy for equity?

It's no wonder that we hate HR. In a 2005 survey by consultancy Hay Group, just 40% of employees commended their companies for retaining high-quality workers, just 41% agreed that performance evaluations were fair. Only 58% rated their job training as favorable. Most said they had few opportunities for advancement—and that they didn't know, in any case, what was required to move up. Most telling, only about half of workers below the manager level believed their companies took a genuine interest in their well-being.

None of this is explained immediately in Vegas. These HR folks, from employers across the nation, are neither evil courtiers nor thoughtless automatons. They are mostly smart, engaging people who seem genuinely interested in doing their jobs better. They speak convincingly about employee development and cultural transformation. And, over drinks, they spin some pretty funny yarns of employee weirdness. (Like the one about the guy who threatened to sue his wife's company for "enabling" her affair with a coworker. Then there was the mentally disabled worker and the hooker—well, no, never mind. . . .)

But then the facade cracks. It happens at an afternoon presentation called "From Technicians to Consultants: How to Transform Your HR Staff into Strategic Business Partners." The speaker, Julie Muckler, is senior vice president of human resources at Wells Fargo Home Mortgage. She is an enthusiastic woman with a broad smile and 20 years of experience at companies such as Johnson & Johnson and General Tire. She has degrees in consumer economics and human resources and organizational development.

And I have no idea what she's talking about. There is mention of "internal action learning" and "being more planful in my approach." PowerPoint slides outline Wells Fargo Home Mortgage's initiatives in performance management, organization design, and horizontal-solutions teams. Muckler describes leveraging internal resources and involving external resources—and she leaves her audience dazed. That evening, even the human-resources pros confide they didn't understand much of it, either.

This, friends, is the trouble with HR. In a knowledge economy, companies that have the best talent win. We all know that. Human resources execs should be making the most of our, well, human resources—finding the best hires, nurturing the stars, fostering a productive work environment—just as IT runs the computers and finance minds the capital. HR should be joined to business strategy at the hip.

Instead, most HR organizations have ghettoized themselves literally to the brink of obsolescence. They are competent at the administrivia of pay, benefits, and retirement, but companies increasingly are farming those functions out to contractors who can handle such routine tasks at lower expense. What's left is the more important strategic role of raising the reputational and intellectual capital of the company—but HR is, it turns out, uniquely unsuited for that.

Here's why.

1. HR people aren't the sharpest tacks in the box. We'll be blunt: If you are an ambitious young thing newly graduated from a top college or B-school with your eye on a rewarding career in business, your first instinct is not to join the human-resources dance. (At the University of Michigan's Ross School of Business, which arguably boasts the nation's top faculty for organizational issues, just 1.2% of 2004 grads did so.) Says a management professor at one leading school: "The best and the brightest don't go into HR."

Who does? Intelligent people, sometimes—but not businesspeople. "HR doesn't tend to hire a lot of independent thinkers or people who stand up as moral compasses," says Garold L. Markle, a longtime human-resources executive at Exxon and Shell Offshore who now runs his own consultancy. Some are exiles from the corporate mainstream: They've fared poorly in meatier roles—but not poorly enough to be fired. For them, and for their employers, HR represents a relatively low-risk parking spot.

Others enter the field by choice and with the best of intentions, but for the wrong reasons. They like working with people, and they want to be helpful—noble motives that thoroughly tick off some HR thinkers. "When people have come to me and said, 'I want to work with people,' I say, 'Good, go be a social worker,'" says Arnold Kanarick, who has headed human resources at the Limited and, until recently, at Bear Stearns. "HR isn't about being a do-gooder. It's about how do you get the best and brightest people and raise the value of the firm."

The really scary news is that the gulf between capabilities and job requirements appears to be widening. As business and legal demands on the function intensify, staffers' educational qualifications haven't kept pace. In fact, according to a survey by the Society for Human Resource Management (SHRM), a considerably smaller proportion of HR professionals today have some education beyond a bachelor's degree than in 1990.

And here's one more slice of telling SHRM data: When HR professionals were asked about the worth of various academic courses toward a "successful career in HR," 83% said that classes in interpersonal communications skills had "extremely high value." Employment law and business ethics followed, at 71% and 66%, respectively. Where was change management? At 35%. Strategic management? 32%. Finance? Um, that was just 2%.

The truth? Most human-resources managers aren't particularly interested in, or equipped for, doing business. And in a business, that's sort of a problem. As guardians of a company's talent, HR has to understand—how people serve corporate objectives. Instead, "business acumen is the single biggest factor that HR professionals in the U.S. lack today," says Anthony J. Rucci, executive vice president at Cardinal Health Inc., a big health-care supply distributor.

Rucci is consistently mentioned by academics, consultants, and other HR leaders as an executive who actually does know business. At Baxter International, he ran both HR and corporate strategy. Before that, at Sears, he led a study of results at 800 stores over five years to assess the connection between employee commitment, customer loyalty, and profitability.

As far as Rucci is concerned, there are three questions that any decent HR person in the world should be able to answer. First, who is your company's core customer? "Have you talked to one lately? Do you know what challenges they face?" Second, who is the competition? "What do they do well and not well?" And most important, who are we? "What is a realistic assessment of what we do well and not so well vis à vis the customer and the competition?"

Does your HR pro know the answers?

2. HR pursues efficiency in lieu of value. Why? Because it's easier—and easier to measure. Dave Ulrich, a professor at the University of Michigan, recalls

STUPID HR TRICKS

Can Your Highly Trained Human-Resources Professional Do This? Or Has He Already?

In 2003, **FedEx** for the first time asked employees to make $10 copayments for doctors' visits. But Dave Haynes, a FedEx sales rep and author of *The Peon Book* (Berrett-Koehler, 2004), notes that "in order to ensure that all employees understood the policy and its impact, HR sent us three separate glossy four-color brochures and went to the expense of creating a Web site." Says a FedEx spokeswoman, "We do send four-color brochures to get the attention of employees and their families."

An editor at Disney Press, the **Walt Disney Co.**'s publisher of children's books, was worried about his relationship with his increasingly erratic supervisor. One morning, he arrived at work to find a voice mail from the boss that threatened physical violence. He played the voice mail to a human-resources manager, who told him, "Well, I think it's time for you to start looking for another job." "I said, 'You're kidding, right?'" the editor says now. "She said, 'That's my best solution.' I couldn't believe it." Disney declined to comment.

Regina Blus was managing a large software project across several departments at **Sun Microsystems**. In one department, a new manager, widely disliked, consistently berated and harassed the workers, Blus says, even while engaging one in an affair. Blus approached the local HR manager. "He said, 'Well, I certainly don't think it's appropriate to get involved in these witch hunts. And anyway, it's none of your business.'" The incident was never investigated. Sun says there is no record of Blus's complaint, that any such report would have sparked an investigation, and that it takes such issues seriously.

---

meeting with the chairman and top HR people from a big bank. "The training person said that 80% of employees have done at least 40 hours in classes. The chairman said, 'Congratulations.' I said, 'You're talking about the activities you're doing. The question is, What are you delivering?'"

That sort of stuff drives Ulrich nuts. Over 20 years, he has become the HR trade's best-known guru and a leading proponent of the push to take on more-strategic roles within corporations. But human-resources managers, he acknowledges, typically undermine that effort by investing more importance in activities than in outcomes. "You're only effective if you add value," Ulrich says. "That means you're not measured by what you do but by what you deliver." By that, he refers not just to the value delivered to employees and line managers, but the benefits that accrue to investors and customers, as well.

So here's a true story: A talented young marketing exec accepts a job offer with Time Warner out of business school. She interviews for openings in several departments—then is told by HR that only one is interested in her. In fact, she learns later, they all had been. She had been railroaded into the job, under the supervision of a widely reviled manager, because no one inside the company would take it.

You make the call: Did HR do its job? On the one hand, it filled the empty slot. "It did what was organizationally expedient," says the woman now. "Getting someone who wouldn't kick and scream about this role probably made sense to them. But I just felt angry." She left Time Warner after just a year. (A Time Warner spokesperson declined to comment on the incident.)

Part of the problem is that Time Warner's metrics likely will never catch the real cost of its HR department's action. Human resources can readily provide the number of people it hired, the percentage of performance evaluations completed, and the extent to which employees are satisfied or not with their benefits. But only rarely does it link any of those metrics to business performance.

John W. Boudreau, a professor at the University of Southern California's Center for Effective Organizations, likens the failing to shortcomings of the finance function before DuPont figured out how to calculate return on investment in 1912. In HR, he says, "we don't have anywhere near that kind of logical sophistication in the way of people or talent. So the decisions that get made about that resource are far less sophisticated, reliable, and consistent."

Cardinal Health's Rucci is trying to fix that. Cardinal regularly asks its employees 12 questions designed to measure engagement. Among them: Do they understand the company's strategy? Do they see the connection between that and their jobs? Are they proud to tell people where they work? Rucci correlates the results to those of a survey of 2,000 customers, as well as monthly sales data and brand-awareness scores.

"So I don't know if our HR processes are having an impact" per se, Rucci says. "But I know absolutely that employee-engagement scores have an impact on our business," accounting for between 1% and 10% of earnings, depending on the business and the employee's role. "Cardinal may not anytime soon get invited by the Conference Board to explain our world-class best practices in any area of HR—and I couldn't care less. The real question is, Is the business effective and successful?"

3. HR isn't working for you. Want to know why you go through that asinine performance appraisal every year, really? Markle, who admits to having administered countless numbers of them over the years, is pleased to confirm your suspicions. Companies, he says "are doing it to protect themselves against their own employees," he says. "They put a piece of paper between you and employees, so if you ever have a confrontation, you can go to the file and say, 'Here, I've documented this problem.'"

There's a good reason for this defensive stance, of course. In the last two generations, government has created an immense thicket of labor regulations. Equal Employment Opportunity; Fair Labor Standards; Occupational Safety and Health; Family and Medical Leave; and the ever-popular ERISA. These are complex, serious issues requiring technical expertise, and HR has to apply reasonable caution.

But "it's easy to get sucked down into that," says Mark Royal, a senior consultant with Hay Group. "There's a tension created by HR's role as protector of corporate assets—making sure it doesn't run afoul of the rules. That puts you in the position of saying no a lot, of playing the bad cop. You have to step out of that, see the broad possibilities, and take a more open-minded approach. You need to understand where the exceptions to broad policies can be made."

Typically, HR people can't, or won't. Instead, they pursue standardization and uniformity in the face of a workforce that is heterogeneous and complex. A manager at a large capital leasing company complains that corporate HR is trying to eliminate most vice-president titles there—even though veeps are a dime a dozen in the finance industry. Why? Because in the company's commercial business, vice president is a rank reserved for the top officers. In its drive for bureaucratic "fairness," HR is actually threatening the reputation, and so the effectiveness, of the company's finance professionals.

The urge for one-size-fits-all, says one professor who studies the field, "is partly about compliance, but mostly because it's just easier." Bureaucrats everywhere abhor exceptions—not just because they open up the company to charges of bias but because they require more than rote solutions. They're time-consuming and expensive to manage. Make one exception, HR fears, and the floodgates will open.

There's a contradiction here, of course: Making exceptions should be exactly what human resources does, all the time—not because it's nice for employees, but because it drives the business. Employers keep their best people by acknowledging and rewarding their distinctive performance, not by treating them the same as everyone else. "If I'm running a business, I can tell you who's really helping to drive the business forward," says Dennis Ackley, an employee communication consultant. "HR should have the same view. We should send the message that we value our high-performing employees and we're focused on rewarding and retaining them."

Instead, human-resources departments benchmark salaries, function by function and job by job, against industry standards, keeping pay—even that of the stars—within a narrow band determined by competitors. They bounce performance appraisals back to managers who rate their employees too highly, unwilling to acknowledge accomplishments that would merit much more than the 4% companywide increase.

Human resources, in other words, forfeits long-term value for short-term cost efficiency. A simple test: Who does your company's vice president of human resources report to? If it's the CFO—and chances are good it is—then HR is headed in the wrong direction. "That's a model that cannot work," says one top HR exec who has been there. "A financial person is concerned with taking money out of the organization. HR should be concerned with putting investments in."

4. The corner office doesn't get HR (and vice versa). I'm at another rockin' party: a few dozen midlevel human-resources managers at a hotel restaurant in Mahwah, New Jersey. It is not glam in any way. (I've got to get a better

HOW TO DO HR RIGHT

Say the Right Thing

At the grand level, what HR tells employees has to match what the company actually believes; empty rhetoric only breeds discontent. And when it comes to the details of pay and benefits, explain clearly what's being done and why. For example, asks consultant Dennis Ackley, "When you have a big deductible, do employees understand you're focusing on big costs? Or do they just think HR is being annoying?"

Measure the Right Thing

Human resources isn't taken seriously by top management because it can't demonstrate its impact on the business. Statistics on hiring, turnover, and training measure activity but not value. So devise measurements that consider impact: When you trained people, did they learn anything that made them better workers? And connect that data to business-performance indicators—such as customer loyalty, quality, employee-replacement costs, and, ultimately, profitability.

Get Rid of the "Social Workers"

After Libby Sartain arrived as chief people officer at Yahoo, she moved several HR staffers out—some because they didn't have the right functional skills, but mostly because "they were stuck in the old-school way of doing things." Human resources shouldn't be about cutting costs, but it is all about business. The people who work there need to be both technically competent and sophisticated about the company's strategy, competitors, and customers.

Serve the Business

Human-resources staffers walk a fine line: Employees see them as stooges for management, and management views them as annoying do-gooders representing employees. But "the best employee advocates are the ones who are concerned with advancing organizational and individual performance," says Anthony Rucci of Cardinal Health. Represent management with integrity and honesty—and back employees in the name of improving the company's capability.

Make Value, Not Activity

University of Michigan professor Dave Ulrich, coauthor of *The HR Value Proposition* (Harvard Business School Press, 2005), says HR folks must create value for four groups: They need to foster competence and commitment among employees, develop the capabilities that allow managers to execute on strategy, help build relationships with customers, and create confidence among investors in the future value of the firm.

travel agent.) But it is telling, in a hopeful way. Hunter Douglas, a $2.1 billion manufacturer of window coverings, has brought its HR staff here from across the United States to celebrate their accomplishments.

The company's top brass is on hand. Marvin B. Hopkins, president and CEO of North American operations, lays on the praise: "I feel fantastic about your achievements," he says. "Our business is about people. Hiring, training, and empathizing with employees is extremely important. When someone is fired or leaves, we've failed in some way. People have to feel they have a place at the company, a sense of ownership."

So, yeah, it's corporate-speak in a drab exurban office park. But you know what? The human-resources managers from Tupelo and Dallas are totally pumped up. They've been flown into headquarters, they've had their picture taken with the boss, and they're seeing *Mamma Mia* on Broadway that afternoon on the company's dime.

Can your HR department say it has the ear of top management? Probably not. "Sometimes," says Ulrich, "line managers just have this legacy of HR in their minds, and they can't get rid of it. I felt really badly for one HR guy. The chairman wanted someone to plan company picnics and manage the union, and every time this guy tried to be strategic, he got shot down."

Say what? Execs don't think HR matters? What about all that happy talk about employees being their most important asset? Well, that turns out to have been a small misunderstanding. In the 1990s, a group of British academics examined the relationship between what companies (among them, the UK units of Hewlett-Packard and Citibank) said about their human assets and how they actually behaved. The results were, perhaps, inevitable.

In their rhetoric, human-resources organizations embraced the language of a "soft" approach, speaking of training, development, and commitment. But "the underlying principle was invariably restricted to the improvements of bottom-line performance," the authors wrote in the resulting book, *Strategic Human Resource Management* (Oxford University Press, 1999). "Even if the rhetoric of HRM is soft, the reality is almost always 'hard,' with the interests of the organization prevailing over those of the individual."

In the best of worlds, says London Business School professor Lynda Gratton, one of the study's authors, "the reality should be some combination of hard and soft." That's what's going on at Hunter Douglas. Human resources can address the needs of employees because it has proven its business mettle—and vice versa. Betty Lou Smith, the company's vice president of corporate HR, began investigating the connection between employee turnover and product quality. Divisions with the highest turnover rates, she found, were also those with damaged-goods rates of 5% or higher. And extraordinarily, 70% of employees were leaving the company within six months of being hired.

Smith's staffers learned that new employees were leaving for a variety of reasons: They didn't feel respected, they didn't have input in decisions, but mostly, they felt a lack of connection when they were first hired. "We gave them a 10-minute orientation, then they were out on the floor," Smith says. She addressed the weakness by creating a mentoring program that matched new hires with experienced workers. The latter were suspicious at first, but eventually, the mentor positions (with spiffy shirts and caps) came to be seen as prestigious. The six-month turnover rate dropped dramatically, to 16%. Attendance and productivity—and the damaged-goods rate—improved.

"We don't wait to hear from top management," Smith says. "You can't just sit in the corner and look at benefits. We have to know what the issues in our business are. HR has to step up and assume responsibility, not wait for management to knock on our door."

But most HR people do.

Hunter Douglas gives us a glimmer of hope—of the possibility that HR can be done right. And surely, even within ineffective human-resources organizations, there are great individual HR managers—trustworthy, caring people with their ears to the ground, who are sensitive to cultural nuance yet also understand the business and how people fit in. Professionals who move voluntarily into HR from line positions can prove especially adroit, bringing a profit-and-loss sensibility and strong management skills.

At Yahoo, Libby Sartain, chief people officer, is building a group that may prove to be the truly effective human-resources department that employees and executives imagine. In this, Sartain enjoys two advantages. First, she arrived with a reputation as a creative maverick, won in her 13 years running HR at Southwest Airlines. And second, she had license from the top to do whatever it took to create a world-class organization.

Sartain doesn't just have a "seat at the table" at Yahoo; she actually helped build the table, instituting a weekly operations meeting that she coordinates with COO Dan Rosensweig. Talent is always at the top of the agenda—and at the end of each meeting, the executive team mulls individual development decisions on key staffers.

That meeting, Sartain says, "sends a strong message to everyone at Yahoo that we can't do anything without HR." It also signals to HR staffers that they're responsible for more than shuffling papers and getting in the way. "We view human resources as the caretaker of the largest investment of the company," Sartain says. "If you're not nurturing that investment and watching it grow, you're not doing your job."

Yahoo, say some experts and peers at other organizations, is among a few companies—among them Cardinal Health, Procter & Gamble, Pitney Bowes, Goldman Sachs, and General Electric—that truly are bringing human resources into the realm of business strategy. But they are indeed the few. USC professor Edward E. Lawler III says that last year HR professionals reported spending 23% of their time "being a strategic business partner"—no more than they reported in 1995. And line managers, he found, said HR is far less involved in strategy than HR thinks it is. "Despite great huffing and puffing about strategy," Lawler says, "there's still a long way to go." (Indeed. When I asked one midlevel HR person exactly how she was involved in business strategy for her division, she excitedly described organizing a monthly lunch for her vice president with employees.)

What's driving the strategy disconnect? London Business School's Gratton spends a lot of time training human-resources professionals to create more impact. She sees two problems: Many HR people, she says, bring strong technical expertise to the party but no "point of view about the future and how organizations are going to change." And second, "it's very difficult to align HR strategy to business strategy, because business strategy changes very fast, and it's hard to fiddle around with a compensation strategy or benefits to keep up." More than simply understanding strategy, Gratton says, truly effective executives "need to be operating out of a set of principles and personal values." And few actually do.

In the meantime, economic natural selection is, in a way, taking care of the problem for us. Some 94% of large employers surveyed this year by Hewitt Associates reported they were outsourcing at least one human-resources activity. By 2008, according to the survey, many plan to expand outsourcing to include activities such as learning and development, payroll, recruiting, health and welfare, and global mobility.

Which is to say, they will farm out pretty much everything HR does. The happy rhetoric from the HR world says this is all for the best: Outsourcing the administrative minutiae, after all, would allow human-resources professionals to focus on more important stuff that's central to the business. You know, being strategic partners.

The problem, if you're an HR person, is this: The tasks companies are outsourcing—the administrivia—tend to be what you're good at. And what's left isn't exactly your strong suit. Human resources is crippled by what Jay Jamrog, executive director of the Human Resource Institute, calls "educated incapacity: You're smart, and you know the way you're working today isn't going to hold 10 years from now. But you can't move to that level. You're stuck."

That's where human resources is today. Stuck. "This is a unique organization in the company," says USC's Boudreau. "It discovers things about the business through the lens of people and talent. That's an opportunity for competitive advantage." In most companies, that opportunity is utterly wasted.

And that's why I don't like HR.

EXPLORING THE ISSUE

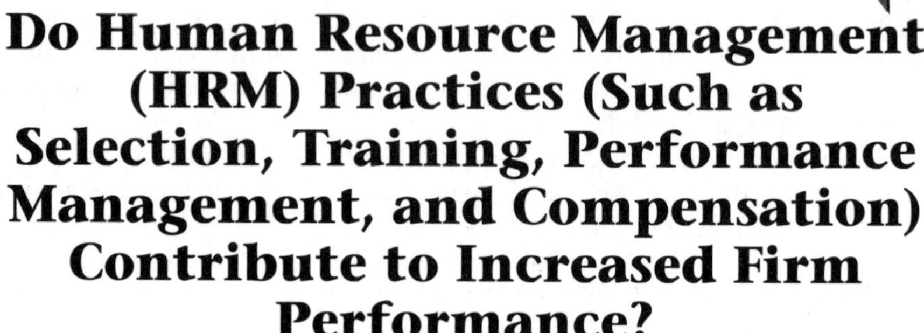

Do Human Resource Management (HRM) Practices (Such as Selection, Training, Performance Management, and Compensation) Contribute to Increased Firm Performance?

Critical Thinking and Reflection

1. Define the resource-based view of the firm.
2. Explain three effective HRM practices of Google Inc.
3. What is the main criticism of the HRM roles in organizations?
4. What are some alternatives that HRM professionals may consider in actually enhancing firm performance?

Is There Common Ground?

The resource-based view theory suggests that organizations can enhance their competitive advantage and firm performance with strategic HRM practices that are valuable. Google Inc., a company founded by doctoral students Larry Page and Sergey Brin from Stanford University in 1998, is a successful multibillion dollar company today. The company has spent elaborate efforts in their people management. On the other hand, in most organizations they are considered as the administrative experts and not as change agents as strategic experts would like them to. Most small and mid-sized organizations do not have an HRM department. Are they not successful? Experts suggest alternatives are to clearly establish financial metrics for HRM practices. Did employee referral applicants add value to the firm's performance? Did providing telecommuting benefits enhance profits?

Additional Resources

Berry, J. (2011). Transforming HRD into an economic value add. *T + D, 65*(9), 66–69.

Morris, A. (2009). Strategic HR Planning at Google Inc.: A Descriptive Case Study of Human Resource Strategy at Google Inc.: http://www.scribd.com/doc/13286610/Strategic-HR-Planning-at-Google-Inc

Pettengell, T. (2007). OOMPH! Heroes or zeroes? *Personnel Today*, 36–38, September 7, 2007.

http://www.jobbankusa.com/News/Hiring/google_adjusts_hiring_process.html: Google Adjusts Hiring Process as Need Grows.

http://www.washingtonpost.com/wp-dyn/content/article/2006/10/20/AR2006102001461.html: Building a 'Googley' Workforce.

http://hr.blr.com/news.aspx?id=3863: Companies Increasingly Outsourcing HR, Study Shows.

http://www.ewin.com/articles/whnHR.htm: When Is an HR Department Necessary?

http://www.thebaileygroup.com/stepping-up-to-the-table/: Stepping Up to the Table: The HR Professional's Role in Corporate Strategy.

Internet References . . .

History of Outsourcing

These Web sites provide a detailed analysis of how outsourcing began in the United States.

http://www.brighthub.com/office/human-resources/articles/100143.aspx
http://www.zdnet.com/news/top-10-risks-of-offshore-outsourcing/299274

Top Ten Risks of Offshore Outsourcing

This Web site provides details on the risks in doing outsourcing and offshoring.

http://www.fenwick.com/docstore/Publications/Corporate/Outsourcing_Alternatives.pdf

Historical Development of the Sweatshop

This Web site provides a historical perspective on how sweatshops began in the industrial world and its journey over the times.

http://www.unc.edu/~andrewsr/ints092/sweat.html

Sweatshop Best Alternatives for Workers in Many Countries

Scholars discuss in this Web site how sweatshops are helpful to the local economies. The authors argue that it acts as the best alternative for many of these underprivileged workers.

http://wichitaliberty.org/economics/sweatshops-best-alternative-for-workers-in-many-countries/

Geert Hofstede's Cultural Dimensions

The Dutch scholar, Hofstede, provides a detailed cultural analysis of several countries. He identifies how local cultures impact host country practices.

http://www.geert-hofstede.com/geert_hofstede_contrarian_position.shtml

How Multinational Corporations Survive and Develop in China

This Web site discusses localization strategies of several leading companies that have established successfully in China.

http://www.btmbeijing.com/contents/en/business/2004-06/coverstory/localization

UNIT 7

Global HRM

U.S. *companies are increasingly making their presence felt in several countries. The technological revolution witnessed in the early 2000s has created the trend of business service outsourcing. Economists are now concerned that many U.S. jobs are being lost to the overseas markets. U.S. manufacturing companies are also largely using the low-skilled labor available in other countries to produce cheaper products and services. How are the labor practices in these countries? Do U.S. companies demonstrate double standards in their manufacturing operations? How adaptive have U.S. companies become in their overseas operations? Do they follow local or global practices?*

- Is Overseas Outsourcing a Good U.S. Business Strategy?
- Is the Sweatshop Concept Adopted by the U.S. Manufacturers Overseas Ethical?
- Are U.S. Companies Adaptive to Local Practices Overseas?

ISSUE 18

Is Overseas Outsourcing a Good U.S. Business Strategy?

YES: John E. Gnuschke, Jeff Wallace, Dennis R. Wilson, and Stephen C. Smith, from "Outsourcing Production and Jobs: Costs and Benefits," *Business Perspectives* (Spring 2004)

NO: Murray Weidenbaum, from "Outsourcing: Pros and Cons," *Executive Speeches* (August/September 2004)

Learning Outcomes

After reading this issue, you should be able to:

- Define outsourcing and offshoring.
- Understand what jobs can be outsourced.
- Identify the positive aspects of outsourcing.
- Gain an understanding of the negative aspects of outsourcing.
- Provide alternatives that organizations can pursue in understanding this concept.

ISSUE SUMMARY

YES: Professor John Gnuschke and colleagues from the University of Memphis insist that outsourcing is a good business strategy as it creates higher profits, delivers cheaper products, and reduces customer response time. Most multinationals are taking advantage of the outsourcing trends as the benefits surpass the costs.

NO: Professor Murray Weidenbaum from Washington University suggests that there are several barriers to a smooth outsourcing process such as language barriers, technology glitches, and intellectual rights. Outsourcing has become a national topic, making employees aware of this global labor trend.

Economists suggest that current outsourcing trends have their roots in early trading patterns. The Europeans established trade with the United States and the rest of the world realizing that other countries have inimitable products and services to offer. This established the concept of trade, exchange, and multilateral relations among nations. The technological revolution introduced by the Internet in the 1990s and subsequent Y2K crisis (computer mediation problem) set the stage for global technical communities to collaborate in an unprecedented way. Currently, Western nations are using overseas labor for outsourcing their work as these economies have the qualified talent performing the labor at much reduced costs.

Outsourcing can be defined as using vendors (domestic or overseas) to complete any specific organizational tasks (either in manufacturing or service). Traditionally, offshoring, a type of outsourcing, is shifting of blue-collar manufacturing jobs as the labor costs are more cost-effective overeseas. Currently, outsourcing development has moved professional white-collar jobs to overseas places where it is more cost-effective.

Thomas Friedman, the distinguished author of *The World Is Flat*, identifies the launching of the World Wide Web as the most important contributing factor for the current state of overseas outsourcing trends. In 1995, when the Internet became globally accessible, it made it possible for organizations to use overseas vendors to complete domestic organizational tasks. Professional jobs that are most likely to be outsourced are: (1) jobs that do not require much face-to-face contact, (2) jobs that can be performed with technology, (3) jobs that can be performed at much lower rates overseas. Currently, the largest percentages of jobs that are being outsourced are office administration (32 percent), information technology (28 percent), and human resource functions (15 percent). Experts predict that 3.3 million service jobs will be outsourced by 2015.

Scholars from the University of Memphis suggest that overseas outsourcing helps organizations in several ways. First, it allows organizations to pursue the most effective labor costs as labor costs vary significantly among countries. For instance, professional labor costs in emerging economies are 25 percent lower than those in the United States. Second, using lower labor costs allow organizations to provide their final products or services at much reduced prices to their customers. Third, lower labor cost ultimately allows organizations to enhance their business profits. Further, such positive outcomes, such as increased profits and customers, will definitely have a positive effect on the domestic economy. Some U.S. organizations that have used overseas outsourcing very effectively are GE Capital, American Express, Bank of America, and CitiGroup, among others. Outsourcing contributes to enhancing competitive business advantage as it allows organizations to remain focused on their core strategic activities.

Practitioners also suggest that overseas outsourcing is driven by current business demands of organizations wanting to provide a 24×7 customer service culture. It could also be that other countries have the required qualified talent that United States does not have currently. Further, today many global communities speak the same business language making outsourcing tasks a very viable option. Finally, businesses that have used domestic outsourcing successfully may want to try overseas vendors also.

On the other hand, several disadvantages have been associated with overseas outsourcing. The primary concern is that thousands of local people are losing their jobs, creating a recession in the domestic economy. While organizations traditionally have been moving blue-collar work overseas, current overseas trends include moving of white-collar professional jobs. This labor issue has been discussed in national debates causing locals to be increasingly insecure of their jobs. Public discussions on outsourcing has created a greater sense of national pride about local jobs and also a feeling of prejudice toward outsourcing trends.

Second, many businesses have expressed concerns that overseas employees have not been able to communicate with U.S. customers effectively even though they speak the English language. For instance, Dell moved its overseas customer support back to the United States as customers frequently complained of difficult accents and miscommunication problems. Third, many emerging economies, where usually most of the outsourcing is done, experience tremendous energy shortages with frequent power outages. This definitely would cause interruption of the outsourcing work unless contingent plans are clearly established. Finally, U.S. organizations must be very mindful about intellectual and privacy rights regarding their outsourcing projects, which may not be strictly enforced in emerging economies.

Experts also imply that common public may have become very sensitive to this topic as it became a national issue at the presidential debates. While outsourcing may be causing professional jobs to move overseas, it also helps in creating a robust local economy. Policymakers have suggested federal interventions in terms of placing a cap on outsourcing activities. However, this defeats the very essence of a capitalistic system that dictates business freedom, market competition, and consumer choice.

There are alternatives for organizations to consider instead of adopting overseas service outsourcing. Scholars and practitioners suggest that domestic outsourcing might be an excellent method to retain the service jobs within the United States. Organizations must identify locations within the United States where they can get qualified talent at much reduced costs. For instance, information technology (IT) employees will be very expensive to hire in California or New York. However, the same qualified talent can be recruited at much reduced costs in the Midwest. IT experts suggest locating domestic talent that are equally cost-effective is an alternative for organizations to consider as it will mitigate overseas outsourcing. Thomas Friedman also provides evidence in his book of Jet Airways that has implemented domestic service outsourcing effectively by identifying qualified female applicants from the Midwest. These female employees, who are traditional homemakers, were hired at much reduced costs than those from the east or west coast. Hence, the company has not only boosted the local employment but also retained the jobs within the United States.

Practitioners suggest that offshoring also can have domestic options. Organizations seek offshore labor to keep labor costs at a minimum so that their products and services can be delivered to customers at much lower costs. However, if organizations implement rigorous manufacturing standards of Six Sigma, just-in-time, and lean manufacturing in their domestic plants their products and services can be produced cost-effectively. The Japanese automobile industry has implemented meticulous manufacturing standards to reduce labor costs which have proven it to be very lucrative. Thus, organizations can produce within the United States thereby enhancing the local economy and providing domestic jobs.

An international perspective suggests that other countries also outsource professional jobs to countries where labor is most cost-effective. The most popular outsourcing destinations are India, China, and the Philippines. The main reason outsourcing jobs are moving to such emerging economies is because employees in these countries may have the adequate educational backgrounds and labor to be employed in such fields.

YES 

John E. Gnuschke et al.

Outsourcing Production and Jobs: Costs and Benefits

The current economic expansion has generated an atypically anemic quantity of new employment opportunities. Compounding the loss of over two million actual jobs since 2000 is the loss of six to seven million potential jobs that would have been created in a typical economic recovery. In the absence of strong job creation, the weak labor market and the prolonged economic recovery have generated an enormous amount of concern about the outsourcing of production and jobs to other countries. If the economy had expanded rapidly and started creating job opportunities after the recession ended in the fall of 2001, the intensity of concerns about outsourcing would have been swept away by the euphoria of the economic expansion. Since job creation has been non-existent since 2000 for most areas of America, it is understandable that American workers, businesses, and government officials are increasingly concerned about the welfare of the U.S. economy.

What actually is outsourcing? Simply defined, outsourcing occurs when an organization transfers some of its tasks to an outside supplier. Offshore outsourcing occurs when these tasks are transferred to other countries. This outsourcing may take the form of constructing facilities and hiring labor offshore to produce services or products for sale and consumption offshore. Alternatively, offshore outsourcing may involve the utilization of offshore facilities and labor for the importation of goods and services into the U.S. In both scenarios, the purpose of offshore outsourcing is to take advantage of lower production costs, increase profits, and remain competitive in an increasingly global economy.

Economists and managers easily focus on the gains that may be generated from meeting global competition in an unencumbered world economy where all competitors face the same set of constraints. Cheaper and frequently better products are generated for consumers both domestically and in the world economy. New employment and income generating opportunities in foreign markets generate new market opportunities for domestic and international producers of goods and services. Finally, international outsourcing of production and employment causes the domestic economy to undergo a new wave of evolution that sets the stage for the next surge of economic growth. An example might be that the outsourcing of parts of the manufacturing supply chain have shifted

U.S. jobs from manufacturing to services and simultaneously prepared the U.S. economy to shift its attention to activities that have a higher market value.

Financial institutions and service providers subsequently found outsourcing to be a source of competitive advantage for their businesses. The Boston Consulting Group cites the following companies (and the locations where they outsourced) as among the most prominent early movers:

- GE Capital (India, China, and Ireland);
- American Express (India and the Philippines);
- Bank of America (India and the Philippines);
- Citigroup (India, the Philippines, Malaysia, Taiwan, and Singapore);
- HSBC (India and China); and
- Standard Chartered Bank (Malaysia, India, and China).

Based upon this history, outsourcing will likely increase, continuing in the manufacturing sectors and expanding significantly into the service sectors including healthcare.

What factors are driving these sectors to outsource their production and employment? According to Bill Sweeny, Vice President of EDS—Global Government Affairs, the decision to outsource is based upon the following factors:

- The demand of the customer;
- The type of local talent available;
- Cost;
- Productivity;
- Political risk; and
- Infrastructure delivery.

Ashok D. Bardhan and Cynthia Kroll with the Fisher Center for Real Estate and Urban Economics at the University of California, Berkeley, further develop this thought by explaining that the "push" factors for outsourcing services are cost driven much like they are for manufacturing, but the "pull" factors provided by the countries where services are being outsourced are somewhat different. As Bardhan and Kroll clarify, the "pull" factors include the following:

- Widespread acceptance of English as a medium of education, business, and communication;
- A common accounting and legal system, with the latter based on either the U.K. or U.S. common law structure;
- General institutional compatibility and adaptability;
- Time differential determined by geographical location leading to a 24/7 capability and overnight turnaround time;
- Simpler logistics than in manufacturing; and
- A steady and copious supply of technical-savvy graduates.

All of these factors result in the potential for significant cost savings by taking advantage of skilled, quality labor at a fraction of the cost associated with producing domestically.

Understandably, from producers and consumers points of view, moving jobs to minimize production costs means some combination of higher profits, lower prices, and improved economic conditions around the world. From the perspective of the workers displaced and the families forced to downsize their expectations, the losses are much more personal and difficult to justify on the basis of the gains in other countries. In previous periods of economic disruption, critics voiced concern over jobs being moved overseas but understood that domestic economic growth would soon accommodate the workers who were displaced. In addition, the majority of the jobs shipped elsewhere were either high-wage, (frequently unionized) blue-collar jobs in manufacturing that generated abundant envy and little public understanding or sympathy, and low-wage and low-skill jobs that could not be protected in a world market overrun by a glut of low-wage workers. Outsourcing was a necessary evil for the betterment of consumerism and capitalism. As long as white-collar, high-wage professional, managerial, and service jobs were immune, there was no real alarm.

Now, however, white-collar jobs are very much at stake and are a newfound cause for concern. As John C. McCarthy noted, these once sacred jobs are now moving to other locations. In Tables 1 and 2, Bardhan and Kroll provide more detail regarding specific industries and jobs at risk to outsourcing, primarily to India and East Asia. Globalization, faster communications, lower costs, and the Internet have all been contributing factors in this evolution. Daniel W. Drezner adds, "The reduction of communication costs and the standardization of software packages have now made it possible to outsource business functions such as customer service, telemarketing, and document management". As Thomas F. Siems and Adam S. Ratner note:

> Specialized tasks—such as software development, financial research and call centers—can often be accomplished elsewhere in the world at a fraction of U.S. costs. . . . It is often in a firm's best interest to outsource certain tasks and use the abilities of its remaining workers in other, more productive activities.

Service-sector jobs that are subject or most vunerable to the risk of outsourcing share some common attributes. Among these are:

- No face-to-face customer servicing requirement;
- High information content;
- Work progress is telecommutable and Internet enabled;
- High wage differential with similar occupation in destination country;
- Low setup barriers; and
- Low social networking requirements.

Unquestionably, workers who have lost and will lose jobs to offshore outsourcing have suffered and will suffer economically, especially in the short run. Consumers ultimately benefit from the lower market prices as a result of businesses seeking the lowest-cost methods for producing goods and services. But, all of this depends on the assumption that U.S. workers can retain the means to earn a living in an increasingly competitive global economy.

Table 1

Employment Change in Industries at Risk to Outsourcing*

Industry Name	U.S. Employment (000) Q1–2001	Q2–2003	% Change 2001–2003
Non-manufacturing Sectors			
Software Publishers (except Internet)	276.1	247.9	−10.2
Internet Publishing and Broadcasting	50.6	33.7	−33.4
Telecommunications	1,323.4	1,138.9	−13.9
ISPs, Search Portals, and Data Processing	516.0	433.2	−16.0
Data Processing and Related Services	320.9	292.2	−8.9
Accounting, Bookeeping, and Payroll	976.3	875.7	−10.3
Payroll Services	158.9	124.6	−21.6
Computer Systems Design and Related Services	1,341.2	1,148.1	−14.4
Business Support Services	784.4	746.2	−4.9
Telephone Call Centers	406.2	363.2	−10.6
Telephone Answering Services	54.8	50.9	−7.1
Telemarketing Bureaus	351.4	312.3	−11.1
Manufacturing Sectors			
Computer and Electronic Products	1,862.1	1,415.9	−24.0
Semiconductors and electronic components	308.7	237.9	−22.9
Subtotal: At-risk Industries	6,853.9	5,791.8	−15.5
All Non-farm	131,073.0	130,513.3	−0.4
Manufacturing	16,932.3	14,757.7	−12.8
Nonmanufacturing	114,141.3	115,757.7	1.4

*These industries have been most often noted as outsourcing to India and East Asia.
Source: US Bureau of Labor Statistics

How many U.S. service jobs will be outsourced? The most frequently cited figures have been those from Forrester Research that estimates almost 600,000 U.S. service jobs will be outsourced by 2005 and up to 3.3 million jobs will be outsourced by 2015. Although this news seems dismal at best, Drezner tempers the Forrester number with the following observation:

> The Forrester prediction of 3.3 million lost jobs, for example, is spread across 15 years. That would mean 220,000 jobs displaced per year by offshore outsourcing—a number that sounds impressive until one considers that total employment in the United States is roughly

Table 2

U.S. Employment in Occupations at Risk to Outsourcing

	Average Annual	
Sectors	**Employment 2001**	**Salary 2001**
All Occupations (Total U.S. Employment)		
Occupations at Risk of Outsourcing	127,980,410	$34,020
Office Support*	8,637,900	$29,791
Computer Operations	177,990	$30,780
Data Entry Keyers	405,000	$22,740
Business and Financial Support**	2,153,480	$52,559
Computer and Math Professionals	2,825,870	$60,350
Paralegals and Legal Assistants	183,550	$39,220
Diagnostic Support Services	168,240	$38,860
Medical Transcriptionists	94,090	$27,020
Total in Outsourcing Risk Occupations	14,063,130	$39,631
Percent of All Occupations	11%	

*Office support aggregates data from 22 detailed Office and Administrative Support categories.
**Business and financial support aggregates data from 10 detailed Business and Financial Occupations.
Source: U.S. Bureau of Labor Statistics

> 130 million, and that about 22 million new jobs are expected to be added between now and 2010. Annually, outsourcing would affect less than .2 percent of employed Americans.

While it is clear that Drezner's observations about job creation seem wildly optimistic, it is true that the disruptions caused by the flight of jobs overseas is probably equally overstated.

> Gartner [Consultants] assumed that more than 60 percent of financial-sector employees directly affected by outsourcing would be let go by their employers. But Boston University Professor Nitin Joglekar has examined the effect of outsourcing on large financial firms and found that less than 20 percent of workers affected by outsourcing lose their jobs; the rest are repositioned within the firm. Even if the most negative projections prove to be correct, then, gross job loss would be relatively small.

Although the U.S. has overcome more challenging obstacles, the nation (especially policymakers and businesses) cannot ignore the responsibilities and needs of the labor force. The key to the success of the U.S. will be how the nation deals with the challenge. Bardhan and Kroll offer some possible scenarios:

1. Services job outsourcing proves more costly to the economy than the earlier round of manufacturing outsourcing. The U.S. will no longer dominate the next wave of innovations since centers of skilled, high-tech professionals build up in other parts of the world. As a result of outsourcing, workers displaced through outsourcing face prolonged periods of unemployment. Such workers would finally be absorbed in lesser-paying service jobs. Alternatively, there could be a downward adjustment of salaries and wages, making the outsourced occupations internationally competitive again.
2. A backlash against globalization could occur within the U.S. and worldwide, slowing down the process of business services outsourcing. Protectionism, although inefficient from an economic point of view, may result in the retention of some outsourceable jobs.
3. Industry shrinkage may come in part from a redistribution of jobs within the U.S. rather than a net loss. This scenario could result from the shifting of jobs from large employers to smaller firms in support sectors, as well as domestic outsourcing from high-cost regions within the U.S. to relatively low-cost regions elsewhere in the U.S.

Some critics of outsourcing suggest that while the gains from free trade are clearly true, the issue of fair trade must be considered. As strong and patriotic as it sounds, protectionism results in increased prices and ultimately long-term jobs losses. But, the long-term benefits of participating in the international exploitation of either people or resources are equally dubious.

Largely ignored in this article, but keenly understood, is India's relation to the U.S. in regard to offshore outsourcing. Indeed, most articles written and comments cited use India as the main comparison. With support from the U.S. and by nurturing a large, educated technical workforce, India became the market it is by being the second-largest English-speaking nation in the world. However, somewhat neglected in discussions and consideration are other Asian nations, particularly China, that are also emerging as serious contenders in the global economy. Simply put, a nation hungry to grow economically will compete at many levels. For the U.S., complacency is not an option, and time is definitely not a luxury.

Globalization means that the U.S. is no longer the only significant economic power and must be innovative in its actions to remain competitive. The first solution must be the creation of new jobs. The next administration, either Bush or Kerry, must not only promise new jobs, but actually deliver them. U.S. Secretary of State Colin Powell recognizes this as a priority:

> Outsourcing invariably does result in the loss of jobs and we have to do a better job in the United States, a good job in the United States, of creating opportunity in the United States to provide more jobs, so that those who have lost jobs will have opportunities in the future.

Retraining of displaced workers must occur. In the past, retraining sometimes meant transferring a displaced worker from one low-skilled job to another. This type of retraining is no longer an option. Retraining must be for high-tech and high-skilled positions and will require increased funding for post-secondary education.

Foresight in dealing with ongoing globalization means the challenge must also be met at the primary and secondary levels of education. The global market has a focus on Math and Sciences; U.S. education must also focus on Math and Sciences. U.S. education has fallen short of its goals. Lael Brainard, Senior Fellow with the Brookings Institution, makes a dire observation: In five years, we're going to be having a debate about one of the worst skill shortages we've ever seen because the demographics are actually going to start moving in the other direction and demographers are forecasting that starting in five years, and certainly 10 and 20 years out we are going to be seeing skill shortages of the sort that we didn't even really begin to see in the late '90s. So this issue about trying to integrate our labor force with international labor forces is going to become absolutely critical to our competitiveness into the longer-term future.

In order for the U.S. to remain competitive, it must meet this new challenge. Proactive, sound, successful measures must be implemented immediately. Realistically, businesses will continue to minimize costs to maximize profits. As Siems and Ratner note:

> Businesses in India and elsewhere are developing an important competitive advantage in outsourcing by providing quality services at low costs. In the Internet Age—where a company's physical location is of little relevance and information travels quickly and cheaply—firms will continue to boost productivity and keep costs low by doing what they do best and outsourcing the rest.

And consumers reap the benefits.

Murray Weidenbaum

Outsourcing: Pros and Cons

Overseas outsourcing of jobs has quickly become a controversial national issue. Some see outsourcing as a way of maintaining or increasing a company's competitiveness. Many others view outsourcing in a far more negative light, focusing on the people who lose their jobs.

Clearly, outsourcing is not a subject that can be dealt with on a bumper sticker or even on a 30-second sound bite. Let us start with a little background before we try to come up with any firm conclusions. Outsourcing involves far more complicated advantages and disadvantages than the debaters on either side are willing to admit.

Why Do Companies Outsource?

Many service companies started creating jobs overseas to gain access to foreign markets. They had to audit, consult, and repair where customers are located. To state the matter mildly, they did not tell their overseas customers that they had to come here. Moreover, many foreign markets have been growing quickly while some domestic areas have become relatively saturated or at least mature.

Simultaneously, some domestic businesses hired specialized workers stationed overseas to respond to U.S. limits on immigration. When these American employers could not get those workers to come here, they had to send the work to them. While doing so, the companies learned how to use modern technology to shift the location of work economically. They thus became accustomed to taking advantage of lower costs, domestic and foreign.

Moreover, the shift of some telemarketing and customer service jobs overseas followed an earlier pattern within the United States when such work was outsourced from urban to rural areas where labor costs were lower. Telecommuting from employees' homes also helped pave the way for some enterprises to extend the process to new suppliers, at home and abroad.

Viewing these matters in a broader perspective, the age of economic isolationism has long since passed. In various industries—ranging from banking to consumer products to job placement services—leading firms report that their overseas revenues exceed their domestic sales. Despite the shift to India of some domestic call center work, approximately 60 percent of the revenue of American information technology companies originates overseas.

From *Executive Speeches,* vol. 19, issue 1, August/September 2004, pp. 31–35.

Most fundamentally, many companies are focusing their efforts on their core competence. It is the rare enterprise that produces an entire product by itself—or even half of the end value. Most businesses subcontract out most of their activities to other companies, mainly domestic. Viewed from that perspective, overseas sourcing is a minor part of the trend to decentralize business operations.

Nevertheless, over time many American corporations came to appreciate how frequently the higher productivity of U.S. workers offset the wage differentials and other costs of operating overseas. Thus they quickly encountered practical limits to offshore outsourcing. To put the matter bluntly, no company can outsource the management, responsibility, or accountability of its activities.

On the other hand, outsourcing can help a company operate in an increasingly competitive global marketplace. Many U.S. companies learned the benefits of drawing on workers stationed in other countries. Outsourcing can enable a business to provide 24/7 coverage, especially for consumers who need around-the-clock support. It is frequently impractical for a firm to adopt a unilateral policy against outsourcing work especially when its foreign and domestic competitors are doing it.

There is also a growing division of labor. For example, system designers in the United States working closely with the retailer may conceive the inventory-management software that helps use electronic product tags more effectively. But once the system has been mapped out, the actual software code can be written by programmers in India. All sorts of adjustments are being made in this complicated world. For example, in 2003, Delta Airlines outsourced 1,000 jobs to India, but the $25 million in savings allowed the company to add 1,200 reservation and sales positions in the United States. Large software companies Microsoft and Oracle have simultaneously increased both outsourcing and their domestic payrolls.

It is important to gain some perspective by seeing the relative importance of domestically and internationally produced services. Much of the current controversy focuses on information technology (IT). In 2003, approximately $120 billion was spent on IT in the United States. Approximately 1.4 percent was moved offshore. However, the 98.6 percent of the work that stayed here was not deemed newsworthy.

In total, about 400,000 U.S. positions in information technology have gone offshore. Meanwhile, total U.S. employment rose from 129 million in 1993 to 138 million in 2003, mainly in services. It turns out that, contrary to much of the heated public discussion, the international movement of services is very positive to the American economy.

That is so because American corporations are not the only companies that engage in offshoring. In 2003, for example, the United States imported (that is, offshored) $87 billion of business services. Yes, that included a lot of relatively low-skilled call center and data entry work done in lower-cost developing countries.

But, in the same year, we exported (that is, companies in other nations offshored to us) $134 billion of business services. That "insourcing" generated a substantial array of relatively high-skilled jobs in engineering, management consulting, banking, and legal services. On average, "insourced" jobs pay 16 percent above the national average. A net balance of $47 billion flowed to the United States. That is more than a 60 percent increase over 1994, a decade earlier. This good news rarely surface in the often emotional debates on offshoring.

The Limits to and Dangers of Outsourcing

A word of warning, however, is necessary in the face of the current business enthusiasm for overseas workers. Companies who outsource just because "everybody is doing it" may be surprised by unexpected costs and complications. About one-half of the outsourcing arrangements are terminated, for a variety of reasons. Some new overseas vendors encounter financial difficulties or are acquired by other firms with different procedures and priorities.

Businesses that arbitrarily set a fixed percentage of work to be outsourced likely will regret it. Newcomers to overseas contracting may find themselves dealing with unreliable suppliers who put their work aside when they gain a more important client or their overseas vendor may suffer rapid turnover of skilled employees who find jobs with more desirable firms. Typical Indian operations in business processing—including call centers and offices handling payroll, accounting, and human resources functions—often lose 15–20 percent of their work forces each year. While software programming skills are plentiful in some parts of Asia, good managerial experience is very limited.

Other costly complications can arise. Local highways and transportation networks may be inadequate. Some overseas companies wind up busing their employers to and from work. Also, electricity may not be available as assuredly as in the United States, where blackouts are very infrequent.

Some American companies are paying much more for real estate for their offshoring activities than they would in the United States. That negative differential occurs for two reasons. One is the cost of upgrading poor infrastructure overseas. The second reason is the fact that inexpensive overseas labor pools are usually found in very large cities, while facilities such as call centers back home are located in lower-cost suburban and rural areas.

Some U.S. companies limit their outsourcing to routine engineering and maintenance tasks because they worry that their core technology may be swiped by vendors in Asia that do not respect intellectual property rights. U.S. firms also may encounter a variety of unanticipated difficulties, such as dealing with arcane legal systems and meeting the requirements of different tax and regulatory agencies. Moreover, they may more frequently encounter corrupt officials in the public sector.

Furthermore, overseas managers often do not understand the American business environment—our customers, lingo, traditions, and high quality control and expectations for prompt delivery of goods and performance of services. Dell moved its call center support for corporate business from India back to the United States in 2003. Its clients had complained about foreigners speaking English in hard-to-follow accents and giving vague answers to technical questions. Given the continued flow of complaints from individual customers, we may wonder what further pullbacks may occur.

What Happens to the Company's Employees?

The effect of outsourcing on U.S. employment is far more complicated than it appears at first. The visible part (the tip of the iceberg) is widely known. Some U.S. employees lose their jobs or get shifted to less desirable work. In recent years, this iceberg may have a very large tip. However, any serious analysis must extend to the rest of the iceberg.

Looking at the total employment effects of outsourcing, the less visible part of the impact is much larger. Far more U.S. employees keep their jobs because outsourcing helps the company stay competitive. Some get new or better jobs because the firm enhances its financial strength. For example, as companies upgrade their software systems, there may be less domestic demand for basic programmers—but more need for higher paid systems integrators.

Corporate IT departments report that they are changing their mix of in-house skills. They now give more emphasis to managerial experience, business process knowledge, and understanding the domestic customer. These capabilities rarely can be provided effectively from an overseas location.

Outsourcing and the savings it generates are the beginning—not the end—of the adjustment process. Cost reductions from outsourcing can open up new market opportunities for U.S. companies and thus generate additional jobs here at home. The companies also can afford to buy new equipment and expand training programs. Hence, higher domestic labor costs can be offset by higher worker productivity. Over time, there is a positive feedback effect from outsourcing. As poor countries overseas develop their economies, new markets are created for U.S.-made products and services. China already has become a major importer of industrial and consumer goods as well as of agricultural products and raw materials. In time, India is likely to do the same.

Moreover, economic trends rarely move in a straight line for long periods of time. Salaries of IT personnel in India are reported to be rising at 15–20 percent a year. In addition, a lot of hidden costs arise, such as the need for U.S.-based managers to visit the overseas sites from time to time to assure that the work being performed meets the standards of the American firm.

Some historical perspective is also useful. In the early 19th century, the United States was a poor developing country. European capital helped finance our canals, railroads, steel mills, and other factories. American workers began to manufacture goods that competed with European production.

Because markets were relatively open, Europeans as well as Americans benefited in the process. Economic growth and job creation occurred on both sides of the Atlantic Ocean. Currently, service providers overseas require American-made computers, telecommunications equipment, and software. They also obtain legal, financial, and marketing services from United States sources. Their employees and their families increasingly are customers of American products.

What Is the Net Effect on the USA?

On reflection, most service jobs cannot be outsourced. Personal contact is vital in virtually all business activities. It takes domestic companies to tailor new products and services to the needs of local customers. Most of the people we work with regularly remain close by. We normally do not take long domestic trips to see our doctor or dentist or lawyer or accountant. Much less do we go to New Delhi or Manila for those purposes.

One of the great strengths of the American economy is that we have a very open labor market. That characteristic is basic to this nation's economic vitality. Approximately one million workers are laid off or quit each week and an equal number is hired in their place. It is much harder to lay off workers in Europe or Japan than here. However, there is another side to the coin. Employers there are very reluctant to take on new workers. In striking contrast, American companies are much more likely to add personnel—and they do so.

Over the years, far more new jobs are created in the United States than are outsourced. Moreover, many foreign companies have been setting up operations in the United States and they hire American workers to staff these operations. Our more realistic labor policies do work, while their labor policy "straightjackets" do not. By its nature, a strong and flexible labor market has plenty of movement—out of some jobs and into others.

The bottom line is clear: the United States creates far more new jobs (net of layoffs) than Europe and Japan combined. We have the highest proportion (66 percent) of the population employed of all industrialized countries.

The record also shows that groundbreaking technology—rather than international competition—is the major cause of layoffs, and of new hires. Technological progress is the heart of the dynamic American job-creating economy. Our positive technology environment also encourages foreign manufacturers, such as pharmaceutical companies, to set up laboratories here.

Let me add a factual note to the emotional debate on the loss of manufacturing jobs. Despite lower wages abroad, foreign firms have chosen to produce automobiles made by high-wage American workers. Examples include Honda in Ohio, Mercedes Benz in Alabama, BMW in South Carolina, and Toyota in California.

Moreover, while direct manufacturing employment has been declining, total U.S. production of manufactured goods has risen about 40 percent over the past decade. This is a tribute to rapidly advancing productivity. By the way, this combination of trends is an international phenomenon. In recent years, China, Japan, and Brazil each lost more manufacturing jobs than did the United States.

A portion of the reported decline in manufacturing employment is a statistical quirk. So is a part of the rise in service employment. That offsetting change results when a manufacturing company contracts out some of its support activities. After all, converting a business function from an overhead burden center in an industrial corporation to a profit center in a service firm is a prod to achieving greater efficiency. It helps keep American businesses more competitive. As for the corporate profits that may result from outsourcing, we tend to forget that the typical shareholder is a pension fund or a mutual fund representing ordinary Americans.

What Should We Do?

Do those who advocate laws against American business outsourcing overseas really believe that foreign governments would not retaliate? My guess is that they never even thought about the fact that, in a global marketplace, companies all over the world are outsourcing. The United States is both the world's largest exporter as well as the world's largest importer. In other words, we have the greatest stake in maintaining open markets—at home and abroad.

As in many other forms of regulation, proposed government restraints on outsourcing would have all sorts of unanticipated adverse consequences. Recently, the University of Maryland requested an exemption from a proposed prohibition on outsourcing by agencies and departments of the federal government. It turns out that the university maintains a network of training centers at many U.S. overseas installations. The alternative to increasing the skills of Americans stationed overseas via "outsourcing" would be to hire foreigners with the needed skills!

Hysterics aside, the Information Technology Association reports that setting up the "do-not-call" list already has eliminated more call-center jobs than all of the outsourcing to India. Conversely, not every job created overseas means that an American job has been lost. For example, in the past, U.S. airlines traditionally did not pursue small billing discrepancies with travel agencies because it was not worth the cost. Now, using cheaper Indian workers, the airlines can afford to correct small billing errors. For the airlines, it is a welcome saving, while those are new jobs in India.

Ironically, experts on offshoring report that all of the publicity on offshoring—unfavorable as well as favorable—has been generating more awareness on the part of U.S. companies of the potential benefits of outsourcing overseas!

Nevertheless, the national debate on offshoring requires a constructive response, especially in a presidential election year. Many of the people who lose their jobs are truly hurting. If old-style protectionism is not a good answer, what should we do?

The positive approach is to enhance the productivity and competitiveness of American workers. IBM recently announced the creation of a new $25 million retraining program for employees who worry about losing their jobs to outsourcing.

More fundamentally, the fact that we have the highest high school dropout rate of all industrialized nations is nothing that can be blamed on foreigners. Nor can we be proud of the fact that, at the other end of the skill spectrum, the United States has fallen from third to seventeenth among nations in terms of the share of 18 to 24 year olds who earn degrees in science and engineering. Also, let us not overlook all the regulatory and tax barriers to innovation and to more efficient domestic production of goods and services that have been erected by the U.S. government.

An agenda of economic reforms is long overdue in order to make the United States a more attractive place to hire—and keep—productive employees. It is fascinating to contemplate that, if we would adopt such a positive approach to the outsourcing debate, the unexpected results would be real and positive for American workers.

EXPLORING THE ISSUE

Is Overseas Outsourcing a Good U.S. Business Strategy?

Critical Thinking and Reflection

1. Define outsourcing and offshoring.
2. What are the positive and negative characteristics of outsourcing?
3. What do experts suggest as alternatives to overseas outsourcing and offshoring?
4. Why do you think jobs are being outsourced so rapidly today?

Is There Common Ground?

Outsourcing allows organizations to become more strategic and focus on their core business activities. It allows organizations to take advantage of differing labor costs and therefore maximize their profits. Outsourcing is considered controversial as it takes away jobs from the local economy. This has created quite a stir among professional white-collar employees who have never experienced any external threats to their jobs before. Experts offer alternatives such as domestic outsourcing and lean manufacturing in order to reduce labor costs, which seem the main reason that multinationals pursue overseas labor. The main question employees need to ask today and in the future is "Will my job be outsourced?" Employees of tomorrow need to focus on developing job-related skills to ensure that their jobs cannot be outsourced.

Additional Resources

Blackman, A., Freedman, M., and Levy, J. (2004). Outsourcing by CPAs: Are we a business or a profession? *The CPA Journal, 74*(5), 6–8.

Masi, C. (2006). Pros and cons of global outsourcing. *Control Engineering, 53*(12), 14–16.

Prentis, D. (2009, January). Look before you leap. *Public Finance,* 26–27.

Shamis, G., Green, M. C., Sorensen, S., and Kyle, D. (2005). Outsourcing, offshoring, nearshoring: What to do? *Journal of Accountancy, 199*(6), 57–61.

www.cyfuture.com/outsourcing-statistics.htm: Outsourcing Statistics.

www.prlog.org/10181084-outsourcing-pros-and-cons.html: Outsourcing Pros and Con.

www.entrepreneur.com/humanresources/hiring/article49616.html: The Pros and Con of Outsourcing.

http://ezinearticles.com/?Outsourcing-Statistics—What-Figures-Will-Tell-You&id=2621948: Outsourcing Statistics—What Figures Will Tell You.

http://itonshore.wordpress.com/2009/02/05/are-there-domestic-employment-alternatives-to-offshore-outsourcing/: How Domestic I.T. Workers Can Compete with Offshore Resources.

http://leanman.hubpages.com/hub/Disadvantages-of-Outsourcing-overseas-What-are-the-Alternatives-to-offshoring-your-business: Disadvantages of Outsourcing Overseas—What Are the Alternatives to Offshoring Your Business.

http://leanman.hubpages.com/hub/Is-Outsoucing-to-China-a-Lean-Decision: Is Outsourcing Overseas to China a Lean Decision.

ISSUE 19

Is the Sweatshop Concept Adopted by the U.S. Manufacturers Overseas Ethical?

YES: Tara J. Radin and Martin Calkins, from "The Struggle Against Sweatshops: Moving Toward Responsible Global Business," *Journal of Business Ethics* (vol. 66, nos. 2–3, pp. 261–272, 2006)

NO: Dennis G. Arnold and Laura P. Hartman, from "Beyond Sweatshops: Positive Deviancy and Global Labor Practices," *Business Ethics: A European Review* (vol. 14, no. 3, pp. 206–210, July 2005)

Learning Outcomes

After reading this issue, you should be able to:

- Define the concept of sweatshops.
- Understand the positive aspects of sweatshop manufacturing.
- Identify the negative aspects of establishing sweatshops.
- Provide alternatives that organizations can pursue in understanding this concept.

ISSUE SUMMARY

YES: Professor Radin and Professor Calkins provide a very informative view as to why sweatshops still exist despite all their controversies. They also provide several alternatives for organizations while adopting sweatshop manufacturing facilities overseas.

NO: The Web sites showcase how women are generally exploited in sweatshops and how Walmart abused its employees in its overseas facilities.

The word "sweatshops" can be defined as overseas manufacturing facilities where labor conditions are not deemed satisfactory by international labor standards. The unsatisfactory practices could be very long work hours, unsafe work conditions, employee abuse, and a lack of labor rights. Sweatshops are considered very oppressive as employees working in these facilities seem to be exploited tremendously. Most of the products made in sweatshops require repetitive labor and involve making of shoes, clothing, rugs, and toys, among others. Western multinationals are criticized a lot because they demonstrate double standards in their treatment of employees between their home and overseas manufacturing plants. The debatable question often asked is, "Why do sweatshops exist?" when organizations realize the immense negative consequences they carry.

Sweatshops exist as they provide several economic advantages to the multinational organizations and also to the host employees. Sweatshops have shown to enhance local economies by creating domestic employment, establishing local infrastructures, and enhancing international trade. In several underdeveloped economies, unemployment and poverty is very extensive with their living conditions considered barely essential. Individuals from such cultures do not have the education or required skills to find any kind of employment. Further, in several agriculture-based economies, only seasonal labor is available. Individuals in such conditions consider getting any kind of employment as a huge boon to their daily existences. The labor conditions or management practices of their employment does not seem to matter as long as they receive any monetary compensation. It is this piece of the puzzle that sweatshops have successfully provided. They provide these individuals with a sense of livelihood. In creating these manufacturing facilities, multinationals have also established the domestic infrastructures by providing transportation, creating health facilities, and opening schools to provide essential standard conditions to their new employees. Sweatshops also provide products that not only are consumed by the local economy but also help increase the domestic exports. Multinationals consider using overseas labor as opportunities to provide their products at much reduced costs, thereby enhancing their business profits. After all, any business is trying to ultimately increase its profits and revenues.

Critics of the sweatshop movement overseas suggest that employees have a right to be treated justly and fairly regardless of where they work and how they have been treated in the past. The word sweatshop emerged as it was considered an employer's right to make their employees "sweat" for their wages. The very concept seems so appalling and inhumane to many labor experts. The main uproar by international labor organizations against multinationals using sweatshops is that they establish working conditions that are considered extremely offensive by international standards. For instance, in many instances, the housing accommodations that multinationals provide to their employees are often squalid, creating unsanitary living conditions. In other cases, young women working in these plants are customarily sexually harassed by their managers. Moreover, opponents assert that workers do not receive their pay and many times are not even aware of their rights. In extreme cases, employees are physically abused if their jobs are not done properly. Walmart, the giant retailer, has been accused of making the employees in their Bangladesh plant work unusually long hours (almost 19 hours) to meet their aggressive domestic demands in sales. The international labor associations suggest that about 250 million children between the ages of 5 and 14 work in sweatshop facilities. In many of these economies, children work in these factories with no breaks, nourishment, or education. The Asian economies are considered the most exploitive of their child labor.

There are alternatives that organizations may pursue while adopting the sweatshop labor concept. Experts suggest that multinationals (MNCs) should take proactive efforts in becoming the change agents in the countries they operate. MNCs should strive to provide best labor practices in these manufacturing facilities regardless of the accepted overseas work practices. These employees may never have experienced "good labor" practices as their lives have been dominated by oppressive conditions. Levi Strauss, the clothing retailer, has been a leader in making sure that it enhances the work conditions of its overseas operations. Second, MNCs can also provide training and developmental opportunities for these employees so that the local employees feel truly empowered. Employees in these economies usually have not had any learning or educational opportunities. Finally, customers can act as powerful change agents too by refusing to buy products from organizations that endorse sweatshop practices. In China, Nike and Adidas, the leading shoe retailers, made radical changes in the working conditions of their overseas operations and also enhanced the local infrastructures. The main themes of the alternative options are that businesses should behave in an ethical and accountable manner wherever they operate, whether it is New York, Nairobi, or New Delhi.

Labor professionals also suggest that multinationals hire external labor contractors to inspect the working conditions of their overseas manufacturing facilities. Many of multinationals alleged with adopting sweatshop conditions claim they were unaware of the deplorable working conditions of their overseas plants. Therefore, international labor organizations suggested that implementing objective third party evaluations will definitely mitigate exploitive practices. However, experts still caution that the external labor inspectors sometimes are under a lot of pressure by multinationals to modify any labor malpractices they notice to appease their customers, local governments, and media. Many labor reformers have taken the onus to report any unfavorable working conditions they observe worldwide.

YES 

Tara J. Radin and Martin Calkins

The Struggle Against Sweatshops: Moving Toward Responsible Global Business

Much of today's discussion of sweatshops steps from a simple question: "What's wrong with sweatshops?" Those engaged in sweatshop labor practices ask, "What's *wrong* with sweatshops?" to be able to shift the burden to critics to construct the opposing arguments. Opponents, on the other hand, ask rhetorically, "What's wrong with *sweatshops*?"—skeptically leaving the emphasis on the end—as if to say, "Where do I start?" Regardless, "What's wrong with sweatshops?" remains the wrong question. It misses the crux of the issue and remains overly abstract. Further, it leaves people debating sweatshops without prompting them to reconsider decision-making and action.

Sweatshops are wrong for a host of reasons. They perpetuate the violation of basic human rights as people are exploited for their labor. This constitutes a breach of the simple Kantian practical imperative that people are supposed to treat others as ends valuable in and of themselves, not only as means to ends. In practice, sweatshops promulgate mental and/or physical abuse and contradict our considered notions of basic morality and strategic business purposes.

A more pertinent question to ask is "Why do sweatshops continue to exist?" Such a question moves us away from broad, abstract theories and concepts toward the more practical and important identification of vexing causes for the existence, longevity, and widespread distribution of sweatshops.

The purpose of this paper is to further the fight against sweatshops. We begin with an examination of the factors that contribute to the survival of sweatshops in spite of widespread censure and condemnation. Through this discussion, we point out how sweatshop labor practices have become integrated in many societies, particularly in developing and emerging countries. We argue that as much as we might deplore sweatshops, the answer is not as simple as unilaterally eliminating them. Rather, we need gradually to transition away from such labor practices in ways that empower workers. In the end, we maintain that by fortifying stakeholder relationships and by making workers more demanding of firms, sweatshops can be eradicated.

From *Journal of Business Ethics,* vol. 66, nos. 2–3, 2006, pp. 261–272 (261–263, 265–267).

Why Do Sweatshops Continue?

Many people are puzzled by the continuing existence of sweatshops in the wake of considerable negative press. For more than a decade, media coverage has decried despicable working conditions around the world. One of the early scandals involved the cruel and inhumane treatment of female workers in sewing factories in Honduras. Both Kathy Lee Gifford and Wal-Mart suffered as a result of the negative press surrounding the manufacturing of Gifford's clothing line distributed by Wal-Mart.

In spite of such experiences, companies continue to engage in questionable labor practices for a number of reasons. For one, there is not a bright-line distinction between acceptable and unacceptable treatment of workers. While many people agree on general principles (i.e., worker safety, fair wages, reasonable hours, and so on), they rarely agree on where to draw the line between appropriate and inappropriate behavior. Another reason has to do with the reluctance of Westerners to impose their values on non-Western business practices. Finally, there are the problems associated with the immediate abandonment of sweatshops. Not least among these includes the crippling of communities as companies move out in search of even more favorable labor conditions, similar to what we experience in the United States when companies relocate operations as part of the general trend toward increased outsourcing.

Absence of a Definition

One major reason for the continued existence of sweatshops has to do with our inability to identify and name them as such. It is not that sweatshops are difficult to locate, but that they are "slippery," or difficult to grasp. Not unlike pornography, we can recognize sweatshops when we see them, but we are not able to define them precisely. If sweatshops were easier to identify, we might be able to leverage moral analyses against them and do away with them. The problem, however, is that they are complex and an exact definition eludes us.

A search for a definition of sweatshops illustrates their complexity. Typical definitions are excessively broad, overly particular, skewed toward a narrow set of workplace abuses, and/or overtly aligned with a particular political, economic, or ideological agenda. For our purposes, we rely upon a fairly representative description of sweatshops as work environments that violate laws and where workers are subject to:

- Extreme exploitation, including the absence of a living wage or long work hours;
- Poor working conditions, such as health and safety hazards;
- Arbitrary discipline, such as verbal or physical abuse; and/or
- Fear and intimidation when they speak out, organize, or attempt to form a union (www.sweatshopwatch.com).

Characterizing sweatshops in such a way facilitates a general understanding of their attributes, but leaves us guessing about the moral status of particular, real-world organizations with harsh work conditions. It is not just

Figure 1

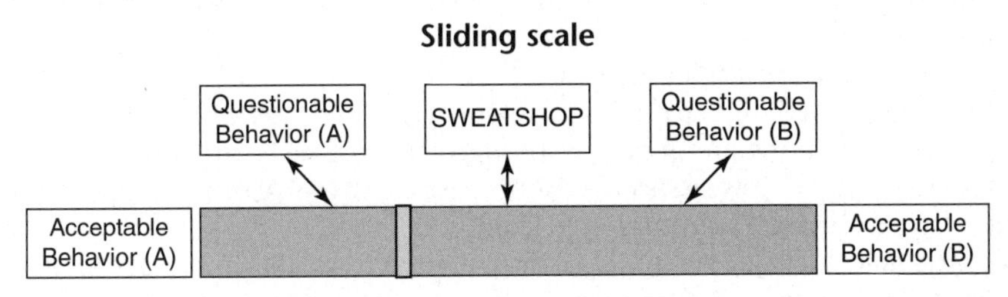

the word "sweatshop" that has multiple interpretations; other words, such as "exploitation," are particularly troublesome as well. The above definition's focus on exploitation, for example, is helpful to the extent that it highlights the harmful and selfish misuse of a workforce. As Karl Marx has shown, however, exploitation is characteristic of capitalism and every employment situation can be considered to exploit workers to some extent. The inclusion of exploitation as an identifying feature of sweatshops is to suggest that this characteristic is beyond the norm, excessive, and harmful to the extreme. Naming "absence of a living wage" and "long work hours" as elements of exploitation is helpful, too, but these also need to be approached with discretion. Jobs that have traditionally been second or supplemental incomes and those that require people to work more than eight consecutive hours might fit the criteria for "absence of a living wage" and "long work hours," but not necessarily "be exploitative, sweatshop jobs." Similarly, firemen and policemen who work under conditions that jeopardize their health and safety might qualify as sweatshop workers if we were to take the criteria literally. So, too, might those who work in call centers that subject employees to the arbitrary verbal abuse of customers.

Because it is difficult to arrive at a definition, sweatshops are better described in terms of their mix of attributes and behaviors. As the sliding scale in Figure 1 illustrates, treatment of workers tends to fall along a spectrum. Many firms engage in questionable business practices that approach sweatshop conditions in one way or another without actually reaching that point. Further, sweatshops are not locatable always in the same spot; rather, they emerge at various places along a continuum of questionable behaviors. Such behaviors are "questionable" because they are comprised of a mix of benefits and harms to various interested parties. They become objectionable when the perceived harms become excessive and tip the balance from acceptability to unacceptability. The exact point when and where this occurs is difficult to ascertain. That is why the nature of sweatshops is regarded as "slippery" and why we can label workplaces as "sweatshops" (like pornography) in the absence of an exact guiding definition. . . .

Local Environmental Conditions

Sweatshops also persist because of social and economic conditions, especially in developing and emerging countries, that leave workers particularly vulnerable. In short, sweatshops are attractive to people in places with few employment options, a lack of social services, and impoverished living conditions.

Sweatshops are often established to lower the cost of labor in production and to bring about higher profits for managers and shareholders. Those who maintain sweatshops are generally thought to be greedy victimizers. While this is often the case, sweatshops exist because they receive broad support from a number of disparate self-interested groups.

At a macro level, governments and other political associations sometimes allow and encourage the promulgation of sweatshops because sweatshops generate tax revenues and other sources of income for state coffers and individual bank accounts. Setting aside issues of graft, sweatshops often receive the tacit approval of societies attempting to improve their economic standing because sweatshops are viewed as a way to enliven a nation's domestic markets and export activity. As economic activity spurred on by sweatshops takes hold, outside investors are drawn to the country in search of opportunities for new markets and production savings. To meet the demands of business interests, the public sector typically secures funding to build or expand essential infrastructure: power plants and electric systems, sewage and water treatment facilities, phone and internet networks, public transportation systems, education, and so forth. These not only benefit the businesses coming into an area, but also the people already living there.

In addition, the output of sweatshops brings about greater economic prosperity to society as increased personal wealth spurs consumer spending, investment, and savings. Although sweatshops are regarded publicly as dehumanizing workplaces, they receive the tacit approval of society because they attract investors, increase GNP, bring or expand essential services, and provide a greater variety of goods to a society. In the view of some, sweatshops are a necessary evil—a way a nascent industrial economy can quickly build itself up from next to nothing.

So, too, at the level of the individual worker, sweatshops can be regarded as a blessing of sort, for they might be the only way for illiterate people lacking marketable skills to enter the global industrial marketplace. In many less developed countries with large populations, agriculture is the only economic activity available to people. Employable for only part of the year, outside of the planting and harvesting seasons, there is little for them to do and they stream into cities looking for work. Young (demographics are such that the populations tend to be youthful and illiterate) and lacking skills useful in the marketplace, they find few alternatives for work outside of sweatshops. Knowing there are plenty of others willing to work in their stead, they willingly (even gratefully) accept sweatshop conditions. In their view, any job is better than no job; for the alternative means no income at all and the very real possibility of starvation.

Separation Thesis

In addition to these economic issues, sweatshops exist because of a prevailing mindset that maintains a clear distinction between business and ethics. This so-called "separation thesis" holds that business decisions can and should be based on the bottom line (profit-making) without consideration of ethics. In effect, businesses are regarded as money-generating machines and managers (indeed, all workers) as functionaries bound by a principal–agency agreement that obliges them to act on behalf of the owner (the principal). Ultimately, this perspective relies on the further separation of the manager/worker from those aspects of self that define him or her as a human being.

The notion that business and ethics, personal and organizational values, and the role of self at work and at home, can be segmented in the way the separation thesis would have it, relies on a highly abstract, individuated, unworkable, and false worldview and characterization of the individual. At the individual level, for example, the dissonance produced from maintaining different, opposing values at the same time is debilitating and psychologically unhealthy. At minimum, it inclines the individual toward self-deception.

Personal versus Firm Values

The separation thesis is accompanied by adherence to a false dichotomy between personal and firm values. Managers and employees tend to adopt the view that they as individuals are different from themselves as employees. They act as if they can check their values at the door. In other words, the values that they apply in the workplace are often not the values they claim as their own. Employees and managers view themselves as mere agents, and they act according to what they perceive are the values and interests of the principals.

This is problematic on a number of levels. It causes layers of managers and employees throughout organizations to act in accordance with perceived values, not the actual values themselves. Individuals thus become interpreters of values without connecting values (and the actions derived from them) to existing guiding moral frameworks. This can lead to inconsistencies as well as to amoral, if not immoral, behavior.

In addition, this way of thinking ignores the intrinsic value of the employees and managers who are hired by the firm. Firms hire people because of their distinct and defining attributes. These include their moral dispositions. For people as employees of the firm to divorce themselves from their moral leanings while at work is to deprive the firm of some of the contributions for which they were hired. Under such conditions, firms might as well employ robots, not vibrant, thinking moral beings.

Furthermore, this sort of thinking robs organizations of the opportunity to self-correct. If employees and managers observe behavior as inappropriate according to their own values but do not endeavor to change such practices, their organization remains entrenched in those practices. Organizations rely upon their people to follow their moral compasses and exercise their moral imaginations in order to ensure that business practices correlate with laws and conventional morality. It is therefore ironic that, by acting as mere agents, employees and managers can actually jeopardize the long-term interests of the principals.

Respect for Cultural Diversity

Deference to cultural diversity is also to blame for the continuing presence of sweatshops. Although Western thinking tends to censure sweatshop labor practices, Westerners are sometimes hesitant to interfere in other cultures. The imposition of Western values on non-Western cultures (also referred to as cultural imperialism) is widely regarded as inappropriate and undesirable. This results because a deep respect for diversity and an inherent respect for the values of the other cultures lie at the heart of Western values.

A difficulty emerges here, though, as a result of our inability to distinguish between cultural values and behavior that can legitimately be deemed inappropriate even from outside the culture. For example, many people who witness business practices that involve physical abuse—particularly in developing or emerging countries—are reluctant to challenge those practices for fear of appearing guilty of cultural imperialism. They err on the side of caution in not imposing their values, when they would do well to err on the side of caution in protecting human life.

How Do We End the Stalemate?

The reality is that sweatshops are not simply the product of greed on the part of business people. They exist because they receive the tacit approval and support of governments, societies, and even the individuals that work in them. They are difficult to confront because of enduring notions that hold business and ethics, personal and organizational values, and the roles of the individual at work and at home to be distinct and separate. They also endure because many of the vulnerable and victimized participate in the perpetuation of sweatshops. They do so because, as harmful as sweatshops are, they provide benefits that are not easily found in alternative work places. Lacking forceful moral theoretical arguments, timid of adopting personal values in the workplace, and fearful of offending those belonging to other cultures, we remain stuck in a stalemate, with the result being the continued promulgation of sweatshops. . . .

Dennis G. Arnold and Laura P. Hartman

NO

Beyond Sweatshops: Positive Deviancy and Global Labor Practices

Disputes concerning global labor practices are at the core of contemporary debates regarding globalization. Attention frequently focuses on the real or alleged unjust exploitation of workers in developing economies by multinational corporations (MNCs) and their suppliers. Critics charge MNCs with the unjust exploitation of workers in developing nations and seek laws restricting the use of sweatshop labor. Many economists retort that the existence of sweatshops is an important and inevitable feature of economic development, and that laws that seek to restrict the production of goods in sweatshops will harm the very people they were intended to help. As a result, MNCs that wish to address the issue are left with little direction or guidance regarding appropriate responses to global labor challenges. However, useful models can be found. For example, some MNCs have been prompted by this attention to improve workplace conditions and wages, had begun the process of improvement at the time the recent media uproar began, or have always maintained superior standards in the workplace. Insufficient attention has been paid to firms that engage in truly good and beneficial activities with regard to their global workforces, where the result is not a sweatshop environment but is instead a safe and healthy workplace where laborers are treated with respect.

Workers have basic rights that should not be violated, notwithstanding the geographical locale of their workplace. The labor practices of "positive MNC deviants" can serve as models for other MNCs that wish to respect human rights while taking advantage of the economic benefits of a global workforce. Such creative approaches to global labor practices allow MNCs to move beyond sweatshops and to provide workers with wages and working conditions that respect their basic human dignity. In addition, such practices may result in numerous strategic advantages such as enhanced productivity, better employee morale, and improved corporate reputation.

In this essay, we outline the conventional case for tolerating sweatshops, as well as arguments for the mandated improvement of those conditions. Next, we provide a normative defense of the basic human rights that ought to be respected by employers. After explaining the concept of positive deviancy and applying it to global labor practices, we use recent empirical field studies of

MNC factories in developing nations conducted by one of the present authors, together with other recent research, as a basis for arguing that MNCs are capable of voluntarily respecting the basic rights of workers while remaining economically competitive. We then provide a summary of the numerous strategic advantages that respect for worker rights may have for MNCs.

The Conventional Dialogue Regarding Sweatshops

The Case for Sweatshops

The exploitation of a national resource—labor—allows developing countries to expand export activities and to improve their economies. Economic growth brings more jobs, which will cause the labor market to tighten, which in turn will force companies to improve conditions in order to attract workers. Though an unpopular sentiment with the general consuming public, economist Paul Krugman claims that the maintenance of sweatshops is clearly supported by economic theory: "The overwhelming mainstream view among economists is that growth of this kind of employment is tremendous good news for the world's poor." In fact, when asked whether there were too many "sweatshops" in poor nations, economist Jeffrey D. Sachs replied that his concern is "not that there are too many sweatshops but that there are too few."

These conclusions are based on the contention that free trade without labor restrictions generates future prosperity and better working conditions for the host nation by providing developing nations with access to cheaper goods and, in turn, opportunities to exploit cost advantages in export markets. Theoretical and empirical research suggests that one of the most effective ways to increase the competitiveness of a developing economy and to improve job prospects is to create a better-trained work force through work experience and training. Jobs—even terrible jobs—provide some positive externalities for a society, benefits that accrue to others who are not parties to the transaction between a laborer and [an] employer. Job-related skills, and the general ability of individuals to function as elements of the global economy, provide benefits to the host nation society at large that are not specifically part of the contractual agreement between laborer and employer. Overall, from this perspective, the best hope for workers in sweatshops lies in the improved economic and social conditions that economic growth brings. Moreover, durable economic growth will occur only if developing countries can capitalize on their low cost advantage to attract foreign development.

In addition, the argument against intervention contends that people work in sweatshops because it is the most rational means available to them for furthering their own ends. These choices prove optimal for a developing nation's economy, as they represent agreements among many producers and consumers of labor regarding desirable exchanges of labor (from the labor producers) and wages or other benefits (from the consumers of labor, in this case, multinational enterprises and the purchasers of their goods and services). In short, the argument states that, however much we may not like some of

Figure 1

The Argument for Sweatshops

We have a moral obligation to perform actions that best enhance the preference satisfaction of the most people possible.

Creating and maintaining sweatshops best enhances the preferences satisfaction of those affected by sweatshops (sweatshop employees, via higher wages than they would otherwise receive; consumers, via lower prices for sweatshop goods; and MNCs and their shareholders, through lower labor costs).

Therefore, as many sweatshops as possible should be created and maintained.

what we see in the labor conditions of developing nations, this is the market at work; and the market works to generate overall improvements in economic welfare for a society.

There are two distinct features of the case for permitting sub-standard working conditions that should be noted. First, there is consequentialist ethical reasoning at work in such arguments. Second, there are empirical assumptions at work as well. To better understand the assumptions involved, it is helpful to explicitly state the main argument for sub-standard working conditions under consideration (see Figure 1).

The consequentialist ethical presupposition captured by the first premise in Figure 1 is, of course, a widely held presumption of most economists (we will refer to this as the ethical premise). The second premise is grounded in various empirical assumptions regarding micro-economics, and is typically taken by economists to be so obvious as to not warrant further attention (we will refer to this as the empirical premise). We will return to evaluate the legitimacy of these premises after exploring the primary competing perspective.

The Case for the Mandated Improvement of Working Conditions

Free markets, either in labor or in products, generate many benefits; but their ability to generate those benefits presumes that certain boundary conditions hold firm. For example, transactions among workers and employers optimally satisfy the interests of each only if there is a free flow of information (e.g., workers get accurate descriptions of occupational health risks), the transaction is truly voluntary (e.g., workers are not forced to work through coercion), people are able to make rational decisions about their self-interest (young children, for example, cannot be held to the terms of any "contract" they enter into), and there are many buyers and sellers (e.g., no potential for exploitative monopoly exists). Criticisms of MNC labor practices in developing countries often stem from the fact that one or more of the conditions for efficient free markets does not hold, or is in some way circumvented by the MNC. In that case, the normally expected benefits of a free market are not guaranteed; there is a market failure. For these reasons, critics of sweatshops contend that the empirical premise is false. Instead, they argue for the mandated improvement in working conditions via regulation.

One argument for regulating the improvement of MNC labor practices is premised on the claim that the preconditions for efficient markets are not met in many developing nations. For example, workers may agree to labor under poor conditions, but only because they have no other option for securing income. Alternatively, when they have a choice (e.g., leave a poor rural area for factory work in a far-away industrial center), they may not be able to make a fully informed choice because of their lack of information about what lies ahead. Furthermore, such labor choices, once made, can be difficult to undo when additional information is learned "on the job" (e.g., it can be extremely difficult to get out of a labor agreement and to return to one's rural home). Thus, critics argue the fact that workers agree to labor under poor conditions does not necessarily mean that this is the kind of agreement that constitutes the normal workings of a well-functioning free market in jobs and labor.

A second argument offered by critics of sweatshops challenges the assumption that creating and maintaining sweatshops best enhances the preferences satisfaction of those affected by them. For example, critics challenge the idea that sweatshops result in many positive externalities. They argue that the kinds of skills developed through much routine factory work hold no promise of greater economic and social development, either for the individual employee or [for] the entire society. Moreover, the transition from agricultural and cottage-industries to factory-based work is argued to have numerous negative externalities; that is, social costs that are not covered by the wages paid by a MNC to its employees. The social disruption caused by urban migration is one such negative consequence, as people move from lives characterized by the informal social support networks of family and village to lives characterized by urban anonymity and dependence upon overstressed public social services. Further, as populations increase in urban centers, existing sanitation and housing resources are stressed beyond capacity. Finally, job losses in the manufacturing sectors of the countries where factories were closed because of higher labor costs frequently result in significant social disruption. These varied social costs are typically unaccounted for in the cost-benefit analyses of economists, and call into question the empirical premise of the argument in support of sweatshops. Accordingly, the global market may not be an effective arbiter of the trade-offs between improved working conditions and levels of economic development, production cost, and product price. Some economists claim that, over time, markets will correct even the worst sweatshop practices; but other economists and many non-economists remain unconvinced.

These are some of the reasons that MNC critics focus on public policy as a means of discouraging the abuse of workers. For example, there is a long history of attempts to harmonize international labor standards via trade agreements such as the North American Free Trade Agreement and the General Agreement on Tariffs and Trade. Indeed, in as early as 1933 activists succeeded in persuading the U.S. Congress to add a fair labor standards provision to the National Industrial Recovery Act (NIRA). The act specified that imports would only be permitted from nations that guaranteed workers the right to organize and bargain collectively, limited maximum working hours, and provided minimum wages. However, the NIRA was ruled unconstitutional by the U.S. Supreme Court in 1935. Recently the Campaign for the Abolition of Sweatshops & Child Labor, a coalition of labor activists, religious groups and academics, has announced a new campaign to push for laws that restrict the ability of MNCs to sell products made in alleged sweatshops. Contemplated regulations include import bans, forced disclosure of the factories where the goods are made, and bans on government purchases of the products of sweatshops.

Moreover, critics argue that, regardless of the kinds of benefits that do or do not accrue from the use of sweatshops, it is simply morally impermissible to subject individuals to extended periods of grueling and mind-numbing labor in conditions that put their health and welfare at risk and which provide them with inadequate compensation. In short, any person deserves better conditions than those found in sweatshops. Thus, in addition to the various contentious arguments as to the real or illusory benefits and costs of poor working conditions for MNCs and developing nations, there remain fundamental objections to certain labor practices, the cogency of which does not depend on cost-benefit calculations. Concern for human dignity and basic rights simply rules some practices "out of bounds."

EXPLORING THE ISSUE

Is the Sweatshop Concept Adopted by the U.S. Manufacturers Overseas Ethical?

Critical Thinking and Reflection

1. Define the sweatshop concept.
2. What are the positive and negative aspects of using sweatshops?
3. What do labor experts suggest as alternatives for organizations wanting to adopt the sweatshops?
4. What suggestions do you have for organizations to provide fair working environments in their sweatshops?

Is There Common Ground?

Sweatshops have been a controversy as they adopt extremely offensive labor practices. However, economists suggest that the host economies usually benefit from the trade and exports of their products. Further, in many economies, consistent employment is so hard to find that usually such multinationals are encouraged to establish their own business operations. Critics condemn the unacceptable working conditions that have caught the attention of several media. Labor professionals suggest that multinationals adopt a proactive stand and remain responsible for the labor conditions they provide overseas. Independent third-party inspectors also might help to moderate this labor problem that is overwhelming the overseas operations of most of the giant retailers. What suggestions do you have to solve this problem?

Additional Resources

http://www.veganpeace.com/sweatshops/sweatshops_and_child_labor.htm: Sweatshops and Child Labor.

http://heartsandminds.org/articles/sweat.htm: Harsh Conditions Create Public Support for Reform.

http://www.pbs.org/itvs/storewars/: Store Wars: When Walmart Comes to Town.

http://www.businessweek.com/bwdaily/dnflash/content/oct2008/db2008109_219930.htm: Walmart Supplier Accused of Sweatshop Conditions.

ISSUE 20

Are U.S. Companies Adaptive to Local Practices Overseas?

Yes: Mike Hughlett, from *Strong Amid Slowdown Worries Sitting Pretty: McDonald's Overseas Sales Are Surging as It Adapts Successful U.S. Operations to Local Tastes, Styles of Its International Restaurants* (McClatchy—Tribune Information Services, 2008)

No: Jaya Halepete, K. V. Seshadri Iyer, and Soo Chul Park, from "Wal-Mart in India: A Success or Failure?" *International Journal of Retail & Distribution Management* (vol. 36, no. 9, pp. 701–713, 2008)

Learning Outcomes

After reading this issue, you should be able to:

- Define ethnocentric and polycentric staffing approaches.
- Explain how McDonald's has become such a successful global company.
- Identify why Walmart was not successful in Germany and Korea.
- Identify what alternatives organizations can pursue in establishing overseas.

ISSUE SUMMARY

YES: Hughlett, a food reporter, provides evidence of how McDonald's has innovatively created different menus to ensure their consumers are happy. Further, the company also has paid attention to local management practices to enhance its corporate success.

NO: Assistant Professor Halepete and her colleagues do an excellent case analysis of Walmart in Germany, Korea, and India, providing evidence of how important cultural values are in making or breaking a company.

McDonald's, the 52-year-old successful multinational, has implemented a global strategy of local adaptation of their main products in several markets. This is a commendable quality of their management, suggesting that the company is sensitive to and appreciative of different cultures. For instance, in Japan, McDonald's provide Tamago burgers with fried eggs catering to local tastes and preferences. In India, they offer Maharaja Mac burgers with chicken as serving beef is against local religious sentiments. For their vegetarian customers in India, they offer Mc Aloo Tikki with potatoes and spices. In every market, they have tactfully adapted their products and services to make their customers happy.

The company has indicated that the motto in their international operations is the same—the customer's choice finally prevails. Many a time multinationals are not willing to change their international brand as standardization is the main ingredient to their global success. In 2008, McDonald's experienced a substantial profit increase of 21% in their international markets. McDonald's has also paid attention to the aesthetic aspects of how appealing their restaurants are to their customers. Instead of the usual Golden Arches found in the United States, their European restaurants have earthy tones and different colors to accommodate to domestic expressions of aesthetic styles. In several countries, they branded their overseas eating places as family restaurants abiding with local cultural values of customers wanting to eat with their families.

Apart from their products and restaurants that they have modified, they have taken another adaptive step while operating overseas. They chose a polycentric staffing strategy of hiring and developing local talent. Usually multinationals prefer to use an ethnocentric staffing approach or hiring of management executives from their own home country. An ethnocentric approach allows for better control of their local subsidiaries and also allows for standardization of management practices. McDonald's follows a decentralized approach in its international branches, indicating a preference of locals managing their own operations. Experts suggest that host employees (employees in the country of operation) will implement human resource management practices that are harmonious with the domestic cultural values, resulting in better organizational outcomes.

U.S. multinationals operating in China also have been very adaptive to local practices and norms. The Chinese business model requires the government to be an active participant in any business ventures between local companies and multinationals. U.S. companies have abided by partnering with the government for their local operations in China. The classic example is that of Google Inc., which quit China in 2010 temporarily when the government mandated restrictions on expression on the Internet. However, Google returned to China after its CEO stated explicitly that the company would completely abide by the local practices.

In China, U.S. multinationals are recognized for providing elaborate training opportunities to their employees, which is congruent with the local culture of wanting to learn and to be skilled. U.S. companies are trying to attract local talent with developmental opportunities as they also realize only if they hire local employees will they create a strong bond with the host country.

On the other hand, Assistant Professor Halepete and her colleagues suggest that U.S. multinationals may fail to adapt adequately as required by the local culture. They illustrate this thesis by using the case study of Walmart in its expansion strategies to Germany and Korea. In Germany, they did not create a positive environment for shoppers to come to their stores. Their stores needed a complete restoration, which they did not consider an immediate priority. They also try to enforce the employment practices that have been used in their U.S. stores for their German stores. For instance, they tried to establish corporate rules whether men and women can date within the organization. Organizations creating rules around dating practices was something the local workforce had not experienced before. They also did not pay attention to the German labor laws, which are very powerfully controlled by their unions and work councils. The German labor organizations have the last word on wages, hours of work, vacations, benefits, and any other employment-related practices. Further, Walmart had not done sufficient market research to understand what kind of products appeal to the German customers. Walmart left Germany with a staggering loss of more than a hundred billion dollars.

Walmart had similar problems in South Korea as it failed to pay sufficient attention to the local consumers' values. It established huge indoor stores similar to those in the United States while missing important Korean retail preferences. In Korea, retail stores are much smaller and also serve as a place for families to socialize and mingle. Moreover, Walmart maintained its low-price strategy to attract customers while Korean customers value a differentiation approach. The stores that they initially established began to offer huge consumer items while Korean customers were expecting to shop for grocery products also. Once again, it seems Walmart did not research satisfactorily the market they were planning to operate in and offered similar practices that were successful in their U.S. operations.

There are other entry strategies multinationals may pursue when establishing overseas. Experts suggest that establishing joint ventures may alleviate much of the cultural problems multinational encounter in operating wholly owned subsidiaries. Joint ventures are usually two organizations (an organization from the home country and an organization from the host country) that combine their resources, capital, and labor to jointly produce products or services. The collaborative spirit of the joint venture organization will be allowed for insightful analysis of the local market making the international companies get a complete flavor of domestic preferences. McDonald's used a joint venture strategy of a 50–50 partnership in their successful 14 years of operations in India. These joint venture partners provided them with a realistic estimate of the expectations of the Indian consumers. U.S. multinationals have used this strategy very effectively in their entry of the Chinese and Mexican markets.

U.S. companies may also pursue a complete decentralized approach in operating overseas. In such a strategy, they hire and train locals to run their overseas operations. This strategy allows international companies to accommodate local practices and also helps create that tacit bond with their customers. McDonald's has shown the positive effects of allowing locals to run its operations in several countries. For instance, in India, the company color-codes the uniforms of the employees who make meat and nonmeat dishes, so that their customers may not have any doubt about the quality of their services. Also, in the United States, the drive-through windows are considered the most popular eating options for customers. But in contrast, in European and in Asian countries, restaurants are considered a place not only to eat and but also to socialize. McDonald's adapted accordingly by providing and creating family restaurant environments in these places. This was possible only because they had a good understanding of the local markets by adopting the polycentric strategy.

Mike Hughlett

Strong Amid Slowdown Worries Sitting Pretty: McDonald's Overseas Sales Are Surging as It Adapts Successful U.S. Operations to Local Tastes, Styles of Its International Restaurants

Whether it's the Maharaja Mac in India, the Croque McDo in France or the Tamago Double Mac in Japan, they're all part of the same recipe: an overseas golden age for U.S. fast-food giant McDonald's Corp.

Oak Brook-based McDonald's in recent years has taken the same winning template devised in the United States—longer hours, quicker service, a healthier menu, etc.—and applied it across the globe. Plus, analysts say ifs benefited from a decentralized approach, with more menu choices culled from local tastes and managers hired from local ranks.

And this year, with McDonald's U.S. sales slowing because of a weak economy, international has particularly been a star.

But European economies are expected to slow considerably in the coming months, while the Japanese economy looks vulnerable too. Plus, currency translation benefits enjoyed by McDonald's and scores of other U.S. multinational companies may go out the window as the U.S. dollar strengthens.

Still, Jim Skinner, McDonald's chief executive, doesn't seem worried. "We operate better in a robust economy, but in some ways we are recession resistant," he said in an interview with the *Tribune* last week. "We are capable of operating in any [economic] environment and we have proved that for 52 years."

As the U.S. economy weakened this year, McDonald's U.S. same-store sales fell in March, the first decline in that key year-over-year gauge since 2003. Since then, sales have bounced back, and overall U.S. revenues through June were up 3 percent over the same six months in 2007, while operating income had risen 5 percent.

But McDonald's overseas performance has been more impressive this year, analysts say. Sales in Europe alone, which is McDonald's biggest market by revenue since 2004, climbed 9 percent for the six months of 2008, while operating profits jumped 21 percent even after adjusting for currency benefits.

And while the U.S. remains McDonald's most lucrative market, the combined operating profits of its European and Asian segments seem likely to surpass those of the U.S. this year. "It's just really good execution across the brand and across the globe," said John Owens, a stock analyst at Morningstar Inc. "They took a lot of pages from their playbook here and implemented them overseas."

That playbook, dubbed "Plan to Win," was forged in 2003 when McDonald's was floundering. Instead of focusing on constantly opening new stores, McDonald's opted to concentrate on the basics: better customer service, tastier food, better-looking restaurants and so on.

The company has "re-imaged" thousands of its existing stores here and abroad, dumping the orange-red fiberglass motif. And that new upscale look—think earth tones and coffeehouse—seems particularly pronounced in Europe, said David Palmer, a stock analyst UBS Securities.

"Their assets are spectacular in Europe versus other markets," he said. "I'm talking about the restaurant buildings. They're often newer and better than what we see in the U.S." Food in those restaurants isn't radically different from those here, but part of McDonald's overseas success comes from its "locally relevant menu choices," said Morningstar's Owens. So, for the French, there is the Croque McDo, which is ham and melted Swiss cheese on round toast; the Japanese get two beef patties and a fried egg between two buns in the Tamago burger; and Indians can avoid beef with the double chicken patties of the Maharaja Mac.

It's not just the food that's gotten more regional over the years, it's McDonald's management. Back in 2001, when Skinner ran McDonald's European operations, he did so from Oak Brook. Since 2005, they've been run from London by Denis Hennequin, a French native often praised for McDonald's European turnaround.

Locally-based leadership goes down to a countrywide level, and "it is very important," said Palmer, the UBS analyst. "They have established accountability and very effective local leadership."

And if an innovative idea works in one country, it often makes its way to another, Palmer said. For instance, specialty coffee—the caramel cappuccinos and such that McDonald's is rolling out in the U.S.—originated from a successful initiative in Australia.

While McDonald's operates in 118 countries, its most promising growth opportunity seems to be China. It's one of the few markets where it's not ranked No. 1; that title goes to KFC. But it will have 1,000 stores in China by the end of the year and plans to add several hundred more in the years to follow. "China is coming on strong, and we have a huge opportunity there," Skinner said.

Today, Asia represents 12 percent to 13 percent of McDonald's profits. Within 10 years, Skinner estimated the region would comprise 30 percent to 35 percent of profits, with China accounting for a big chunk of that growth.

In the short term, though, McDonald's may have to ride out an economic slowdown that could even affect China, albeit not nearly as much as more developed nations. Official forecasts call for the European economy to barely creep forward, with Britain a leading candidate for recession.

"European consumers are tightening up their wallets and lowering their spending," said David Kolpak, managing director of Victory Capital Management, which owns 1.1 million McDonald's shares.

Still, for all the angst about a global economic slowdown, McDonald's same-store sales results for August, released Tuesday, were "blowout numbers" as Kolpak called them.

Overall, same-store sales, which are from stores open at least a year, were up 8.5 percent globally, 11.6 percent in Europe and 10 percent in Asia and the pacific.

Said Skinner, "We hear the same things, 'Oh, the economy in Europe, that's the next shoe to drop, they're going to go into a recession, the U.S. is in a recession, consumer confidence is at an all-time low.' And yet our traffic and our growth not only here, but in European countries, is very strong."

Jaya Halepete, K. V. Seshadri Iyer, and Soo Chul Park

NO

Wal-Mart in India: A Success or Failure?

In times of cut throat competition in the retail industry and saturation of domestic markets, retailers have been looking to expand internationally. Many American retailers have ventured internationally and established presence in several countries. While some retailers have been highly successful, others have faced failures. This paper analyzes Wal-Mart as a company that has been expanding internationally for several years with its share of successes and failures. This paper analyzes the main reasons for Wal-Mart's failures in Germany and South Korea utilizing the eclectic theory, and then applies the learnings to evaluate Wal-Mart's entry into the Indian retail market.

Wal-Mart Company Background and History

Wal-Mart's business model is founded on providing the lowest prices to its customers. The company's primary expansion strategy has been to continuously open new stores, especially its massive, 100,000–200,000 square foot supercenters. Starting in 1962 when Sam Walton opened the first Wal-Mart discount city in Rogers, Arkansas, a city of only 6,000 residents, Wal-Mart today operates a total of 971 discount stores, 2,447 supercenters, 591 Sam's Clubs and 132 neighborhood markets in the US and 3,020 retail stores internationally. Wal-Mart's growth has been nothing less than spectacular.

In the beginning, most stores were located in small towns with populations of up to about 5,000 people offering typical department store merchandise but no groceries. With the introduction of supercenters in the 1980s, with sizes of over 200,000 square feet, Wal-Mart began selling groceries. Over time, Wal-Mart expanded into larger metropolitan areas with store formats that included both Sam's Club membership stores, selling at a very low-price level with most products sold in bulk, and neighborhood markets offering about 20,000 products.

Wal-Mart's International Expansion

Wal-Mart's international expansion began as an attempt to generate sales growth outside its well-established base in the USA Wal-Mart's international operations are spread across countries such as Canada, Mexico, Brazil, Costa

From *International Journal of Retail & Distribution Management*, 2008, pp. 701–713.

Rica. International stores represent about 45 percent of the company's total retail outlets.

The company's current stated goal is to increase its international business from the current level of about 20–33 percent of its revenues or roughly $103 billion. Wal-Mart's approach to achieving this growth goal is based on three strategies:

1. expanding into new markets with multiple formats;
2. opening new stores in existing markets; and
3. increasing sales at existing international stores.

To achieve this goal, Wal-Mart aggressively increased its international presence by expanding into Latin America in 2005 through the purchase of an interest in 413 stores of a regional retailer. This increased the company's international footprint from ten countries to 15 countries at that time. Though, Wal-Mart has been able to succeed in close-to-home markets like Canada and Mexico, the company's Asian and European business units have been much more difficult to manage. In the late 1990s, Wal-Mart expanded into the South Korean and the German retail markets and has since exited both markets because of poor financial performance. These exits have reduced Wal-Mart's international presence to 13 markets.

Wal-Mart had planed to open 320–330 international stores in 2007, of which 10 percent were relocations or expansions of existing stores and the remaining units were new operations for the company. Wal-Mart officials have indicated that India, where government reforms lifting restrictions on foreign ownership of retail operations are underway, is a major target market for the company.

Dunning's Theory of the Eclectic Firm for International Expansion

Dunning's theory of eclectic firm approach has been widely accepted as a conceptual framework for explaining foreign direct investment and international expansion. The model of theory of eclectic firm includes three dimensions associated with foreign direct investment. These are:

1. ownership;
2. location; and
3. internalization.

Ownership covers the firm's assets and transactions. Asset ownership provides advantages due to the reputation of the company whereas transactions cover the way a store carries out its operations. The location dimension includes factors that cover the overall attractiveness of a country to a retailer. These are grouped into pull and push factors. Pull factors include factors related to location that make the market more attractive such as market size, low cost of land, and labour, whereas push factors are related to location that make the market less attractive such as cultural differences and stringent regulations. Finally, the internalization dimension relates to how company's secrets are handled. This may be important for companies that have assets that need to be protected. Based on the level of protection required, the companies choose different methods for foreign expansion such as franchising and joint ventures.

In this paper, we closely examine Wal-Mart's expansion in Germany and South Korea using relevant dimensions from Dunning's theory of the eclectic firm, and then analyze Wal-Mart's Indian context.

Wal-Mart in Germany

Wal-Mart chose Germany for its entry into the European market because it is the biggest market in Europe and has a central location. The thinking was that it would be possible to expand into other markets in Europe from Germany. Wal-Mart entered the German market by buying 21 Wertkauf hypermarkets at the end of 1997 and 74 interspar hypermarkets a year later in 1998. Many of the stores they purchased were not working profitably and most of the stores were in need of renovation. Wal-Mart operated in Germany as a wholly owned subsidiary of the parent company.

Utilizing the eclectic theory, we analyze the ownership, locational, and internalization dimensions of Wal-Mart's entry into Germany. First, we analyze the ownership and internalization dimensions together. Since Wal-Mart entered Germany through a completely owned German subsidiary, it owned all assets, and has the ability to implement its own approach to transactions within its operations in Germany. Wal-Mart seems to have failed to take advantage of the benefits arising from ownership. To start, there were delays in changing the name of the stores to Wal-Mart. Further, considering that several stores were in need to substantial renovation, Wal-Mart missed on renovating the stores immediately, which seems to have resulted in a poor image of the Wal-Mart brand. Customers began to associate the name of Wal-Mart with the image of run-down stores. Also, even though Wal-Mart constantly increased the share of store brands, they still accounted for only 15 percent of all articles and Wal-Mart never became a well-known brand name in Germany. Finally, Wal-Mart was not really able to differentiate itself in terms of the service it provided compared to competition. Its return policies were viewed as identical to other German retailers, and its quality of service was mediocre. The only difference cited between Wal-Mart and other retailers was that Wal-Mart's shopping bags were free. Overall, Wal-Mart was not able to create a positive, well-known image or to find a niche of its own in the fragmented German retail market.

Second, we analyze the locational dimension. Wal-Mart's natural approach in Germany was to focus on improving operations through the rationalization of stores by closing some of them to open new ones. One locational parameter that Wal-Mart seems to have underestimated was the strict zoning laws and the scarcity of development sites. The resulting delays in the opening of new stores rapidly did not allow for Wal-Mart to scale up fast enough. The inability to scale effectively reduced Wal-Mart's ability to obtain sufficient volume discounts from suppliers or to achieve efficiencies in logistics—two key factors that have driven Wal-Mart's success in the USA. Owing to the small number of Wal-Mart stores, the company was at a disadvantage when compared to other German discount chains. Furthermore, the lack of scale power resulting in Wal-Mart's failure to achieve price leadership. Wal-Mart's capability to reduce prices was limited because of the low-profit margins and it is illegal to sell below the buying price in Germany. Whenever Wal-Mart reduced prices, competitors did so as well. This ties back to the first dimension of ownership where transactional advantages could not be achieved. Although, Wal-Mart had 92 stores by 2003, the inability to scale to the right size in a timely manner within a strongly regulated environment resulted in significant annual losses of between $130 million and $260 million. Further, Wal-Mart's lack of market success made it difficult to find partners willing to invest with them. One of the distinct and critical attributes of localization is culture, where again Wal-Mart seemed to have faced challenges in Germany; cultural differences between American and German consumers was a significant reason that prevented the successful acceptance of the Wal-Mart culture in Germany.

The cultural factor affected Wal-Mart internally as well. Knorr and Arndt attributed Wal-Mart's failure to the company's management, writing that "Wal-Mart's attempt to apply the company's proven US success formula in an unmodified manner to the German market turned out to be nothing short of a fiasco." Wal-Mart's American managers pressured German executives to enforce American-style management practices in the workplace. Employees were forbidden, for instance, from dating colleagues in positions of influence. Workers were also told not to flirt with one another. Several workers resisted the management's demands which they felt were unjust. Two senior managers of Wal-Mart in Germany were quoted as saying:

> Corporate culture not only requires supportive action (intercultural training, coaching) but also time and patience in order to grow within an acquired company with a cultural history of its own. There is no such pill as a pill for cultural transformation.

Besides, running up against German tradition, analysts say Wal-Mart also misfired when it came to knowing the market they were attempting to crack. American styles do not always translate well. Many of the product buyers in Germany were Americans, resulting in a lack of understanding of the German consumer markets. As an example, in the US supercenters, food accounts for about 40 percent of sales. In its German competitors, food accounted for 50–360 percent of sales. While Wal-Mart kept this ratio—in contrast to its home stores in the US—it slightly changed the assortment of about 60,000 different articles in order to meet the requirements of the German consumer as much as possible. German refrigerators are usually much smaller than American ones and Germans tend to have less storage room and therefore, are not used to buying large quantities of food or other items. For this reason, Wal-Mart offered smaller sizes in Germany but they did not reduce the share of food in the stores and this resulted in lower operating margins. Also, Wal-Mart did not sufficiently research the German market to tailor its merchandise mix. The company was stuck with millions of dollars worth of merchandise which was not desired by German consumers.

Finally, Wal-Mart has traditionally operated in the US market where it has exploited local labour laws to its benefit. The labour laws in Germany seemed to have been much harsher which directly increased Wal-Mart's labour costs. Strict local business regulations concerning store operating hours and employee protections prevented the chain from achieving profits similar to their US operations.

When Wal-Mart departed the German market, the revenue lost was just 0.8 percent of Wal-Mart's annual $103 billion in sales.

Wal-Mart in South Korea

Wal-Mart entered South Korea in 1998 when the South Korean Government opened up retail markets to foreign investments. It purchased an 85 percent stake in Korea Makro, which had four stores located in the Seoul metro area. A number of other retailers entered the market at the same time. Eventually in 1998, there were five major foreign retailers actively operating in Korea along with numerous domestic rivals.

Utilizing the eclectic theory, we specifically analyze the locational dimensions of Wal-Mart's entry into Korea. The ownership and internalization dimension really do not seem to have any significant impact compared to the locational dimension. Wal-Mart's natural approach in Korea was to offer a warehouse based store setting—very similar to its settings in the USA. Wal-Mart seems to have missed fully understanding the local Korean retail culture which thrives as a festive and social setting. Korea's retail market is composed of thousands of small retailers that are typically dispersed in local neighborhoods and form both a marketplace and a social center. The successful domestic retail supercenters aimed to recreate the festive, noisy atmosphere of the outdoor markets within their stores.

Wal-Mart's value proposition of price leadership did not seem to work well, as it failed to adapt to some of the unique peculiarities of the South Korean market. While Korean consumers are price sensitive like their American counterparts, they tend to equally value fashion trends, quality, variety, and personalized service over cost. Several of the local competitors—who better understood Korean customers' tastes, buying preferences, and fashion/trend consciousness—improved their offerings to cater to these specific needs of the Korean customer. Also, the Korean retailers very astutely instituted campaigns such as "Buy-Korean" that encouraged Koreans to support their domestic industry, which hurt Wal-Mart. When Wal-Mart using discounted pricing as a lever, it found it difficult to sustain. The domestic retailers reacted very aggressively to Wal-Mart's discount pricing strategy by quickly offering lower prices. This escalated into a price war among the major retailers, limiting Wal-Mart's ability to attract new customers to its stores and limiting the return on their investment.

Besides, running up against the Korean tradition, Wal-Mart seems to have misfired when it came to offering the right products in the Korean market. When Wal-Mart opened its first stores in Korea in 1998, it tried to build its business model around dry goods, such as electronics, which was not at all aligned with the expectation of Korean shoppers, who were looking to the discount giant to supply them with value-priced food and beverages. Also, there were some reports that Koreans were disappointed with the quality of customer service at Wal-Mart.

Another significant locational parameter that Wal-Mart seems to have been hurt by was a high cost of real estate compared to the domestic retailers. Some domestic retailers were able to purchase or lease prime real estate at low prices after the 1998 Korean economic crisis to establish a lower, sustainable base fixed cost than the foreign competition.

Finally, in 2006, Wal-Mart sold its South Korean unit consisting of 16 stores to the country's biggest domestic retailer in 2006.

Wal-Mart in India

In 2005, India was rated the top international investment opportunity among 30 emerging markets for mass merchant and food retailers looking to expand globally. The Indian economy is one of the world's fastest growing, with gross domestic product (GDP) expanding at an average annual rate of about 7.5 percent for the past three years and the retail market expanding 10 percent on average. The Indian retail market, an estimated $250 billion annually, is the world's eighth largest market and is projected to grow by more than 7 percent annually. All these factors show the strong economic conditions of the country which is a pull factor for companies like Wal-Mart that are interested in expanding into the Indian retail market.

Although the Indian economy has been growing rapidly in the face of substantial deregulation, the Indian retail economy remains protected from foreign competition by rules that mostly prohibit direct investment by foreigners. Currently, multi-brand retailers are prohibited from direct investment in the country and cannot own and operate their own stores. To circumvent this regulation, Wal-Mart has announced a partnership with Bharti Enterprises, an Indian business group that is the country's largest mobile phone company. The joint venture between Wal-Mart and Bharti will manage the supply chain together while Bharti Enterprises will be franchised to run the retail portion. This operating model in India will expose Wal-Mart to potential challenges on the ownership and internalization dimensions of the eclectic model. Since Wal-Mart has not really seen any such issues in Germany or South Korea, it needs to ensure that the operating model is one that is clearly defined with coupling with Bharti that is aligned with its classic operating model's strengths. In addition, most joint ventures fail, and using the joint venture model to enter India will require Wal-Mart to closely manage the venture, and be patient in terms of how it works with Bharti. Moreover, Wal-Mart brings a tremendous amount of supply chain and information technology intellectual property to the joint venture, which it will need to protect. This has been a challenge in the Indian context, and Wal-Mart needs to carefully understand the management of the relationship from this specific dimension.

On the location dimension, the sheer market size makes India an attractive country, but one that is riddled with several limitations that need to be effectively managed for success. India's population is over a billion (Table 1). Although a large percentage of population is poor, the middle class has been estimated to include 300,000,000 people, larger than the total population of the US. This is a immense advantage for Wal-Mart as there is a large population in the segment it typically serves.

Although large in size, the diversity and heterogeneity of the Indian market is tremendously complex. Religion, language, dialect, value system, food habit, economic buying power, clothing selection, fabric, tradition, and access to transportation are all attributes that clearly demonstrate the complexity in India; there are sub-markets within markets in India. Segmenting the market along a variety of attributes will be key—Wal-Mart's ability to develop localised merchandise and source and supply the 75,000 products sold in a typical supercenter will truly be tested. While, the Indian middle class customer is a value-conscious shopper, she/he is very hard to please. This is best expressed

Table 1

Demographic comparison of Germany, South Korea, and India

	Germany	South Korea	India
Population	82,422,299	48,846,823	1,095,351,995
Age structure			
0–14 years (percent)	14	19	31
15–64 years (percent)	66	72	64
65+ years (percent)	19	9	5
Population growth rate (2006) (percent)	−0.02	0.42	1.38
Language(s)	German	Korean w/English widely taught	English is most important language for commerce 30 percent speak Hindi 14 other official languages 1,600+ dialects
Literacy (>age 15) (percent)	99	97.9	60
Religions	34 percent Protestant 34 percent Roman Catholic 4 percent Muslim 28 percent other or none	26 percent Christian 26 percent Buddhist 48 percent other or none	81 percent Hindu 13 percent Muslim 2 percent Christian 2 percent Sikh 2 percent other or none
GDP per capita (2006) ($)	31,400	24,200	3,700

Source: CIA Factbook (2007)

by this customer's mindset of "wanting a world-class product at Indian prices." So, Wal-Mart's traditional business model, offering the lowest prices, may not work well in India without substantial modifications. The model did not work well in South Korea, where consumers were as price sensitive as their American counterparts and at the same time a lot more fashion conscious. In the case of Germany, while consumers were noted for being very value-conscious, which should have helped Wal-Mart, the company did not sufficiently research the German market to tailor its merchandise mix to the German consumer market. Getting its product offering right to align with the Indian consumer's preferences would be key driver for success in the Indian market.

The above driver's importance is further reinforced by the competition that Wal-Mart will face from unorganized retail which includes "kirana stores" and small size family-owned stores. The 12 million small, local businesses in India, known as "kirana" stores, are spread across 5,000 towns and 600,000 villages throughout India. Small stores, slightly larger and better organized than "kirana" stores, are family-owned, and depend on unpaid family labour and often, free land for a small stall for selling various products. Both these types of stores maintain low prices and are able to offer a variety of staples and household items very conveniently to their local consumers. There is still a large population that [is] currently shopping from small mom and pop stores, and this is the segment whose needs Wal-Mart will ideally choose to cater to. While Wal-Mart's joint venture with Bharti may help alleviate this problem, it would be very important for Wal-Mart to change, not only its offerings, but also its mindset to operations, to suit the Indian multi-dimensional and multi-characteristic consumer.

Another front of competition comes from large organized retail stores. While these stores currently make up only 2–3 percent of the total primarily is in the ten biggest cities in India, they are growing at 18–20 percent a year. Spencer's retail, a traditional south Indian brand is planning to expand nationwide and open 1,900 stores in the next three years across all of India, while Reliance retail, the country's largest non-state owned company and a quick reacting, fierce competitor has already opened 25 stores and plans to invest $5 billion over the next four years to build a range of store formats, including supercenters. Trent, the retail portion of the Tata Group, has announced plans to change product offerings, open more outlets, and expand the range of their retail formats, including supercenters. Future Group and Shoppers' Stop, the retail branch of the K Raheja construction company, an established player in the retail market with 160 stores has announced plans to increase to 3,300 stores by 2010, including increasing the number of their supercenters from 37 to 100 in the next year. The organized retail space seems to be getting very crowded and the competition very intense. Since, the Wal-Mart model is very dependent on real estate because:

- stores must be large enough to display the huge variety of merchandise; and
- stores must be located near where people live for easy access, frequent visits, and convenience, availability and cost of retail space becomes an important factor.

The competitive situation discussed above has put tremendous pressure on the available retail space, and has significantly driven up commercial and residential property prices 80–100 percent in the past year. These factors may delay both the ability of Wal-Mart/Bharti to expand its distribution network and the ability of Bharti to acquire land for development of new supercenters. While retail space, currently estimated to be about 10 million square feet, is expected to grow to 200 million square feet over the next five years, the growth of Wal-Mart is going to be constrained by this rate of growth. Furthermore, the difficulties involved in acquiring and developing land for retail use in India are another hindrance to retail development. In many areas of India, land titles are obscure and disputed. Also, there are restrictions placed on how the land may be used. A complex web of central, state and local government rules and regulations where retailers have to acquire multiple licenses, covering general trading, specific products, and pollution clearances creates another level of complexity.

Higher real estate costs as well as a constraint on retail space capacity will increase the fixed costs associated with retail and distribution operations, consequently lowering return on investment as well as limiting the number of storefronts. This was a problem for Wal-Mart in Germany and South Korea that contributed to their exiting those markets (Table 2).

Developing a supply system that can reliably supply goods throughout the country will be another challenge for Wal-Mart. Some of the biggest infrastructure problems in India include airports, electricity supply, adequate roads and working sea ports. Transport delays and inadequate cold storage mean that between 35 and 40 percent of fruit and vegetables grown in India rots where it is harvested or in transit. Transporting goods from one end of India to another by truck can take as long as 45 days. Such issues have potentially significant consequences. For example, the high proportion of groceries sold in Wal-Mart's stores in Germany was one of the factors responsible for their poor economic performance in that market due to the inherently low margins associated with food products. India is a country where more than 70 percent of the people are vegetarians and fruits and vegetables account for about 75 percent of retail sales as compared to only 25 percent in the USA. Ensuring that goods are able to reach their retail destinations with minimal spoilage is a critical factor for success. This one issue demonstrates the importance of establishing a reliable supply and distribution system such that good can get to the consumers in a timely manner.

While there are several other minor locational factors that will need to be considered, getting the location dimension figured out correctly the first time around will be key to drive operational, customer, and financial health of Wal-Mart in India.

Conclusion

Consumers are different in different parts of the world. To be successful, it is important for companies to completely understand their consumers. Wal-Mart has always tried to keep their format standard in their international operations.

Table 2

Retail market comparison of Germany, South Korea, and India

	Germany	South Korea	India
Mode of Wal-Mart market entry	Purchase of existing retailer	Purchase of existing retailer	Joint venture for supply and franchising of Wal-Mart brand
Supply chain	Well developed and established system of distributors and producers	Well developed and established system of distributors and producers	Unreliable and mostly undeveloped business and supplier infrastructure
Retail mix	50–60 percent food and vegetables	High proportion of purchases are fresh meats and vegetables	75 percent of retail sales overall are food, 70 percent of consumers are vegetarian
Retail store formats	Mix of grocery store chains, department store chains, and supercenters	Mix of local retailers, local produce markets, grocery store chains, department store chains, and supercenters	Fragmented market with primarily small local retailers and few chain stores
Retail fixed costs	High fixed costs due to unions and wage controls, real estate costs, and local taxation	High fixed costs due to limited available real estate and competitors with lower established base costs	High fixed costs due to real estate speculation and local business taxation and regulations
Competitors	Established departments stores and discount chains	Established local retailers, department stores and discount chains	Traditional small shops plus newly formed companies and business groups
Culture	Germany's more collectivist society discouraged German consumers from exploring different retailers, preferring the security of existing stores	Korea's more collectivist society and higher uncertainty avoidance combined to deter Korean consumers from changing their buying habits	Indian society is likely to be more open to new situations, such as exploring new retailers, than Wal-Mart has experienced in Germany and Korea

Cultures that are similar to the American culture or those that are highly influenced by the American culture have accepted the Wal-Mart formats as is. But, countries like Germany and South Korea have not accepted this format. To be successful in India, Wal-Mart will have to learn from their German and South Korean experiences, and make suitable changes to meet the need of the Indian consumer. Entering into a joint venture with an Indian company is a positive step in this direction, but one that comes with additional management overhead.

If Wal-Mart is to be successful in India, it will need to compete not only on price, but also on other key levers. Based on our analysis of Wal-Mart's recent failures, there are four key areas where Wal-Mart will need to perform well in order to have a chance to succeed in India:

1. Establishing a mutually satisfying, efficient, and productive working partnership with Bharti Enterprises.
2. Developing a rapidly functioning, capable, and reliable supply and distribution network.
3. Building convenient store locations and rapidly establishing a presence in the Indian market.
4. Thoroughly research their target consumer markets to be able to offer Indian consumers the type of products they desire at the appropriate level of quality, service, and value.

It remains to be seen what value proposition from domestic or international retail chain stores will appeal to Indian consumers as their retail marketplace undergoes massive change in the next decade.

EXPLORING THE ISSUE

Are U.S. Companies Adaptive to Local Practices Overseas?

Critical Thinking and Reflection

1. Define polycentric and ethnocentric staffing strategies.
2. Why is McDonald's so successful in its global operations?
3. Why was Walmart not successful in Germany and Korea?
4. What alternate suggestions do experts offer for multinationals establishing overseas?

Is There Common Ground?

Multinational organizations have the options of standardizing or localizing for their operations overseas. Successful companies have demonstrated the power of integrating the local values as it creates a strong bond with the customers. This might imply organizations have to change their products, services, and practices to domestic market values. In the long run, such market adaption might be very beneficial for organizations. On the other hand, several U.S. companies take their domestic recipe of success and try to implement it in other countries. This might not work well as local laws, values, and preferences contribute to the success or failure of a product or service. Experts suggest using joint ventures or decentralized approach as excellent method of entering new markets. If you were on the Walmart HRM team establishing in Germany, what would you have proposed differently? What suggestions would you have if you were working with Walmart's HRM team in Korea?

Additional Resources

Kulkarni, S., and Lassar, W. (2009). *McDonald's ongoing marketing challenge: Social perception in India.* Miami, FL: Department of Management and International Business, Florida International University.

http://www.nytimes.com/2010/03/23/technology/23google.html: Google Shuts China Site in Dispute Over Censorship.

http://online.wsj.com/article/SB10001424052748704075604575356552939507706.html?mod=djem_jiewr_MG_domainid: China Renews Google License.

http://www.shrm.org/Publications/hrmagazine/EditorialContent/Pages/0907cover.aspx: China: Land of Opportunity and Challenge.

Contributors to This Volume

EDITOR

PRAMILA RAO is working as an associate professor of human resource management (HRM) at Marymount University, Arlington, VA, since August 2005. She graduated from George Washington University, Washington D.C., in May 2005 with a major in human resource management and minor in international business. Her subject research has been published in *Employee Relations, Cross-Cultural Management, The Business Journal of Hispanic Research, International HRM Best Practices Series of Routledge, Journal of Indian Business Research,* and *Multicultural Educational and Technology Journal,* among others. She is very interested in student-centered teaching and frequently adopts this pedagogy in her classes. Her research interest focuses on HRM practices in a cross-cultural context with special focus on Mexico and India. She has also authored learning modules on HRM practices of India and Mexico for SHRM (Society of Human Resource Management). She is the author of the first edition of McGraw Hill's *Taking Sides: Clashing Views in Human Resource Management.*

AUTHORS

SARAH ANDERSON is the Director of the Global Economy Project at the Institute for Policy Studies.

DENNIS K. BERMAN is the *Wall Street Journal*'s Global Deals editor, responsible for M&A coverage in the world's leading business paper. He is author of a biweekly column, "The Game," which covers Wall Street. Mr. Berman joined the *Journal* in 2001 as a telecom reporter and technology columnist. He covered the historic financial collapse and subsequent accounting scandals at companies such as Lucent, Global Crossing, and WorldCom. Mr. Berman was one of the *Journal* reporters who shared in the 2003 Pulitzer Prize in explanatory journalism for a series on corporate scandals. His work is honored in the 2005 anthology of "Best Newspaper Writing" published by the American Society of Newspaper Editors. He is a magna cum laude graduate of the University of Pennsylvania, a guest lecturer on journalism at New York University, and a Kentucky Colonel. In March 2009, Mr. Berman and a team of reporters won the annual contest sponsored by the Society of American Business Editors and Writers in the category of breaking news for articles that ran on September 15, 2008, covering the collapse of Lehman Brothers.

DINA BERTA was the senior editor of *National Restaurant News* for nine years. She is an award-winning writer who has developed, wrote, and photographed stories on restaurant industry trends in human resources and culinary arts, as well as best business practices among companies in the Rocky Mountain region. Dina Berta continues to pursue freelancing and specializes in features, news, and corporate communications. She currently holds the marketing and HR director position at Frank's Kitchen.

IRA BLANK is a litigation attorney with Lathrop & Gage with an emphasis in employment law. Blank has extensive experience in the areas of employee coaching, discipline and discharge, managing unionized employees, labor arbitration, workplace harassment risk avoidance, and union avoidance. He was formerly industrial relations manager for a *Fortune* 100 manufacturing company. He also served as vice president of human resources and human resources counsel for a service company that was one of *Inc*. magazine's 500 Fastest Growing Companies in America. Blank received his undergraduate degree from the University of Alabama School of Business. He received a Master of Industrial and Labor Relations (M.I.L.R.) from the School of Industrial and Labor Relations at Cornell University. He obtained his juris doctorate from the Washington University School of Law.

ALEX BLYTH has been a freelance writer for eight years and works for several magazines such as *Accountancy, B2B Marketing, Financial Director, First Voice, Growing Business, New Business, Personnel Today, PR Week*, and *Revolution,* among others. As well as a prolific writer, Alex is an award-winning public speaker, and is regularly called upon to speak at conferences, product launches and workshops. He also runs a series of monthly open training courses on PR skills such as writing effective copy, getting coverage in the business press, and successful media interviews. His first book—*How to Grow Your Business for Entrepreneurs* was released by Pearson in July 2009.

MICHAEL C. BUDDEN is the Dean of the College of Business and Technology at Southeastern Louisiana University.

MARTIN CALKINS is the assistant professor in the College of Management at the University of Massachusetts Boston. He earned a Ph.D. in management from the University of Virginia, M.Div. and Th.M. degrees in theology from the Weston School of Theology, and an M.I.M. in international management from the American Graduate School of International Management. His academic interests include moral theory (in particular, casuistry and virtue theory) as well as contemporary international business issues such as international codes, whistle blowing, sweatshops, and the impact of computer and Internet technologies on societies.

JOHN CAVANAGH has been director of the Institute for Policy Studies (IPS) since 1998. In this capacity, he oversees programs, outreach, and organizational development.

DAVID L. CHAPPELL is the principal of Chappell & Associates in San Francisco, California. Through his speaking, writing, and consulting, he helps people around the world understand, use, and make better decisions about new technology. David has also been a series editor for Addison-Wesley and a columnist for several publications. David's comments have appeared in *The New York Times*, CNN.com, and many other publications.

CHUCK COLLINS is a senior scholar at the Institute for Policy (IPS) and directs IPS's Program on Inequality and the Common Good.

DALIA EIKERSH was an MBA candidate who has obtained her degree in December 2010. She wishes to pursue a career in marketing and public relations after graduation.

MARTHA J. FRASE is a freelance writer in Martinsburg, West Virginia. She is currently the editor of *The New Physician*.

JOHN E. GNUSCHKE, Ph.D., director, Jeff Wallace, Ph.D., Senior Research Associate, Dennis R. Wilson, Ph.D., Senior Research Associate, and Stephen C. Smith, Editor/Research Associate, Sparks Bureau of Business and Economic Research/Center for Manpower Studies, Fogelman College of Business and Economics, The University of Memphis. Dr. John E. Gnuschke is the director of the Bureau of Business and Economic Research and the Center for Manpower Studies and the professor of Economics at The University of Memphis.

LESSING E. GOLD is an attorney and partner of Mitchell Silberberg Knupp and has legal expertise on shareholder disputes, mergers and acquisitions, representation of nonprofit associations, representation before regulatory agencies, and contractual negotiations. Some of his key professional achievements have been the formation of several major security alarm and integration companies and serving as leading counsel in the acquisition of one of the largest security alarm companies in the United States. He publishes a monthly column in *SDM Magazine,* a national trade publication for the security industry.

ROBERT J. GROSSMAN, a contributing editor of *HR Magazine,* is a lawyer and a professor of management studies at Marist College in Poughkeepsie, New York. Mr. Grossman holds a masters degree in law (LL.M) from NYU Law School, a J.D. from the University of Buffalo, and a bachelor's degree in history from Hobart College in Geneva, NY. He has written for *HR Magazine* since 1996.

JAYA HALEPETE is an assistant professor in the College of Arts and Sciences at Marymount University. Her research focus is on international retailing and consumer behavior. Jaya Halepete is the corresponding author and can be contacted at: jaya.halepete@marymount.edu.

KEITH H. HAMMONDS was the executive editor of *Fast Company* magazine for eight years. He has an MBA from Harvard Business School. Right now he is the director of Ashoka, a nonprofit organization on news and knowledge.

FAY HANSEN is a contributing editor for *Workforce Management* and is very prolific in writing about employment-related issues.

PAUL HEMP, a Harvard Law School graduate, is a contributing editor to the *Harvard Business Review* and was the senior editor of the same for nine years. He is the author of several *HBR* articles. He also has appeared as a commentator on CNN, CNBC, NPR, and BBC and as a panelist at the Yale CEO Leadership Summit.

MIKE HUGHLETT, a reporter in the food industry, covers the food industry for the *Star Tribune,* including General Mills and Supervalu. Previously, he was a food reporter for the *Chicago Tribune.*

HERMINIA IBARRA is the Cora chaired professor of leadership and learning, professor of organizational behavior, faculty director of the INSEAD Leadership Initiative, and a member of the INSEAD Board. She received her M.A. and Ph.D. from Yale University, where she was a National Science Fellow. Prior to joining INSEAD, she served on the Harvard Business School faculty for 13 years. She is a member of the World Economic Forum Global Agenda Councils and the Visiting Committee of the Harvard Business School.

K. V. SESHADRI IYER is a management consultant. His research focus includes the retail industry, outsourcing, and globalization.

GAIL JOHNSON was the managing editor of *Training* and currently is the president/CEO at Face to Face Communications and Training. Ms. Johnson has designed and delivered thousands of communication-related workshops throughout the United States. Ms. Johnson earned her B.A. degree in journalism and M.A. in communication studies from Northern Illinois University.

JONATHAN KAUFMAN is education editor at Bloomberg News, overseeing a team of reporters and editors covering higher education and K–12. Prior to joining Bloomberg News, Mr. Kaufman was a Pulitzer Prize winning reporter and editor at *The Wall Street Journal* where he served as deputy Page One editor and helped oversee coverage of the 2008 campaign as well as writing stories about the election for Page One. He served as China Bureau Chief for the *Journal,* based in Beijing, and covered race and class issues in the workplace and on college campuses as senior special writer.

DANA KYLES is a published writer for *BusinessWeek and Strategic Finance* magazines. She works as a principal analyst in the utilities industry with a decade of leadership, valuation, financial modeling, strategy, and project management experience. She is a frequent public speaker on multigenerational workforces.

MICHELLE LABROSSE, PMP, is the founder of Cheetah Learning, a virtual company of about 100 employees, contractors, and licensees worldwide. The Project Management Institute recently selected Michelle as one of the 25 Most Influential Women in Project Management in the World, and only one of two women selected from the training and education industry. She is a graduate of the Harvard Business School's Owner President Managers (OPM) program and also holds engineering degrees from Syracuse University and the University of Dayton. Her articles have appeared in hundreds of publications from around the world. Her monthly column, the *Know How Network,* is carried by over 500 publications, and her monthly newsletter subscription list includes more than 50,000 people.

MIKE LAPHAM is an associate fellow at the Institute of Policy Studies.

JESSICA MARQUEZ is the New York bureau chief for *Workforce Management.*

OTILIA OBODARU, graduated with her doctorate from INSEAD in 2010, specializes in organizational behavior.

SOO CHUL PARK is an undergraduate student at Marymount University majoring in fashion merchandising.

RANGARAJAN (RAJ) PARTHASARATHY is a process improvement manager with a leading retail business in Chicago, Illinois. He is a senior member of ASQ and a certified quality manager and quality engineer. Parthasarathy has worked in manufacturing engineering, quality engineering, and process improvement for more than 10 years. He may be contacted by e-mail at rpartha463@aim.com.

SAM PIZZIGATI is an associate fellow at the Institute for Policy Studies (IPS).

ANN POMEROY is senior writer for *HR Magazine.* She has provided several in-depth analytical articles on various work-related issues. She was the former managing editor of *SHRM Professional Emphasis Group* newsletters.

C. J. PRINCE, who has been a versatile writer and editor for more than 15 years, covers everything from small-business finance to big corporate mergers, from glass ceiling myths to CEOs and alcoholism, for national magazines. Formerly executive editor of CEO Magazine (6+ years), he initiated coverage of personal finance, technology, and corporate diversity. He is now a full-time freelancer seeking to bring his expertise, creativity, and knowledge of industry to national business and consumer publications.

TARA J. RADIN is visiting assistant professor in the Legal Studies and Business Ethics department at the Wharton School and assistant director of The American College Center for Ethics in Financial Services. She earned a J.D. from the University of Virginia School of Law and an M.B.A. and Ph.D. in management from the Darden School at the University of Virginia. Her research encompasses topics such as employment, global labor practices, technology, privacy, corporate governance, and stakeholder theory, and includes publications in journals such as *Business Ethics Quarterly, Journal of Business Ethics,* and *American Business Law Journal*. She is also co-author of *Employment and Employee Rights*, published by Blackwell Publishers, Ltd.

ROBERT D. RAMSEY is a freelance writer from Minneapolis with extensive frontline experience in supervision and personnel administration. He is the author of several successful trade books and a frequent contributor to *Supervision* and numerous other popular journals and newsletters.

ROBERT B. REICH, professor of public policy at the University of California at Berkeley and former U.S. Secretary of Labor under President Clinton, is author of the just-published *Supercapitalism: The Transformation of Business, Democracy, and Everyday Life* (Alfred A. Knopf).

STEPHEN C. SMITH is the editor/research associate for the Sparks Bureau of Business and Economic Research/Center for Manpower Studies, Fogelman College of Business and Economics, at the University of Memphis.

DANIEL J. SOLOVE is a professor of law at the George Washington University Law School, Washington, D.C. He is the author of many books, including *Nothing to Hide: The False Tradeoff Between Privacy and Security* (Yale University Press, 2011), *Understanding Privacy* (Harvard University Press, 2008), *The Future of Reputation: Gossip, Rumor, and Privacy on the Internet* (Yale University Press, 2007), and *The Digital Person: Technology and Privacy in the Information Age* (NYU Press, 2004). His book, *The Future of Reputation,* won the 2007 McGannon Award. An internationally known expert in privacy law, Solove has been interviewed and quoted by the media in several hundred articles and broadcasts, including the *New York Times, Washington Post, Wall Street Journal, USA Today, Chicago Tribune,* the Associated Press, ABC, CBS, NBC, CNN, and NPR. He joined the GW Law faculty in 2004 and teaches information privacy law, criminal procedure, criminal law, and law and literature.

CHAD TERHUNE is currently a senior writer at Smartmoney. He was a senior writer for *BusinessWeek* for three years. Terhune previously worked for *The Wall Street Journal* for 11 years. He won a National Press Club award in 2003 for his coverage of abuses in the health insurance industry. Terhune graduated from the University of Florida.

JAMIE VICKNAIR was an MBA candidate who obtained her degree December 2010. She has three years of recruiting experience. After graduation she hopes to go into the field of human resources.

JEFF WALLACE, Ph.D., is a senior research associate at the Sparks Bureau of Business and Economic Research/Center for Manpower Studies, Fogelman College of Business and Economics, at the University of Memphis.

MURRAY WEIDENBAUM holds the Mallinckrodt Distinguished University Professorship at Washington University, where he is also honorary chairman of the Weidenbaum Center on the Economy, Government, and Public Policy.

SUSAN J. WELLS, a contributing editor of HR Magazine since 1998, has more than 20 years of experience as an award-winning editor, writer and correspondent for national news sources, leading business-to-business publications, web sites and specialty information providers. Her current reporting centers on employment and workforce strategies, business and financial news, industry forecasts and market trends, management advice, and consumer change.

ERIN WHITE is a staff reporter covering management and workplace issues for the *Wall Street Journal* in New York. She graduated cum laude from Yale University.

DENNIS R. WILSON, Ph.D., is a senior research associate at Sparks Bureau of Business and Economic Research/Center for Manpower Studies, Fogelman College of Business and Economics, at the University of Memphis.

CHARLES WOODRUFFE is the managing director of Human Assets Ltd. that he founded in 1987. Human Assets is a team of result-oriented and highly qualified business psychologists who help organizations choose, develop, and engage the winning talent they need. Woodruffe is a well-respected expert and author of many books such as *Identifying and Developing Competence* and *Winning the Talent War* as well as countless articles on HR strategy, executive development, coaching, talent management and the talent war, and recruitment and employee engagement. He has his Ph.D. in psychology from the London University.

KATIE YANCEY was an MBA candidate with a concentration in marketing. She graduated in May 2010 and works in the field of marketing.

VICTORIA ZELLERS is a labor and employment attorney in Cozen O'Connor's Philadelphia office. Victoria has significant federal and state court litigation experience representing both private and public employers under Title VII, the Americans with Disabilities Act, and the Age Discrimination in Employment Act, among other employment-related claims. She earned her law degree from Temple University Beasley School of Law, cum laude, where she was a member of the *International and Comparative Law Journal*.